YOUNG, BLACK, AND MALE IN AMERICA:

AN ENDANGERED SPECIES

YOUNG, BLACK, AND MALE IN AMERICA

An Endangered Species

Edited by

Jewelle Taylor Gibbs
University of California, Berkeley

Ann F. Brunswick
Columbia University

Michael E. Connor
California State University, Long Beach

Richard Dembo
University of South Florida

Tom E. Larson
California State University, Los Angeles

Rodney J. Reed
University of California, Berkeley

Barbara Solomon
University of Southern California

 AUBURN HOUSE
New York • Westport, Connecticut • London

Library of Congress Cataloging-in-Publication Data

Young, Black, and Male in America.

Bibliography: p.
Includes index.
1. Afro-American men.   2. Afro-American youth.
I. Gibbs, Jewelle Taylor.
E185.86.Y68   1988   305.2'3508996073   87-19340
ISBN 0-86569-169-X

Library of Congress Catalog Card Number: 87-19340
ISBN: 0-86569-169-X (case)
ISBN: 0-86569-180-0 (pbk.)

First published in 1988

Auburn House, 88 Post Road West, Westport, CT 06881
An imprint of Greenwood Publishing Group, Inc.

Printed in the United States of America

The paper used in this book complies with the
Permanent Paper Standard issued by the National
Information Standards Organization (Z39.48-1984).

10 9 8 7 6 5 4 3 2

This book is dedicated to my husband,
James Lowell Gibbs, Jr.,
who modeled competence, courage, and
commitment,
and to my sons, Geoffrey and Lowell,
who learned their lessons well.

CONTENTS

FOREWORD

Jewelle Taylor Gibbs and the authors who contributed to this volume make a convincing case that it is no exaggeration to call young black males an "endangered species." In many ways the conditions of these youths have deteriorated markedly since the 1950s and 1960s, and they are caught up in a complex mix of forces and circumstances that will, in the absence of policy changes, make their conditions even worse in the future. While the conditions of all other groups (including women and recent immigrants) have improved in the past 25 years, 6 million young black males age 15 to 24 are more likely than their counterparts in 1960 to be unemployed, to be involved with the criminal justice system, and to commit suicide. In November 1987 the black teenage unemployment rate (34.0 percent) was nearly twice the rate for all teenagers (17.4 percent); the black unemployment rate was three times as high as in 1960, and both unemployment and labor force participation rates of young black males had deteriorated dramatically relative to whites since 1960. Almost half (46.2 percent) of young black males under 18 are in households below the poverty line; 42 percent live in female-headed households, two-thirds of which have below-poverty incomes.

One of the most important conclusions to be drawn from the rich materials presented in this volume is that the conditions of young black males are due to a complex constellation of mutually reinforcing factors. Failure to appreciate this reality often causes policymakers, the media, and even scholars who should know better to analyze problems such as dropping out of school, teenage pregnancy, high crime rates, unemployment or unemployability as unitary problems with single solutions such as "better education" or a "willingness to work." The reality is that relative to whites, many young black males face serious cumulative problems all of their lives. They are more likely to be born to unwed teenage mothers who themselves have limited education and even more limited life choices. The children of teenage mothers are more likely to be underweight and to suffer from inadequate nutrition and health care; consequently they are more likely to start life with serious disadvantages. Unstable family lives and poor health and nutrition cause them to have very restricted learning opportunities as infants and young children. They are therefore more likely to be stigmatized or placed in classes for the "educable mentally retarded"; to have learning problems in school; to fall increasingly behind their age group in achieving basic educational competencies; to drop out of school; to get involved with drugs, crime, and the criminal justice system; and to be convicted and incarcerated in prison. Young black males having problems in school and in life are more likely to be teenage parents and to be either unemployed or unemployable. It should be noted that the problems of young black males from two-parent families, while less serious on the average than those in single-parent families, are nevertheless much worse than young white males from similar families. And two wage earners are more likely to be required to raise the incomes of these black families above the poverty line.

In terms of education, although young black males have improved their dropout rates in the past 25 years, in 1980 over a fifth of black males aged 12 to 17 were unable to read at the fourth grade level and over a fifth of black 18- to 21-year-old black males had not graduated from, or were not enrolled in, high school. Moreover, black college enrollment in four-year institutions has declined since 1980, and the gap between the proportions of black and white high school graduates going to college, after having narrowed to 3.6 percent in 1975, widened to 7.9 percent in 1983. Limited financial support aggravated by reductions in federal aid programs plays a role in lower black college enrollments—in 1981, 48 percent of black college-bound students, but only 10 percent of whites, were from families with incomes below $12,000 a year. These deficiencies are particularly serious because of the rising education levels required to obtain good jobs and the fact that well-educated blacks have been able to improve their condition relative to both whites and less-educated blacks since the 1960s. There is, in addition, mounting evidence that positive income and employment outcomes are associated with educational achievement. On the other hand, educational deficiencies and the inability to become gainfully employed cause young black males to "be increasingly tempted to participate in the underground alternative economy of urban ghettos—that is, the illegal system of barter in stolen goods, drugs, gambling, and prostitution." Moreover, ". . . up to 15 percent of all black males will spend some time in an adult prison, while only 2 to 3 percent of white males are expected to do so." Teenage pregnancy, another growing problem among young whites and blacks, is highly correlated with the factors associated with low incomes and low educational achievement. Although birth trends among black teenagers have declined absolutely and relative to whites, adolescent pregnancy rates are still twice as high among blacks as whites. In 1983, 85.7 percent of black babies born to females under age 19 were out of wedlock, compared with 39.7 percent for whites. Infant mortality rates among teen mothers are nearly twice as high for blacks as whites.

It should be emphasized, however, that solutions to unwanted teen pregnancies must involve young males as well as young females. The typical unwed teenage father is a high school dropout and unemployed, with low skills. Joblessness among young black males greatly reduces the available marriage partners for young black women.

While the authors of the chapters in this volume uniformly emphasize the limitations of our understanding of all of young black males' problems, the evidence suggests a number of contributing factors, which Professor Gibbs classifies as historical, sociocultural, economic, and political. Historically, the expectations of significant improvements in black fortunes raised in the 1960s by economic progress, the civil rights movement, and the Kennedy-Johnson administrations, have been dashed by slow economic growth and rising unemployment in the 1970s and 1980s. From a sociological perspective, the conditions of the most disadvantaged blacks have been worsened by the widening income gaps between the poor and middle-class blacks and the movement of middle-class blacks out of the geographic areas where poor blacks are concentrated. This outmigration has destabilized those areas by removing important leaders, role models, supportive networks, and social institutions. As indicated in Chapter 1, with the breakdown or weakening of these traditional institutions within inner-city communities, there has been a concomitant breakdown of traditional black community values of the importance of family, religion, education, self-improvement, and social cohesion through extensive social networks. "Thus, we see situations where young black men sell drugs openly on major thoroughfares without fear of apprehension; teenage girls have multiple out-of-wedlock pregnancies without fear of ostracism;" youthful gangs terrorize neighborhoods without fear of retaliation; and no one seems to disapprove of young men who loiter aimlessly on street corners.

From an economic perspective, the conditions of young blacks have been worsened by slow economic growth (rapid growth has generally been favorable to black employment and income growth) and structural changes which have moved jobs out of central cities or put out of reach many of the manufacturing, agricultural, and service jobs formerly available to young blacks with limited formal education.

The political factors are associated with the conservative trend that started with the election of Richard Nixon in 1968. This trend has been "strongly reinforced by the Reagan administration." Conservatives "have quite deliberately and effectively transformed the national debate from a proactive emphasis on preventive policies to a reactive emphasis on retrogressive policies and punitive programs." Again, as stated in Chapter 1, conservative political analysts have shifted the focus from the complex social and economic causes of the problems of the poor and minorities to blaming the poor and disadvantaged for their lack of motivation, their dysfunctional family systems, and their dependency on welfare programs.

The second main conclusion from this valuable book is that, despite their grim statistics and analyses, Jewelle Taylor Gibbs and her fellow authors actually have a hopeful message. They point out that while much remains to be learned about the causes of young black males' maladies, we understand much that could provide bases for constructive remedies. It is, moreover, very clear that a failure to address the problems for these young men will be very costly in material and human terms to society as a whole. We must view interventions as *investments*, not merely as *costs*. According to abundant documentation, many constructive interventions yield high social and individual returns. This is particularly true of health care for mothers and children, education enrichment programs like Head Start, training and education programs like the Job Corps, and numerous successful programs to prevent problems and to remedy their consequences—many of which are detailed in this book. Failure to intervene will therefore debase the quality of life for all of us. Young black males will be an increasing proportion of the youth population. They will either be an increasing proportion of those who are constructively employed or they will be an increasing proportion of those involved in destructive social and economic activity. History demonstrates the wisdom of *preventing* these problems rather than concentrating on their symptoms and attempting to ameliorate their consequences.

The evidence in this volume demonstrates the complexity of the problems and the need for systematic, comprehensive approaches that involve all of the principal participants in fashioning solutions based on realistic assessments of causes and remedies. The main impetus for change must undoubtedly come from the black community, but whites will pay a high price if they ignore this very serious problem and fail to be responsive to constructive remedial approaches. We must remove the social and institutional barriers society has created for these young people and we must create the conditions that enable them to have realistic chances of participating in the mainstream of American life.

October 1987
RAY MARSHALL
Audre and Bernard Rapoport Centennial
Professor of Economics and Public Affairs
Lyndon B. Johnson School of Public Affairs
University of Texas, Austin

FOREWORD

The black community is now reaping the bitter harvest of decades of neglect of the plight of its young people by national policies that have failed to eradicate their poverty, failed to equip them with education for an information society, and failed to replace discriminatory barriers with equal opportunity. The result is that young black males, as the title of this book suggests, have become an endangered species, with more young black men added each year to the ranks of the poor, the jobless, and the homeless. The impact on the black family, the black economy, and on individual lives has been devastating.

The black family is the subject of much concern these days, especially with the rise in single female-headed households, but a major reason for the deterioration of black family stability is the deterioration in economic opportunities for black men. The rise of single-headed families parallels the decline in the black male work force. It takes two to form a family, and when a young man cannot get work or earn enough to support a family, fewer families are formed.

A Children's Defense Fund study in 1987 found that the economic position of young black males is far worse than it has been in years. Back in 1973 the majority of young males earned enough to keep a three-person family out of poverty. Now, less than half do. Young men age 20 to 24 who earn enough to stay above the poverty line marry at rates three and four times higher than young men with below-poverty-line earnings. Constricted opportunities for young men have cut their marriage rates in half over the past 15 years.

Young black males have been trapped between the rock of poor educational backgrounds and the hard place of a changing job structure that demands higher educational levels. Black high school dropout rates are nearly double those for whites and approach fifty percent or more in some cities. Black students score 80 to 100 points lower than whites on SAT college entrance exams.

Although the black college-eligible population has increased over the past decade, black college entrance rates have fallen. Once young black men do enroll in college, they drop out at higher rates than whites. Few major in mathematics and the physical sciences, and fewer still go on to earn doctorates in such crucial fields of the future as computer science, physics, and engineering. It seems that the more employers talk about the need to hire people with highly developed technical and analytical skills, the less blacks appear to be acquiring those skills. Despite some signs of improvement in black students' test scores, especially in the lower grades, there is a clear pattern of black educational deficiency that places the economic future of all black people in jeopardy.

Despite the advocates of school reforms, it is clear that the situation young blacks find themselves in can be ameliorated only through broad programs that attack the causes of their underachievement. The majority of young black males today grow up in poverty. Significant numbers live in substandard housing conditions—many in chaotic, crime-torn neighborhoods.

Community organizations such as the National Urban League and others are mounting important programs oriented toward helping young blacks overcome these disadvantages. Programs aimed at encouraging better school performance, male responsibility, reduced teen pregnancy, family stability, and work-readiness are important. But equally as important must be sweeping national policies designed to assure quality education for all, elimination of poverty for children, decent housing, and broader horizons for our beleaguered young people. It is my hope that the essays in this volume will help focus national attention on the plight of young black men and help to move our society to harness their talents and their abilities.

JOHN E. JACOB
President and Chief Executive Officer
National Urban League

PREFACE

This book evolved out of a presentation on the psychosocial problems of black adolescents and youth at a colloquium jointly sponsored by the Bay Area Black United Fund and the School of Social Welfare at the University of California at Berkeley in the Spring of 1982. In preparing that presentation, I was surprised to learn that most of the major social indicators for black youth were worse in 1980 than they were in 1960. It was difficult to comprehend that the status of black youth had deteriorated in employment, delinquency, homicide, and suicide despite 20 years of antipoverty programs, 15 years of affirmative action programs, and two decades of economic progress. The colloquium presentation evolved into an article, "Black Adolescents and Youth: An Endangered Species," published in the *American Journal of Orthopsychiatry* in January 1984, which evoked so much interest and debate that it became clear that there was a need for a more comprehensive, in-depth analysis of the deteriorating status of black youth, particularly young, black males in the 15 to 24 age group.

Until the recent mass media attention to these issues, the public perception has been that blacks were making progress toward equality and integration into mainstream American society. These perceptions have been informed by some accurate impressions about the growth of the black middle class since 1960, yet they did not take account of the growing gap between the middle class and the poor blacks, whose numbers have grown and whose conditions have worsened since that time.

Some naive people still believe that the urban riots of the 1960s solved all the problems of inner-city blacks, but many of the programs initiated in response to those riots were not well conceived, not well developed, and not effectively implemented. There was a great deal of radical rhetoric, political posturing, and bureaucratic bungling during the 1960s, but 20 years later there are very few long-term positive effects of these programs, with a few notable exceptions such as Head Start. In 1968 the Kerner

Commission warned that the nation was "rapidly moving toward two increasingly separate Americas." Two decades later, that prophecy seems chillingly accurate as blacks in the inner cities are more removed from mainstream America than they were before the riots.

In fact, the problems of young black inner-city males are so severe that society seems to have decided simply to ignore them, to isolate them in ghettos, to put them out of sight. In 1987, as the nation celebrated the bicentennial of the signing of the American Constitution, young black males were treated as "invisible" persons on urban "welfare plantations," just as they were treated as "3/5ths of a person" on rural slave plantations in 1787.

In writing and editing this book, I have been struck by the similarities of the inner city "welfare plantations" of the 1980s to the southern slave plantations of the 1780s: Blacks in the ghettos are still "separate but not equal," still dependent on the paternalism of the white power elite, still disenfranchised and powerless, still treated as second-class citizens in the land of their birth, and still dehumanized and depersonalized, exploited and extorted, neglected and narcotized. In 1987, two hundred years after the signing of the U.S. Constitution, blacks—and particularly young black males—have still not realized the promises of democracy and are still not beneficiaries of "liberty and justice for all."

Meanwhile, more and more black youth are unemployed, unskilled, and unproductive in a society which rewards hard work, competence, and productivity. The so called "underclass" has not only become a convenient label for this group, but it has also developed into a growth industry for social scientists and public policy specialists who have generally spent more effort on describing the symptoms than on attempting to analyze the underlying causes of many of the apparent self-destructive and dysfunctional behaviors.

Too much emphasis has been placed on "blaming the victims" for their own victimization and for the consequences of over three centuries of discrimination, deprivation, and denial of equal opportunity. Double standards have been applied in a blatantly hypocritical attempt to attribute immoral and deviant motives to black youth for the same kinds of behaviors for which white youth are ignored, excused, tolerated, or exonerated.

This book is an attempt to redress the balance by presenting a comprehensive, interdisciplinary perspective on the major social and economic problems of young black males in America. All of the contributors to this book have conducted research in their areas of expertise, and their chapters are based on in-depth analyses of the problems experienced by black youth. Similarly, their recommendations for preventive policies and remedial programs to address the problems of black youth are grounded in their thoughtful evaluations of the implications of their research results rather than on political platitudes or reactionary rhetoric. These contributors all recognize the need to develop policies and programs to attack the *underlying* social and structural factors in American society which create barriers to equal opportunity for black youth, reinforce their dependency and passivity, and destroy the potential for their development as competent and self-sufficient adults.

The book is organized as follows: In Chapter 1, Jewelle Taylor Gibbs presents an overview of the social indicators for young black males, notes the deterioration in these indicators since 1960, shows their interrelationship, and emphasizes the need for a set of comprehensive, well-coordinated policies and programs to reverse the pattern of deterioration in their status.

In Chapter 2, Rodney Reed describes the educational status and academic problems of young black males. In addition to a demographic profile of black students, Dr. Reed presents a comprehensive picture of the factors which mitigate against positive educational experiences and outcomes for young black males. He proposes specific recommendations for educational policies and practices to improve the school performance of these youth.

In Chapter 3, Tom Larson analyzes the employment problems of young black males. The results of his recent research indicate that declining employment rates among black youth are primarily caused by structural changes in the economy and other social and economic factors over which they have no control. Dr. Larson discusses policy implications and proposes recommendations to increase employment opportunities and employment rates for young black males.

In Chapter 4, Richard Dembo reports on the results of an innovative screening project for delinquents at a regional juvenile detention center in Tampa, Florida. His multivariate analysis of the correlates of delinquency and drug use in black and white youth is related to major theories of delinquency among black youth. From his findings, Dr. Dembo suggests implications for research, policy formulation, and program development to prevent delinquency in this group.

In Chapter 5, Ann Brunswick describes the results of a longitudinal study of young black male drug users in Harlem. She has developed a conceptual model which offers an understanding of the factors related to the patterns of substance use among young black males, their lifestyle, and their health concomitants. Dr. Brunswick suggests that policies to prevent school failure and to promote employment opportunities for black youth are the most effective strategies for preventing substance abuse.

In Chapter 6, Michael Connor reviews the literature on young black unwed fathers and reports on several studies of fathers who are involved with their children. Dr. Connor offers suggestions for policy changes and programs to educate these black youth about family planning and to provide supportive services so that they can function more effectively as parents.

In Chapter 7, Dr. Gibbs describes the multiple physical and psychological problems which occur disproportionately among young black males, particularly emphasizing the impact of poverty and discrimination on the health and mental health of these youth, from high rates of infant mortality to high rates of sexually transmitted diseases, chronic diseases, and psychiatric disorders. Recommendations are proposed to extend health benefits and to improve access to health care facilities for these youth and their families, as well as to ameliorate the underlying causes of their poor health and mental health.

In Chapter 8, Dr. Gibbs discusses the "new morbidity"—that is, the incidence of mortality and serious injuries caused by homicide, suicide, accidents, and substance abuse among young black males. Her analysis of the multiple causes of these self-destructive behaviors focuses on the interrelationship among social, psychological, cultural and economic factors in contributing to this phenomenon. Recommendations are proposed to address these underlying factors, which range from introducing conflict resolution techniques in public schools to passing gun control legislation.

In Chapter 9, Barbara Solomon proposes a framework for developing policy solutions to the severe problems of young black males. The policies she recommends are aimed at improving the status of all low-income families and youth and are thereby designed to be "racially neutral" yet beneficial to the millions of disadvantaged black youth. Dr. Solomon's proposals emphasize the importance of a comprehensive family income policy, education, and training in order to provide a solid foundation for positive change in the status of black youth.

In Chapter 10, Dr. Gibbs summarizes the recommendations of all the contributors and integrates them into a comprehensive set of policies and programs designed to reverse the current cycle of despair among young black males, as well as to provide long-term solutions to prevent further deterioration in the functioning of these youth. Many of these policies and programs have previously been proposed as solutions to unidimensional problems by dozens of social scientists, public policy specialists, educators, and health professionals, but very few serious efforts have been made to propose them as a package and to document the futility of piece-meal solutions to multi-dimensional problems which are indisputably interconnected and indivisible. In this final chapter, a strong argument is made for the need for a comprehensive, well-coordinated set of policies and programs—sponsored by the government, business, foundations, and voluntary organizations—to address the complex, chronic, and severe problems of young black males in America.

Portions of this book have been previously presented by the author as a keynote speaker, workshop leader, or panelist at the following conferences and annual meetings: National Urban League Annual Conference in Los Angeles, California, August 1982; Children's Defense Fund Conference on "Children Having Children" in Atlanta, Georgia, June 1984; Annual Civil Rights Institute, NAACP Legal Defense and Educational Fund, Inc. in New York City, May 1985; Conference on Future Social Welfare Policy Options, sponsored by the Ford Foundation at the Wingspread Conference Center, Racine, Wisconsin, November 1985; Conference on Social Welfare Policy and the American Future, cosponsored by the Ford Foundation and Jackson State University in Jackson, Mississippi, February 1986; Council of Foundations Annual Meeting in Kansas City, Missouri, April 1986; the Annual Meeting of the American Association of Suicidology in San Francisco, California, May 1987; and the Annual Conference of the National Black Child Development Institute in Detroit, Michigan, October 1987. I want to express my appreciation to all of these organizations and institutions for inviting me to participate in these programs and to the other participants who provided me with valuable feedback about my presentations.

There are three final points to make about this book: (1) Why is such a book significant at this time? (2) Who is the intended audience for this book? (3) What is the anticipated impact of this book? The answers to these questions are fairly straightforward, yet not without qualifications.

First, I consider this book significant for several reasons, but primarily because I hope that it will alert the nation's leaders in education, business, and government that a sizable proportion of black youth are failing in nearly every area, falling between the cracks of society's indifference and neglect and facing an inevitable future of welfare dependency, penal incarceration, or marginal

social adaptation. More importantly, these black youth will constitute at least one out of five *American* youth by the year 2000, yet
many of them will not be able to contribute productively to the
economy and will constitute a major drain on the nation's resources. The health and stability of the social security system for
the country's growing number of older citizens is directly linked
to the earning capacity of these black youth in the 21st century. If
the current problems of black youth do not evoke sympathy or
compassion from the "moral majority," perhaps they will at least
provoke concern or consternation among those policymakers who
must plan for the future manpower needs, social welfare costs, and
social insurance programs of this society.

Second, this book is intended for a wide audience of professionals and those people who have some interest or involvement in the
problems of black youth and their families. This includes a wide
spectrum of government officials, legislators, public policy specialists, social scientists, educators, health care professionals, criminal
and juvenile justice officials, labor leaders, business executives,
foundation executives, civic and political leaders, clergymen, social
workers, civil rights leaders, and youth advocates. In addition, it
is our hope that this book will be useful for graduate and undergraduate courses in social sciences, ethnic studies, health sciences,
public policy, law, education, and social work. Organizations which
serve inner-city youth and their families, such as the Urban
League, NAACP, Boys Clubs, YMCA, and Boy Scouts, as well as
those organizations dedicated to youth advocacy, should also find
this book useful.

Third, this book is deliberately designed to provoke debate over
what needs to be done to reverse the negative trends for black
youth. It will evoke anger and outrage in some readers, depression
and despair in others. Whatever the reactions are to this book,
however, it is our sincere hope that it will not only raise the
public's consciousness about the plight of black youth but also
ultimately appeal to the consciences of American leaders in all
areas of the society to translate their awareness and concerns into
constructive policies and programs which will improve the status
of black youth.

Finally, a personal note. From its initial conceptualization
through each stage of its research, writing, and editing, this book
has often been a painful and disturbing experience for me. It has
long been difficult for black scholars and community leaders to
discuss and to debate these issues publicly, particularly because of
their negative implications of deviance and dysfunction in the black
community. However, it is essential for us to bring this topic "out

of the closet," to analyze its causes and consequences, and to examine public policy options to solve the problems of young black males. Moreover, as a parent of two young adult sons and seven young nephews, who are vulnerable simply because they are black males in a white society, it has not always been easy to maintain a posture of dispassionate objectivity about this material. In the final analysis, I have made a concerted effort to separate my personal feelings from the data, but these feelings are clearly reflected in my interpretations of the data and in my recommendations in those chapters which I authored and for which I take the sole responsibility.

A generation of black youth is truly endangered. These youth cannot continue to be demeaned, denied, and deprived of the basic essentials of life, liberty, and the pursuit of happiness. I hope that readers of this book will realize that the hour is late and the time for action is *now*. In America we have the knowledge, the technology, and the resources to improve life chances for young black males. What we need is the compassion, the motivation and the consensus to create a humane and nurturant environment not only for black youth but for all youth in this country. We hope that this book will provide a significant impetus to the development of just such a national consensus.

December 1, 1987　　　　　　　　　JEWELLE TAYLOR GIBBS
University of California
Berkeley, California

ACKNOWLEDGMENTS

This book is the result of the collaborative efforts of many people and the sustained encouragement and support of many others. I would like particularly to thank the following people for their direct contribution to this project: The contributing authors for their scholarly analyses of the major social problems of young black males; Dean Harry Specht and my colleagues at the School of Social Welfare for their enthusiastic support and critical feedback on these issues; the research and teaching assistants who helped me to collect data, check references, and meet deadlines, including Gloria Aguilar, Helen Ahn, Christine Carillo, Holly Danforth, Alice Hines, Ann Jackson, Frances Merriweather, Sue Skinner, and Jane Weil; Sharon Ikami, my efficient secretary, who typed countless versions of my chapters with equanimity and grace under pressure; Jim Steele, Betty Harrison, Kris Hughes, Lora Graham, and the administrative staff of the School of Social Welfare for their support, patience, and good humor in responding to requests for resources and extensions of deadlines; John Harney, the publisher who had faith in the concept and has been so consistently supportive of the project; and Eugene Bailey, the editor, who has been so constructive and cooperative in making the manuscript more cohesive, more consistent, and more concise.

My interest and enthusiasm for this specific project, as well as for the broader area of the psychosocial problems of minority youth, have been fostered and nurtured over a period of years by the following colleagues and friends: Dr. David A. Hamburg and the late Dr. David Dorosin, who both encouraged me to pursue scholarly research in the area of ethnicity and adolescent mental health; Professor Sheldon J. Korchin, my mentor and adviser, who has made such outstanding contributions to the field of minority mental health and to the training of minority psychologists; Professor Rhona S. Weinstein and colleagues in the Community Psychology Interest Group, who encouraged me to publish the article which gave an impetus to this book; colleagues from the American

Orthopsychiatric Association, whose insightful comments have helped to define the scope of the issues and to sharpen the focus of my analysis, including Dr. James P. Comer, Dr. Ferdinand Jones, Charles King, Dr. Vera Paster, Dr. Chester M. Pierce, and Professor Elaine Pinderhughes; Dr. Charles V. Hamilton, Dr. Leslie McLemore, and Dr. Robert Reischauer and other colleagues from the Wingspread Conference on Future Social Welfare Policy Options, who expanded my knowledge and challenged my thinking about traditional social welfare policies; Eddie N. Williams and the staff of the Joint Center for Political Studies, who have enriched my work through their enlightening discussions and excellent publications; colleagues and staff members at the Mary I. Bunting Institute at Radcliffe College, Cambridge, Massachusetts, who provided a forum for many of these ideas and a scholarly setting in which to pursue them in the Spring of 1985.

Finally, I would like to acknowledge the most significant and continuous contributions of my family and friends to my career and to this book: my mother, Margaret Taylor Hancock, and my late father, the Reverend Dr. Julian A. Taylor, who encouraged me to aspire to excellence and gave me the strong foundation to make it possible; my husband, James Lowell Gibbs, Jr., and my sons, Geoffrey Taylor Gibbs and Lowell Dabney Gibbs, who have provided me with constant support of every variety and have endured some unintended vicissitudes due to my two-year immersion in this project; my family and close friends, near and far, who have been sympathetic and sensitive to my needs for concentrated periods of work and intensive periods of introspection in order to complete this book.

To all my colleagues, family, and friends I owe a debt of gratitude for their direct and indirect contributions, their support, and their love. I hope that they will share with me the pleasure and satisfaction that the book has been completed and the hope that it will contribute toward a meaningful dialogue on the problems of young black males.

JEWELLE TAYLOR GIBBS

ABOUT THE AUTHORS

Ann F. Brunswick, Ph.D. is Senior Research Scientist in Public Health (Sociomedical Sciences) at Columbia University, where she has been conducting the Longitudinal Study of Harlem Health since 1967. A Fellow of the American Psychological Association, she has served on Advisory Boards of the American Public Health Association and the American Association for Public Opinion Research and on review panels for the U.S. Dept. of Health and Human Services, Office of Maternal and Child Health, and National Institute on Drug Abuse. Dr. Brunswick is on the Board of Directors of the State of Illinois Ounce of Prevention Program and of the New York State Narcotics and Drugs Research agency. She has authored numerous research articles in public health, social problem and drug abuse journals and in books on adolescence and drug abuse.

Michael E. Connor, Ph.D. is a Professor of Psychology at Cal State University, Long Beach, California, where he has developed and teaches courses on Cross-Cultural Psychology and on Fathers and Fathering. Additionally, he is a clinical psychologist in private practice working primarily with children and adolescents and their families. Dr. Connor is cofounder of the Southern California Divorce Mediation Group, which specializes in minimizing conflict in the dissolution of marriage where children are involved. His research interests and publications focus on the reduction of teenage pregnancy, positive attitudes of black men who are fathers, issues in dual careers, successful male/female adult relationships, and methods for non-litigated divorce procedures.

Richard Dembo, Ph.D. is a professor in the Department of Criminology at the University of South Florida in Tampa, Florida. He received his Ph.D. in sociology from New York University in 1970. He has conducted research on the relationship between drug use and delinquency and has published numerous articles and chapters for books in the fields of criminology, substance use, mental health, and program evaluation. For the past several years, Dr. Dembo has been engaged in research and service projects involving detained juveniles, with the goal of developing innovative intervention programs for youths at high risk of future delinquency and drug use.

Jewelle Taylor Gibbs, Ph.D. a native of Connecticut, was educated in public schools in Ansonia, Connecticut, then was graduated with honors from Radcliffe College. She received a master's degree in social work and a doctorate in clinical psychology from the University of California at Berkeley. Since 1979 she has been on the faculty of the School of Social Welfare at the University of California at Berkeley, where she is currently an associate professor and chairperson of the M.S.W. curriculum. Dr. Gibbs has served on the Board of Directors of the American Orthopsychiatric Association and on the Board of Publications of the National Association of Social Workers, and is currently a member of the Advisory Board of the National Resource Center for Children in Poverty. She was a member of the Task Panel on Special Populations of President Carter's Commission on Mental Health. She has been a Fellow at the Mary I. Bunting Institute at Radcliffe College and is listed in *Who's Who of American Women* and *Who's Who Among Black Americans*. She has also served as a consultant to the Carnegie Corporation of New York and the Ford Foundation on programs for disadvantaged minority youth. Dr. Gibbs, the author of numerous publications on the psychological problems and treatment of minority youth, was the recipient of the 1987 McCormick Award from the American Association of Suicidology for her scholarly contributions to minority suicide.

Tom E. Larson, Ph.D. recently received his doctorate in economics from the University of California at Berkeley. His dissertation was on changes in employment patterns among black male youth in the post-World War II period. He also received a postdoctoral fellowship from *California Tomorrow* and studied minority and youth employment in California. Dr. Larson served on the Youth Subcommittee of the California State Job Training Coordinating Council. Currently, he is an assistant professor in the Department of Economics and Statistics at California State University, Los Angeles, and is doing research on youth training programs.

Rodney J. Reed, Ph.D. (University of California at Berkeley), is currently professor of Educational Administration, School of Education, University of California at Berkeley. His teaching and research focus on school leadership and management, human resources management, and educational equity for minority students, faculty, and staff at all levels of education. Dr. Reed has been actively involved in a number of professional and civic organizations and has served as an educational consultant at local, state, and federal levels. He is presently directing a California statewide research-based project entitled, "Shaping Teacher Expectations for Minority Students," which is designed to improve the academic performance of black public school students. He is founder and director of the Institute for School Administrators at the University of California, which has operated since 1978. Dr. Reed serves on several editorial boards of scholarly and professional journals and has published widely. He is author of the recently published *School and Competency Testing Programs: Perceptions and Effects on Black Students in Louisiana and North Carolina* and is co-author (with James W. Guthrie) of *Educational Administration and Policy, Effective Leadership for American Education*.

Barbara Solomon earned her doctorate in social work from USC in 1966, her M.S.W. degree in social welfare from USC in 1956, and her B.S. degree in psychology *magna cum laude* from Howard University in 1954. Acting dean of graduate studies at the University of Southern California, she has direct responsibility for all degree programs offered through the Graduate School and oversight responsibilities for all other post-baccalaureate degrees awarded by USC's professional schools.

Dr. Solomon, who joined the USC faculty as an assistant professor of social work in 1966, is currently a professor of social work and director of the research center in the School of Social Work. Her primary research and teaching interests are social service delivery systems in health and mental health settings, particularly minority and aged populations. She has published extensively in these and other areas and has won numerous professional awards, including Social Work Educator of the Year from the National Association of Social Workers and, from USC, a Distinguished Faculty Award, a USC Associates Award for Teaching Excellence, and membership in the Phi Kappa Phi Honor Society.

Chapter 1

YOUNG BLACK MALES IN AMERICA: ENDANGERED, EMBITTERED, AND EMBATTLED

Jewelle Taylor Gibbs

> *I am an invisible man. . . . I am a man of substance, of flesh and bone, fiber and liquids—and I might even be said to possess a mind. I am invisible, understand, simply because people refuse to see me. . . . When they approach me, they see only my surroundings, themselves, or figments of their imagination—indeed, everything and anything except me.*
>
> RALPH ELLISON in *Invisible Man* (New York: Random House, 1972).

An endangered species is, according to Webster, "a class of individuals having common attributes and designated by a common name . . . [which is] in danger or peril of probable harm or loss." This description applies in a metaphorical sense, to the current status of young black males in contemporary American society. They have been miseducated by the educational system, mishandled by the criminal justice system, mislabeled by the mental

NOTE: This chapter includes portions of a paper by the author previously published as "Black Adolescents and Youth: An Endangered Species" in *American Journal of Orthopsychiatry*, and an invited lecture on "Young Black Males: An Endangered Species," presented at the Annual Civil Rights Institute, NAACP Legal Defense and Educational Fund, Inc., New York, May 1985.

1

health system, and mistreated by the social welfare system. All the major institutions of American society have failed to respond appropriately and effectively to their multiple needs and problems. As a result, they have become—in an unenviable and unconscionable sense—rejects of our affluent society and misfits in their own communities (Gibbs, 1984).

Who are these black youth who are increasingly subjected to the belated scrutiny of social scientists, educators, policymakers, and the mass media? They are black males in the 15–24-year-old age group who live predominantly in urban inner-city neighborhoods but can also be found in rural areas, working-class suburbs, and small towns all over America. They are the teenagers and young adults from families at the lower end of the socioeconomic spectrum, many of whom are welfare-dependent and live below the poverty line. They are the black youth who are seen when one drives through inner-city ghetto neighborhoods, hanging out on dimly lit street corners, playing basketball on littered school lots, selling dope in darkened alleys, and "rapping" in front of pool halls and bars. The media refer to them by a variety of labels: "dropouts," "delinquents," "dope addicts," "street-smart dudes," "welfare pimps," and, even more pejoratively, as members of the "underclass." They refer to themselves as "home boys," "hardheads," "bloods," and "soul brothers." Labels are powerful clues to the ways in which groups are perceived, valued, and treated, but labels cannot convey the feelings of frustration, humiliation, and anger of these black youth who experience daily doses of failure, rejection, and discrimination. From the brutal lynching of Emmett Till in Mississippi in 1955 to the "justifiable" police killing of Michael Stewart on a New York City subway in 1983, young black males in America have been the primary victims of mob violence, police brutality, legal executions, and ghetto homicide.

Black males are portrayed by the mass media in a limited number of roles, most of them deviant, dangerous, and dysfunctional. This constant barrage of predominantly disturbing images inevitably contributes to the public's negative stereotypes of black men, particularly of those who are perceived as young, hostile, and impulsive. Even the presumably positive images of blacks as athletes and entertainers project them as animal-like or childlike in their aggressiveness, sensuality, "natural rhythm," and uninhibited expressiveness. Clearly, the message says: If they entertain you, enjoy them (at a safe distance); if they serve you, patronize them (and don't forget to leave a tip); if they threaten you, avoid them (don't ride on the subway). Thus, young black males are stereotyped by the five "d's": dumb, deprived, dangerous, deviant, and disturbed. There is no room in this picture for comprehension, caring, or compassion of the plight of these young black men.

A few vignettes illustrate the impact of these stereotypes on community attitudes and behaviors toward this group:

- Just five days before Christmas 1986, three young black men (ages 19, 23, and 37) stopped at a pizza parlor to call for help when their car broke down in the predominantly white neighborhood of Howard Beach, Queens. While there, they ordered pizza and chatted briefly with the counterman, but became apprehensive when a crowd of white youth gathered outside and began chanting: "Niggers, go home." As they left the restaurant, they were beaten and chased by the angry youth in various directions. One of the black youth, 23-year-old Michael Griffith, after pleading to an onlooker for help, ran onto the nearby freeway to escape his assailants and was killed by an oncoming car. Subsequently, four white teenagers, none older than 18, were arrested and charged with manslaughter. In their defense, neighbors were quoted as saying that they were "just average boys from respectable families," and that they probably thought that the three black men were "up to no good."
- In October 1986, the *Washington Post* inaugurated a new Sunday magazine section with a feature story on the problems of operating small businesses in the downtown areas of the capital city, where merchants customarily installed bars on their windows and frequently refused to open their doors to young black males whom they viewed as potential assailants. Although the *Post* was heavily criticized by local black leaders for this inflammatory article, the paper was only revealing a practice that is common in central city shopping areas of New York, Chicago, Los Angeles, and many others.
- The sheriff of Jefferson Parish, Louisiana, a predominantly white suburb of New Orleans, called a news conference on December 2, 1986 to announce that his deputies would henceforth arrest any young black males seen in the residential areas of his community after dark. When civil rights groups objected to this policy, the sheriff defended his position on the grounds that most of the crime in the New Orleans area was committed by young black men and, therefore, it seemed perfectly reasonable and justifiable to arrest anyone fitting that description, as a preventive measure.
- In Liberty City, Florida, a riot broke out in the predominantly

black area after a young black male died in police custody in May 1980. The police claimed that his death was an accident, but witnesses swore that he had been subdued with a choke hold and brutally beaten by the police. This incident was one of a series of confrontations between blacks and the local police, with black males consistently complaining of police brutality and discrimination.

• In December 1984, a young black man approached a white man riding on a New York City subway, asking him for five dollars. Three of the black youth's friends sitting nearby were watching, perhaps planning to join in the panhandling, as the white man pulled out a gun and shot all four of them. One youth is paralyzed for life, but Bernhard Goetz, a 37-year-old electrical engineer, was hailed as a hero by many New Yorkers and was treated as a celebrity by the mass media. In his defense, Goetz's lawyer claimed that he felt his life was threatened because of the "gleam in their eyes." Nearly two and a half years later, in June 1987, a jury of his peers found him "not guilty" of attempted murder and assault.

In 1985 there were 8.5 million black youth in the 10–24-year-old age range, with nearly 3 million each in the 15–19 and 20–24-year-old age groups. Black males accounted for nearly 3 million in the 15–24 category, or 50 percent of the total group. Since nearly half of the total black population is composed of children and youth, the median age for blacks is 25.8 years compared to a median age of 31.8 for whites (U.S. Census Bureau, 1987). Thus, any social and economic problems in the black community will have a disproportionate impact on black youth under the age of 25, and more particularly on the additional unenumerated black males (Gibbs, 1985).

Nearly half (42.7 percent) of black youth under 18 live in families who are below the poverty line, while two-thirds (67.1 percent) of those living in female-headed families are classified as poor. Two of every five (42 percent) black youth live in female-headed families (U.S. Census Bureau, 1987). Clearly, this type of family structure tends to have a negative impact on the economic status and opportunities for all black youth, and it may have particularly negative effects on black males (CDF, 1986c).

Children in black female-headed families are five times as likely to be welfare-dependent than those in intact black families. Thus, males in female-headed families are not only reared without fathers as role models, but are also reared in families triply stigmatized by being black, single-parent, and on welfare. Furthermore, youth in these families are more likely to live in substandard housing, to attend inferior schools, to have inadequate health and dental care, to have higher rates of chronic illnesses, to have more behavioral problems, and to live in deteriorating neighborhoods with high crime rates, poor services, and inadequate public transportation (CDF, 1985a and 1986a).

Even for those black youth who live in intact nuclear families, economic stability and quality of life are much less predictable and permanent than for comparable white youth (CDF, 1985b). For such youth, total family income is more likely to depend on both parents working, but their fathers are 2.5 times more likely than adult white males to be unemployed. Both parents are more likely than parents of white youth to be employed in lower-status, lower-income jobs in the white-collar, blue-collar, and unskilled sectors of the economy. In 1986, the median black family income of $17,604 was only 57 percent of white family income of $30,809, a decrease from 61 percent in 1970. Thus, it is an illusion that the gap between black and white family income has narrowed in the past 15 years. In fact, black family income is lower than it was in 1978, and its modest gains since 1980 remain heavily dependent on two parents working, a stable economy, and the security of government employment (U.S. Census Bureau, 1987).

Just as the modest economic gains experienced by the black family in the late 1960s and early 1970s have largely been offset by the increasing rate of poverty among single-parent families, black youth have also lost ground on five out of six social indicators. What is particularly dramatic and demoralizing is that, while all other groups (including women and recent immigrants) have made progress since 1960 in all of these areas, young black males in particular are now more likely than they were in 1960 to be unemployed, to be addicted to drugs, to be involved in the criminal justice system, to be unwed fathers, and to die from homicide or suicide. The educational statistics indicate a reduction in high school drop-out rates among black males during this period, but this improved high school completion rate has been offset by a decline in the college enrollment rates of black high school graduates and a continuing high rate of illiteracy among 18–21-year-old black youth, both of which are more characteristic of black males.

A brief summary of each of these social indicators for black youth will provide a background for the in-depth treatment of these issues in the following chapters.

Social Indicators for Young Black Males

Education

A surface familiarity with the statistics on the educational attainment of black youth suggests that there has been some improvement in the past 25 years. For example, the proportion of high school dropouts among black youth in the 14–24 age group steadily declined from 23.8 percent in 1960 to 13.2 percent in 1984, and for 16–17-year-olds, from 22.3 percent to 5.2 percent in the same period (College Entrance Examination Board, 1985). In recent years the gap between black and white overall drop-out rates in the high school age group has reached parity, in spite of disproportionately high rates for inner-city black youth. However, these figures do not reveal the number of black high school graduates who were functionally illiterate or barely able to fill out a job application. While an earlier survey estimated that more than 20 percent of black male adolescents in the 12–17 age group were unable to read at the fourth-grade level (Brown, 1979), more recent statistics indicated that 21 percent of all 18- and 19-year-old and 25 percent of all 20- and 21-year-old black youth had neither completed nor were presently enrolled in high school in 1980 (U.S. Census Bureau, 1981). Thus, more than one out of five black youth in the 18–21 age group currently do not have either the basic certificate or basic skills which in our society are necessary for most entry-level jobs, apprenticeship programs, military service, or postsecondary education.

While reasons for dropping out of high school are varied, a recent Urban League Study pointed out that many black male teenagers leave because of family economic problems, academic difficulties, or disciplinary problems, and females often drop out due to pregnancy (Williams, 1982). This study also reported that nearly one-third of black families with incomes below $6,000 and 18 percent of black families with incomes above $20,000 had at least one child suspended from school. These figures suggest that black students have attitudes or behaviors which school administrators and teachers define as problematic and which they are either unwilling or unable to deal with effectively. On the other hand, inner-city students are confronted with nearly insurmountable barriers to learning and achievement in schools which are characterized by poorly prepared teachers, inadequate educational facilities, low teacher expectations, ineffective administrators, and chronic violence. Lack of communication between parents and school authorities, as well as prevailing community attitudes toward the schools, probably contribute to bureaucratic inflexibility, student alienation, and hostility in a continuously escalating cycle of mistrust and maladaptive behaviors.

Whether black teenagers drop out of school or obtain a meaningless high school diploma based on "social promotion," the consequences are higher rates of unemployment, fewer options for jobs, greater welfare dependency, and long-range limitations on their social and economic mobility (see Bane and Ellwood, 1983; McLanahan, 1985). What has caused this massive alienation of black males from the educational system? In a nation which boasts of universal education and equal opportunities, how is it that this group has not seized those opportunities to improve their status? In the most advanced technological society in the world, where we can build rockets to send a man to the moon, planes to break the sound barrier, and ships to raise the "Titanic," why can't we teach black children how to read, write, and use computers? Chapter 2 presents a comprehensive analysis of the factors contributing to the current educational status of black youth, with a particular focus on the implications for black males.

Employment/Unemployment

In November 1987, the U.S. Labor Department announced a national unemployment rate of 6.0 percent. Unemployment among black youth, however, was 34.0 percent—twice the rate of 17.4 percent among all teenagers. This national rate is nearly three times higher than the 12.1 percent employment rate among 16–19-year-old black youth in 1960, but lower than the local unemployment rates in many large metropolitan areas of the country, which have consistently ranged between 40 and 50 percent in the past decade. Since 1960, unemployment rates of black male youth have consistently been higher than black females by a ratio of 2 to 1.

Unemployment statistics obviously reflect the labor force participation rates of black youth, which have fallen dramatically since 1960. At that time, 82.0 percent of black males 20–24 participated in the labor force, but in 1980 only 73.5 percent of this group participated (Wilson and Neckerman, 1984). Labor force participation rates for black males 16–19 also dropped from 42.4 percent in 1960 to 36.5 percent in 1980. In the early 1960s, over half of the black high school graduates 16–24 were employed, but by 1980 fewer than one-third were able to find jobs. In 1983 black high school dropouts were twice as likely to be unemployed, with only 26 percent in the labor force (U.S. Dept. of Labor, 1987). Ironically, employment rates increased for all white youth, including high school dropouts, during this same period from 67 to 71 percent.

A recent study found that in 1984 nearly half of the black youth in the 16–24 age group had no work experience at all (Larson, 1986). These extremely high unemployment rates, affecting from over one-third to one-half of the nation's young black males, have significant implications for these young people and for the society at large in the next few decades (Sum, Harrington, and Goedicke, 1987). If black youth are unable to find jobs, they will not develop the work skills, attitudes, and habits that are appropriate and necessary in a competitive, highly technological economy. Moreover, recent studies have indicated that chronically unemployed black males constitute a disproportionately high percentage of those workers who become "discouraged" and completely drop out of the job-seekers' market (Auletta, 1982). Without gainful employment, black youth are increasingly tempted to participate in the underground alternative economy of the urban ghettos—that is, the illegal system of barter in stolen goods, drugs, gambling, and prostitution (Glasgow, 1981; Clark, 1965).

The prospect of a rapidly increasing cadre of unemployed and unemployable urban youth, socialized to a nonproductive life-style on the streets, has major implications in terms of the development of a permanent urban underclass with the accompanying sociopolitical consequences (Glasgow, 1981; Wilson and Aponte, 1985). How has this "underclass" developed in the richest industrial nation in the world? Why are black men, who have labored in the cotton fields, the coal mines, and the steel factories, now unwanted and unemployable in American industry? Do these young black males reject the Protestant work ethic or are they unwitting victims of structural economic changes and technological progress in America? Chapter 3 offers fresh insights into the deteriorating economic status of young black men from a recent study of structural and social constraints on their participation in the labor force.

Delinquency and Crime

The rate of delinquency among black youth has increased from 19.6 percent of all juvenile arrests in 1960 to 23.2 percent in 1985; thus 407,807, or approximately 7 percent of all black adolescents in the 10–19 age group, were arrested in 1985 (FBI, 1986).

Black juveniles were arrested more frequently than whites for robbery, rape, homicide, and aggravated assault. They were also more likely than white juveniles to be arrested for other violent personal crimes, disorderly conduct, sexual misbehavior, and handling stolen property. National data, compiled from 1977 to 1982 by the FBI on juvenile arrests by race for Part I offenses (violent crimes against persons and property), indicate that blacks accounted for nearly one-third of all arrests; yet black juveniles represent less than one-fifth of the total youth population (Krisberg et al., 1986). During that same period, over half of the juvenile arrests for the most violent crimes were among black youth. However, arrest rates tend to give a biased view of the actual prevalence of delinquent behavior in black youth.

Another perspective on black youth crime rates is provided by the National Youth Survey (NYS), a longitudinal study of self-reported delinquency and substance use among a probability sample of 11–17-year-olds in the United States. Data collected from 1976 to 1983 indicate that black youth reported a slightly higher rate of general delinquency, index offenses, and felony offenses than white youth, but few of these offense differences were consistent or statistically significant across age subgroups and over the seven-year period (Krisberg et al., 1986). Despite official statistics indicating that black youth are disproportionately represented among violent and high-frequency offenders, Huizinga and Elliott (1985) analyzed the NYS data for 1976–1980 and found no statistically significant racial differences in high-rate offenders except for one year (1976). These researchers conclude:

> *Overall, these findings suggest that there are few if any substantial and consistent differences between the delinquency involvement of different racial groups. This finding is not unique. Other large scale self-report studies of delinquency have reached similar conclusions.—As a result*, it does not appear that differences in delinquent behavior can provide an explanation for the observed race differential in incarceration rates. *(p. 13) (emphasis supplied)*

These authors assume that self-report surveys of delinquency are equally valid for black and white youth, which may be arguable, particularly since the most violent offenders are least likely to remain subjects in a longitudinal study. However, given their well-documented conclusion, it is particularly disturbing to note that black youth are significantly more likely than any other ethnic group to be incarcerated in public juvenile facilities for both overall delinquency and for Part I offenses (Krisberg et al., 1986). Further, these authors note that, while 71 percent of incarcerated black youth are confined in public facilities, only 54 percent of whites are in these facilities. In 1979 black males had the highest rate of incarceration for all sex/race subgroups (587.9 per 100,000) and black females were highest among females incarcerated (76.9 per 100,000) in public juvenile facilities. By 1982, these incarceration rates had increased dramatically to 810 per 100,000 for black males and 98.4 per 100,000 for black females, more than double the rate of increase among whites of either gender.

By 1982, when black males comprised about 14 percent of youth under the jurisdiction of the juvenile court, they represented 39 percent of all incarcerated male juveniles, a ratio of 44 to 1 compared to the rate of white male juvenile incarceration. Further, the rate of black youth incarceration for Part I offenses in 1982 was 8.6 per 100, which was 69 percent higher than the 5.1 per 100 rate of incarceration for white youth for the same offense category (Krisberg et al., 1986).

The proportion of minority youth in public correctional facilities increased 26 percent from 1977 to 1982, with nearly two-thirds of this increase due to black youth. Of even greater concern, a recent report noted that on any given day the state prison population contains more than 5 percent of all black males in their 20s. Projected lifetime rates predict that up to 15 percent of all black males will spend some time in an adult prison,while only 2 to 3 percent of white males are expected to do so (Krisberg et al., 1986).

Some studies have suggested that black teens are more likely to be arrested, booked, and remanded for trial and to receive harsher dispositions than whites. It has also been suggested that the more frequent arrests of black youth for minor offenses occur both because inner-city neighborhoods are patrolled more intensively and because police tend to overreact to the perceived negative attitudes and "anti-authority demeanor" of black youth (Piliavin and Briar, 1964; Thornton, James, and Doerner, 1982). Whether or not these factors can reasonably account for the widespread discrepancy between arrest rates of black and white youth, the fact remains that black youth are disproportionately involved in the juvenile justice system, resulting in severe limitations on their educational and occupational opportunities and creating a vicious cycle of delinquency, incarceration, recidivism, and chronic criminal careers—or unemployment and marginal social adaptation in adulthood (Tolmach, 1985).

Moreover, the primary victims of black juvenile crime are the juveniles themselves and the black community. In addition, the rate of victimization for crimes of violence is generally greater for blacks than whites at all income levels, and the victimization rate of residents of central cities was roughly twice that of residents of urban and suburban areas (FBI, 1981). In 1980, 95 percent of those who committed crimes against blacks were themselves black, and the majority of these crimes were committed by youth under the age of 24. Inner-city neighborhoods are increasingly becoming brutalized by youth who burglarize stores and homes, vandalize schools and churches, and terrorize those who are old, sick, and vulnerable. The major victims of these antisocial youth are black females, age 25 and older, black males in the 50–64 age group, and other black male teenagers in the 12–15 age group (FBI, 1981).

The crucial question is, Who are the real victims in these statistics—those who are brutally victimized or those who are brutally aggressive? What kinds of social realities, family situations, and personal traumas might account for the violence, the amorality, and the contempt for community norms of these young men? Why have so many chosen to live outside the laws, to engage in self-destructive behaviors, and to embrace a deviant life-style? Chapter 4 provides a partial answer to these questions in its analysis of the relationship between sociodemographic factors and early delinquency in a study which demonstrates the differential treatment of young black males in the juvenile justice system.

Substance Abuse

Recent data from the National Institute on Drug Abuse indicate that nonwhite youth in the 18–25 age group have higher or equal rates of drug abuse than white youth in every major drug category except for inhalants and hallucinogens (NIDA, 1979). For the younger age group, 12–17, 31 percent of black teens reported they had used marijuana, and 29 percent said they had used alcohol in this 1979 NIDA survey. Although a number of recent studies have indicated that in early adolescence the overall rate of drug and alcohol use is actually lower among black than white youth, the rates of heroin and cocaine (including the recent derivative "crack") are disproportionately high among older black male youth (Brunswick, 1979). Reliable estimates of drug use in this population are difficult to obtain due to sampling problems and other methodological issues, but studies of selected samples of young black inner-city males in major metropolitan areas suggest high lifetime rates of these drugs. For example, a study of drug use in a Harlem sample of black males in the mid–1970s found that heroin and cocaine rates were three times higher than reported by a national sample of selective service registrants (Brunswick, 1979).

The issue is not simply a legal or moral issue. Society's concern should be focused on the damage these young people are inflicting on themselves physically, psychologically, and socially (Brunswick and Messeri, 1986). Drug use among black youth is highly correlated to low school achievement, delinquency, and accidental deaths. Moreover, drug addiction inevitably involves teenagers in activities that will increase access to drugs, whether these involve stealing, dealing, or hustling sex in order to "get high" (Beschner and Friedman, 1979; Gandossy, Williams, and Harwood, 1980; Thornton, James, and Doerner, 1982). Addicts lose interest in school, work, and gradually deteriorate so that "getting high" becomes the major motivation of each day; eventually, they become walking zombies, worthless to themselves, their families, and their communities. Drug addiction among black youth also substantially increases the risk of arrest and imprisonment, physical and mental illness, and death by overdosing (Gandossy, Wiliams, and Harwood, 1980; Nelson et al., 1974).

The newest drug-related threat to young black males is the spectre of AIDS (acquired immunodeficiency syndrome), which is increasing rapidly among intravenous drug users in the inner cities. In 1986, the Centers for Disease Control (1986b) reported that black males accounted for nearly one of four (23 percent) of all males with AIDS. The rate of infection of the AIDS virus is also reported to be higher among blacks than whites in samples of military recruits and potential blood donors (Centers for Disease Control, 1986a). Since few of these young black men practice preventive health care or engage in drug treatment programs, they are virtually unreachable for public health education campaigns (CDF, 1986b).

The implications of AIDS among young black male drug addicts, especially those who are sexually active and adamantly opposed to any form of male contraception, are truly frightening for the black community, furtively ticking away with the insidious danger of a time bomb primed to explode in the 21st century. These implications are discussed in Chapter 7 in an analysis of the health and mental health status of young black males.

How have drugs become so entrenched among black youth in the inner cities? What larger social forces have shaped the vulnerability of young black males to the high-risk life-style of the drug addict and his involvement in the underworld economy? Why haven't effective drug prevention and treatment programs been developed for these black youth? Chapter 5 reports the results from a longitudinal study of drug use in Harlem youth, pointing out both the risk factors and the consequences of drug addiction for black youth, as well as the social factors which foster and reinforce the addict's life-style.

Unwed Teenage Parenthood

In 1985, the Guttmacher Institute published a startling report that the pregnancy rate for American teenagers in the 15–19-year-old age group was the highest of all industrialized nations at 96 per 1,000 pregnancies per year. In 1980, America was also the only country where the rate was increasing and, contrary to popular stereotypes, it was increasing more rapidly among white than black adolescent females. Despite the decreasing birth trend among black teenagers, pregnancy rates are still twice as high among blacks as whites (163 per 1,000 vs. 83 per 1,000), and out-of-wedlock pregnancy is a major problem in the black community (CDF, 1986d). In 1980, for example, nearly one out of ten black teenage females gave birth (9.5 percent) compared to one out of 25 white females (4.5 percent). Black teens are more likely to have their babies, while white teens are more likely to terminate their pregnancies by abortions. In 1983, 85.7 percent of babies born to black females under age 19 were out-of-wedlock compared to 39.7 percent born to white teenage mothers (CDF, 1986d).

These are children having children, with profound physical and psychosocial consequences for the girls themselves, as well as negative implications for their babies and their families (Family Impact Seminar, 1979). Teenage mothers are more likely to drop out of high school, more likely to go on welfare, and more likely to experience complications in pregnancy and associated physical and psychological problems than adult women who bear their first child (Chilman, 1983; Furstenberg, Lincoln, and Menken, 1981). Moreover, teen mothers are more likely than adult women to have larger families, to experience less occupational stability and economic mobility, and to be less competent and effective as parents.

Babies born to teenage mothers are more likely to have low birth weight and other perinatal and postnatal problems, to have poor health, and to experience abuse or neglect. Infant mortality rates are highest among teen mothers and nearly twice as high among blacks as among whites (19.2 vs. 9.7 per 1,000 live births in 1983). If they survive, these children tend to be less healthy, less academically successful in school, more likely to grow up in a single-parent, welfare-dependent family, and more likely than children born to adult women to become single parents themselves.

The effects of premature fatherhood on the youthful male partners of these teenage mothers has only recently been of interest to researchers. Several studies have found that, compared with their peers who have not fathered children, these young men are more likely to attain a lower educational level and lower occupational status, to have larger families, and to experience unstable marriages (Chilman, 1983; Furstenberg, Lincoln, and Menken, 1981).

Much less is known about the male partners who father these out-of-wedlock children. Contrary to popular belief, one study suggests that a significant number of these men are young adults and older men who become sexually involved with younger women. The typical profile of the teenage/young adult unwed father, drawn from ethnographic studies and reports of teenage parenting programs, is a high school dropout who is unemployed, low-skilled, and lives with his family. Such a characterization may be both inaccurate and biased, however, because it is based on small samples of young men willing to participate in studies or motivated to cooperate in parenting programs with the teenage mothers of their children.

Several studies have indicated that young black males not only have negative attitudes toward using contraception, but also discourage their female sexual partners from using any contraceptive measures (Shapiro, 1980; CDF, 1986a; Gibbs, 1986). Ethnographic studies suggest that black males are very interested in having children to demonstrate their virility, yet many do not exhibit a similar level of commitment to supporting them after they arrive. More recently, however, there is some evidence that these young fathers often do have continuing involvement with their children, contribute to their support when their financial status permits, and play a significant role in their lives over an extended period of time (CDF, 1986c). Thus, the stereotype of the "irresponsible teenage father" may be more of a myth than a reality, based on false assumptions and inadequate empirical data from nonrepresentative samples.

Nonetheless, the impact of these illegitimate births on black families has yet to be fully understood and documented. Some sociological studies suggest that children reared in single-parent homes have fewer competent role models and fewer social supports, which, in turn, limits their ability to grow up in successfully functioning families, to develop satisfactory heterosexual relationships, and to form stable family units of their own (Ladner, 1971; Williams, 1982). The recent prediction that 94 percent of all black children born in 1980 will spend part of their lives before age 18 in a single-parent family (predominantly female-headed) has very serious implications for the stability of black families and for the health and welfare of black youth (Hofferth, 1985).

How has illegitimacy become such a widespread pattern in black communities, rural and urban? What factors have contributed to the decline in marriage rates for young black males and females? Are black teenage fathers uncaring and uncommitted to their children or are they unequipped and unprepared to assume the responsibilities of parenthood? Chapter 6 discusses these issues in the context of historical, cultural, and economic factors which have influenced the responses of young black men to marriage and parenthood.

Homicide and Suicide

The final and most alarming social indicator is the increase in mortality rates among young black males, particularly from homicide and suicide. Homicide is now the leading cause of death for black male teenagers and young adults.

In 1960 the homicide rate for black males 15–24 was 46.4 per 100,000 (DHHS, 1986). This rate increased through the next two decades, reaching a peak of 102.5 per 100,000 in 1970 and then declining to 61.5 per 100,000 in 1984. However, the current rate is still 33 percent higher than it was 25 years ago, a level unacceptable in a civilized society. A young black male has a 1 in 21 chance of being murdered before he reaches the age of 25. In 1985 alone, more than 1,900 black youth 15–24 were murdered—over 90 percent of them by other black youth (NCHS, 1986).

While white youth die primarily from accidents, black youth die primarily from homicide. With the increase in drug trafficking in the inner cities, drug dealers employ violence with impunity in cities like New York, Detroit, Oakland, and Washington, D.C., where they now use Uzi machine guns to protect their turf and to terrorize their neighborhoods, often killing innocent bystanders.

Despite the recent decline in the homicide rate, it is still unacceptably high and represents a clear and present danger to the black community. This wanton violence suggests a pervasive disregard for human life and a profound alienation from shared community norms and values. What factors can account for this violent behavior among young black males? What are the psychological, physical, and sociodemographic factors which place young black males at such high risk for a homicidal death? Is there any relationship between the increased rates of homicide and suicide for this population group? An analysis of suicide rates may shed some light on these questions, but leaves unanswered the more troubling question of the underlying causes of the overall increase in mortality rates among young black males.

In 1960 the suicide rate for black males was 4.1 per 100,000, and for black females it was 1.3 per 100,000 in the 15–24 age group. After peaking in 1971 and 1976, the suicide rate in this age group declined slightly but by 1982 had nearly tripled to 11.0 per 100,000 for black males and nearly doubled to 2.2 per 100,000 for black females (NCHS, 1986). Even though suicide rates among black males are still lower than whites of the same age, it has been suggested that the figures would be much higher if causes of death among blacks, in general, were reported as reliably as are causes of death among whites. For example, if suspected cases of suicide by single-car accidents, deliberate drug overdoses, victim-precipitated homicides, and other violent accidents were included in these statistics, the suicide rates would be significantly higher, particularly since the rates of homicide and other types of violent accidents are higher among nonwhite youth (Holinger, 1979).

In an analysis of long-term trends in adolescent suicide, Holinger and Offer (1982) demonstrated the correlation between adolescent population changes and adolescent suicide rates in the United States and suggested that higher rates may reflect increased peer competition—for colleges, jobs, and access to services—that occurs during periods of adolescent population growth. Since young black males are clearly in a more disadvantaged competitive position compared with whites, this may very well contribute to their feelings of hopelessness and thereby increase their vulnerability to suicidal behavior.

In spite of the increase in suicide rates among young black males, their rates are consistently lower than the rates of white males and higher than those of black females. What factors might account for these differential rates, particularly since black males are demonstrably more disadvantaged than their white counterparts? What is the relationship between suicide and homicide among young black men? What are the psychological, physical, and sociodemographic risk factors which are predictors of violent and self-destructive behavior in this group? Chapters 7 and 8 discuss the interrelationship among health, mental health, and life-threatening behaviors in black youth, with a particular focus on the psychological, psychosocial, and environmental antecedents and consequences of suicide, homicide, and drug abuse.

In summary, these six social indicators—education, unemployment, delinquency, drug abuse, teenage parenthood, and mortality rates from homicide and suicide—are bellwethers of the serious problems experienced by many black youth in American society, but particularly afflicting young black males. Like the biological food chain, each problem contributes to a larger problem and, in turn, is encompassed by it. None of these problems can or should be viewed in a vacuum—they are all inextricably connected. For a young black male, dropping out of school increases the probability of unemployment, which increases the risk of delinquency and criminal behavior, which in turn, increases the vulnerability to drug abuse. Young black men who are unemployed and involved in a delinquent or addictive life-style are more likely to be sexually irresponsible and less likely to marry if their partners become pregnant. Finally, suicide may be perceived as the only option for a young black man who has no skills, no options, and no future. In order to improve the status of young black males, it is first necessary to understand the complex set of factors which have contributed to these problems and, second, to develop a set of comprehensive and well-coordinated strategies for their amelioration.

Contributing Factors to the Deteriorating Status of Young Black Males

Four major sets of factors can account for this downward spiral of black youth, and particularly black males, since 1960: historical, sociocultural, economic, and political. These factors are briefly discussed below.

Historical Factors

Black youth today are the ultimate victims of a legacy of nearly 250 years of slavery, 100 years of legally enforced segregation, and decades of racial discrimination and prejudice in every facet of American life. Countless authors have documented the brutality of slavery, the cruelty of segregation, and the injustice of discrimination. Generations of blacks have endured inferior schools, substandard housing, menial jobs, and the indignities of poverty. Yet, through all of these travails, each generation of blacks made some progress and believed that their children would eventually merge into the mainstream of American society. These beliefs were infused with new life by the New Deal programs of the 1930s, nurtured by the economic opportunities of World War II, and fostered by the postwar policies of the Truman administration. By 1960, many blacks were optimistic that "Jim Crow" was in a terminal stage, that opportunities were increasing for minorities, and that black youth would finally be able to share in the American dream. No one could have anticipated that the tremendous civil rights and economic gains of the 1960s would have been seriously eroded and ideologically challenged by the mid-1980s, leaving black youth in a worse economic and social situation than they had experienced since before President John F. Kennedy initiated his New Frontier.

The past two and one-half decades since 1960 have been one of the most turbulent periods in American history, encompassing the rise of the civil rights movement, the urban riots, the women's movement, the Vietnam War, the war on poverty, and major political and economic changes in the society. The era began with a liberal Democratic administration committed to increasing opportunities for minorities, but it has gradually evolved into a conservative Republican administration which has aggressively dismantled or diluted many of the most effective civil rights and social welfare programs.

Black youth, who lived through a period of heightened expectations and increased opportunities in the 1960s and early 1970s, began to see their dreams of major social change gradually fade as the economy stopped expanding and other groups (e.g., women, immigrants) began competing for the same limited resources. While much of the civil rights legislation and many of the anti-poverty programs primarily benefited working and middle-class blacks (who were in a better position to take advantage of them), the unanticipated effect of these changes was to create a wider gap between middle-class and poor blacks. Middle-class blacks moved out of the inner cities into integrated urban and suburban areas, leaving poor blacks behind in blighted neighborhoods without effective leadership, successful role models, or the supportive institutions and social networks that provided social stability, economic diversity, and traditional values to the community (see Clark, 1965; Glasgow, 1981). Thus, with increased isolation from the black middle class and alienation from the white community, black inner-city ghettos have gradually become "welfare reservations" where black youth have few, if any, positive role models; where they lack access to high-quality educational, recreational, and cultural facilities; where they do not have job opportunities or adequate transportation to locate jobs; and where they are confronted daily with adult role models who are openly involved in drugs, prostitution, gambling, and other forms of deviant behavior.

Sociocultural Factors

These recent historical and demographic developments have undoubtedly contributed to sociocultural changes in the black community. As the black middle class has drifted away from the inner cities, it has left a vacuum not only in terms of leadership but also in terms of values and resources. For example, in these transformed ghettos, the black church, which had formerly been the center of activity in the black community, has lost much of its central function as a monitor of norms and values. The power of political organizations has been diminished, as their constituencies no longer include the better educated and wealthier blacks who are more likely to participate actively in the political process. In cities with shrinking tax bases, civic and social organizations have fewer resources to improve neighborhoods, initiate youth programs, or provide incentives to attract external sources of support.

With the breakdown or weakening of these traditional institutions within inner-city communities, there has been a parallel breakdown of the traditional black community values of the importance of family, religion, education, self-improvement, and social cohesion through extensive social support networks. Many blacks in inner cities no longer seem to feel connected to each other, responsible for each other, or concerned about each other. Rather than a sense of shared community and a common purpose, which once characterized black neighborhoods, these inner cities now reflect a sense of hopelessness, alienation, and frustration. It is exactly this kind of frustration that exploded in the urban riots of the 1960s from Watts, California, to Detroit, Michigan, to Washington, D.C.

It is also this kind of frustration that erupts into urban crime and violence, family violence, and self-destructive violence. Thus, we see situations in which young black men sell drugs openly on major thoroughfares without fear of apprehension; teenage girls have multiple out-of-wedlock pregnancies without fear of ostracism; youthful gangs terrorize neighborhoods without fear of retaliation; and young teenagers loiter aimlessly at night on street corners without fear of reprobation.

The poverty and the powerlessness of black youth are inextricably linked to the safety and security of the rest of the society, since the frustration-bred violence will ultimately spill over the invisible walls of the ghetto. The violence which young black males now direct mainly against the black community (black-on-black crime), against relatives and friends (homicide), and against themselves (suicide), will inevitably erupt and spread throughout urban and suburban America, leaving behind damage, destruction, and distrust in its wake. In anxious anticipation of this rising tide of black rage, urban dwellers now put bars on their doors and windows, shopkeepers turn their stores into fortresses, and politicians build new prisons. The causes of these antisocial behaviors are ignored, denied, or blamed on the black youth, who are written off as being intellectually deficient, culturally deprived, and pathologically deviant. Short-term remedies are devised for the consequences of their behaviors, with little understanding that these band-aid solutions are very temporary, very perishable, and very ineffective to cure the underlying causes of frustration and anger in these black youth.

Economic Factors

The post–World War II economic revolution in the United States is the third major factor contributing to the problems of black youth. Two parallel developments created chronic unemployment among black males, both young and old: the structural change in the economy from a predominantly manufacturing and industrial base to a predominantly high-technology and service base, and the movement of these newer jobs from the central cities to the suburbs and peripheral areas (Kasarda, 1985; Sum, Harrington, and Goedicke, 1987). Black youth did not have the skills to compete in the new industries; nor did they have the transportation to follow the jobs to the suburbs. As these jobs moved away from the central cities to the suburbs and exurbs, new services were developed to supply the needs of employers in these industrial and technical companies. These new employment opportunities were increasingly filled by white women and young immigrant workers. After the urban riots of the 1960s, many of the "Mom-and-Pop" stores were forced to close or moved away from the inner cities, removing another source of employment for black youth. As these convenience stores have gradually been replaced, the new owners are predominantly Asian, Hispanic, and Middle-Eastern immigrants who tend to employ family members rather than black youth from the community. Some black leaders have accused these immigrant shopkeepers of commercial exploitation of the black community without returning any economic benefits to the community by hiring black youth.

Black youth, who once had the monopoly on menial service and domestic jobs in restaurants, airports, and department stores, are increasingly being displaced by Asian and Hispanic youth. Although there is some controversy about the displacement theory, statistics indicate that black youth employment rates have decreased as the employment rates of other nonwhite youth have increased. In any case, whether the competition for jobs between black and immigrant youth is perceived or actual, interethnic tensions have increased between blacks and these other minority groups in many urban areas. However, some employers have suggested that immigrant youth are more cooperative, less aggressive, and willing to work for lower wages than black youth. In their analysis of the employment problems of poor youth in America, Sum and his colleagues (1987) conclude that "it is poor black teens who were experiencing the most severe employment problems in March 1985 in both an absolute sense and relative to whites and Hispanics in similar family income positions" (p. 217). Clearly, there are some "noneconomic" factors operating in the severe employment problems of young black males—problems which reflect discriminatory hiring practices as much as they reflect economic and technological changes. The complexity of these factors, in combination with negative employer attitudes toward black youth, are elaborated on more fully in Chapter 3.

Political Factors

The fourth major factor which has exacerbated already existing problems for black youth is the conservative political climate in this country, which began with the election of Richard Nixon in 1968 and has been strongly reinforced by the Reagan administration. Many political analysts interpret this growing conservatism as a backlash to the antipoverty programs and affirmative action policies of the Johnson and Carter administrations, a not-so-subtle protest of the "middle-American majority" to the civil rights and economic gains of minority groups (Omi and Winant, 1986). Threatened with the loss of their special status, these "middle Americans" have been manipulated by politicians and lobbyists for their own self-serving goals. Framing their rationale in neoconservative dogma, these policymakers have shifted the emphasis from the goal of providing all citizens with a decent standard of living through federally subsidized health and welfare programs to the need to blame the poor and disadvantaged for their perceived lack of motivation, their "dysfunctional" family systems, and their dependency on welfare programs. By shifting the focus from society's responsibility for its most vulnerable citizens to an emphasis on the so-called "social pathology" of minority youth and their families, advocates of this view (such as Murray, 1984) have quite deliberately and effectively transformed the national debate from a proactive emphasis on policies of prevention and early intervention to a reactive emphasis on retrogressive policies and punitive programs. As a result, politicians who support cuts in social programs aimed primarily at disadvantaged and minority families have found increasing favor with the voters in the past 20 years; thus programs with a direct impact on black youth, such as CETA, the Job Corps, federally subsidized loans for college, and youth employment programs, all have been severely cut back or eliminated.

The impact of these political and economic changes has resulted in direct negative consequences of fewer educational and employment opportunities for young black males. It has also affected their perceptions of opportunity and their access to the American dream of social and economic mobility. Several national surveys and opinion polls have shown that black families believe they are worse off economically and politically in the 1980s than they were in the 1970s. Consequently, black youth have responded by withdrawing from the labor market, reducing their applications to four-year colleges, and increasing their involvement in self-destruction and deviant behavior. As noted in Chapter 7, peak suicide rates of black youth are also correlated with periods of political conservatism in the past two decades. Thus, there is a reciprocal relationship between the political backlash against minority gains and the social indicators for black youth; that is, these youth respond in a *rational manner* to perceived prejudice and socioeconomic barriers to their mobility by dropping out of the labor market and choosing not to attend college. This reciprocal relationship suggests a self-fulfilling prophecy, which could be reversed if policies and programs were to change, as suggested in later chapters of this book.

Implications of the Problems of Young Black Males

This summary of the major social and economic problems of young black males clearly demonstrates that they are an endangered group and a population "at risk" for an escalating cycle of deviance, dysfunction, and despair. What are the implications of these problems, if they are left unsolved, for black youth, black families, and the larger society? The major implications can be projected in four areas: economic, social, sociocultural, and political.

Economic Implications

Demographers predict that nonwhite youth (80 percent of whom will be black) will constitute 20 percent of the youth population under age 17 by the year 2000 and 23 percent by 2020 (Ozawa, 1986). Similarly, 16 percent of the labor force in the 16–24-year-old age group will be nonwhite by 2000. In fact, the net increase in the labor force between 1985 and 2000 will come primarily from nonwhites, immigrants, and women, with native nonwhite males constituting 8 percent of the labor force in 2000. Moreover, an increasing proportion of these nonwhite workers, particularly blacks and Hispanics, will be recruited from disadvantaged backgrounds from which they have experienced poverty, school failure, and minimal work experience (U.S. Dept. of Labor, 1987).

At the same time, the economy is moving from an industrial/manufacturing-based economy to a service/technology-based economy, in which 90 percent of the newer jobs will be found in those latter occupations by 2000 (Marshall, 1986). Since many of the black youth will not have adequate education or work skills to compete for high-tech jobs, they will not be employable. Since they will be unable to earn income, they will also be unable to contribute to the economy and to support the social security program, which will be expanding as the proportion of elderly retired people increases rapidly during this same period. Thus, black youth will not only be locked out of an increasingly technological labor market, but will also create a major drain on an economy with a shrinking population base to support ever-expanding social insurance and social welfare programs for the elderly. Chapter 3 contains a structural analysis of unemployment among black males and proposes policies needed to address unemployment and to alleviate its negative consequences.

Social Implications

What is the relationship, if any, between the alarming increase in female-headed households among blacks and the statistics on black male unemployment? Sociologists William Wilson and Kathryn Neckerman (1984) of the University of Chicago recently presented a well-documented scholarly analysis concerning this relationship. After examining demographic trends in employment and in family patterns since before World War II, they concluded that the increase in female-headed households is strongly associated with the deteriorating status of black males in the labor market. They show, for example, that participation of black males in the labor force declined from 84 percent in 1940 to 67 percent in 1980. This decline has been especially dramatic among black young men in the 18–19-year-old age group—for example, from 75.7 percent in 1955 to 50.2 percent in 1983. Labor force participation for 20–24-year-old black males also declined from 88.5 percent in 1940 to 73.5 percent in 1980. In 1985, only 43.3 percent of black males 16–19 were participating in the labor force, compared to 59.7

percent of white male teenagers (Sum, Harrington, and Goedicke, 1987).

Wilson and Neckerman also point out that the historical relationship between unemployment and marital instability has been consistently found for black and white families. Moreover, they have also devised a "male marriageable pool index," which is the number of employed single civilian men to the number of single women of the same race and age group. If black males between 16 and 24 who are unemployed, incarcerated, or victims of homicide or suicide are subtracted, this index shows a sharp decline in the ratio of black males to black females since the 1960s. For example, in the 20–24 age group, these authors estimated in 1982 that there were only 47 employed black males for every 100 "marriageable" females, a decline from 69 in 1960. In the 25–34 age group, the figures were 59 males for every 100 females, down from 68 in 1960. The ratio improves somewhat among older black men and women, but it remains very unfavorable in the 20–34 age range, which is the prime period for marriage and family formation in the United States.

The significant point is that there has been an absolute long-term decline in the proportion of young black men who are both available and eligible to support a family. Wilson and Neckerman make a compelling argument that this imbalance in the pool of young black "marriageable" men results in higher rates of out-of-wedlock births, because so many of these young men are not able or willing to support a family. The lack of older black "marriageable" males also results in lower rates of remarriage among divorced and widowed black women, who are also unwilling to marry a man unable to assume family obligations.

Recently, scholars and politicians have been decrying the rise in the number of female-headed households among blacks—a group that has increased from 22 percent in 1960 to 28 percent in 1970 to 42 percent in 1983. This trend is particularly troublesome because much of the increase in this group comes from two major sources: never-married teenage mothers, and divorced or widowed women who have lower remarriage rates than white women. Statistics indicate that the increase in female-headed households is inextricably tied to the "feminization of poverty"—that is, half (50.1 percent) of all black female-headed households are below the poverty line as compared to 28.2 percent among whites, and two-thirds (67.1 percent) of black female-headed families with children under 18 live in poverty, which is nearly 1.5 times the rate for whites (46.3 percent) in similar households (Census Bureau, 1987). In fact, an even more startling figure indicates that 71 percent, or nearly three out of every four, poor black families were headed by females in 1982 (CDF, 1986a).

To put this figure in even starker perspective, as of 1986, one of every two black children in America was born into poverty, and the average poor black child today can expect to remain poor for about 20 years (APWA, 1986). The chance that a black child will experience poverty increases to 90 percent if he or she lives in a family headed by a single woman under age 30. In addition, as Bane and Ellwood (1983) of Harvard's Kennedy School of Government have documented, these children have longer spells in poverty, are more likely to be welfare-dependent, and are more likely to suffer from all the negative consequences of poverty, including malnutrition, chronic diseases, and inadequate housing, medical care, and educational facilities.

Thus, we can see that the deteriorating employment status of young black males is mirrored in the increasing incidence of out-of-wedlock pregnancy and female-headed families among blacks. While all the concern has been focused on the plight of the unwed teenage mother and her problems as a parent, it is time for us to take a critical look at teenage fathers, particularly focusing on their lack of sexual responsibility and lack of motivation or ability to become involved in a joint parenting venture (Barret and Robinson, 1982). The plight of young fathers of babies born out of wedlock to black teenage mothers is discussed in Chapter 6, along with proposed policies and programs that might increase their sexual responsibility and foster their involvement in child rearing.

Sociocultural Implications

One of the major consequences of lack of education and lack of employment among young black males is their disproportionate involvement in the juvenile justice system, which results in severe limitations on their future educational and occupational opportunities; creates a vicious cycle of delinquency, incarceration, and recidivism; and results in an adult life-style of chronic criminality or chronic unemployment and marginal social adaptation. Scholars have debated for many years as to whether these behaviors reflect a "culture of poverty," a "dysfunctional" black family structure, or behavioral responses to socioeconomic forces. The cultural deficit and deprivation theories of the 1960s have largely been replaced by the more recent cultural variant and adaptation theories of black family functioning (Allen, 1978; Stack, 1974).

Despite scholarly efforts to reconceptualize the structure and functioning of the low-income black family, it is both naive and dangerous to ignore the symptoms of social disorganization, frustration, and social alienation in inner-city ghettos. The life-style of many young black inner-city males is frequently characterized by antisocial behaviors, drug addiction, exploitative and hostile relationships with women, confrontational relationships with police and other authorities, and very high-risk activities. These attitudes and activities may well be individual and/or collective responses to structural forces and environmental constraints which combine to deny these black males access to equal opportunity and social mobility. Yet they are *socially* reinforced through the black community's tolerance and tacit acceptance. They are *economically* reinforced by the educational and business institutions that fail to provide adequate training programs or employment opportunities to prepare these young men for making the transition from school to the world of work. And they are *politically* reinforced by the "benign neglect" policies of the federal, state, and local governments that fail to develop comprehensive policies and programs to strengthen vulnerable families and youth.

While the term "underclass" has been variously defined, Carson (1983) describes it as having two dimensions: "a *demographic dimension*, consisting of such characteristics as low earned income, low educational attainment and limited labor market participation; [and] a *psychological* dimension which has an attitudinal and behavioral component such as alienation or lack of motivation." He further suggests that the psychological dimension should be broken down into two separate dimensions of attitudes and behavior. This definition encompasses the three primary characteristics attributed to the underclass by some researchers, yet it is more specific and more easily operationalized than the pejorative label used by other authors (see McLanahan, 1985; Wilson and Aponte, 1985). It is clear that this definition of the underclass can be appropriately applied to a sizable group of young black males who are both educationally and economically disadvantaged and in danger of being permanently consigned to the urban underclass— chronically unemployed, unmotivated, and unsocialized. However, the term "underclass" does imply some serious conceptual and methodological issues and should be used selectively and cautiously.[1]

The implications for educational and economic policies which will address the *demographic* factors that have contributed to the growth of the underclass are discussed in Chapters 2 and 3, while the implications for attitudinal and behavioral change which will address the *psychological* dimension of membership in the underclass are discussed in Chapters 4, 5, and 8.

Political Implications

The implications of a potential disaffected and dysfunctional under-class, located in the rapidly expanding urban areas of the nation, are truly disturbing. If this trend is not reversed, these young black males might very well find themselves in a second period of involuntary servitude. Only this time it would be based on invol-untary dependence on and subjugation to government social wel-fare programs. Urban ghettos are rapidly becoming "welfare plan-tations," cut off from the vital urban centers of culture and commerce by inadequate transportation, lack of an economic base, and lack of political power. Young blacks would have to compete for jobs with a labor force increasingly dominated by white women and immigrants, who will account for nearly all of the net increase in the labor force in the next three decades (Marshall, 1986). Without the necessary literacy and job skills, black youth would be forced to accept the most menial domestic and service jobs, placing them in a position of servitude and submission to a middle-class white majority. It is quite probable that a highly specialized technological economy will gradually evolve in American society, in which positions will increasingly be awarded on demonstrated competency and merit. Furthermore, this highly qualified meri-tocracy, which will be predominantly white, will probably feel neither compassion nor tolerance for a nonproductive underclass, which will be predominantly nonwhite.

Thus, these young black males could presumably find them-selves locked into the lowest stratum of society, with very little access to mobility, completely dependent on the government for their sustenance, and growing more and more alienated from the mainstream of society. Just as black males in 1787 were treated as "nonpersons" on slave plantations, in 1987 they are increasingly ignored as "invisible persons" on "welfare plantations." In fact, these young black males *are invisible* in America, in a literal as well as a figurative sense, because many are simply not counted in the decennial census. In 1987 the U.S. Census Bureau estimated that 11.2 percent of the black population in major metropolitan areas was not counted in 1980, and the majority of these "under-enumerated citizens" were young transient black males (*New York Times*, 1987a). As a number of big city mayors pointed out, this underenumeration of blacks (and Hispanics) not only deprives the cities of political representation in Congress and state legislatures, but also costs these cities millions of dollars in federal and state aid, which is also allocated on the basis of population. Yet in October 1987, the Commerce Department announced that it would not make any attempts to adjust for the acknowledged undercount of minorities because the adjustments "might create more problems than they would solve" (*New York Times*, 1987b). Thus, two hundred years after blacks were first counted as only three-fifths of a person by the framers of the U.S. Constitution in 1787, young black men are still being discounted by the U.S. Census Bureau in 1987 with the same effect of denying their existence and disenfranchizing them as citizens.

Conclusions

The power elite has unfortunately been very slow to recognize that the future of the American economy and the American city is inextricably tied to the fate of young black males. If they cannot contribute to the economy, they will drain more and more of its resources. If they cannot participate in the revitalization of the cities, they will oversee urban decay and urban chaos. If they are locked out of the technological and scientific advances of the next decade, the United States will enter the 21st century with more serious social, political, and economic problems, placing the nation at an even greater competitive disadvantage and threatening its position as the leader of the Western world (Marshall, 1986).

Such a scenario may seem particularly pessimistic and farfetched to some, but already discomfiting signs of this growing disaffection of young black males from society and society's repressive reaction to them are appearing. Recent decisions of the Supreme Court have eroded the civil liberties of people arrested for crimes, including a dilution of the Miranda warning and an approval of pretrial detention, all of which will impact more heavily on poor black defendants. In 1987 the same Supreme Court which accepted a statistical argument based on the proportion of women in certain management positions to justify its decision in an affirmative action case, less than two months later rejected a similar statistical argument based on the racial proportions of victims and offenders to abolish the death penalty, a decision which clearly impacts differentially on blacks accused of capital crimes, especially when the victims are white. Thus, scores of young black men currently on death row are slated for execution, not just for the violent crimes they committed, but more fundamentally for the social and economic crimes of being black and poor. In fact, of the 86 executions which have been carried out in the United States since 1977, 33 have been black males, a disproportionate 38 percent of all executions, nearly all involving the murder of a white victim (*New York Times*, 1987c). Owners of retail stores in inner-city commercial areas routinely put bars on their windows and some even refuse to admit young black male customers. Reports of police brutality and unprovoked fatal shootings of young black males are frequently noted in the mass media. Bernhard Goetz, after being acquitted of shooting four black teenagers on a New York subway in 1984, was convicted only of carrying an unlicensed concealed pistol and sentenced to six months in jail by a jury of his peers in October of 1987, nearly three years after the incident.

A number of states, including New York, California, and Texas, are building more prisons to house disproportionate numbers of young black males, who are incarcerated at significantly higher rates than whites who commit similar crimes. State legislatures willingly authorize funds for new prisons, knowing it will cost an average of $20,000 per year to house one inmate, but these same legislative bodies seldom consider using those same funds to set up a Job Corps Program or college scholarship funds for disadvantaged students, both of which would cost less than $20,000 per year. Ironically, it currently costs less to send a young man to Harvard or Stanford University for one year than to incarcerate him in a penal institution.

Increased tensions between black youth and immigrant groups have been reported in high schools, work sites, and housing projects in California, Texas, and New York. Unemployment rates among black youth continue to rise while white teenagers and immigrant teenagers manage to find jobs. Even on liberal college campuses such as the University of Michigan, the University of Massachusetts, and the University of Chicago, where most of the black students are middle class, blacks have been the targets of overt racist remarks and physical harassment.

Most of the hostility has been directed against young black males, who are viewed with ambivalence, fear, or hostility by so many groups in this society. As long as they serve as the screen on which other Americans project their own anger, anxieties, and fantasies, young black males will provide the lightning rod for racial prejudice and the justification for racial oppression. As the competition for scarcer resources increases in this society, and as American political and economic supremacy is challenged by Asian and European nations, black youth are in the unenviable position to serve as society's scapegoats. Thus, the conservative backlash against civil rights and social welfare programs is not just a transient reaction of the moral majority but more likely a harbinger of a more fundamental atavistic response to the integration of blacks into the mainstream of American life.

Ironically, while census takers cannot manage to locate black males, schools cannot manage to teach them, and businesses cannot manage to hire them, draft boards seem to be very successful at recruiting them in times of war or national emergencies. Black soldiers played a major role in both the Korean and the Vietnam wars, where they were underrepresented in the officer corps but overrepresented in the "body count." In fact, 5,640 black servicemen died in the Vietnam War, most of them barely out of their teens, dying in a vain effort to ensure the freedom—for strangers in a foreign land—which they could not fully enjoy for themselves in America (Solomon, 1987). Young black men from inner cities and rural towns, mostly uneducated and unskilled, were sacrificed on the alter of American imperialism, while middle-class white boys manipulated the system and beat the draft through college deferments, medical exemptions, and flights to Canada.

While today's young black males may not be enumerated in the census, may not achieve in the classroom, and may not be counted in the labor force, they are still far from invisible. They cannot be dismissed by the rhetoric of politicians or the analysis of social scientists. They intrude on the nation's consciousness and appeal to the nation's conscience. Their plight is worsening, their pain is growing, and their anger is escalating. Our society must make "the invisible visible" and must bring these black youth into the social, economic, and political mainstream.

Further documentation of the endangered status of young black males would be both repugnant and redundant. The challenge lies not in describing the scope of the problems, but in developing some realistic and creative solutions. How much longer can this nation allow the systematic destruction and exclusion of one of its major sources of human capital? What kinds of radical policies and programs are needed to salvage this group? What strategies are required to marshall support for a massive program of social engineering? Chapter 9 discusses the policy implications of the multiple social problems facing black youth and traces the relationship between political ideology and social programs. The final chapter proposes a comprehensive set of policies and programs to address the problems of black youth, with special emphasis on young black males. These proposals not only build on the analysis of the social indicators and their proposed solutions, but also provide a framework for viewing the interrelationship among all the problems, rather than a unidimensional picture of a single issue.

The problems of young black males are challenging, complex,

and chronic, confounding scores of educators, researchers, and policymakers. In the following chapters of this book, thoughtful scholars offer some original and insightful analyses of these problems and propose a series of reasonable recommendations for their amelioration.

Endnote

1. The term "underclass" still remains a very pejorative, imprecise, and controversial term, precisely because it has so many different connotations and interpretations. In March 1987, the Joint Center for Political Studies convened a group of social scientists with the goal of developing a common definition of the term "underclass" for research purposes. After prolonged debate, the group proposed a consensus definition of the underclass as "poor people who live in a neighborhood or census tract with high rates of unemployment, crime, and welfare dependency" (McFate, 1987). However, several researchers continue to place more emphasis on the behavioral rather than the economic aspect of the definition. This emphasis is particularly problematic because it portrays the behaviors of members of the underclass as basically deviant, immoral, and egregious violations of the norms of the dominant majority culture. Yet, there seems to be a very clear unacknowledged double standard operating here, so that the behaviors of poor blacks are evaluated and interpreted quite differently from similar behaviors of middle-class whites. Even a cursory knowledge of highly publicized activities of the middle-class majority in the past decade indicates a fairly widespread contempt for laws by highly placed lawyers and government officials who are sworn to uphold them (e.g., Watergate and the Iran-Contra Affair); unparalleled greed and illegal manipulation of the stock market by Ivy League trained financiers on Wall Street (e.g., Dennis Levine and Ivan Boesky); endemic levels of cocaine use and alcoholism among the social and cultural elite, whose wealth can afford them anonymous treatment at the Betty Ford Treatment Center in Palm Springs, California; fraudulent business practices among executives of major corporations; and rampant white-collar crime in the private sector and in the government, where illegal profits and embezzlements were estimated at ten times the cost of street crime in 1985 alone.

   In the past decade the mass media have also reported innumerable scandals involving middle-class white youth: mass cheating on college campuses, widespread shoplifting in suburban shopping malls, sophisticated computer sabotage by "computer whizzes," cocaine addiction among "yuppie professionals," and gang rapes by athletes and fraternity boys at elite colleges. It is obvious that many of the "best and the brightest" are quite capable of lying, cheating, stealing, getting drunk, getting stoned, and assaulting women. However, should they get caught breaking any laws or violating any norms, they are much less likely than black youth to be expelled from school, arrested or convicted for a crime, and barred for life from any meaningful employment because of a criminal record. To the contrary, their behavior is more likely to be attributed to momentary lapses of judgment, which naturally occur because "boys will be boys" or they are "just going through a phase." Even if they are punished for their transgressions, they will still usually manage to overcome these temporary setbacks and will graduate from college, obtain coveted jobs, and fulfill their manifest destiny: to be the future leaders of America by virtue of their race, class, and education.

Moreover, as social problems and antisocial behaviors have increased among white youth since the counterculture movement of the 1960s, social scientists and policymakers have adopted an entirely new vocabulary to describe socially undesirable behaviors: "drug addicts" are now "substance abusers"; "unwed mothers" are now "single parents by choice"; "illegitimate children" are now "children born out of wedlock"; "matriarchal families" are now "female-headed households"; "rape" is now "sexual misconduct." I would contend that this change in language is not simply the development of new phraseology for conceptual clarity, but rather it reflects the historical tendency of the power elite to redefine social norms and public morality according to their own changing standards of behavior.

When a Harvard-trained young stockbroker bilks his clients out of millions of dollars, sympathetic editorials attribute his behavior to poor judgment due to the competitive pressures of Wall Street. When a young government lawyer has to resign because he was a prominent cocaine dealer, sympathetic friends attribute his behavior to financial problems. When a son of a prominent political family is found dead of an overdose of drugs, his death is attributed to severe emotional problems. It does seem curious that such behaviors among middle-class white youth can always be excused for psychological and personal reasons, while similar behaviors among blacks are always attributed to social and cultural causes. It is also well to recall that the young black guard who discovered the Watergate burglary has since suffered a series of economic and personal misfortunes, while all the major White House staffers convicted in that scandal are now rehabilitated and successfully pursuing careers as consultants, journalists, businessmen, and even ministers.

Thus, use of the term "underclass" should not obscure the facts that poor blacks, and especially young black males, are particularly vulnerable to the vicissitudes of persistent poverty, particularly exposed to public agencies which monitor their activities, particularly at risk for arrest and imprisonment, and particularly powerless to challenge the legal system or to reverse the negative consequences of conviction and incarceration in the juvenile or criminal justice system.

Young blacks also experience multiple personal, financial, and psychological pressures, yet they do not have the education, the family background, or the financial resources to extricate themselves from the kinds of problems they face. It would be far more constructive and humane to interpret the behaviors of black youth in terms of their environmental deprivation, chronic stress, and barriers to mobility, rather than in terms of their personal deficiencies, pathology, or deviance. As long as there are double standards for the behaviors of whites and blacks in American society, social scientists should exercise restraint in their attribution of immorality and deviance solely to the behaviors of black youth and should focus more attention on the underlying causes of persistent poverty as the major factor contributing to the growth of the so-called "underclass."

References

Allen, W. R. (1978). The search for applicable theories of Black family life. *Journal of Marriage and the Family* 40: 117–29.

American Public Welfare Association (APWA). (1986). *One child in four*. New York: APWA.

Auletta, K. (1982). *The underclass*. New York: Random House.

Bane, M. J., and Elwood, D. (1983). Slipping into and out of poverty: The dynamics of spells. Working Paper 1199. Washington, D.C.: National Bureau of Economic Research.

Barret, R., and Robinson, B. (1982). Teenage fathers: Neglected too long. *Social Work* 27: 484–88.

Beschner, G., and Friedman, A., eds. (1979). *Youth drug abuse*. Lexington, Mass.: Lexington Books.

Brown, S. (1979). The health needs of adolescents. In *Healthy people: The surgeon general's report on mental health promotion and disease prevention*. Publication 79-55071A. Washington, D.C.: U.S. DHEW.

Brunswick, A. (1979). Black youths and drug-use behavior. In *Youth and drug abuse*, edited by G. Beschner and A. Friedman. Lexington, Mass.: Lexington Books.

Brunswick, A., and Messeri, P. (1986). Drugs, lifestyle and health: A longitudinal study of urban black youth. *American Journal of Public Health* 76: 52–57.

Carson, E. (1983). Possible approaches for social science research on the underclass. Paper presented at the Population Association of America, Pittsburgh.

CDF. See Children's Defense fund.

Census Bureau, See U.S. Bureau of the Census.

Centers for Disease Control (1986a). Acquired immunodeficiency syndrome (AIDS) among blacks and Hispanics—United States. *Morbidity and Mortality Weekly Report* 35: 656–58.

———. (1986b). Update—Acquired immunodeficiency syndrome—United States. *Morbidity and Mortality Weekly Report* 35: 757–65.

Children's Defense Fund. (1985a). *A children's defense budget*. Washington, D.C.: CDF.

———. (1985b). *Black and white children in America*. Washington, D.C.: CDF.

———. (1986a). *A children's defense budget*. Washington, D.C.: CDF.

———. (1986b). *Building health programs for teenagers*. Washington, DC.: CDF.

———. (1986c). *Declining earnings of young men: Their relation to poverty, teen pregnancy and family formation*. Washington, D.C.: CDF.

———. (1986d). *Welfare and teen pregnancy: What do we know? What do we do?* Washington, D.C.: CDF.

Chilman, C. (1983). *Adolescent sexuality in a changing American society*. New York: John Wiley & Sons.

Clark, K. B. (1965). *Dark ghetto: Dilemmas of social power*. New York: Harper & Row.

College Entrance Examination Board. (1985). *Equality and excellence: The educational status of Black Americans*. New York: The College Board.

Congressional Budget Office. (1982). *Improving youth employment prospects: Issues and options*. Washington, D.C.: Congress of the United States.

Deal, T. (1975). An organizational explanation of the failure of alternative secondary schools. *Educational Researcher* 4: 10–16.

Department of Health and Human Services (DHHS). (1981). Statistical series, annual data, 1980, Ser. E-21. Washington, D.C.

Edmonds, R. (1979). Effective schools for the urban poor. *Educational Leadership* 37: 15–24.

Family Impact Seminar. (1979). *Teenage pregnancy and family impact: New perspectives on policy*. Washington, D.C.: George Washington University.

FBI (1986). Crime in the U.S., 1985 *Uniform Crime Reports*, Washington, D.C.

Furstenberg, F., Jr., Lincoln, R., and Menken, J. (1981). *Teenage sexuality, pregnancy and childbearing*. Philadelphia: University of Pennsylvania Press.

Gandossy, R., Williams, J., and Harwood, H. (1980). *Drugs and crime: A survey and analysis of the literature*. Washington, D.C.: U.S. Dept. of Justice.

Gibbs, J. T. (1984). Black adolescents and youth: An endangered species. *American Journal of Orthopsychiatry* 54: 6–21.

———. (1985). Young black males: An endangered species. Invited lecture at Annual Civil Rights Institute, NAACP Legal Defense and Educational Fund, Inc., New York (May).

———. (1986). Psychosocial correlates of sexual attitudes and behaviors in urban early adolescent females: Implications for intervention. *Journal of Social Work and Human Sexuality* 5: 81–97.

Glasgow, D. (1981). *The black underclass*. New York: Vintage Books.

Hofferth, S. L. (1985). Updating children's life course. *Journal of Marriage and the Family* 47: 93–115.

Holinger, P. (1979). Violent deaths among the young: Recent trends in suicide, homicide, and accidents. *American Journal of Psychiatry* 136: 1144–47.

Holinger, P., and Offer, D. (1982). Prediction of adolescent suicide: A population model. *American Journal of Psychiatry* 139: 302–07.

Huizinga, D., and Elliott, D. (1985). *Juvenile offenders' prevalence, offender incidence and arrest rates by race*. Boulder, Colo.: Institute of Behavioral Science.

Kasarda, J. (1985). Urban change and minority opportunities. In *The new urban reality*, edited by P. E. Peterson. Washington, D.C.: The Brookings Institute.

Krisberg, B., Schwartz, I., Fishman, G., Eiskovits, Z., and Guttman, E. (1986). *The incarceration of minority youth*. Minneapolis: H. H. Humphrey Institute of Public Affairs, University of Minnesota.

Ladner, J. (1971). *Tomorrow's tomorrow: The black woman*. Garden City, N.Y.: Doubleday.

Larson, T. (1986). Employment and unemployment of young black men. Unpublished paper, Berkeley, Calif.

Marshall, R. (1986). Economic change and education. Address at the Carnegie Forum on Education and the Economy, May 14–16 San Diego.

McAndrew, G. (1986). Turning dropouts into graduates. *Youth Policy* 9: 3–4.

McFate, K. (1987). Defining the underclass. *Focus* 15: 8–12 (Newsletter of the Joint Center for Political Studies, Washington, D.C.).

McLanahan, S. (1985). Family structure and the reproduction of poverty. *American Journal of Sociology* 90: 873–901.

Murray, C. (1984). *Losing ground: American social policy 1950–1980*. New York: Basic Books.

National Center for Health Statistics (NCHS). (1986). *Monthly vital statistics report*. Washington, D.C.

National Institute of Drug Abuse (NIDA). (1979). *National survey on drug abuse, 1979*. Washington, D.C.: NIDA.

New York Times, National Edition. (1987a). Big city mayors ask census change. July 24, p. 7.

———. (1987b). U.S. rejects pleas to adjust 1990 census for undercount. October 31, p. 1.

———. (1987c). Louisiana leads U.S. in a surge of executions. August 9, p. 7.

Omi, M., and Winant, H. (1986). *Racial formation in the United States: From the 1960s to the 1980s*. New York: Routledge & Kegan.

Ozawa, M. (1986). Nonwhites and the demographic imperative in social welfare spending. *Social Work* 31: 440–46.

Piliavin, I., and Briar, S. (1964). Police encounters with juveniles. *American Journal of Sociology* 70: 206–14.

Shapiro, C. (1980). Sexual learning: The short-changed adolescent male. *Social Work* 25: 489–93.

Snowdon, L. R. (editor). (1982). Reaching the underserved: Mental health needs of neglected populations. Beverly Hills, Calif.: Sage Publications.

Solomon, I. D. (1987). Blacks in the military. *The Crisis* 94: 15–26.

Stack, C. (1974). *All our kin*. New York: Harper & Row.

Sum, A., Harrington, P., and Goedicke, W. (1987). One-fifth of the nation's teenagers: Employment problems of poor youth in America, 1981–1985. *Youth and Society* 18: 195–237.

Thornton, W. James, J., and Doerner, W. (1982). *Delinquency and justice*. Glenview, Ill.: Scott, Foresman.

Tolmach, J. (1985). There ain't nobody on my side. *Journal of Child Clinical Psychology* 14: 214–19.

U.S. Bureau of the Census. (1981). School enrollment: Social and economic characteristics of students, 1980 (advance report). *Current population reports, ser. P-20*. Washington, D.C.

———. (1987). *Statistical abstract of the United States, 1987*. 107th ed. Washington, D.C.: U.S. Government Printing Office.

———. (1987). *Money income and poverty status of families and persons in the United States: 1986. Current population reports*, ser. P-60, 157. Washington, D.C.

———. (1986). *Report of the Secretary's Task Force on Black and Minority Health*, vol. V. Washington, D.C.

U.S. Dept. of Labor. (1987). *Youth 2000: Challenge and opportunity*. Washington, D.C.

Williams, J., ed. (1982). *The state of black America, 1982*. New York: National Urban League.

Wilson, W. J., and Aponte, R. (1985). Urban poverty. *Annual Review of Sociology* 11: 231–58.

Wilson, W. J., and Neckerman, K. M. (1984). Poverty and family structure: The widening gap between evidence and public policy issues. Paper prepared for conference on Poverty and Policy: Retrospect and Prospects, 6–8 December, Williamsburg, Virginia.

Chapter 2

EDUCATION AND ACHIEVEMENT OF YOUNG BLACK MALES

Rodney J. Reed

> *The educational system presents a fundamental paradox for Blacks. It continues to be held up by the broader society and by Blacks themselves as the institution that makes possible upward mobility, yet Black youths' encounters with it have resulted too often in destroyed aspirations and failure. . . . In the final analysis, the ghetto educational system has, whether or not consciously, immobilized ghetto youth, creating a technically obsolete class.*
>
> D. G. GLASGOW, in *The Black Underclass* (San Francisco: Jossey-Bass, Inc., Publishers, 1980).

Education is the key that unlocks the door to social, economic, and political mobility. It is requisite to self-fulfillment, employability, and one's full participation in a rapidly growing informational and technological society. For most American youngsters, basic formal education is acquired in public schools. This is not to diminish the importance of family, church, neighborhood, peer group, television and the mass media, and other formal and informal out-of-school educational influences. Rather, it is to assert that schools deliberately provide a structured pattern of formal education for children—the youth of today and, we hope, the productive, ethical, well-rounded adults of tomorrow.

37

Public schools, in tandem with other educational influences, have generally been quite effective in educating large numbers of students. More recently, however, public schools have come under substantial criticism because of students' comparatively low standardized test scores, overall grade point averages in core subjects, scores on college entry tests, and a general lack of such employability attributes as high level of literacy, problem-solving skills, positive work attitudes, ability to adapt to change, and foundation for continuous learning.

The political and educational response to the slippage in educational or school quality, as indicated in such areas as the foregoing, has been a call to excellence. Thus, what have been proposed by various commissions and studies, enacted by state legislatures, and adopted by public schools and colleges are increased high school graduation and college entry requirements, extension of school class periods and length of the school day, minimum competency testing for students and teachers, reformulation of the manner in which school teachers are prepared and deployed in school systems, and the like.

The movement toward excellence is not without merit. But the move toward excellence must not abridge equity considerations. Equity and excellence are both important school aims. All students can be excellent. Students with special needs, however, require sufficient support to build the bridges that will lead to excellence. The movement toward excellence must not distort our vision; nor must we sacrifice effort and resources necessary to bring about educational equity.

It is reassuring that considerable attention is now being given to the quality of public school education and teaching. Whereas public schools have been effective for many students, they have been, and continue to be, ineffective for large percentages of students disproportionately represented by minorities—blacks, Hispanics, native Americans—and the poor. For many students in these categories, schools represent an acrimonious environment in which educational success is thwarted by a lack of, among other things, intellectual rigor and expectations for success, teacher and staff respect for students and vice-versa, meaningful parental participation and oversight of school processes, and attention to individual student differences and needs. We would hope, therefore, that the heightened awareness of problems that beset public education will hasten effective solutions.

The need for public schools to be more effective for minorities and the poor is imperative. Because of changing population statistics, the nation's future work force not only will depend on these students, but also its future leaders. Thus, the degree to which blacks, Hispanics, native Americans, and the poor are successful in the schools, and in life, is crucial to the social, economic, and political viability of the nation.

In this chapter several facets related to the public school performance of black students, in general, and black males, in particular, are examined. The initial foray into this arena is a demographic profile of black students within the general population and within the public schools. Next is a discussion of school enrollment and completion, including grades in core subjects and scores on standardized tests, years of education completed and Carnegie units earned, drop-out rates, and enrollment in postsecondary education (institutions of higher education, vocational education, and continuing education). This is followed by a discussion of issues related to school performance—tracking, teacher attitudes and expectations, and school discipline. The chapter concludes with recommendations for educational policies and practices for improving the school performance of black males, particularly in the crucial 15–24 age range where educational achievement or the lack thereof will largely determine later adult occupational attainment and socioeconomic status.

Black Students in the General Population and in Public Schools

Before considering present and projected public school enrollment, it is instructive first to examine overall U.S. population estimates. Three U.S. population projections are calculated by the U.S. Bureau of the Census—low, middle, and high. Using middle-series estimates, the total U.S. population is projected to reach 249,657,000 by 1990, 267,955,000 by the year 2000, and 301,394,000 by 2025 (see Table 2–1). For whites, total middle-level estimates are 210,790,000 (84.4 percent of the total U.S. population) for 1990 and 222,654,000 (83.1 percent of the total U.S. population) for 2000. By gender, these projections translate into 102,979,000 (48.9 percent) white males and 107,811,000 (51.1 percent) females in 1990, and 108,879,000 (48.9 percent) white males and 113,775,000 (51.1 percent) females in 2000 (see Table 2–2).

It is estimated that the total U.S. black population, using the Census Bureau's middle-series estimates, will reach 31,412,000 (12.6 percent of the total U.S. population) in 1990 and 35,753,000 (13.3 percent of the total U.S. population) in 2000. By gender,

Table 2–1   Projections of the Total Population by Race, Sex, and Age, 1986 to
                2025 (In thousands, as of July 1. Includes Armed Forces overseas.)

Year	Lowest series (series)	Middle series (series)	Highest series (series)	Zero migration series (series)
1986	239,366	240,856	242,722	238,993
1987	241,068	243,084	245,534	240,728
1988	242,704	245,302	248,381	242,444
1989	244,268	247,498	251,249	244,127
1990	245,753	249,657	254,122	245,764
1991	247,154	251,767	256,984	247,342
1992	248,466	253,817	259,825	248,852
1993	249,690	255,800	262,636	250,288
1994	250,825	257,714	265,411	251,646
1995	251,876	259,559	268,151	252,927
1996	252,849	261,339	270,859	254,137
1997	253,750	263,060	273,544	255,282
1998	254,587	264,731	276,213	256,370
1999	255,368	266,360	278,876	257,411
2000	256,098	267,955	281,542	258,412
2005	259,181	275,677	295,276	263,085
2010	261,482	283,238	310,006	267,468
2015	262,795	290,406	325,423	271,335
2020	262,695	296,597	340,762	274,118
2025	260,904	301,394	355,503	275,436

SOURCE: U.S. Bureau of the Census, *Current Population Reports*, series P-25, No. 952.
Reported in Census Bureau (1987, p. 15).

given middle-level estimates, it is projected that the black male
population in 1990 will be 14,926,000 (47.5 percent) and females,
16,485,000 (52.5 percent). In 2000 the number of black males is
projected to be 17,040,000 (47.7 percent) and females, 18,714,000
(52.3 percent). Whereas the total U.S. population is expected to
increase by about 7.3 percent between 1990 and 2000, using
Census Bureau middle-level estimates, the white population will
increase by 5.6 percent during this period and the black population
by 14 percent (see Table 2–2).

Examining the foregoing data on the basis of gender, it is readily
apparent that females will continue to outnumber males in the
population, regardless of ethnicity. In fact, as displayed in Table
2–3, the number of males per 100 females has been declining since
1950. As of July 1, 1985, there were 95.4 white males and 90.0
black males of all ages for every 100 females. Respectively, these

Table 2–2 Projections of the Total Population by Age, Sex, and Spanish Origin, 1990–2000 (In thousands, as of July 1. Includes Armed Forces overseas.)

Age, Sex, Race, and Spanish Origin	Lowest Series (series 19)			Middle Series (series 14)			Highest Series (series 9)		
	1990	1995	2000	1990	1995	2000	1990	1995	2000
Total population[1]	245,753	251,876	256,096	249,657	259,559	267,955	254,122	268,151	281,542
Under 5 years old	17,515	16,193	14,942	19,198	18,615	17,626	20,615	20,815	20,530
5–17 years old	44,486	46,125	44,951	45,139	48,518	49,763	46,055	50,990	54,434
18–24 years old	25,547	23,347	24,157	25,794	23,702	24,601	26,137	24,233	25,326
25–34 years old	43,147	39,887	35,596	43,529	40,520	36,415	44,329	41,672	37,850
35–44 years old	37,570	41,500	42,972	37,847	41,997	43,743	38,229	42,870	45,128
45–54 years old	25,226	31,044	36,533	25,402	31,397	37,119	25,578	31,763	37,813
55–64 years old	20,910	20,655	23,326	21,051	20,923	23,767	21,189	21,190	24,212
65 years old and over	31,353	33,127	33,621	31,697	33,887	34,921	31,989	34,618	36,246
16 years old and over	190,198	196,242	203,526	191,819	199,188	208,185	194,035	203,249	214,597
Male, total	119,620	122,608	124,871	121,518	126,368	130,491	123,696	130,577	137,163
Under 5 years old	8,964	8,288	7,647	9,827	9,529	9,022	10,550	10,653	10,508
5–17 years old	22,745	23,586	22,989	23,082	24,815	25,458	23,549	26,074	27,842
18–24 years old	13,016	11,904	12,314	13,127	12,072	12,530	13,283	12,325	12,881
25–34 years old	21,722	20,155	18,009	21,892	20,443	18,384	22,261	20,959	19,044
35–44 years old	18,598	20,649	21,508	18,732	20,879	21,866	18,927	21,322	22,537
45–54 years old	12,268	15,152	17,903	12,350	15,327	18,196	12,441	15,518	18,563
55–64 years old	9,804	9,733	11,048	9,871	9,865	11,227	9,936	10,000	11,511
65 years old and over	12,503	13,143	13,255	12,637	13,440	13,762	12,751	13,725	14,277
16 years old and over	91,205	94,152	97,779	91,929	95,480	99,906	92,964	97,378	102,913
Female, total	126,133	129,268	131,427	128,139	133,191	137,464	130,424	137,574	144,379
Under 5 years old	8,551	7,906	7,295	9,371	9,086	8,604	10,065	10,161	10,022
5–17 years old	21,741	22,539	21,962	22,056	23,703	24,305	22,506	24,915	26,592
18–24 years old	12,532	11,443	11,843	12,667	11,630	12,071	12,854	11,908	12,445
25–34 years old	21,426	19,731	17,586	21,637	20,077	18,031	22,068	20,713	18,806
35–44 years old	18,971	20,851	21,465	19,116	21,119	21,877	19,302	21,548	22,591
45–54 years old	12,958	15,891	18,630	13,051	16,071	18,923	13,137	16,245	19,251
55–64 years old	11,105	10,922	12,279	11,180	11,059	12,495	11,253	11,190	12,702
65 years old and over	18,850	19,984	20,366	19,061	20,447	21,158	19,238	20,893	21,969
16 years old and over	98,993	102,090	105,747	99,890	103,708	108,279	101,071	105,871	111,684
White, total	207,799	211,481	213,498	210,790	217,412	222,654	213,753	223,236	231,980
Under 5 years old	14,046	12,884	11.760	15,390	14,797	13,843	16,451	16,417	15,958
5–17 years old	36,028	37,062	35,876	36,523	38,941	39,667	37,149	40,716	43,061
18–24 years old	20,989	19,008	19,485	21,170	19,267	19,806	21,369	19,578	20,238
25–34 years old	36,027	32,867	29,009	36,289	33,312	29,590	36,768	33,998	30,442
35–44 years old	32,097	35,037	35,822	32,292	35,379	36,355	32,509	35,895	37,180
45–54 years old	21,868	26,822	31,239	21,994	27,077	31,662	22,090	27,286	32,071
55–64 years old	18,432	18,014	20,273	18,536	18,213	20,605	18,605	18,362	20,868
65 years old and over	28,313	29,787	30,032	28,596	30,424	31,126	28,810	30,984	32,162
16 years old and over	162,971	166,987	171,734	164,160	169,181	175,245	165,486	171,695	179,346
Male	101,518	103,352	104,369	102,979	106,266	108,879	104,460	109,175	113,536
Female	106,281	108,129	109,129	107,811	111,146	113,775	109,292	114,061	118,445
Black, total	30,836	32,506	33,957	31,412	33,651	35,753	31,974	34,780	37,602
Under 5 years old	2,948	2,771	2,620	3,215	3,165	3,079	3,440	3,525	3,570
5–17 years old	6,942	7,498	7,553	7,042	7,871	8,321	7,159	8,222	9,031
18–24 years old	3,766	3,495	3,715	3,798	3,542	3,773	3,849	3,620	3,865
25–34 years old	5,809	5,683	5,208	5,860	5,768	5,316	5,932	5,884	5,479
35–44 years old	4,254	5,096	5,701	4,295	5,169	5,811	4,339	5,261	5,954
45–54 years old	2,600	3,210	4,036	2,626	3,262	4,124	2,646	3,307	4,211
55–64 years old	1,978	2,035	2,292	1,996	2,073	2,355	2,013	2,103	2,407
65 years old and over	2,538	2,717	2,833	2,579	2,802	2,975	2,597	2,857	3,085
16 years old and over	21,922	23,230	24,996	22,138	23,618	25,613	22.372	24,055	26,317
Male	14,645	15,451	16,156	14,926	16,013	17,040	15,204	16,573	17,958
Female	16,191	17,055	17,802	16,485	17,638	18,714	16,769	18,207	19,644
Spanish origin, total[2]	19,148	21,149	23,065	19,887	22,550	25,223	22,053	26,475	31,208
Under 5 years old	2,047	2,039	2,033	2,282	2,412	2,496	2,690	3,129	3,510
5–17 years old	4,682	5,158	5,436	4,825	5,554	6,206	5,337	6,605	7,973
18–24 years old	2,289	2,376	2,602	2,386	2,511	2,766	2,811	3,069	3,499
25–34 years old	3,517	3,514	3,529	3,629	3,717	3,804	4,242	4,782	5,129
35–44 years old	2,721	3,309	3,602	2,788	3,430	3,803	2,900	3,771	4,590
45–54 years old	1,629	2,091	2,687	1,668	2,165	2,811	1,720	2,262	2,993
55–64 years old	1,160	1,297	1,547	1,183	1,341	1,619	1,209	1,394	1,709
65 years old and over	1,101	1,367	1,627	1,126	1,419	1,719	1,144	1,463	1,804
16 years old and over	13,070	15,663	16,434	13,453	15,322	17,419	14,763	17,597	20,807
Male	9,580	10,586	11,548	9,947	11,285	12,627	11,137	13,425	15,869
Female	9,568	10,562	11,516	9,940	11,265	12,596	10,916	13,050	15,339

[1]Includes other races not shown separately.

[2]Persons of Spanish origin may be of any race.

SOURCE: U.S. Bureau of the Census, *Current Population Reports*, series P-25, No. 952. Reported in Census Bureau (1987, p. 16).

Table 2–3   Ratio of Males to Females, by Age Group, 1910 to 1985, and by Race, 1985
(Represents number of males per 100 females. Total resident population)

Age	1910 (Apr. 15)	1920 (Jan. 1)	1930 (Apr. 1)	1940 (Apr. 1)	1950 (Apr. 1)	1960 (Apr. 1)	1970 (Apr. 1)	1980 (Apr. 1)	1985 (July 1) Total[1]	1985 (July 1) White	1985 (July 1) Black
All ages	106.0	104.1[2]	102.5[2]	100.7	98.6	97.1	94.8	94.5	94.8	95.4	90.0
Under 14 years	102.1	102.1	102.6	103.0	103.7	103.4	103.9	104.6	104.9	105.4	102.6
14–24 years	101.2	97.3	98.4	98.9	98.2	98.7	98.7	101.9	102.2	102.8	97.4
25–44 years	110.2	105.1	101.8	98.5	96.4	95.7	95.5	97.4	98.5	100.5	86.5
45–64 years	114.4	115.2	109.1	105.2	100.1	95.7	91.6	90.7	91.5	92.8	81.6
65 years and over	101.1	101.3	100.5	95.5	89.6	82.8	72.1	67.6	67.8	67.7	67.0

[1]Includes other races, not shown separately.

[2]Includes "age not reported."

Source: U.S. Bureau of the Census, *U.S. Census of Population: 1930*, vol. II; *1940*, vol. II, part 1, and vol. IV, part 1; *1950*, vol. II, part 1; *1960*, vol. I, part 1; *1970*, vol. I, part B; and *Current Population Reports*, series P-25, No. 985, Reported in Census Bureau (1987, p. 17).

statistics highlight the fact that there are proportionately fewer black males than females or white males in the U.S. population. Scrutiny of the data shown in Table 2–4 reveals that the total 1985 U.S. population of 238,740,000 consisted of 116,161,000 males and 122,579,000 females for all age categories. However, in 1985 males outnumbered females for the age categories of under 5 years to 25–29 years. This majority male pattern, irrespective of ethnicity, is reversed beginning with the 30–34-year-old category and continues to the 75-years-and-over age category (see Table 2–4). A similar pattern holds for blacks, except that black females begin to outnumber black males earlier, during the 20–24-year-old category.

Turning now to school enrollments, we find in Table 2–5 that in fall 1982 a total of 40,132,000 K-12 students were registered in the nation's public schools. By 1984 that number had decreased to 39,793,000, and by 1985 to 39,788,000.

With respect to race or ethnicity, as revealed in Table 2–6, percentages of the total public elementary and secondary school enrollment in 1980 (39,832,482) by ethnic groups were: white, 73.3 percent; black, 16.1 percent; Hispanic, 8.0 percent; Asian or Pacific Islander, 1.9 percent; and American Indian/Alaskan native, 0.8 percent. By fall 1984 the public elementary and secondary school enrollment had dropped to 71.2 percent and black student representation was virtually unchanged at 16.2 percent. Hispanic population grew to 9.1 percent, Asian or Pacific Islander population grew to 2.5 percent, and the American Indian/Alaskan native population grew to 0.9 percent. The largest percentages of black students were found in the District of Columbia (92.5 percent) and in the following states: Alabama (34.5 percent), Arkansas (25.3 percent), Delaware (25.8 percent), Florida (23.1 percent), Georgia (35.8 percent), Illinois (24.8 percent), Louisiana (42.5 percent), Maryland (37.2 percent), Mississippi (50.4 percent), North Carolina (30.0 percent), South Carolina (40.6 percent), Tennessee (20.9 percent), and Virginia (23.8 percent) (Snyder, 1987, p. 46).

Not only does the public school population of several of the states mirror a sizable number of black students, but also many of the nation's largest cities enroll large percentages of total minority students. These cities, given 1982 statistics, include Boston (70.2 percent), Baltimore (79.5 percent), Newark (91.4 percent), Philadelphia (72.8 percent), Chicago (83.7 percent), Cleveland (74.1 percent), Detroit (89.1 percent), St. Louis (80.2 percent), Atlanta (92.2 percent), Dade County, Miami (71.2 percent), New Orleans (89.4 percent), Dallas (74.0 percent), Houston (78.3 percent), San Antonio (90.3 percent), and Los Angeles (78.2 percent) (National Center for Education Statistics, 1985, p. 26).

Black students enrolled in the nation's public schools are thus heavily concentrated in about one-fourth of the states (and the District of Columbia) and in many of the nation's largest cities. We will return to the implications of this enrollment pattern, but let us first examine the school performance of black students.

School Enrollment and Performance

Four themes are explored in this section: grades in core subjects and scores on standardized tests, years of education completed and units earned in high school, drop-out rates, and enrollment in postsecondary education.

School Performance of Black Students

In general, black students display lower academic performance in high school than do other racial or ethnic groups. Based on total 1982 high school graduates, black students, in comparison with other racial or ethnic groups, receive proportionately fewer A averages and more D or F averages in various subject matter areas. Asian or Pacific Islanders receive the highest percentage of A averages (35.8 percent) and non-Hispanic whites the next highest (27.1 percent). These two groups are followed by American Indian/ Alaskan natives (20.9 percent), Hispanics (18.5 percent), and non-Hispanic blacks, (16.3 percent). By contrast, the percentages of 1982 high school graduates receiving D or F averages in various subject matter areas, in descending order from high to low, are as follows: non-Hispanic blacks (28.6 percent), Hispanics (25.5 percent), American Indian/Alaskan natives (23.4 percent), non-Hispanic whites (14.5 percent), and Asian or Pacific Islanders (12.0 percent). The subject matter areas upon which these grade averages are based include English, foreign language, mathematics,

Table 2–4 Resident Population, by Age, Sex, and Race: 1970 to 1985 (in thousands, except as indicated. 1970 and 1980 data based on enumerated population as of April 1; other years based on estimated population as of July 1. Excludes Armed Forces overseas. For definition of median, see Guide to Tabular Presentation.)

Year, Sex, and Race	Total, all years	Under 5 years	5-9 years	10-14 years	15-19 years	20-24 years	25-29 years	30-34 years	35-39 years	40-44 years	45-49 years	50-54 years	55-59 years	60-64 years	65-74 years	75 years and over	5-13 years	14-17 years	18-24 years	16 years and over	65 years and over	Median age (yr.)
1970, total[1,2]	203,235	17,163	19,969	20,804	19,084	16,383	13,386	11,437	11,113	11,988	12,124	11,111	9,979	8,623	12,443	7,530	36,675	15,851	23,714	141,268	19,972	28.0
Male	98,926	8,750	10,175	10,598	9,641	7,925	6,626	5,599	5,416	5,823	5,855	5,351	4,769	4,030	5,440	2,927	18,687	8,069	11,583	67,347	8,367	26.8
Female	104,309	8,413	9,794	10,206	9,443	8,458	6,859	5,838	5,697	6,166	6,269	5,759	5,210	4,593	7,002	4,603	17,987	7,782	12,131	73,920	11,605	29.3
White	178,098	14,464	16,941	17,724	16,412	14,327	11,850	10,000	9,749	10,633	10,868	10,019	9,021	7,818	11,300	6,972	31,171	13,579	20,655	125,520	18,272	28.9
Black	22,581	2,434	2,749	2,812	2,425	1,816	1,429	1,254	1,196	1,199	1,124	990	874	734	1,300	501	5,009	2,073	2,721	14,053	1,544	22.4
1980, total[1]	226,546	16,348	16,700	18,242	21,168	21,319	19,521	17,561	13,965	11,669	11,090	11,710	11,615	10,088	15,581	9,969	31,159	16,247	30,022	171,196	25,549	30.0
Male	110,053	8,362	8,539	9,316	10,755	10,663	9,705	8,677	6,862	5,708	5,388	5,621	5,482	4,670	6,757	3,548	15,923	8,298	15,054	81,766	10,305	28.8
Female	116,493	7,986	8,161	8,926	10,413	10,655	9,816	8,884	7,104	5,961	5,702	6,089	6,133	5,418	8,824	6,400	15,237	7,950	14,969	89,429	15,245	31.3
White[3]	194,713	13,414	13,717	15,095	17,681	18,072	16,658	15,157	12,122	10,110	9,693	10,360	10,394	9,078	14,045	9,117	25,691	13,492	25,381	149,121	23,162	30.9
Male[3]	94,924	6,882	7,034	7,730	9,008	9,102	8,363	7,565	6,014	4,991	4,755	5,016	4,928	4,221	6,095	3,221	13,165	6,906	12,803	71,559	9,316	29.6
Female[3]	99,788	6,532	6,683	7,365	8,673	8,970	8,295	7,592	6,108	5,119	4,938	5,344	5,466	4,858	7,950	5,896	12,526	6,586	12,579	77,562	13,846	32.2
Black[3]	26,683	2,459	2,509	2,691	3,007	2,749	2,342	1,904	1,469	1,260	1,150	1,135	1,041	874	1,344	748	4,629	2,380	3,948	18,425	2,092	24.9
Male[3]	12,612	1,240	1,265	1,353	1,500	1,313	1,095	879	667	571	519	507	469	386	567	281	2,330	1,198	1,903	8,454	849	23.9
Female[3]	14,071	1,220	1,245	1,338	1,506	1,436	1,247	1,025	801	689	632	628	573	488	777	467	2,298	1,181	2,045	9,971	1,243	26.2
1981, total	229,637	16,931	16,093	18,312	20,501	21,614	20,200	18,786	14,381	12,019	10,992	11,616	11,579	10,376	15,914	10,323	30,754	15,598	30,168	174,517	26,236	30.3
1982, total	231,996	17,298	16,020	18,172	19,887	21,587	20,753	18,808	15,599	12,450	11,027	11,455	11,510	10,603	16,197	10,630	30,454	15,040	30,012	176,822	26,827	30.6
1983, total	234,284	17,650	16,147	17,912	19,274	21,488	21,202	19,211	16,165	13,135	11,226	11,213	11,528	10,705	16,494	10,934	30,410	14,720	29,692	178,965	27,428	30.9
1984, total	236,495	17,859	16,464	17,511	18,785	21,327	21,534	19,696	16,932	13,613	11,463	11,030	11,442	10,872	16,733	11,234	30,238	14,704	29,145	180,980	27,967	31.2
1985, total[1]	238,740	18,037	16,822	17,103	18,551	20,993	21,751	20,267	17,708	14,055	11,648	10,942	11,337	10,997	16,995	11,535	30,111	14,866	28,492	183,010	28,530	31.5
Male	116,161	9,230	8,608	8,762	9,445	10,515	10,886	10,096	8,741	6,889	5,679	5,281	5,380	5,120	7,466	4,062	15,415	7,611	14,304	87,631	11,529	30.3
Female	122,579	8,806	8,213	8,340	9,107	10,479	10,865	10,171	8,967	7,166	5,969	5,660	5,957	5,877	9,529	7,473	14,696	7,255	14,188	95,379	17,002	32.7
White	202,768	14,636	13,621	13,830	15,194	17,511	18,316	17,158	15,243	12,168	10,046	9,509	9,990	9,804	15,248	10,495	24,346	12,157	23,653	157,584	25,743	32.4
Male	99,006	7,509	6,990	7,100	7,746	8,815	9,250	8,636	7,608	6,023	4,946	4,637	4,771	4,585	6,720	3,670	12,494	6,233	11,923	75,820	10,390	31.2
Female	103,762	7,127	6,631	6,730	7,448	8,696	9,067	8,522	7,635	6,144	5,099	4,872	5,219	5,219	8,529	6,824	11,852	5,924	11,729	81,764	15,353	33.6
Black	28,887	2,706	2,597	2,655	2,770	2,842	2,749	2,408	1,889	1,442	1,255	1,148	1,101	982	1,463	880	4,669	2,229	3,965	20,380	2,343	26.6
Male	13,683	1,370	1,314	1,346	1,391	1,369	1,301	1,121	862	653	563	514	500	439	619	321	2,364	1,128	1,927	9,374	940	25.2
Female	15,204	1,335	1,283	1,309	1,378	1,473	1,448	1,287	1,027	789	692	634	601	543	844	559	2,305	1,101	2,038	11,006	1,403	27.8
Percent:																						
1970	100.0	8.4	9.8	10.2	9.4	8.1	6.6	5.6	5.5	5.9	6.0	5.5	4.9	4.2	6.1	3.7	18.0	7.8	11.7	69.5	9.8	(x)
1980	100.0	7.2	7.4	8.1	9.3	9.4	8.6	7.8	6.2	5.2	4.9	5.2	5.1	4.5	6.9	4.4	13.8	7.2	13.3	75.6	11.3	(x)
1985, total[1]	100.0	7.6	7.0	7.2	7.8	8.8	9.1	8.5	7.4	5.9	4.9	4.6	4.7	4.6	7.1	4.8	12.6	6.2	11.9	76.7	12.0	(x)
Male	100.0	7.9	7.4	7.5	8.1	9.1	9.4	8.7	7.5	5.9	4.9	4.5	4.6	4.4	6.4	3.5	13.3	6.6	12.3	75.4	9.9	(x)
Female	100.0	7.2	6.7	6.8	7.4	8.5	8.9	8.3	7.3	5.8	4.9	4.6	4.9	4.8	7.8	6.1	12.0	5.9	11.6	77.8	13.9	(x)
White	100.0	7.2	6.7	6.8	7.5	8.6	9.0	8.5	7.5	6.0	5.0	4.7	4.9	4.8	7.5	5.2	12.0	6.0	11.7	77.7	12.7	(x)
Black	100.0	9.4	9.0	9.2	9.6	9.8	9.5	8.3	6.5	5.0	4.3	4.0	3.8	3.4	5.1	3.0	16.2	7.7	13.7	70.6	8.1	(x)

X Not applicable.   [1] Includes other races, not shown separately.   [2] Official count. The revised 1970 resident population count is 203,302,031; the difference of 66,733 is due to errors found after release of the official series.   [3] The race data shown for April 1, 1980 have been modified. See text, section 1 for explanation.

SOURCE: U.S. Bureau of the Census, *Current Population Reports*, series P-25, Nos. 870 and 985. Reported in Census Bureau (1987, p. 18).

Table 2–5   Enrollment in Public and Private Elementary and Secondary
Schools, 1970–1985

October of year	K-12 enrollment (In thousands)			Private school enrollment as a percentage of total K–12 enrollment
	Total	Public	Private	
1970	51,848	46,193	5,655	10.9
1971	51,953	46,575	5,378	10.4
1972	50,546	45,343	5,203	10.3
1973	49,890	44,945	4,945	9.9
1974	49,825	44,958	4,867	9.8
1975	49,522	44,521	5,001	10.1
1976	49,006	44,202	4,804	9.8
1977	48,178	43,153	5,025	10.4
1978	46,954	41,976	4,978	10.6
1979	46,006	41,343	4,663	10.1
1980	45,181	—	—	—
1981	45,598	40,897	4,701	10.3
1982	44,834	40,132	4,702	10.5
1983	44,569	39,701	4,868	10.9
1984	44,099	39,793	4,306	9.8
1985	44,660	39,788	4,872	10.9

—Not available.

SOURCE: U.S. Department of Commerce, Bureau of the Census, *School Enrollment—Social and Economic Characteristics of Students: October 1984* (Current Population Reports, Series P-20, No. 404), 1985 and unpublished tabulations. Reported in Center for Education Statistics (1986, p. 188).

natural science, health, home economics, industrial arts, personal and social development, philosophy, physical education, psychology, public affairs, and religion. The foregoing grade average distributions are graphically illustrated for the major subject areas in Figure 2–1 (A grade averages), and Figure 2–2 (D or F grade averages).

With respect to reading proficiency, as measured in the 1983–84 school year, approximately 15 percent of black students scored below the national average at grades 4, 8, and 11 (National Center for Educational Statistics, 1985, p. 54). At each age, 9, 13, and 17, black students also scored below the national mean in reading/literature comprehension (1979–80), music and art (1978–79), citizenship and social studies (1975–76), science (1975–76), and mathematics (1981–82) (Grant and Snyder, 1986, pp. 19–21).

As can be seen in Table 2–7, at age 9, between 1976–77 and 1981–82, black male scores increased in science inquiry by 3.4 percentage points (37.4 to 40.8). In the area of science, technology,

Table 2–6 Enrollment in Public Elementary and Secondary Schools, by Race or Ethnicity and by State, Fall 1980

State	Total[a]		White[b]		Black[b]		Hispanic		Asian or Pacific Islander		American Indian/Alaskan Native	
	Number	Per-cent	Number	Per-cent	Number	Per-cent	Number	Per-cent	Number	Per-cent	Number	Per-cent
United States	39,832,482	100.0	29,180,415	73.3	6,418,194	16.1	3,179,345	8.0	749,003	1.9	305,730	.8
Alabama	754,595	100.0	501,404	66.4	249,734	33.1	529	.1	1,437	.2	1,488	.2
Alaska	80,036	100.0	57,321	71.6	3,108	3.9	1,270	1.6	1,862	2.3	16,475	20.6
Arizona	481,935	100.0	319,623	66.3	20,348	4.2	116,647	24.2	5,369	1.1	19,952	4.1
Arkansas	410,165	100.0	313,812	76.5	92,231	22.5	1,213	.3	1,279	.3	1,642	.4
California	3,954,586	100.0	2,258,499	57.1	400,691	10.1	1,002,207	25.3	260,609	6.6	32,640	.8
Colorado	550,452	100.0	428,884	77.9	25,205	4.6	84,282	15.3	9,162	1.7	2,930	.5
Connecticut	528,250	100.0	438,265	83.0	53,943	10.2	30,433	5.8	4,853	.9	769	.1
Delaware	96,035	100.0	68,365	71.2	24,900	25.9	1,730	1.8	911	.9	128	.1
District of Columbia	104,907	100.0	3,779	3.6	97,962	93.4	2,048	2.0	1,069	1.0	29	(c)
Florida	1,488,344	100.0	1,008,951	67.8	348,769	23.4	117,561	7.9	11,500	.8	1,560	.1
Georgia	1,073,915	100.0	705,582	65.7	359,890	33.5	3,080	.3	4,911	.5	460	(c)
Hawaii	162,198	100.0	40,297	24.8	2,330	1.4	3,300	2.0	115,889	71.4	382	.2
Idaho	210,997	100.0	193,623	91.8	1,140	.5	9,737	4.6	2,069	1.0	4,432	2.1
Illinois	1,929,853	100.0	1,377,566	71.4	403,067	20.9	117,787	6.1	29,273	1.5	2,157	.1
Indiana	1,028,821	100.0	905,077	88.0	102,322	9.9	15,830	1.5	4,687	.5	919	.1
Iowa	516,309	100.0	495,295	95.9	11,445	2.2	4,054	.8	4,503	.9	1,010	.2
Kansas	371,867	100.0	324,818	87.3	29,160	7.8	11,238	3.0	4,501	1.2	2,156	.6
Kentucky	685,952	100.0	623,327	90.9	59,616	8.7	734	.1	2,085	.3	202	(c)
Louisiana	778,314	100.0	440,223	56.6	322,985	41.5	6,136	.8	6,057	.8	2,912	.4
Maine	204,060	100.0	202,233	99.1	579	.3	294	.1	642	.3	325	.2
Maryland	756,012	100.0	502,719	66.5	231,590	30.6	6,876	.9	13,645	1.8	1,183	.2
Massachusetts	918,127	100.0	819,801	89.3	56,675	6.2	30,098	3.3	10,352	1.1	1,207	.1
Michigan	1,759,442	100.0	1,384,576	78.7	314,205	17.9	31,834	1.8	14,478	.8	14,323	.8
Minnesota	796,860	100.0	749,703	94.1	16,760	2.1	5,955	.7	11,872	1.5	12,564	1.6

State	Total	%										
Mississippi	447,552	100.0	216,523	48.4	228,252	51.0	602	.1	1,567	.4	607	.1
Missouri	832,793	100.0	709,879	85.2	113,356	13.6	4,107	.5	4,489	.5	951	.1
Montana	142,913	100.0	125,635	87.9	454	.3	1,686	1.2	1,204	.8	13,943	9.8
Nebraska	240,226	100.0	214,934	89.5	13,435	5.6	4,473	1.9	1,997	.8	5,385	2.2
Nevada	148,388	100.0	120,310	81.1	14,051	9.5	7,788	5.2	3,212	2.2	3,035	2.0
New Hampshire	156,482	100.0	154,419	96.7	782	.5	620	.4	601	.4	65	(c)
New Jersey	1,223,859	100.0	876,703	71.6	226,823	18.5	96,053	8.0	21,363	1.7	956	.1
New Mexico	270,300	100.0	116,116	43.0	5,928	2.2	125,779	46.5	1,509	.6	20,969	7.8
New York	2,712,925	100.0	1,844,929	68.0	484,296	17.9	325,538	12.0	53,512	2.0	4,674	.2
North Carolina	1,112,193	100.0	757,561	68.1	329,722	29.6	2,136	.2	4,618	.4	18,155	1.6
North Dakota	93,232	100.0	90,012	96.5	424	.5	486	.5	650	.7	1,662	1.8
Ohio	1,907,303	100.0	1,626,107	85.3	249,484	13.1	18,452	1.0	11,095	.6	2,148	.1
Oklahoma	520,025	100.0	411,856	79.2	48,176	9.3	8,502	1.6	4,004	.8	47,490	9.1
Oregon	461,795	100.0	422,494	91.5	9,484	2.1	11,951	2.6	10,249	2.2	7,621	1.7
Pennsylvania	1,868,218	100.0	1,590,782	85.1	231,326	12.4	28,862	1.5	13,651	.7	3,570	.2
Rhode Island	141,841	100.0	130,202	91.8	6,644	4.7	2,974	2.1	1,570	1.1	454	.3
South Carolina	612,153	100.0	345,921	56.5	262,110	42.8	937	.2	2,363	.4	821	.1
South Dakota	117,039	100.0	107,751	92.1	186	.2	283	.2	392	.3	8,430	7.2
Tennessee	849,426	100.0	640,896	75.5	204,019	24.0	978	.1	3,230	.4	311	(c)
Texas	2,846,105	100.0	1,538,758	54.1	408,754	14.4	864,306	30.4	29,977	1.1	4,329	.2
Utah	343,978	100.0	318,892	92.7	1,708	.5	12,014	3.5	5,241	1.5	6,124	1.8
Vermont	74,436	100.0	73,659	99.0	242	.3	104	.1	386	.5	44	.1
Virginia	1,008,853	100.0	731,096	72.5	257,659	25.5	5,152	.5	14,115	1.4	834	.1
Washington	762,733	100.0	655,195	85.9	25,991	3.4	30,428	4.0	27,868	3.7	23,255	3.0
West Virginia	381,970	100.0	365,610	95.7	14,748	3.9	405	.1	1,089	.3	120	(c)
Wisconsin	813,600	100.0	737,796	90.7	50,541	6.2	12,532	1.5	5,583	.7	6,955	.9
Wyoming	100,112	100.0	92,636	92.5	744	.7	5,322	5.3	433	.4	977	1.0

a Data on enrollment by race/ethnicity were calculated independently and may not add across to the totals shown in column 2. Because of rounding, percentages may not add to 100.0. b Excludes persons of Hispanic origin. c Less than 0.05 percent.

Note: The above tabulation excludes approximately 1,152,000 pupils not reported by race or ethnicity.

Source: U.S. Department of Education, Office for Civil Rights, data from the "1960 State Summaries of Elementary and Secondary School Civil Rights Survey." Reported in Grant, W. V. and Snyder, T. D. (1986, p. 39).

Table 2–7   National Assessment of Educational Progress in Science for Ages 9, 13, and 17, by Assessment Area and Selected Characteristics of Participants: United States, 1976–77 and 1981–82

	Assessment area								
	Content			Inquiry			Science, technology, and society		
Selected characteristics of participants	Average percentage correct		Change in percentage points	Average percentage correct		Change in percentage points	Average percentage correct		Change in percentage points
	1976–77	1981–82		1976–77	1981–82		1976–77	1981–82	
1	2	3	4	5	6	7	8	9	10
9-year-olds, average	—	—	—	53.6	52.6	−1.0	57.1	59.9	2.8
Sex									
Male	—	—	—	53.9	52.8	−1.1	57.4	60.5	3.1
Female	—	—	—	53.4	52.5	−0.9	56.8	59.4	2.6
Race and sex									
White male	—	—	—	57.2	55.9	−1.3	59.7	62.7	3.0
Black male	—	—	—	37.4	40.8	3.4	46.3	50.7	4.4
White female	—	—	—	57.0	55.3	−1.7	59.1	61.3	2.2
Black female	—	—	—	39.5	41.4	1.9	47.4	51.7	4.3
Region									
Northeast	—	—	—	56.1	54.9	−1.2	57.7	59.8	2.1
Southeast	—	—	—	48.5	50.5	2.0	54.6	57.2	2.6
Central	—	—	—	56.1	54.6	−1.5	57.6	61.4	3.8
West	—	—	—	52.6	50.6	−2.0	57.9	60.6	2.7
13-year-olds, average	52.8	52.4	−0.4	58.6	58.0	−0.6	56.8	57.4	0.6
Sex									
Male	54.4	54.7	0.3	58.9	58.5	−0.4	58.6	59.5	0.9
Female	51.2	50.2	−1.0	58.4	57.6	−0.8	55.0	55.3	0.3
Race and sex									
White male	57.0	56.8	−0.2	61.2	60.4	−0.8	60.8	61.5	0.7
Black male	42.4	44.6	2.4	48.2	48.8	0.6	48.6	50.1	1.5
White female	53.6	52.4	−1.2	60.8	59.7	−1.1	57.0	57.4	0.4
Black female	41.4	40.6	−0.8	49.2	49.3	0.1	47.6	46.8	−0.8
Region									
Northeast	55.0	53.3	−1.7	61.9	59.9	−2.0	58.4	57.6	−0.8
Southeast	49.6	49.0	−0.6	55.7	54.4	−1.3	55.1	55.2	0.1
Central	54.4	54.1	−0.3	60.4	59.9	−0.5	57.7	59.0	1.3
West	51.8	52.5	0.7	55.7	57.4	1.7	55.7	57.1	1.4
17-year-olds, average	61.7	59.7	−2.0	72.2	69.6	−2.6	67.5	67.0	−0.5
Sex									
Male	64.9	62.7	−2.2	72.8	70.2	−2.6	70.0	68.6	−1.4
Female	58.6	56.9	−1.7	71.5	69.1	−2.4	65.1	65.4	0.3
Race and sex									
White male	67.3	65.8	−1.7	75.4	72.8	−2.6	72.4	71.2	−1.2
Black male	49.6	47.8	−1.8	58.2	58.1	−0.1	55.5	55.8	0.3
White female	60.9	59.3	−1.6	74.1	71.6	−2.5	67.6	67.8	0.2
Black female	45.7	44.4	−1.3	58.6	56.7	−1.9	52.1	54.1	2.0
Region									
Northeast	64.2	60.1	−4.1	74.7	71.1	−3.6	68.6	67.0	−1.6
Southeast	57.4	57.3	−0.1	68.6	66.7	−1.9	63.9	64.6	0.7
Central	62.8	61.9	−0.9	73.5	71.4	−2.1	69.2	68.6	−0.6
West	61.1	58.7	−2.4	70.7	68.2	−2.5	66.9	67.0	0.1

—Data not available.

Note: The change in precentage points is equal to the difference in the average percentage correct for each year but may differ in this table due to rounding.

SOURCE: University of Minnesota, Minnesota Research and Evaluation Center, *Images of Science, 1983* (copyright). (This table was prepared January 1986). Reported in Snyder (1987, p. 90).

and society, a gain of 4.4 percentage points (46.3 to 50.7) over the same time period also can be noted for black males. By contrast, black females at age 9 manifested a slightly smaller gain, 1.9 percentage points, in science inquiry between 1976–77 and 1981–82 (39.5 to 41.5), but they were similar to black males in percentage points gained (4.3) in science, technology, and society (47.4 to 51.7). Although the percentage point gains of black males and females between 1976–77 and 1981–82 in the areas of science inquiry and science, technology, and society were above national average gains, their scores were still considerably lower than national average scores for 9-year-olds. These scores were 53.6 in 1976–77 and 52.6 in 1981–82 for science inquiry, and 57.1 in 1976–77 and 59.9 in 1981–82 for science, technology, and society.

At age 13 the gap between scores earned by black students and national average scores in science inquiry and in science, technology, and society was slightly smaller than at age 9. It was nearly the same at age 17, however, as it was at age 9. Change in percentage points between 1976–77 and 1981–82 continued to be slightly higher for black males than for black females at age 13 in science inquiry (black males, 0.6, black females, 0.1) and in science, technology, and society (black males, 1.5, black females, −0.8). Percentage point changes in scores of black males and females displayed a different pattern, however, at age 17. In science inquiry, black male scores declined by −0.1 percentage point (58.2 in 1976–77 to 58.1 in 1981–82), whereas black female scores declined by −1.9 percentage points. In science, technology, and society, black females showed a 2.0 percentage point gain between 1976–77 (52.1) and 1981–82 (54.1), whereas black males gained only 0.3 percentage points (55.5 in 1976–77 to 55.8 in 1981–82). While gain scores for black students were slightly greater than those for whites, their average scores continued to be considerably lower than average percent correct scores for white students in science content, in science inquiry, and in science, technology, and society at ages 9, 13, and 17.

In the areas of reading/literature comprehension, music, art, citizenship, social studies, and mathematics, black students also scored below national averages at ages 9, 13, and 17 during the 1975–1982 period (see Table 2–8). Irrespective of ethnicity, females consistently scored below national averages at these ages in science, whereas males scored above the average. On the other hand, females at ages 9, 13, and 17, regardless of ethnicity, scored above, and males scored below, national averages in reading/literature comprehension and music. Interestingly, females out-

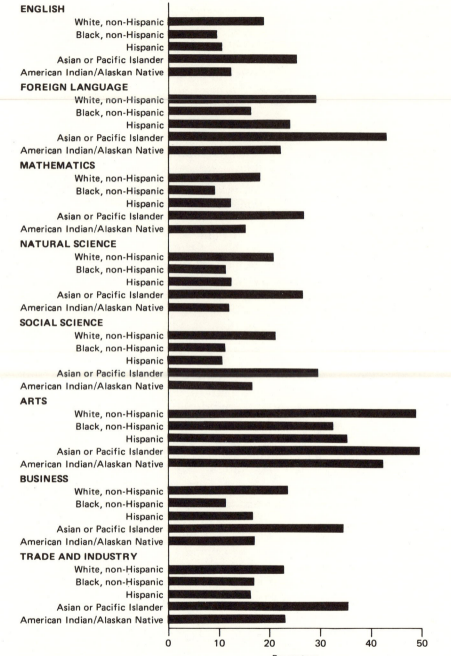

Figure 2-1 Percentage of 1982 High School Graduates Who Received an "A" Average in Various Subject Matter Areas, by Race/Ethnicity (Source: National Center for Education Statistics, U.S. Department of Education. *The Condition of Education, 1985*. A Statistical Report. Washington, D.C.: U.S. Government Printing Office, 1985, p. 51.)

ENGLISH
White, non-Hispanic
Black, non-Hispanic
Hispanic
Asian or Pacific Islander
American Indian/Alaskan Native

FOREIGN LANGUAGE
White, non-Hispanic
Black, non-Hispanic
Hispanic
Asian or Pacific Islander
American Indian/Alaskan Native

MATHEMATICS
White, non-Hispanic
Black, non-Hispanic
Hispanic
Asian or Pacific Islander
American Indian/Alaskan Native

NATURAL SCIENCE
White, non-Hispanic
Black, non-Hispanic
Hispanic
Asian or Pacific Islander
American Indian/Alaskan Native

SOCIAL SCIENCE
White, non-Hispanic
Black, non-Hispanic
Hispanic
Asian or Pacific Islander
American Indian/Alaskan Native

ARTS
White, non-Hispanic
Black, non-Hispanic
Hispanic
Asian or Pacific Islander
American Indian/Alaskan Native

BUSINESS
White, non-Hispanic
Black, non-Hispanic
Hispanic
Asian or Pacific Islander
American Indian/Alaskan Native

TRADE AND INDUSTRY
White, non-Hispanic
Black, non-Hispanic
Hispanic
Asian or Pacific Islander
American Indian/Alaskan Native

0   10   20   30   40   50
Percentage

Figure 2-2   Percentage of 1982 High School Graduates Who Received a
"D" or "F" Average in Various Subject Matter Areas, by Race/Ethnicity.
(Source: National Center for Education Statistics, U.S. Department of
Education. *The Condition of Education, 1985*. A Statistical Report. Wash-
ington, D.C.: U.S. Government Printing Office, 1985, p. 51.)

51

Table 2–8 National Assessment of Educational Progress for Ages 9, 13, 17, by Subject Area and Selected Characteristics of Participants, United States, 1975–1982

	Age 9				Age 13				Age 17			
	National Mean p[a]	Male[b]	Female[b]	Black Students[b]	National Mean p[a]	Male[b]	Female[b]	Black Students[b]	National Mean p[a]	Male[b]	Female[b]	Black Students[b]
Reading/literature comprehension	58.2	−2.5	2.5	−13.8	74.0	−2.1	2.0	−14.3	79.1	−1.4	1.4	−16.6
Music	57.3	−0.9	1.0	−8.2	52.3	−1.2	1.2	−6.0	50.0	−1.8	1.7	−6.6
Art	41.2	0.2	−0.2	−3.4	47.0	−0.9	0.9	−3.5	50.6	−1.3	1.2	−4.6
Citizenship	62.1	0.3	−0.3	−7.4	63.2	−0.1	0.1	−7.6	67.4	0.0	0.0	−8.6
Social studies	63.3	0.3	−0.3	−8.6	62.9	0.0	0.0	−8.2	67.6	0.2	−0.2	−9.4
Science	50.7	1.5	−1.6	−12.9	49.1	1.8	−1.7	−11.7	53.5	2.6	−2.5	−15.7
Mathematics	56.4	−0.6	0.5	−11.2	60.5	−0.1	0.1	−12.3	60.2	1.4	−1.3	−15.2

[a]The mean delta p is a single number used in national assessment to describe a group's performance. The percent correct, or the p, for an exercise (test item) can be expressed for the nation as a whole or for any of the national assessment groups. The difference between these percentages is the delta p for the exercise. The mean delta p for a group is the mean of all delta p's for the group.

[b]Scores reported for males, females, and black students are differences from national means.

Note: Data are for the following years: 1975–76, citizenship, social studies; 1976–77, science; 1978–79, music, art; 1979–80, reading/literature comprehension; 1981–82, mathematics.

Source: Derived from data available in the files of the National Assessment of Educational Progress, July 1983, and data reported in Grant and Snyder (1986, pp. 19–22).

scored males in mathematics at ages 9 and 13. At age 17, however, their scores fell behind the national average, whereas males scored above it (see Table 2–8).

Scores on the Scholastic Aptitude Test (SAT) reveal consistent differences among ethnic groups, with black students receiving the lowest scores, even though their math scores have increased slightly each year since 1977–78. Performance on the SAT is important in that it is used to predict the probable success which students will experience in learning and performing college-level work; thus it is used to make admission decisions to selective colleges and universities. The appropriateness of its use for these purposes is called into question by Willie (1985). He argues that SAT scores predict academic performance for only the first year of college work and explain less than half of the variance in first-year college grades. These views notwithstanding, the SAT is widely used both for college-entry decisions and by some observers to gauge educational effectiveness.

As displayed in Table 2–9, the highest SAT math scores between 1975–76 and 1984–85 were recorded by Asian-Americans. Following these students, in descending order, were white, American Indian, Mexican-American, Puerto Rican, and black students. The average math score over the above ten-year period for Asian-Americans was 514. For black students it was 363.

SAT verbal scores display a similar distribution pattern, except that white students replace Asian-Americans as the highest scorers. They are followed by Asian-American, American-Indian, Mex-

Table 2–9 Scholastic Aptitude Test Score Averages, by Race/Ethnicity: United States, 1975–76 to 1984–85

Racial/Ethnic Background	1975–76	1976–77	1977–78	1978–79	1979–80	1980–81	1981–82	1982–83	1983–84	1984–85
SAT-Verbal, all students	431	429	429	427	424	424	426	425	426	431
White	451	448	446	444	442	442	444	443	445	449
Black	332	330	332	330	330	332	341	339	342	346
Mexican-American	371	370	370	370	372	373	377	375	376	382
Puerto Rican	364	355	349	345	350	353	360	358	358	368
Asian-American	414	405	401	396	396	397	398	395	398	404
American Indian	388	390	387	386	390	391	388	388	390	392
Other	410	402	399	393	394	388	392	386	388	391
SAT-Mathematical, all students	472	470	468	467	466	466	467	468	471	475
White	493	489	485	483	482	483	483	484	487	491
Black	354	357	354	358	360	362	366	369	373	376
Mexican-American	410	408	402	410	413	415	416	417	420	426
Puerto Rican	401	397	388	388	394	398	403	403	405	409
Asian-American	518	514	510	511	509	513	513	514	519	518
American Indian	420	421	419	421	426	425	424	425	427	428
Other	458	457	450	447	449	447	449	446	450	448

SOURCE: College Entrance Examination Board, *National Report on College-Bound Seniors, 1985*. (Copyright © 1985 by the College Entrance Examination Board. All rights reserved.) (This table was prepared October 1986.)

ican-American, Puerto Rican, and black students. The average SAT verbal score over the ten-year period of 1975–76 through 1984–85 was 445 (high), which was earned by white students and 335 (low), earned by black students (see Table 2–9).

The data in Tables 2–7, 2–8, and 2–9 show that, overall, black students receive lower grades in subject matter areas and on the SAT than do other ethnic groups. The SAT math scores of blacks and their grade averages in subject matter areas are rising, however, and gains are to be noted in the areas of science inquiry and science, technology, and society between 1976–77 and 1981–82. These gains exceed national average change in percentage points at ages 9, 13, and 17 with two exceptions—black females fall slightly below the national average in change points for science content and for science, technology, and society at age 13. With respect to actual scores earned by gender, differences reveal that at age 9 black female scores in science inquiry and in science, technology and society are higher than those of black males. At ages 13 and 17 this pattern is reversed: Black males generally earn scores that are higher than those of black females in science content, in science inquiry, and in science, technology and society. The exception to this pattern is in science inquiry at age 13 and at age 17 for 1976–77 when black female scores exceed those of black males (see Table 2–7).

Specific gender differences by ethnicity in other subject matter areas are not included in our data. Overall gender differences are shown, however, in Table 2–8. At ages 9, 13, and 17, Table 2–8 exhibits that females have higher scores than males in reading/ literature comprehension and music, and lower scores in science. At age 9 female scores are lower than males in art, but at ages 13 and 17 female scores are higher. Males have higher scores than females in math and social studies at ages 9 and 17, but not at age 13. In the area of citizenship, males have a higher score than females at age 9, females are higher at age 13, and there is no difference in male and female scores at age 17. It is quite possible that some of the scores are probably lower for black males than for black females ages 9–17 due to what is interpreted as behavioral difficulties in classrooms for which they are singled out more frequently than females. This sort of interpretive leap, however, must be made with caution.

Years of Education Completed and Carnegie Units Earned

The percentage of black Americans 25 years old and over completing four years of high school, regardless of school type (public or private), increased from 12.9 percent in 1960 to 33.9 percent in 1985. For those completing one to three years of high school, the percentage increased from 19 percent in 1960 to 19.2 percent in 1985. Concomitantly, black students completing only eight years of elementary school decreased from 12.9 percent in 1960 to 6.2 in 1985 (see Table 2–10). By contrast, a total of 24.6 percent of the general population completed four years of high school in 1960 and 38.2 percent in 1985. Although the gap between the percentage of black students completing four years of high school and that of the total population narrowed between 1960 and 1983, this gap remains.

On the basis of gender, females in all ethnic groups completed four years of high school at a higher rate than males. For black students, 14.3 percent of the females completed four years of high school in 1960, but only 11.3 percent of the males did so. In 1970, 20 percent of the males and 22.2 percent of the females completed four years of high school. The four-year high school completion rate in 1980 was as follows: male, 28.3 percent, and female, 30 percent; in 1985, male, 31.9 percent, female, 35.5 percent (see Table 2–10). Viewing high school completion rates between black and white males, we find that in 1960, 22.2 percent of white males 25 years and older completed four years of high school; in 1970, 28.5 percent; in 1980, 31.8 percent; and in 1985, 35.3 percent. Comparable proportions for black males are: in 1960, 11.3 percent; in 1970, 20.0 percent; in 1980, 28.3 percent; and in 1985, 31.9 percent.

Examining percentages of the population 18 and 19 and 20–24 years old completing four years of high school (see Table 2–11), we find that, in general, black students show increases similar to those noted earlier. In 1974 the proportion of black students 18 and 19 completing four years of high school was 49.4 percent (491,000). For the category 20–24 years old, it was 71.9 percent (1,565,000). By 1982 the percentage of black students 18 and 19 years old completing four years of high school had grown to 51.8 percent. For black individuals 20–24 years old, it reached 77.3 percent (2,106,000).

The increases in the proportion of black students ages 18 and 19, and 20–24 completing four years of high school are not without merit. It must be noted, however, that black four-year high school completion rates for the ages 18 and 19, and 20–24 years old are still below those of whites. As an illustration, in 1982, 63.5 percent of the white students 18 and 19 years old and 84.7 percent of those 20–24 years old completed four years of high school (see Table 2–11). Yet, as reported in the preceding section, in 1982 only 51.8

Table 2–10 Years of School Completed, by Race, Spanish Origin, and Sex: 1960 to 1985 (Persons 25 years old and over. Persons of Spanish origin may be of any race.)

Year, Race, Spanish Origin, and Sex	Popula-tion (1,000)	Percent of Population Completing—							Median school years completed
		Elementary school			High school		College		
		0–4 years	5–7 years	8 years	1–3 years	4 years	1–3 years	4 years or more	
1960, all races	99,438	8.3	13.8	17.5	19.2	24.6	8.8	7.7	10.6
White	89,581	6.7	12.8	18.1	19.3	25.8	9.3	8.1	10.9
Male	43,259	7.4	13.7	18.7	18.9	22.2	9.1	10.3	10.7
Female	46,322	6.0	11.9	17.8	19.6	29.2	9.5	6.0	11.2
Black	9,054	23.8	24.2	12.9	19.0	12.9	4.1	3.1	8.0
Male	4,240	28.3	23.9	12.3	17.3	11.3	4.1	2.8	7.7
Female	4,814	19.8	24.5	13.4	20.5	14.3	4.1	3.3	8.6
1970, all races	109,899	5.5	10.0	12.8	19.4	31.1	10.6	10.7	12.1
White	98,246	4.5	9.1	13.0	18.8	32.2	11.1	11.3	12.1
Male	46,527	4.8	9.7	13.3	18.2	28.5	11.1	14.4	12.1
Female	51,718	4.1	8.6	12.8	19.4	35.5	11.1	8.4	12.1
Black	10,375	14.6	18.7	10.5	24.8	21.2	5.9	4.4	9.8
Male	4,714	17.7	19.1	10.2	22.9	20.0	6.0	4.2	9.4
Female	5,661	12.0	18.3	10.8	26.4	22.2	5.8	4.6	10.1
Spanish origin	3,946	19.5	18.6	11.5	18.2	21.1	6.5	4.5	9.1
Male	1,897	19.1	18.0	11.3	18.1	19.9	7.6	5.9	9.3
Female	2,050	19.9	19.2	11.6	18.3	22.3	5.4	3.2	8.9
1980, all races	132,836	3.6	6.7	8.0	15.3	34.6	15.7	16.2	12.5
White	114,290	2.6	5.8	8.2	14.6	35.7	16.0	17.1	12.5
Male	53,941	2.8	6.0	8.0	13.6	31.8	16.4	21.3	12.5
Female	60,349	2.5	5.6	8.4	15.5	39.1	15.6	13.3	12.6
Black	13,195	8.2	11.7	7.1	21.8	29.3	13.5	8.4	12.0
Male	5,895	10.0	12.0	6.7	20.5	28.3	14.0	8.4	12.0
Female	7,300	6.7	11.6	7.3	22.9	30.0	13.2	8.3	12.0
Spanish origin	6,739	15.5	16.6	8.1	15.8	24.4	12.0	7.6	10.8
Male	3,247	15.2	16.2	7.7	15.5	22.6	13.4	9.4	11.1
Female	3,493	15.8	17.1	8.4	16.1	26.0	10.6	6.0	10.6
1985, all races	143,524	2.7	4.8	6.4	12.2	38.2	16.3	19.4	12.6
White	124,905	2.2	4.3	6.5	11.5	39.0	16.5	20.0	12.7
Male	59,405	2.3	4.6	6.3	10.8	35.3	16.7	24.0	12.7
Female	65,500	2.1	4.1	6.6	12.1	42.4	16.4	16.3	12.6
Black	14,820	6.2	8.6	6.2	19.2	33.9	14.8	11.1	12.3
Male	6,554	7.8	9.0	6.0	18.7	31.9	15.3	11.2	12.3
Female	8,266	4.9	8.3	6.3	19.6	35.5	14.3	11.0	12.3
Spanish origin	8,455	13.5	15.5	8.7	14.3	28.4	11.0	8.5	11.5
Male	4,063	13.6	15.8	8.2	13.9	27.2	11.5	9.7	11.6
Female	4,392	13.4	15.3	9.3	14.7	29.5	10.6	7.3	11.3

SOURCE: U.S. Bureau of the Census, *U.S. Census of Population: 1960*, vol. I; *1970*, vols. I and II; *1980*, vol. I, chapter C, and *Current Population Reports*, series P-20, forthcoming reports. Reported in Census Bureau (1987, p. 121).

percent of black students 18 and 19 years old and 77.3 percent of those 20–24 years old completed high school. The implication of these statistics is rather clear: Small percentages of black students completing high school translate into small percentages of those pursuing a college education.

A *Carnegie unit* is the measurement standard used to specify the completion of a one-year school course. With reference to the average number of Carnegie units earned by 1982 high school graduates in public, Catholic, and other private schools, black

Table 2–11 Population 18 and 19 Years Old and 20–24 Years Old, and Percent Who Have Completed Four Years of High School, by Race/Ethnicity, March 1974–March 1982 (thousands)

Age and Race/Ethnicity	1974	1975	1976	1977	1978	1979	1980	1981	1982
Total									
Total 18 and 19 years old	7,772	7,956	8,125	8,174	8,150	8,201	8,428	8,229	8,104
Number completing high school	4,990	4,992	5,181	5,072	5,019	5,112	5,116	5,077	5,005
Percent completing high school	64.2	62.7	63.8	62.1	61.6	62.3	60.7	61.7	61.8
Total 20 to 24 years old	17,841	18,360	18,811	19,230	19,561	19,849	20,690	20,985	21,078
Number completing high school	14,932	15,468	15,825	16,122	16,121	16,754	17,333	17,475	17,667
Percent completing high school	83.7	84.2	84.1	83.8	82.4	84.4	83.8	83.3	83.8
White									
Total 18 and 19 years old	6,676	6,826	6,940	6,977	6,934	6.976	7,097	6,889	6,756
Number completing high school	4,433	4,446	4,588	4,517	4,444	4,466	4,481	4,395	4,288
Percent completing high school	66.4	65.1	66.1	64.7	64.1	64.0	63.1	63.8	63.5
Total 20 to 24 years old	15,439	15,883	16,217	16,544	16,790	17,008	17,620	17,723	17,817
Number completing high school	13,169	13,660	13,896	14,082	14,318	14,572	14,988	14,946	15,098
Percent completing high school	85.3	86.0	85.7	85.1	85.3	85.7	85.1	84.3	84.7
Black									
Total 18 and 19 years old	994	1,003	1,064	1,057	1,059	1,073	1,137	1,129	1,137
Number completing high school	491	476	515	463	482	497	525	560	589
Percent completing high school	49.4	47.5	48.4	43.8	45.5	46.3	46.2	49.6	51.8
Total 20 to 24 years old	2,094	2,162	2,229	2,322	2,395	2,427	2,574	2,553	2,725
Number completing high school	1,505	1,550	1,616	1,749	1,758	1,820	1,929	2,025	2,106
Percent completing high school	71.9	71.7	72.5	75.3	73.4	75.0	74.9	76.3	77.3
Hispanic*									
Total 18 and 19 years old	436	484	445	497	494	515	605	581	603
Number completing high school	182	188	196	206	212	242	280	236	243
Percent completing school	41.7	38.8	44.0	41.4	42.9	47.0	46.3	40.6	40.3
Total 20 to 24 years old	934	992	992	1,085	1,185	1,184	1,349	1,434	1,401
Number completing high school	527	590	586	666	728	729	819	799	835
Percent completing high school	56.4	59.5	59.1	61.4	61.4	61.6	60.7	55.7	59.6

*May be of any race

Note: Tabulation includes persons still in school.

Source: U.S. Department of Commerce Bureau of the Census, Current Population Reports, *Educational Attainment in the United States*, Series P-20, various years, and unpublished data from the March 1982 Current Population Survey. Reported in National Center for Education Statistics (1985, p. 74).

students earn slightly fewer units than do other ethnic groups. The total average number of Carnegie units earned by all 1982 high school graduates was 21.0. For public school graduates it was 20.9, for Catholic school graduates, 23.4, and for other private school graduates, 20.4. Black students earned, on average, 20.3 Carnegie units, the lowest of all ethnic groups. Asian or Pacific Islanders earned the highest total average number of Carnegie units at 21.7. They are followed by white graduates, who earned 21.2 Carnegie units (see Table 2–12).

Three-tenths of a Carnegie unit separates black students from the 1982 high school average in foreign language and natural science. In English, mathematics, social science, arts, and trade and industry, black graduates are only one-tenth of a Carnegie unit less than the average. They meet the average in business and exceed it by four-tenths of a unit for a combination of such courses

Table 2–12   Average Number of Carnegie Units Earned by High School Graduates,[1] by Area of Study and Selected Student and School Characteristics: United States, 1982

Characteristic	Total	English	Foreign language	Mathe-matics	Natural science	Social science	Arts	Business	Trade and industry	Other[2]
Average number of units	21.0	3.7	1.0	2.5	1.9	2.6	1.4	1.7	.9	5.4
Student characteristics										
Sex										
Male	20.8	3.6	.8	2.6	1.9	2.6	1.2	1.0	1.6	5.4
Female	21.2	3.7	1.2	2.5	1.9	2.6	1.5	2.4	.2	5.3
Race/ethnicity										
White, non-Hispanic	21.2	3.7	1.1	2.6	2.0	2.6	1.4	1.8	.8	5.2
Black, non-Hispanic	20.3	3.6	.7	2.4	1.6	2.5	1.2	1.7	.8	5.8
Hispanic	20.7	3.6	.8	2.2	1.5	2.5	1.2	1.6	1.1	6.1
Asian or Pacific Islander	21.7	3.6	1.9	3.1	2.4	2.5	1.2	1.1	.7	5.2
American Indian/Alaskan Native	20.6	3.5	.4	2.0	1.6	2.7	1.6	1.5	1.6	5.6
Test performance group[3]										
Low	20.0	3.4	.3	1.9	1.2	2.5	1.3	1.8	1.1	6.4
Low-middle	20.7	3.6	.7	2.2	1.5	2.6	1.3	2.2	1.0	5.6
High-middle	21.3	3.7	1.1	2.6	2.0	2.6	1.4	1.9	.8	5.3
High	22.0	3.8	1.9	3.3	2.7	2.7	1.5	1.2	.5	4.4
Postsecondary education plans										
None	20.0	3.5	.3	1.9	1.3	2.5	1.2	2.0	1.4	6.0
Vocational/technical school	20.7	3.5	.5	2.0	1.4	2.6	1.4	2.0	1.4	6.1
Less than 4 years of college	21.1	3.7	1.0	2.4	1.7	2.6	1.4	2.1	.7	5.5
Bachelor's degree	21.7	3.8	1.5	3.1	2.3	2.7	1.5	1.5	.5	4.9
Advanced degree	21.6	3.8	1.9	3.2	2.6	2.6	1.4	1.2	.3	4.5
Time spent on homework										
Less than 1 hour per week	20.1	3.4	.4	2.0	1.3	2.4	1.3	1.4	1.8	6.1
1 to less than 5 hours per week	21.0	3.6	.9	2.5	1.8	2.6	1.4	1.9	.9	5.5
5 or more hours per week	21.7	3.8	1.8	3.1	2.5	2.6	1.4	1.5	.3	4.6
School characteristics										
Control										
Public	20.9	3.6	.9	2.5	1.8	2.6	1.4	1.8	.9	5.4
Catholic	23.4	4.1	2.0	3.3	2.3	2.7	1.0	1.5	.3	6.2
Other private	20.4	3.9	1.9	3.0	2.4	2.9	1.4	.9	.3	3.7

[1]Data are based on student transcripts for the last 4 years of high school.

[2]Includes courses in architecture, computer and information sciences, health, home economics, industrial arts, personal and social development, philosophy, physical education, psychology, public affairs, and religion.

[3]Test performance as measured by a test battery administered as part of the "High School and Beyond" survey.

Note: Data have been revised slightly from published figures. The Carnegie unit is a standard of measurement that represents one credit for the completion of a 1-year course. Because of rounding, details may not add to totals.

Source: U.S. Department of Education, Center for Education Statistics, "High School and Beyond, 1982" survey. (This table was prepared May 1986.) Reported in Snyder (1987, p. 96).

as architecture, computer and information services, health, home economics, industrial arts, personal and social development, philosophy, physical education, psychology, public affairs, and religion.

Overall, female graduates, irrespective of ethnicity, earned more Carnegie units (21.2) than males (20.8). By subject areas, 1982 female high school graduates earned more units than males in English, foreign language, arts, and business. They earned fewer units in mathematics, trade and industry, and in other courses such as architecture, computer and information sciences, health, and so forth (see Table 2–12). In natural science and social sciences, female and male 1982 graduates earned the same number of units. Although not apparent in the data, it is likely that the gender differences noted would also hold for each ethnic group.

Drop-out Rates

Drop-out rates represent one indication of the failure of schools to meet the educational and social growth needs of youth effectively. Students who are not in school fail to benefit from the formal, deliberately structured education potentially available to them in the school setting. Dropouts lack the credentials necessary to avail themselves of a wide range of occupational and career options, and in the main will have lower lifetime earnings than students who graduate from high school. Dropouts are considered to be individuals not enrolled in school and not having graduated from high school. The focus here is on dropouts at the secondary school level, which generally includes ages 14–19.

Between October 1970 and October 1985, the total percentage of dropouts declined from 8.0 percent for those 16 and 17 years old, and 16.2 percent for the age group 18 and 19 to 7.0 percent, and 14.3 percent, respectively. For students 14 and 15 years old, the drop-out rate remained at 1.8 percent in both 1970 and 1985. Black 14- and 15-year-old dropouts declined slightly from 2.4 percent in 1970 to 2.1 percent in 1985; dropouts 16 and 17 years old from 12.8 percent to 6.5 percent; and those 18 and 19 years old from 31.2 percent to 17.3 percent (see Table 2–13).

In considering gender differences in high school drop-out rates, regardless of ethnicity, the percentage of female dropouts exceeded that of males in 1970 for ages 14–34. By 1985, however, male dropouts overshadowed female dropouts. Yet, the percentage of female dropouts 14–17 years old outpaced males in this age group but fell behind them for the age group 18–29. In the group 20 and 21 years old, male drop-out rates became significantly higher than those of females (20.5 percent male as compared to 15.3 percent female).

The pattern of gender differences among black dropouts generally runs counter to that noted for the total population. In 1970, the percentage of black male dropouts surpassed the percentage of females between the ages 16 and 24. By 1985, the black male drop-out percentage (15.6 percent) continued to be larger than that of black females (15.4 percent) for the age group 14–34 years, but only two-tenths of a percentage point separates them. Although the proportion of black male dropouts (17.7 percent) continued to be higher than that of black females (16.9 percent) for ages 18–24,

Table 2–13 High School Dropouts Among Persons 14 to 34 Years Old, by Age, Race/Ethnicity, and Sex: United States, October 1970, 1975, 1980, and 1985

Year, Race/Ethnicity, and Sex	Total, 14 to 34 years	14 and 15 years	16 and 17 years	18 and 19 years	20 and 21 years	22 to 24 years	25 to 29 years	30 to 34 years
October 1970								
All races								
Total	17.0	1.8	8.0	16.2	16.6	18.7	22.5	26.5
Male	16.2	1.7	7.1	16.0	16.1	17.9	21.4	26.2
Female	17.7	1.9	8.9	16.3	16.9	19.4	23.6	26.8
White								
Total	15.2	1.7	7.3	14.1	14.6	16.3	19.9	24.6
Male	14.4	1.7	6.3	13.3	14.1	15.3	19.0	24.2
Female	16.0	1.8	8.4	14.8	15.1	17.2	20.7	24.9
Black								
Total	30.0	2.4	12.8	31.2	29.6	37.8	44.4	43.5
Male	30.4	2.0	13.3	36.4	29.6	39.5	43.1	45.9
Female	29.5	2.8	12.4	26.6	29.6	36.4	45.6	41.5
October 1975								
All races								
Total	14.1	1.8	8.6	16.0	16.6	14.5	15.4	20.5
Male	13.2	1.6	7.6	15.5	16.4	14.0	14.4	18.9
Female	15.0	2.0	9.6	16.5	16.7	15.0	16.5	22.0
White								
Total	12.8	1.7	8.4	14.7	14.8	12.6	14.0	18.6
Male	21.1	1.4	7.3	13.7	14.5	12.6	13.2	17.4
Female	13.5	1.9	9.6	15.6	15.0	12.7	14.7	19.7
Black								
Total	23.4	2.6	10.2	25.4	28.7	27.8	27.9	36.8
Male	21.9	2.4	9.7	27.7	30.4	25.9	25.5	33.1
Female	24.7	2.8	10.7	23.4	27.3	29.2	29.9	39.6
Hispanic origin[1]								
Total	33.0	4.0	13.2	30.1	31.6	41.7	42.9	48.7
Male	29.9	1.9	11.1	26.3	30.2	40.0	40.6	45.0
Female	35.7	6.2	15.5	33.5	32.7	43.2	44.8	51.9
October 1980								
All races								
Total	13.0	1.7	8.8	15.7	15.9	15.2	13.9	14.6
Male	13.2	1.3	8.9	16.9	17.8	16.4	13.8	14.0
Female	12.8	2.2	8.8	14.7	14.3	14.0	14.0	15.2
White								
Total	12.1	1.7	9.2	14.9	14.5	13.9	12.7	13.4
Male	12.4	1.2	9.3	16.1	15.6	15.4	12.7	13.1
Female	11.8	2.1	9.2	13.8	13.4	12.6	12.7	13.6
Black								
Total	18.8	2.0	6.9	21.2	24.8	24.0	22.6	23.5
Male	19.0	1.5	7.2	22.7	31.3	24.9	22.1	21.9
Female	18.7	2.5	6.6	19.8	19.6	23.3	22.9	24.8
Hispanic origin[1]								
Total	35.2	5.7	16.5	39.0	41.6	40.6	40.9	45.4
Male	35.6	3.3	18.1	43.1	41.4	42.9	40.1	43.9
Female	34.9	7.9	15.0	34.6	41.9	38.6	41.7	47.0
October 1985								
All races								
Total	12.0	1.8	7.0	14.3	13.9	14.1	14.1	12.7
Male	12.3	1.6	6.7	16.3	14.9	14.9	14.2	12.5
Female	11.7	2.0	7.2	12.3	12.9	13.3	13.9	12.9

Table 2–13 *(continued)*

White								
Total	11.5	1.8	7.1	13.8	13.4	13.3	13.6	11.6
Male	11.8	1.6	6.7	16.3	14.2	14.2	14.0	11.5
Female	11.1	2.0	7.6	11.3	12.7	12.5	13.3	11.7
Black								
Total	15.5	2.1	6.5	17.3	17.7	17.8	17.5	20.5
Male	15.6	1.8	7.6	17.7	20.5	18.4	17.0	20.7
Female	15.4	2.4	5.4	16.9	15.3	17.4	18.0	20.4
Hispanic origin[1]								
Total	31.4	3.6	14.5	30.6	27.9	33.9	39.1	41.5
Male	32.1	3.2	10.1	42.2	33.5	33.9	37.6	41.1
Female	30.8	4.0	19.2	19.9	22.8	33.8	40.6	41.9

[1]Persons of Hispanic origin are also included, as appropriate, in the white and black categories.

Note: Dropouts are persons who are not enrolled in school and who are not high school graduates. People who have received GED credentials are counted as graduates. Data are based upon sample surveys of the civilian noninstitutional population.

SOURCE: U.S. Department of Commerce, Bureau of the Census, *Current Population Reports*, Series P-20, Nos. 222, 303, 362, and 409. (This table was prepared October 1986.) Reprinted in Snyder (1987, p. 86).

for ages 14–17 black female dropouts exceeded black male dropouts. This latter statistic may be attributable to the large percentage of black female teenagers who become pregnant and drop out of school (Ladner, 1987). The accuracy of this assumption, however, should be subjected to strict scrutiny. The precise reasons of the higher female drop-out rate between the ages 14 and 17 cannot be ascertained from these data. At another level, and significantly, within the population of males ages 18 and 19, and 20 and 21, in 1970 black males (36.4 percent and 29.6 percent, respectively) dropped out of high school at almost double the rate of white males, 13.3 percent and 14.1 percent, respectively. By 1985, however, the gap had become narrower. Black male drop-out rates among 18- and 19-year-old students was 17.7 percent; for white males, 16.3 percent. Among 20–21-year-old students, the difference was much greater: black males, 20.5 percent; white males, 14.2 percent.

Reviewing overall high school drop-out rates for individuals between 14 and 34 years of age provides a rather depressing picture of reality. Whereas the overall percentage of high school dropouts between the ages 14 and 34 declined between 1970 and 1985, the percentage of black dropouts remained significantly higher than that of whites during that period. In 1970 black high school drop-out figures were nearly twice as high as those of whites (30 percent versus 15.2 percent). By 1985, percentages of black high school dropouts exceeded those of whites by about one-fourth (15.5 percent versus 11.5 percent) (see Table 2–13).

Table 2–14   High School Dropout Rates of 1980 Sophomores, by Selected
School and Community Characteristics, Fall 1982

Characteristic	Total	Male	Female	White, Non-Hispanic	Black, Non-Hispanic	Hispanic
All high school sophomores:						
Total	13.6	14.6	12.6	12.2	16.8	18.7
Control of school						
Public	14.4	15.2	13.5	13.0	17.2	19.1
Catholic	3.4	4.7	2.2	2.6	4.6	9.5
Public high school sophomores:						
Region[a]						
Northeast	11.9	12.8	10.9	9.5	21.7	18.2
North Central	12.3	12.0	12.7	10.8	23.1	16.1
South	16.6	18.3	15.0	16.3	14.5	20.3
West	16.5	17.7	15.1	16.6	14.2	19.5
Community type:						
Urban	18.1	19.0	17.2	15.5	20.3	23.3
Suburban	12.8	14.1	11.5	12.1	14.0	17.2
Rural	14.3	14.7	14.0	13.4	15.4	17.6
Schools with black enrollment:						
Less than 10 percent	12.8	13.5	12.2	12.0	16.9	17.2
10 to 29 percent	15.3	16.9	13.6	14.6	15.7	20.1
30 to 49 percent	18.1	17.0	19.0	18.4	15.3	24.0
50 percent or more	19.7	21.8	17.9	(b)	19.3	(b)
Schools with Hispanic enrollment:						
Less than 10 percent	13.5	14.2	12.7	12.5	16.2	16.7
10 to 29 percent	18.8	20.7	16.9	17.2	22.9	23.1
30 to 49 percent	25.6	23.8	27.5	28.7	29.6	22.8
50 percent or more	21.1	24.1	18.3	15.6	(b)	22.6
County per capita income quartile:						
Low	16.2	17.0	15.4	15.7	17.5	16.2
Low-middle	13.4	14.3	12.5	12.7	14.2	17.2
High-middle	15.7	16.3	15.0	14.0	18.4	22.8
High	12.7	13.8	11.6	10.7	17.1	19.1

[a]The regions correspond to Bureau of the Census definitions. See the Definitions of Selected
Terms in the appendix.

[b]Small sample size precludes showing percent.

SOURCE: U.S. Department of Education, National Center for Education Statistics, High
School and Beyond Study. Unpublished tabulations (September 1984). Reported in National
Center for Education Statistics (1985, p. 208).

Data collected through the National High School and Beyond Study and reported in the *Conditions of Education* (National Center for Education Statistics, 1985) reveal that drop-out rates for black sophomores in 1980 were substantially higher in public schools located in urban communities in the Northeast and North Central states than states in the South and West, and in public schools in which the total black school enrollment was 50 percent or more and the Hispanic enrollment was between 30 and 49 percent. The lowest high school drop-out rates for 1980 sophomores for all ethnic groups were associated with Catholic schools (see Table 2–14).

Returning to the earlier point of income differentials for dropouts and nondropouts, it is significant to note the correspondence between education and income dramatically portrayed in Table 2–15. Given the data displayed in this table, it becomes readily apparent that from 1950 to 1983 the median income for individuals between 25 and 34 years old, with income during the year, was higher for college graduates than for high school graduates and for those with some high school. It was also higher for high school

Table 2–15 Median Income of Male College Graduates, Male High School Graduates, and Those with Some High School, 25–34 Years Old, with Income During the Year, 1950–1983 (figures in current dollars)

Year	College graduates	High school graduates	Some high school	Ratio (1)/(2)	Ratio (2)/(3)
1950	3,510	3,095	2,735	1.13	1.13
1958	5,970	4,688	4,275	1.27	1.10
1961	6,640	5,175	4,425	1.28	1.17
1963	6,947	5,612	4,903	1.24	1.14
1965	7,474	6,151	5,254	1.21	1.17
1967	8,762	6,882	5,922	1.27	1.16
1969	10,228	8,008	6,693	1.28	1.20
1971	10,908	8,556	7,331	1.27	1.17
1973	12,349	10,153	8,448	1.22	1.20
1975	13,232	10,767	8,241	1.23	1.31
1979	17,345	14,280	10,983	1.21	1.30
1981	20,589	15,393	11,173	1.34	1.38
1982	21,149	15,298	10,948	1.38	1.40
1983	21,988	15,789	10,711	1.39	1.47

Source: 1950 Census of Population, Special Reports. *Educational Attainment*, table 12; 1958–82, U.S. Bureau of the Census. Current Population Reports. Series P-60 *Income of Families and Persons in the U.S.* various issues. Reported in Census Bureau (1985a, 11).

graduates than for those with only some high school education, except in the year 1958. In fact, the gap between income based on educational attainment has widened each successive year since 1958.

Black students are thus further jeopardized by failing to complete high school. The high drop-out rates of 18- and 19-year-old black males point to important harsh consequences, such as lowered potential earnings and the lack of credentials necessary for upward educational and economic mobility. Thus the ability of black males who drop out of high school to provide for the basic needs, and some of the advantages beyond this level, to families that many of them either will head or will desire to head becomes problematic.

Potential earnings are not only correlated with educational attainment, as displayed in Table 2–15, but are also associated with type of curriculum studied in secondary schools and postsecondary institutions, a topic we consider next.

Enrollment in Postsecondary Education

The total enrollment in public and private institutions of higher education in fall 1984 was slightly more than 12.1 million (see Table 2–16). This enrollment figure was approximately 1.0 percent higher than the total 1980 enrollment of about 12 million and approximately 10 percent higher than the 1976 enrollment of about 11 million. For black, non-Hispanic students, total fall 1984 enrollment was 1,069,885, a decline of about 3.3 percent from the total 1980 enrollment of 1,106,750. Of concern here is the fact that the 1984 enrollment figure (1,069,885) is relatively close to matching the 1976 (1,033,025) enrollment figure. The declining college enrollment of black students is particularly troubling. Whereas total higher education enrollment increased between 1980 and 1984, it declined for black students during this period. In fact, the percentage of black students enrolled in two- and four-year colleges has been declining since 1978 (National Center for Education Statistics, 1985, p. 104).

By gender, in fall 1984 there were 434,515 black, non-Hispanic males and 635,370 black, non-Hispanic females enrolled in public and private institutions of higher education. In comparison to fall 1980 figures, black male enrollment in 1984 declined about 6.3 percent from 463,739, and black female enrollment declined by about 1.12 percent from 643,011 (see Table 2–16).

By institutional type, as displayed in Table 2–17, blacks (non-Hispanic) in four-year institutions declined as a percentage of total enrollment from 5.5 percent in 1976 to 5.2 percent in 1980 to 5.0 percent in 1984. During the same period, the proportion of non-Hispanic blacks enrolled in two-year institutions has remained fairly constant at about 3.9 percent (see Table 2–17). It is instructive to note that in 1976, as determined from data provided in Table 2–17, 41.5 percent of black undergraduate students were enrolled in two-year colleges and 58.5 percent in four-year colleges. In 1984, 42.7 percent of the black college students were enrolled in two-year institutions and 57.3 percent in four-year institutions. By contrast, the total percentage of all students enrolled in two-year colleges was 37.1 percent in 1984 and 35.3 in 1976. Enrollment figures for students in four-year colleges, irrespective of ethnicity, was 64.7 percent in 1976 and 62.9 percent in 1984. Thus, the proportion of black students attending two-year colleges is greater than that of the overall college-going population. Conversely, a smaller proportion of black students attend four-year colleges.

The percentage of black students as a proportion of overall college enrollment rates is becoming alarmingly smaller. At the same time, however, within the black college enrollment population their representation as a proportion of students enrolling in two-year colleges is growing. What must be questioned in this regard is the degree to which black two-year college students transfer to four-year colleges and enroll in, and successfully complete, high-status vocational/occupational programs.

The general declining trend in black college enrollment becomes more dramatic when viewed in relationship to increases in the population of black high school graduates. In 1970 the completion rate for four years of high school for black students 20–24 years old was 71.9 percent. By 1985, that rate had increased to 33.9 percent (see Table 2–10). Viewed either as a percentage of 18- to 24-year-olds or as a percentage of high school graduates, the percentage of black high school graduates enrolling in institutions of higher education, however, has been decreasing since 1976. In that year 33.5 percent of black high school graduates enrolled in college. By 1985 that percentage had dropped to 26.1 percent. Enrollment figures as a percentage of 18- to 24-year-olds for black students are similar: 22.6 percent in 1976 and 19.8 percent in 1985 (see Table 2–18). During this same period the percentage of white high school graduates enrolling in college has increased slightly from 33.0 percent in 1976 to 34.4 percent in 1985 (see Table 2–18).

With regard to gender, for the period 1960 to 1985, the percentage of black (including other nonwhite groups) male high school graduates between the ages of 18 and 24 initially enrolled in college

Table 2–16   Total Enrollment in Institutions of Higher Education, by Control of Institution, Level of Enrollment, and Race/Ethnicity and Sex of Student: United States, Fall 1976, 1980, and 1984

Year and race/ethnicity and sex of student	Enrollment, by control of institution			Enrollment, by level			
	Total	Public	Private	Undergraduate	Graduate	First-professional	Unclassified
1976 total	10,985,614	8,641,037	2,344,577	8,432,240	1,081,858	244,121	1,227,395
Men	5,794,390	4,499,541	1,294,849	4,420,228	599,778	189,642	584,742
Women	5,191,224	4,141,496	1,049,728	4,012,012	482,080	54,479	642,653
White, non-Hispanic	9,076,131	7,094,521	1,981,610	6,899,743	907,583	220,003	1,048,802
Men	4,813,717	3,714,567	1,099,150	3,645,423	496,260	172,422	499,612
Women	4,262,414	3,379,954	882,460	3,254,320	411,323	47,581	549,190
Black, non-Hispanic	1,033,025	831,212	201,813	866,147	65,352	11,181	90,345
Men	469,881	375,389	94,492	397,084	27,016	7,234	38,547
Women	563,144	455,823	107,321	469,063	38,336	3,947	51,798
Hispanic	383,790	336,818	46,972	323,540	20,274	4,547	35,429
Men	209,714	183,881	25,833	175,940	11,359	3,498	18,917
Women	174,076	152,937	21,139	147,600	8,915	1,049	16,512
Asian or Pacific Islander	197,878	165,716	32,162	152,533	18,487	4,075	22,783
Men	108,434	89,423	19,011	82,558	11,600	2,933	11,343
Women	89,444	76,293	13,151	69,975	6,887	1,142	11,440
American Indian/Alaskan Native	76,110	67,500	8,610	61,267	3,887	1,253	9,703
Men	38,543	34,236	4,307	30,809	2,193	1,032	4,509
Women	37,567	33,264	4,303	30,458	1,694	221	5,194
Nonresident alien	218,680	145,270	73,410	129,010	66,275	3,062	20,333
Men	154,101	102,045	52,056	88,414	51,350	2,523	11,814
Women	64,579	43,225	21,354	40,596	14,925	539	8,519

1980 total	12,086,808	9,456,423	2,630,385	9,262,003	1,095,455	276,844	1,451,506
Men	5,868,095	4,521,632	1,346,463	4,488,357	568,969	198,483	612,286
Women	6,218,713	4,934,791	1,283,922	4,773,646	527,486	78,361	839,220
White, non-Hispanic	9,833,012	7,656,094	2,176,918	7,466,278	898,698	247,655	1,220,381
Men	4,772,918	3,658,136	1,114,782	3,632,900	452,886	179,538	507,594
Women	5,060,094	3,997,958	1,062,136	3,833,378	445,812	68,117	712,787
Black, non-Hispanic	1,106,750	876,070	230,680	932,254	59,993	12,824	101,679
Men	463,739	365,296	98,443	393,397	22,795	7,365	40,182
Women	643,011	510,774	132,237	538,857	37,198	5,459	61,497
Hispanic	471,717	406,150	65,567	390,463	24,263	6,534	50,457
Men	231,609	198,652	32,957	190,224	12,173	4,633	24,579
Women	240,108	207,498	32,610	200,239	12,090	1,901	25,878
Asian or Pacific Islander	286,446	239,710	46,736	215,002	23,494	6,124	41,826
Men	151,287	124,771	26,516	112,522	14,473	4,123	20,169
Women	135,159	114,939	20,220	102,480	9,021	2,001	21,657
American Indian/Alaskan Native	83,903	74,224	9,679	67,917	3,882	805	11,299
Men	37,776	33,417	4,359	30,542	1,909	545	4,780
Women	46,127	40,807	5,320	37,375	1,973	260	6,519
Nonresident alien	304,980	204,175	100,805	190,089	86,125	2,902	25,864
Men	210,766	141,360	69,406	128,772	64,733	2,279	14,982
Women	94,214	62,815	31,399	61,317	21,392	623	10,882
1984 total	12,161,778	9,424,911	2,736,867	9,451,066	1,100,353	276,364	1,333,995
Men	5,824,388	4,448,502	1,375,886	4,518,645	569,469	183,626	552,648
Women	6,337,390	4,976,409	1,360,981	4,932,421	530,884	92,738	781,347
White, non-Hispanic	9,766,845	7,524,802	2,242,043	7,549,607	882,253	241,597	1,093,388
Men	4,667,606	3,542,374	1,125,232	3,620,973	436,893	162,537	447,203
Women	5,099,239	3,982,428	1,116,811	3,928,634	445,360	79,060	646,185
Black, non-Hispanic	1,069,885	841,336	228,549	897,185	52,834	13,243	106,623

Table 2–16   (*continued*)

Year and race/ethnicity and sex of student	Enrollment, by control of institution			Enrollment, by level			
	Total	Public	Private	Undergraduate	Graduate	First-professional	Unclassified
Men	434,515	340,030	94,485	368,089	19,961	7,017	39,448
Women	635,370	501,306	134,064	529,096	32,873	6,226	67,175
Hispanic	528,786	452,514	76,272	436,614	24,402	7,913	59,857
Men	251,030	213,705	37,325	206,337	11,676	5,152	27,865
Women	277,756	238,809	38,947	230,277	12,726	2,761	31,992
Asian or Pacific Islander	381,746	317,454	64,292	301,167	28,543	9,24	42,796
Men	205,542	169,568	35,974	160,564	17,865	5,786	21,327
Women	176,204	147,886	28,318	140,603	10,678	3,454	21,469
American Indian/Alaskan Native	82,672	71,642	11,030	68,815	3,634	980	9,243
Men	37,056	32,262	4,794	30,842	1,706	616	3,892
Women	45,616	39,380	6,236	37,973	1,928	364	5,351
Nonresident alien	331,844	217,163	114,681	197,678	108,687	3,391	22,088
Men	228,639	150,563	78,076	131,840	81,368	2,518	12,913
Women	103,205	66,600	36,605	65,838	27,319	873	9,175

[1] Some 214 institutions did not report the racial/ethnic status of their student body. Data for 195 of these nonreporting institutions, representing about 5 percent of total enrollment, were imputed. For those institutions which reported race data in 1982, data have been estimated by applying their 1982 race distribution to their enrollment reported in 1984.

Note: Because of underreporting and nonreporting of racial/ethnic data, totals in this table may be slightly smaller than totals appearing in other tables. Because of rounding, details may not add to totals.

SOURCE: U.S. Department of Education, Center for Education Statistics. "Fall Enrollment in Colleges and Universities 1984" survey. (This table was prepared September 1986.) Reported in Snyder (1987, p. 152).

has been larger than that of black females, except in 1980, but significantly smaller than that of white males. As displayed in Table 2–19, the percentage gap of black male over female high school graduates enrolled in college has ranged from 4.6 percent in 1970 to 3.1 in 1985. In 1980—the year that the percentage of black female high school graduates exceeded black males—the percentage difference was 2.2 percent. The gap between black and white male high school graduates 18–24 years old enrolling in college ranges from a high of 13.4 percentage points in 1970 to a low of 3.5 percentage points in 1975. Since that time the gap created by more white than black high school graduates enrolling in college has averaged around 7.0 percent. As of 1985, however, 8.4 percent more white male (36.6 percent) than black male (28.2 percent) high school graduates between the ages of 18 and 24 enrolled in college.

College enrollment is related not only to grades and test scores but also to family financial circumstances. By income bracket for all ethnic groups, the highest percentage of high school graduates 18–24 years old enrolled in college in 1985 who were family dependents was 53.8 percent for the family income category of $50,000 and over. By ethnicity, a larger percentage of black students were in the family income bracket of $40,000 to $49,999 (39.3 percent) than were in the $50,000-and-over category (data for this category were to small to meet reliability standards). For white students the greatest percentage (53.8 percent) were in the $50,000-and-over bracket (see Table 2–20). These data strongly suggest that family income should be considered an important factor in the equation relating to who attends college. Students from higher-income families are likely to be enrolled in college in greater percentages than students from lower- to middle-class family income categories. Importantly, the college enrollment of black students from lower- to middle-class family income brackets attests not only to their desire and motivation to attain higher education, but also to a greater willingness of their parents to sacrifice financially for them to do so. The family income of slightly more than half of black college students (313,000, or 53 percent) in 1985 was under $19,999. The proportion of white students in this family income bracket was only 15 percent (7,720).

College persistence rates in part are also associated with financial circumstances, and minorities (black and Hispanic) are more likely than whites to leave college for financial reasons. Among four-year college students in 1974, 38 percent of the black students not receiving financial aid withdrew for nonacademic reasons, compared to 23 percent of their white counterparts. Similarly, of

Table 2–17   Total Enrollment in Institutions of Higher Education, by Type of Institution and Race/Ethnicity of Student: United States, Fall 1976 to Fall 1984

Type of institution and race/ethnicity of student	Number, in thousands				Percentage distribution			
	1976	1980	1982	1984[1]	1976	1980	1982	1984[1]
All institutions	10,986	12,087	12,388	12,162	100.0	100.0	100.0	100.0
White, non-Hispanic	9,076	9,833	9,997	9,767	82.6	81.4	80.7	80.3
Total minority	1,691	1,949	2,059	2,063	15.4	16.1	16.6	17.0
Black, non-Hispanic	1,033	1,107	1,101	1,070	9.4	9.2	8.9	8.8
Hispanic	384	472	519	529	3.5	3.9	4.2	4.3
Asian or Pacific Islander	198	286	351	382	1.8	2.4	2.8	3.1
American Indian/Alaskan Native	76	84	88	83	0.7	0.7	0.7	0.7
Nonresident alien	219	305	331	332	2.0	2.5	2.7	2.7
4-year institutions	7,107	7,565	7,648	7,651	64.7	62.6	61.7	62.9
White, non-Hispanic	5,999	6,275	6,306	6,263	54.6	51.9	50.9	51.5
Total minority	931	1,050	1,073	1,108	8.5	8.7	8.7	9.1

Black, non-Hispanic	604	634	612	613	5.5	5.2	4.9	5.0
Hispanic	174	217	229	241	1.6	1.8	1.8	2.0
Asian or Pacific Islander	119	162	193	217	1.1	1.3	1.6	1.8
American Indian/Alaskan Native	35	37	39	37	0.3	0.3	0.3	0.3
Nonresident alien	177	241	270	280	1.6	2.0	2.2	2.3
2-year institutions	3,879	4,521	4,740	4,511	35.3	37.4	38.3	37.1
White, non-Hispanic	3,077	3,558	3,692	3,504	28.0	29.4	29.8	28.8
Total minority	760	899	987	955	6.9	7.4	8.0	7.8
Black, non-Hispanic	429	472	489	457	3.9	3.9	3.9	3.8
Hispanic	210	255	291	288	1.9	2.1	2.3	2.4
Asian or Pacific Islander	79	124	158	165	0.7	1.0	1.3	1.4
American Indian/Alaskan Native	41	47	49	45	0.4	0.4	0.4	0.4
Nonresident alien	42	64	61	52	0.4	0.5	0.5	0.4

[1]Some 214 institutions did not report the racial/ethnic status of their student body. Data for 195 of these nonreporting institutions, representing about 5 percent of total enrollment, were imputed. For those institutions which reported race data in 1982, data have been estimated by applying their 1982 race distribution to their total enrollment reported in 1984.

Note: Because of underreporting and nonreporting of racial/ethnic data, totals in this table may be slightly smaller than totals appearing in other tables. Because of rounding, details may not add to totals.

SOURCE: U.S. Department of Education, Center for Education Statistics, "Fall Enrollment in Colleges and Universities" surveys. (This table was prepared September 1986.) Reported in Snyder (1987, p. 151).

Table 2–18   Enrollment Rates of 18- to 24-Year-Olds in Institutions of Higher Education, by Race/Ethnicity: United States, 1967 to 1985

Year	All students		White		Black		Hispanic origin[1]	
	Enrollment as a percent of 18- to 24-year-olds	Enrollment as a percent of high school graduates	Enrollment as a percent of 18- to 24-year-olds	Enrollment as a percent of high school graduates	Enrollment as a percent of 18- to 24-year-olds	Enrollment as a percent of high school graduates	Enrollment as a percent of 18- to 24-year-olds	Enrollment as a percent of high school graduates
1967	25.5	33.7	26.9	34.5	13.0	23.3	—	—
1968	26.0	34.2	27.5	34.9	14.5	25.2	—	—
1969	27.3	35.0	28.7	35.6	16.0	27.2	—	—
1970	25.7	32.7	27.1	33.2	15.5	26.0	—	—
1971	26.2	33.2	27.2	33.5	18.2	29.2	—	—
1972	25.5	31.9	26.4	32.3	18.1	27.1	13.4	25.8
1973	24.0	29.7	25.0	30.2	16.0	24.0	16.0	29.1
1974	24.6	30.5	25.2	30.5	17.9	26.6	18.1	32.3
1975	26.3	32.5	26.9	32.4	20.7	32.0	20.4	35.5
1976	26.7	33.1	27.1	33.0	22.6	33.5	19.9	35.8
1977	26.1	32.5	26.5	32.2	21.3	31.5	17.2	31.5
1978	25.3	31.4	25.7	31.1	20.1	29.7	15.2	27.2
1979	25.0	31.2	25.6	31.2	19.8	29.5	16.6	30.2
1980	25.6	31.6	26.2	31.8	19.2	27.6	16.1	29.8
1981	26.2	32.5	26.7	32.5	19.9	28.0	16.7	29.9
1982	26.6	33.0	27.2	33.1	19.8	28.0	16.8	29.2
1983	26.2	32.5	27.0	32.9	19.2	27.0	17.2	31.4
1984	27.1	33.2	28.0	33.7	20.4	27.2	17.9	29.9
1985	27.8	33.7	28.7	34.4	19.8	26.1	16.9	26.9

[1]Persons of Hispanic origin may be of any race.   —Data not available.   *Note:* Data are based upon a sample of the civilian noninstitutional population. Source: U.S. Department of Commerce, Bureau of the Census, *Current Population Reports*, Series P-20, Nos. 404 and 409. (This table was prepared January 1987.) Reprinted in Snyder (1987, p. 155).

Table 2–19 College Enrollment and Percent of High School Graduates Enrolled in, or Completed One or More Years of College, by Sex and Race: 1960 to 1985 [As of October, except as noted. Covers civilian noninstitutional population 14 to 24 years old]

Item and Year	All Persons			Male			Female		
	Total[1]	White	Black	Total[1]	White	Black	Total[1]	White	Black
College enrollment (1,000):									
1960[2]	2,279	2,138	[3]141	1,365	1,297	[3]68	914	841	[3]73
1970	6,065	5,535	437	3,461	3,213	202	2,604	2,322	236
1975	7,228	6,368	699	3,821	3,437	308	3,407	2,931	392
1980	7,475	6,546	718	3,700	3,303	292	3,778	3,243	426
1984	7,844	6,735	826	4,020	3,479	383	3,823	3,256	443
1985	7,799	6,729	755	3,880	3,374	355	3,917	3,357	400
Percent of high school graduates enrolled:									
1960[2]	23.8	24.3	[3]18.7	30.4	31.1	[3]21.1	18.0	18.1	[3]16.9
1970	33.3	33.9	26.7	41.8	42.9	29.5	26.3	26.3	24.7
1975	33.1	33.0	32.5	36.7	36.9	33.4	29.9	29.4	32.0
1980	32.3	32.5	28.3	33.8	34.3	27.0	30.9	30.9	29.2
1984	33.7	34.2	28.0	36.4	36.8	29.6	31.3	31.8	26.8
1985	34.3	35.0	26.5	36.0	36.6	28.2	32.8	33.6	25.1
Percent of high school graduates enrolled in college or completed 1 or more years of college:									
1960[2]	40.4	41.0	[3]32.5	46.1	47.1	[3]33.5	35.3	35.6	[3]31.8
1970	52.3	53.4	40.0	59.2	60.8	41.2	46.5	47.1	39.0
1975	52.5	52.7	48.0	56.1	56.6	50.3	49.2	49.1	46.4
1980	51.1	51.4	46.2	51.4	51.8	44.4	51.0	51.0	47.5
1984	53.0	53.8	45.2	53.6	54.2	45.2	52.4	53.4	45.0
1985	54.3	55.3	43.8	54.6	55.5	43.5	54.0	55.2	43.9

[1]Includes other races, not shown separately.
[2]As of April.
[3]Black and other races.
SOURCE: U.S. Bureau of the Census, *U.S. Census of Population: 1960*, vol. I, *Characteristics of the Population*, part 1; *Current Population Reports*, series P-20, No. 404 and earlier reports; and unpublished data. Reported in Census Bureau (1987, p. 137).

the two-year college students withdrawing in 1974 who did not receive financial aid, 58 percent were black students, compared to 42 percent white students. Moreover, based on a representative sample of students entering four-year colleges in fall 1983, withdrawals by 1977 were 27 percent for black students and 23 percent for whites. At the two-year college level, withdrawal rates were much higher for both black and white students, but considerably higher for black students. One unavoidable conclusion is that the financial resources of black students are inadequate to underwrite

Table 2–20   College Enrollment of High School Graduates Who Are Dependent Family Members, 18 to 24 Years Old, by Family Income: 1985

	All Races[1]			White			Black		
		In college			In college			In college	
Income Class	Total	Number	Percent	Total	Number	Percent	Total	Number	Percent
All income levels	16,179	5,853	36.2	13,014	5,037	38.7	2,726	595	21.8
Under $10,000	2,629	405	15.4	1,512	247	16.3	1,030	129	12.5
$10,000 to $19,999	3,046	755	24.8	2,180	525	24.1	782	184	23.5
$20,000 to $29,999	2,652	886	33.4	2,190	765	34.9	395	91	23.0
$30,000 to $39,999	2,673	1,182	44.2	2,350	1,041	44.3	247	94	38.1
$40,000 to $49,999	1,627	808	49.7	1,466	736	50.2	117	46	39.3
$60,000 and over	2,833	1,524	53.8	2,699	1,452	53.8	65	34	(B)
Not reported	720	291	40.4	616	272	44.2	89	20	22.5
									(X)
Median family income (dol.)	29,104	37,449	(X)	32,660	39,428	(X)	14,258	19,158	

Note: In thousands, except as indicated. As of October. Covers civilian noninstitutional population. Degree creditable enrollment. A dependent family member is a relative of the person maintaining the family other than the spouse. Such persons are generally sons and daughters within the family. Based on Current Population Survey.

B Base too small to meet standard of reliability.

X Not applicable.

[1]Includes other races, not shown separately.

Source: U.S. Bureau of the Census, unpublished data. Reported in Census Bureau (1987, p. 141).

their college education. As a consequence, those who receive no financial aid withdraw from two- and four-year colleges in much larger percentages than whites (College Entrance Examination Board, 1985).

Let us now consider the distribution of participants in various postsecondary programs: academic programs (full- or part-time programs and coursework leading to an undergraduate, graduate, or professional degree), vocational programs (full- or part-time programs of coursework leading to a vocational credential, occupational license, or other vocational diploma or degree), and continuing education programs (college credit courses not classified as vocational or academic and not seeking a degree, or noncredit courses for personal and occupational improvement or for social/recreational purposes).

In October 1982 the largest number of all students 16–65 years of age and over (9,243,000, or 50.8 percent) enrolled in postsecondary education were in academic programs. The next highest number (5,177,000, or 28.4 percent) were enrolled in continuing education, and 3,787,000, or 20.4 percent, were in vocational education (see Table 2–21). Within the academic postsecondary education category, males and females, in general, are represented at virtually the same percentages (males, 50.1 percent; females, 49.9 percent). By contrast, the proportion of females in continuing

Table 2–21 Participants in Postsecondary Academic, Vocational, and Continuing Education, by Sex, Race, and Age Group, October 1982

Sex, Race, and Age Group	Academic[a]		Vocational[b]		Continuing[c]	
	Number (in thousands)	Percentage Distribution	Number (in thousands)	Percentage Distribution	Number (in thousands)	Percentage Distribution
Total	9,243	100.0	3,787	100.0	5,177	100.0
Male	4,629	50.1	1,712	45.2	1,808	34.9
Female	4,614	49.9	2,074	54.8	3,368	65.1
White	7,933	85.8	3,199	84.5	4,731	91.4
Black	918	9.9	449	11.9	255	4.9
Other races	392	4.2	138	3.6	190	3.7
16–24	6,208	67.2	1,833	48.4	848	16.4
25–34	2,145	23.2	1,078	28.5	1,667	32.2
35–44	624	6.8	522	13.8	1,121	21.7
45–54	198	2.1	240	6.3	717	13.8
55–64	56	.6	95	2.5	514	9.9
65 and over	12	.1	19	.5	309	6.0

[a]Academic students pursued coursework, either full- or part-time, for the purpose of obtaining an undergraduate, graduate, or professional degree.
[b]Vocational students took coursework (either full- or part-time) in an occupational or technical field for the purpose of obtaining a vocational credential, such as a vocational certificate, occupational license, or other vocational diploma or degree.
[c]Continuing education students were postsecondary education participants not otherwise classified as academic or vocational students who were taking college credit courses but not seeking a degree or who were taking noncredit courses for job improvement, personal development or social/recreational purposes (excluding adult basic education courses to improve basic skills in reading, writing, or arithmetic).
Note: Data revised from those previously published. Details may not add to totals because of rounding.
SOURCE: U.S. Department of Education, National Center for Education Statistics, Special Report, *Participants in Postsecondary Education, October 1982.* 1984, based on data from Current Population Survey of the Bureau of the Census. Reported in National Center for Education Statistics (1985, p. 90).

education (65.1 percent) is almost twice as large as that of males (34.9 percent). In vocational education, females represent 54.8 percent of all students, and males, 45.2 percent.

By ethnicity, for fall 1982, white students represented 85.8 percent of the total number of students enrolled in academic programs, black students, 9.9 percent, and students from other races, 4.2 percent. Within vocational education programs, white students constituted 84.5 percent of the total, blacks, 11.9 percent, and students of other races, 3.6 percent. The distribution of students in continuing education programs was as follows: white students, 91.4 percent; black students, 4.9 percent; and students of other races, 3.7 percent (see Table 2–21).

Why black students are overrepresented in postsecondary vocational programs is not immediately clear from these data, although several reasons may account for this phenomenon: a need to enter programs that should have an immediate financial payoff; the insufficiency of the high school preparation of many black students;

and high school curriculum placement or tracking practices, which find a disproportionately high percentage of black students in general tracks and special education (*Hobson* v. *Hansen*, 1967; *Larry P.* v. *Riles*, 1979; Oakes, 1985). In addition, low high school grade point averages of many black students disqualify them from meeting academic program entry requirements. The relatively small percentages of black students in postsecondary academic programs foreshadow what may be expected with regard to attainment of four-year college and advanced and professional degrees.

Comparatively few black students obtain four-year college or advanced academic and professional degrees relative to their high school completion rates (Astin, 1982). Black students received 6.56 percent of the bachelor's degrees awarded to college graduates in 1978–79, and 6.49 percent in 1980–81. White students, on the other hand, received 87.26 percent of the bachelor's degrees in 1978–79 and 86.36 percent in 1980–81 (Grant and Snyder, 1986, p. 134; Grant and Eiden, 1982, p. 124; also see Trent, 1984). Black students, who represented 9 percent of the full-time students enrolled in institutions of higher education in 1974, 10.5 percent in 1976, and 10.4 in 1980, thus receive bachelor's degrees at rates well below their college enrollment percentages.

Within the population of black bachelor's degree recipients, females receive that degree at almost 20 percentage points higher than males. In 1978–79, 59.2 percent of the bachelor's degrees among black graduates went to females and 40.8 percent to males. The pattern was similar in 1981–82. Black females received 59.6 percent of the bachelor's degrees and black males, 40.4 percent. These data are particularly troubling given the fact, as discussed earlier, that black male high school graduates 18–24 years old had higher college enrollment rates than black females every year between 1960 and 1983, with the exception of 1980.

Although the experiences of black males in the college setting which are related to their academic performance is not the focus of this chapter, their comparatively low persistence rate clearly needs to be examined more closely. Do black males have greater pressures than females in the college setting? Are they perceived to be less capable than females and hence not supported and encouraged by faculty? Is their high attrition rate due to participation in athletic programs? Must they leave college and seek employment to assist their families? Are student adjustments to college and college adjustments to students greater for black males than for black females? The answers to such questions and others may assist us in understanding black male college attrition and suggest ameliorative interventions. Future research into such areas as suggested by the foregoing questions should become a matter of central rather than peripheral concern. Let us now discuss selected factors related to the performance of black students in elementary and secondary public schools.

School Performance-Related Factors

In many respects, student performance is associated with school practices and expectations held for student success. Out-of-school educational influences that provide supplemental reinforcement of formal in-school education, such as private lessons in music, tutoring in academic subjects, participation in educational programs in churches and in private and community organizations, and the like, also have an impact on student aspirations and school performance (Reed, 1975). Important as these may be, however, in our view school practices are the most powerful determinants of students' school performance. Moreover, these determinants or factors are differentially linked to students' ethnic group or family economic circumstances, particularly if they are black students. Here three factors are briefly discussed: ability group tracking, attitudes and expectations of school officials, and student discipline.

Ability Group Tracking

In a considerable number, if not in most, secondary schools, students are placed or tracked into homogeneous ability groups within the school and within classrooms (Rist, 1970; Fair, 1980; Oakes, 1985). These groups are generally variations of three fundamental curriculum tracks: (1) high ability, academic, or college preparatory; (2) general education; and (3) vocational. Although the assumptions upon which homogeneous ability grouping or tracking are based—that is, facilitation of student learning, enhancement of student self-esteem, accuracy of student ability determination, and ease of teaching and classroom management— have generally been shown to be fallacious, the practice of tracking on these bases continues unabated (Oakes, 1985; National Coalition of Advocates for Students, 1985). In fact, tracking practices begin in first grade, and the ability groups to which individual students are assigned are fixed by third grade (National Coalition of Advocates for Students, 1985).

School and classroom tracking by presumed ability grouping has had, and continues to have, deleterious effects on black students.

That is, black students are more apt to be disproportionally represented in low ability groups in general education and vocational
tracks (Oakes, 1985; National Coalition of Advocates for Students,
1985; Benson and Lareau, 1982). This pattern of grouping and
placement became so pervasive in one school system (although
clearly not the only one) that parents and community members
were driven to seek legal relief. In this instance, the charge was
made and substantiated that the Washington, D.C., public schools
followed a tracking system that was discriminatory and based on
"socioeconomic and racial status rather than ability, resulting in
the undereducation of many District students" (*Hobson* v. *Hansen*,
1967, p. 512). Here the court ruled that the tracking system used
in the Washington, D.C., schools violated the equal protection and
due process rights of students who were poor and those of a
majority of the black students in the District's public schools
(*Hobson* v. *Hansen*, 1967, p. 515); see also, *McNeal* v. *Tate County
School District*, 508 F.2d 1017 (5th Cir. 1975).

Black students are also overrepresented in special education
classes for the educable mentally retarded (EMR) and underrepresented in gifted and talented programs. In comparison to other
students, they are much more likely to be placed in the former
program category than in the latter. In 1981 the percentage of
black students identified by teachers throughout the United States
as *needing* resources for students classified as slow learners or
having learning disabilities (13.5 percent) is nearly four times
greater than black students they identify as needing resources as
gifted students (3.5 percent). The percentage of black students
identified by teachers as *using* the resources for slow learners or
those with learning disabilities in 1981 (8.9 percent) was slightly
more than six times greater than those using resources for the
gifted (1.4 percent) (National Center for Education Statistics, 1985,
p. 194). By comparison, white students identified as *needing* the
resources for slow learners or those having learning disabilities was
9.3 percent, and for the gifted, 7.4 percent. Those identified as
using the resources for slow learners or for students with learning
disabilities was 6.6 percent, and for the gifted, 3.7 percent.

In both 1978 and 1980 the percentage of black students in public
elementary and secondary school programs for the educable mentally retarded (3.4 percent) was more than double that of all
students in this category (1.4 percent). By contrast, only 1.1
percent of white students participated in EMR classes in either
1978 or 1980. For Asian students the proportions were 0.4 percent
in 1978 and 0.3 percent in 1980; Hispanic students, 1.0 percent in
1978 and 0.8 percent in 1980 (National Center for Education

Statistics, 1985, p. 192). With respect to enrollment in gifted and talented programs, black students on an average participate in such programs at about 20 percentage points below their school population representation (College Entrance Examination Board, 1985, p. 30).

Because of the disproportionate placement of black children in EMR classes in California, which was based on IQ test results, placement practices were legally challenged. In the resulting *Larry P.* v. *Riles* case, the court ruled that IQ tests could not be used in the state of California for EMR classification. Appeals to the court's initial decision were unsuccessful, and the court order banning the use of IQ tests for EMR classification purposes in California was made permanent in September 1986 (*Larry P.* v. *Riles*, 343 F. Supp. 1306 [N.D.Cal. 1972]; No. C-71-2270 RFP [Oct. 1979], Order Modifying Judgment [Sept. 1986]).

Specific data on differences in EMR and gifted placement by sex within ethnicity were not available. It is the case, however, that males are more likely to be overrepresented in EMR and learning disabilities programs and underrepresented in gifted programs than are females (National Center for Education Statistics, 1985, p. 192). By inference, then, a greater proportion of black males than females are likely to participate in EMR classes and a smaller proportion in classes for the gifted and talented.

Enrollment in vocational education programs provides another indication of depressed educational opportunity. Whereas black students appear not to be enrolled in secondary-school-level vocational educational programs in percentages greater than their white counterparts, they are clearly disproportionately represented in low-status vocational programs (Benson and Lareau, 1982; Oakes, 1985). At the senior high level, white students more frequently than nonwhites participate in such high-status vocational programs as the managerial and financial facets of business—for example, taxation, marine technology, and aviation. Nonwhite students are more frequent participants in such low-status programs as building maintenance, commercial sewing, and retail sales (Oakes, 1985, pp. 160–63).

Because of homogeneous ability grouping practices, disproportionately large placement in special education classes for the educable mentally retarded, underrepresentation in classes for the gifted and talented, and the greater likelihood of participation in low-status vocational programs, black students are victimized and handicapped in the public school system. As a consequence, for all too many black students, the educational preparation they receive in elementary and secondary schools is inadequate for their maximum growth and development. Nor is it sufficient to provide them with the foundation necessary to meet basic requirements and to compete effectively for college and university entry. Distressingly, future career and occupational options are imperiled and substantially curtailed. From the evidence pertaining to participation rates in the programmatic areas discussed earlier, black males are generally more endangered than nonblack males and females. This suggests that a fruitful area for further investigation is the relationship between participation rates in public school special education classes, low-ability curriculum tracks, low-status vocational educational programs, and drop-out rates from high school and during the transition from high school to college, particularly as these pertain to black males.

Attitudes and Expectations of School Officials

In part, the disproportionate placement of black students in special education classes, in general education and vocational curriculum tracks, and in low-status vocational programs within the vocational track can be linked to the attitudes and expectations of school officials—teachers, counselors, psychologists, administrators—who make placement decisions. Equally important, students' school performance is influenced in significant ways by the feelings which school officials have about student capability and the expectations they transmit verbally and nonverbally about student performance.

The attitudes which school officials have toward students are relatively enduring beliefs they have formed which predispose them to act or react in certain ways (Rokeach, 1968, p. 112). To the extent that school officials develop attitudes that interfere with their fair and impartial assessment of human potential and worth, the inappropriate placement of students in ability groups will be exacerbated, and student encouragement, reinforcement, and accessibility to information and opportunities will be hampered. High drop-out rates, high placement in low-ability curriculum tracks and special education classes, and elementary and secondary school performance, in general, as these pertain to black students, are thus partially the result of stereotypic and ethnocentric attitudes and inappropriate expectations.

Expectations held by individuals shape and define their role or position behavior and the behaviors they believe others should exemplify in relation to that role or position. Expectations held for one's behavior in the school setting are defined and shaped by past experience, organizational culture, personal beliefs, and messages of superiors to subordinates, supervisors to supervisees, leader to follower, parents to school officials, teacher to student, and sometimes student to teacher. Such messages may be subtle or open. They convey expected behavior and task performance in the school and in the classroom. They signal expectations through standards established and maintained by school officials and teachers through the pattern of administrator/teacher-student, administrator/teacher-parent, and student-student interactions established in the school and in the classroom, and through the level of respect demanded by school officials and accorded to students and their parents.

The attitudes and expectations held by school officials toward students in general and minority students in particular appear to be based on an interrelated set of student characteristics. These include, but are not limited to, the following: race or ethnicity, socioeconomic status (SES), physical attractiveness, and initial achievement and test performance. In terms of race or ethnicity, black and minority students are perceived to be less capable and receive less attention in integrated classrooms (Williams and Muehl, 1978; Long and Henderson, 1974; Woodworth and Salzer, 1971); students of low socioeconomic status are more likely to be perceived negatively than middle and upper SES students (Gollub and Sloan, 1978; Mazer, 1971; Rist, 1970; Yee, 1968; Herriot and St. John, 1967). Student attractiveness influences teacher perception of ability and intelligence, future success, and popularity with peers (DeMeis and Turner, 1978; Clifford and Walster, 1973). And from initial achievement and test performance school officials form perceptions of future achievement (Murray, Herling, and Staebler, 1973; Fleming and Anttonen, 1971).

Negative attitudes and low expectations held by school officials relative to the academic and nonacademic performance of black students for reasons such as the foregoing become unconsciously and consciously fixed and transmitted to students. Black students sense these attitudes and expectations and respond by assuming a negative view of classroom performance and school work. Moreover, as young black males experience failure in formal school work, they increasingly seek recognition among their peers in nonacademic areas (Hare, 1987). Thus, young black males develop an "air of coolness," of aloofness; they cultivate the image of the successful athlete, and peer-accepted styles of walking, talking, and dressing. Some may seek to emulate drug dealers and pimps whom they see as being street-smart and successful. These students tend to reject the outward manifestation of being smart in the formal classroom since their efforts in this regard may not be recognized, rewarded, or encouraged. As a consequence, they seek approval and acceptance by their peers.

Although Brophy (1983) concludes that relatively few teachers have major expectation effects on their students' achievement and that what effects they have are minimal, nevertheless, it appears that differential treatment of individual students in the same group or class and of intact groups or classes is mediated by teacher expectations. Thus there are several mediation mechanisms that can be used in training teachers with particular reference to how teachers might inhibit the progress of low-expectation students. For example, these include giving inappropriate feedback to low expectation students, demanding less of them, failing to call on them to respond to questions in class, interacting with them less frequently, providing inadequate verbal and nonverbal reinforcement to them, criticizing them for failure more frequently, giving them less praise, and seating them farther away from the teacher (Brophy, 1983, pp. 641–42).

Low expectations held by school officials for the school success of black youngsters become a self-fulfilling prophecy. These black students, like all youngsters and adults, perform as they are expected and encouraged to perform. Through the use of such enabling behaviors as giving students individual attention, accepting students' feelings, monitoring student progress, clearly establishing a floor for acceptable achievement, and avoiding behaviors that create a negative climate in the classroom and in the school, messages of respect and expectations are transmitted (Ashton and Webb, 1986; Harris and Rosenthal, 1985; Dusek, Hall, and Meyer, 1985; Brookover et al. 1979). The beneficiaries of such actions are, in the short run, students; in the long term, society at large.

Student Discipline

In general, a good school setting is one in which a climate conducive to effective teaching and learning is prevalent, respect for others and their property is a deeply embedded principle, personal safety is a reality, and orderly conduct of students throughout the school is self-evident. In part, school systems and individual schools attempt to ensure that these conditions are met by developing policies pertaining to student conduct, and, concomitantly, negative sanctions to be imposed when these policies are violated. Such sanctions are codified under the umbrella term "student discipline," and include, but are not restricted to, corporal punishment, denial of student privileges, suspensions, and expulsions.

Because of the rights which students enjoy under the Constitution of the United States, due process procedures must be applied before certain sanctions can be administered. For example, in *Goss* v. *Lopez* (1975) the court ruled that before a school can suspend a student for ten days or less, the student must be informed orally or in writing of the charges being made for which the sanction is to be imposed. If the student denies the charges, then he or she must be given an explanation of the basis upon which they were made. Subsequently, the student must have the opportunity to present his or her version of the occurrence. Exceptions to these procedures inhere when the student's presence "poses continuing danger to persons or property or an ongoing threat of disrupting the academic process" (*Goss* v. *Lopez*, 1975, p. 739). In such instances a student may be removed from school with the indisputable understanding that proper notice and hearing will follow in a timely manner. Due process procedures also must be followed for school expulsions which must be formally approved by the school board. The consequences of deprivation of students' constitutional rights in these instances and the potential liability of school board members are clearly expressed by the court in *Wood* v. *Strickland* (1975).

When due process procedures have been followed by school officials, the imposition of such negative sanctions or disciplinary measures as those earlier mentioned has been upheld by the courts. Of concern here, however, is whether sanctions such as out-of-school suspensions are effective in deterring students' inappropriate school behavior and whether application of disciplinary measures is discriminatory.

Despite the use of a variety of negative sanctions by schools, parents in the 1987 annual Phi Delta Kappa/Gallup Poll of the Public's Attitudes Toward the Public Schools identified the lack of discipline as second only to the use of drugs as the most important problem facing local public schools (Gallup and Clark, 1987, p. 28). In fact, in 16 of 17 of the preceding annual Phi Delta Kappa/Gallup polls, the lack of discipline has been rated as the most important local school problem. The definition of disciplinary problems, however, presumably varies by individuals and groups.

By their admission, as shown in Table 2–22, most 1982 high school seniors reported that they had cut classes or attended class with their homework incomplete. Relatively few of them had experienced disciplinary problems (14 percent) or had been suspended for disciplinary reasons (12 percent). Even fewer of them had been suspended for academic reasons (4 percent) or had been in serious trouble with the law (5 percent). More males than

Table 2–22   High School Seniors' Self-Reports of Discipline and Behavior Problems, by
Selected Student and School Characteristics, 1982

| | | *Percent of Students Who Reported They Had:* | | | | |
Characteristic	Cut Classes	Attended Class Without Homework Completed	Disciplinary Problems	Been Suspended for Academic Reasons	Been Suspended for Disciplinary Reasons	Been in Serious Trouble with the Law
All students	42	28	14	4	12	5
Student Characteristics						
Sex						
Male	46	35	18	6	17	8
Female	38	21	10	2	8	2
Race/ethnicity						
White non-Hispanic	42	28	12	3	12	5
Black, non-Hispanic	36	25	18	6	13	5
Hispanic	43	32	20	8	14	7
Asian or Pacific Islander	42	24	15	6	7	4
American Indian/Alaskan Native	52	31	19	5	12	12
Socioeconomic status group[a]						
Low	37	32	18	6	14	5
Low-middle	40	30	14	4	13	4
High-middle	44	29	13	4	12	5
High	44	26	12	3	11	4
Test performance group[b]						
Low	42	32	21	8	15	7
Low-middle	43	29	15	4	15	5
High-middle	44	27	12	2	12	4
High	37	23	9	1	7	3
High school program[c]						
Academic	37	22	9	2	8	2
General	47	36	16	5	15	5
Vocational	41	33	17	6	14	6
High school characteristics						
Control						
Public	43	28	14	4	12	5
Catholic	24	26	11	4	11	3
Other private	43	24	14	2	14	5
Community						
Urban	46	26	16	5	11	5
Suburban	43	29	13	4	13	5
Rural	37	28	14	4	12	5

[a]Socioeconomic status was measured hy a composite score on parental education, family income, father's occupation, and household characteristics.

[b]Test performance was measured by a test battery administered as part of the High School and Beyond survey.

[c]High school program as reported by student.

SOURCE: U.S. Department of Education, National Center for Education Statistics. High School and Beyond Study, unpublished tabulations (October 1985). Reported in National Center for Education Statistics (1985, p. 66).

females and more minority than nonminority students, however, reported having disciplinary problems and being suspended.

According to a report by the Children's Defense Fund (1975, p. 9), in 1972–73 school districts enrolling more than half the nation's public school students suspended over 1 million students. Reasons for student suspension encompassed the following categories: fighting (36.6 percent), truancy and tardiness (24.5 percent), behavior problems such as disobeying the teacher and acting up in class (13.6 percent), arguments or verbal confrontations such as insulting, talking back to, and disagreeing with the teacher (8.5 percent), and other reasons such as smoking and punishment-related incidents (16.8 percent). The most frequent single reason for suspension was fighting with other students (185 or 31.5 percent).

More recent data compiled by the National Coalition of Advocates for Students (1987) reveal that in 1984 the proportion of black students suspended, by state level, ranged from a high of 21.3 percent in Wisconsin to a low of .94 percent in North Dakota, the only state in which the figures for black student suspensions were less than those of white students. Black students are suspended at rates well in excess of white students in all but 2 of the nation's 50 states and the District of Columbia: North Dakota and Massachusetts. For example, in Wisconsin 18 percent (9,826) more black than white students were suspended. In Pennsylvania the proportion was 14 percent (33,342), and in Michigan, 13 percent (33,323). In an aggregate of 50 states and the District of Columbia, 585,039 black students were suspended from school in 1984, a number which exceeded white suspensions by 324,403 (National Coalition of Advocates for Students, 1987).

A considerable number of reasons students are suspended can be classified as nonviolent offenses. This suggests that sanctions other than removal from school and consequent loss of school instruction might have been effectively imposed. Furthermore, the incidence of students cutting classes, being truant from school, and being tardy to class may be symptomatic of problems relating to teaching and student treatment within the classroom rather than to problems which reside with the student. Suspensions here may address the symptom rather than the cause, and thus may be of dubious value.

Examining the question of who gets suspended, the Children's Defense Fund Report (1975, p. 63) indicates that in elementary school, blacks were suspended three times as often as whites (1.5 versus 0.5) and in secondary school twice as often (11.8 versus 6.0). In addition, at both elementary and secondary school levels, boys were suspended at higher rates than girls (5.4 percent versus 3.4 percent) (p. 61). Black students, according to the same report, were also suspended for longer periods of time and more repeatedly than were white students at both elementary and secondary school levels.

According to the report, the average length of suspensions for black students was 4.46 days; for white students, 3.55 days. Viewed as school days lost per 100 enrolled students, black students lost

26.74 days as compared to 11.04 days for white students. In addition, black students (27 percent) were repeatedly suspended three or more times, while only 11 percent of white students were repeatedly suspended. For single suspension rates, 58 percent of black students and 73 percent of white students were suspended only once (p. 71). More recent data indicate that, at the high school level, black students are suspended three times as frequently as white students. Whereas they represent about 25 percent of the school population, about 40 percent of all students suspended or expelled are black (National Coalition of Advocates for Students, 1985, p. 10).

The picture that emerges is not a pleasant one. Black students, as other minority students, are more apt to be suspended and expelled from school at rates far higher than nonminority students. They are also suspended for longer periods of time and are repeatedly suspended more frequently than nonminority students. Since more males than females are suspended, we can infer that black male suspensions outpace their nonminority male and female counterparts.

Suspensions typically remove students from school. On occasion this is no doubt necessary for their safety, or the safety of others. But removal from school, particularly for nonviolent offenses, may not address the underlying problem(s) which a suspension is supposedly used to correct. Perhaps the problems that should be addressed are teacher-school negative attitudes toward, and expectations held for, minority students, inconsistent and inequitable application of school and classroom policies, a lack of respect for students, intolerance, and bigotry.

Students and their parents generally desire to acquire the advantages which education can bring. The important questions to be answered and problems to be solved revolve around school and environmental antecedents of student behavior, which are, in fact, inappropriate and dysfunctional. Importantly, we must also consider alternatives to out-of-school suspensions which disproportionately affect black students.

Conclusions

The portrait painted by the preceding statistics is not a pretty one. In fact, it is rather troubling. What is evident is that all black students continue to be at risk in the public schools, but black males tend to be at greater risk. While there are encouraging signs with respect to the educational progress of black students, there are also many discouraging signs.

In general, black high school graduation rates have improved over the past two decades, and the gap between graduation rates by ethnicity has narrowed. Nevertheless, the gap remains. Black females complete high school at higher rates than black males, but it is clear that both groups complete high school at rates below those of whites. Percentage gain points in science content, inquiry, and technology and society between 1976–77 and 1981–82 for black students have been positive and have exceeded gains made by other groups. Yet it is abundantly clear that overall mean scores for black students are below those of other groups, not only in the area of science, but also in reading and literature comprehension, mathematics, social studies, citizenship, music, and art at ages 9, 13, and 17. And although SAT scores have gradually been increasing for black students since 1975–76, particularly in the area of math, SAT scores for black students are consistently below those of other groups.

The school performance of black students is influenced by a number of variables. As has been described, black students are far more likely than whites to be placed in general education and vocational high school curricular tracks than in an academic track. Within the vocational education track they are more apt to participate in low-status programs. They are much more likely to be placed in classes for the educable mentally retarded and for students with learning disabilities than in classes for the gifted and talented. They earn fewer Carnegie units in high school than do their counterparts. They have higher drop-out rates than white students. (This is particularly the case for black males.) Black students are suspended from school more frequently and for longer periods of time than majority students. They are frequently the recipients of negative attitudes by school staff, who also frequently hold low levels of expectation for their school performance. Because of such factors and conditions, it is regrettably understandable that black students receive fewer A grades and more D and F grades than do their counterparts.

At the postsecondary level the college enrollment rates of black students as a percentage of high school graduates have been declining roughly since 1978. A fairly large percentage of black students is enrolled in two-year colleges in which drop-out rates are high and transfer rates to four-year colleges low. Black students are also enrolled more frequently in vocational education programs than in academic programs. Moreover, while more black males

enter college, black females earn bachelor's degrees at higher rates
than do black males.

Black students in general, and black male students in particular,
face many stumbling blocks and obstacles in the public schools.
That as many make it as do is testimony to their determination and
resilience. It is clear, however, that many do not make it—that
many become frustrated, lose hope, and drop out or are pushed
out of the schools. The question to be asked, then, is: Can
conditions in the school be improved to halt the continuing waste
of human potential and the frequent imposition of negative sanctions against students who desperately need to be recognized in
positive ways? Hopefully, the answer is yes, and in the next and
concluding section recommendations are provided for implementation at local, state, and federal levels.

Recommendations

Recommendations at the Local and School Level

1. *Recruit and select competent, caring, confident, and creative
teachers and school site and district level administrators.* Black
students, as do all students, need to be placed in the classrooms of
competent, caring, confident, and creative teachers—teachers who
respect and value them as human beings of great worth. In
particular, minority teachers who meet the foregoing criteria
should be heavily recruited and selected, as the percentage of such
teachers is rapidly declining and relatively few are entering into
teacher preparation programs.

It is also increasingly clear that the degree to which schools are
effective is a function not only of creative, competent, confident,
and caring teachers, but also of school principals and superinten-
dents and their support staffs. School administrators in part create
the organizational climate and develop the support systems that
enable effective teaching and learning to prosper. They also provide the mechanisms to ensure that school programs and fiscal and
human resources are appropriately assigned to maximize the educational growth of all students. Such administrators must be vigorously recruited and selected for public school positions.

2. *Implement heterogeneous ability grouping.* Except in cases
in which students cannot be placed in a regular classroom because
of some handicapping condition, student tracking by presumed
ability level should be eliminated. The evidence is rather clear that
homogeneous ability grouping is not an essential requirement for

meaningful teaching and learning. While such grouping may make the teacher's job a little easier, the social and educational skills to be gained in a heterogeneous setting are equally, if not more, important considerations. In such settings students come to know and value others from whom they are typically isolated. Students grouped, for example, for cooperative learning, develop a strong sense of group belonging and responsibility for the group's academic progress, and cooperation, long valued in several minority communities, rather than competition, can be more readily facilitated. Heterogeneous ability groups may also provide a more acceptable, supportive, and nonthreatening environment for the serious performance of academic work. Finally, the implementation of such classroom groupings would significantly reduce the frequent and misused practice of placing black students in general education and low-ability tracks.

3. *Ensure that teachers, administrators, and school staff are cognizant of the importance of expectations on student achievement*. In order to enhance the academic achievement of black students, and in particular black males, teachers, administrators, and school staff must become aware of the important role of expectations. In many respects, students respond in ways that are consonant with expectations held for them. Without high expectations, positive reinforcement, support, teacher-student, administrator-student, and staff-student interaction and appropriate feedback, excellence in student performance will not be encouraged. Teachers, administrators, and staff, therefore, should become cognizant of how their expectations for student performance are conveyed and the effects these expectations have upon students. In-service programs in teacher, administrator, and staff expectations, along with continuous monitoring of how expectations are being transmitted and their effects on students, are of utmost importance in maximizing student achievement. Programs such as Teacher Expectations and Student Achievement (TESA), developed by Kerman, Kimball, and Martin (1980), represent an important resource in this regard.

4. *Value school academic performance*. Upon entering many secondary schools across the nation, students, faculty, parents, and others frequently are greeted by a display case of trophies won in athletic competitions of various kinds. One message which this transmits, particularly when students have few other options, is that recognition in the school comes from participation in sports. Ironically, some administrators and coaches believe this generates community support and patronage. Yet when parents who have options are examining schools for their children, it is the school

with the strong academic program, with solid and reputable teachers, with a climate that supports effective teaching and learning,
that is selected. Schools attended by black and other minority
students, particularly in central cities, must become lighthouses of
academic brilliance. Students must recognize that they are expected to be excellent students. Schools must provide the necessary resources and create the necessary environment to enable all
students to develop academically. Academic success must be rewarded, encouraged, expected, and valued throughout the school,
within the community, and within the home.

5. *Implement early childhood education programs.* The early
years are crucial in establishing the foundation for educational
attainment. There is convincing evidence that students participating in preschool programs display improvements in a variety of
areas: cognitive performance during early childhood, scholastic
performance during the school years, high school graduation,
enrollment in postsecondary programs, and employment. Concomitantly, these students are less likely to be involved in delinquency and crime, to become pregnant as teenagers, or to use
welfare assistance (Berrueta-Clement et al., 1984). Given the
benefits of preschool programs and the growing number of single-
parent, female-headed households, the establishment and maintenance of preschool programs are essential. Parents who must work
are unable to be at home with their children. Early childhood
education programs should be available to such parents at each
school site or in the workplace. As part of these programs, parents
should receive guidance from school personnel in techniques to
assist the educational development of their children.

6. *Use resources from the business community.* Because the
business community depends on the schools for its basic future
labor pool, it is in its interest to provide assistance for school
improvement. For business, investments in schools and in efforts
to improve the quality of education are investments in their future
economic viability, and, in turn, in the social and political well-
being of the nation. When necessary and where possible, schools
should avail themselves of the resources the business community
can offer. These might include, for example, instructional assistance in specialized courses in vocational education, career exploration for students, incentives and rewards through adopt-a-school
programs, and commitments to employ high school graduates, as
exemplified by the Boston Compact (Research and Policy Committee of the Committee for Economic Development, 1985).

7. *Develop and use a resource bank of role models.* Many black
·students are concentrated in large urban areas in which profes-

sional role models are virtually nonexistent. Many find role models among their peers and from among those who accumulate financial assets by selling drugs and engaging in other questionable activities. Black males are particularly vulnerable in this setting. Anxious to be accepted by peers and to display their manhood, many of them follow a path of least resistance and succumb to the illegal temptations to which they are exposed. To counter this, schools should work with churches, social and civic organizations, and businesses to develop a resource bank of role models who would regularly interact with students at the school site and in the community, beginning with the elementary grades. Through such interaction, career possibilities and their requisites could be discussed and explored. In addition, students should be able to develop an understanding of personal characteristics necessary for upward social, educational, and career mobility.

8. *Improve parental involvement in the schools and their knowledge of postsecondary educational requirements.* It is a rather widely accepted assumption that the majority of parents desire the best of everything for their children, even though they may be unable to translate that desire into reality. Education continues to be viewed by parents as a vehicle for social and economic mobility for their children. Hence, their interest and desire serve as opportunities for schools to involve them in planning, decision making, and establishing and monitoring school goals and objectives. Further, the participation of parents in school matters reinforces the expectations they hold for the school success of their children.

Schools can also provide significant assistance to parents in helping them to plan for educational options for their children. The need for parents to become aware and better informed in this area is highlighted in a recent study by Brouder (1987). Schools have an excellent opportunity to assist parents to become informed about post-high school options for their children, academic requirements for various educational and career choices, and the costs of post-high school education and how they might plan to meet them. This, of course, is not a typical school role. It is, nonetheless, an important one.

Recommendations at the State Level

States have an obligation to assist local school districts to implement recommendations, such as the foregoing, that are designed to raise students' academic performance and to improve the future labor pool. Although many of the recommendations can be implemented through local initiatives, state policy and funding can be of great assistance in implementing some of them.

1. *Ensure that teachers, administrators, and school staff are cognizant of the importance of expectations on student achievement.* States should seriously consider including in their pre-service teacher, administrator, and pupil personnel credential requirements, specific knowledge areas pertaining to the effects of expectations on student achievement. Beyond this, states should make available to local districts funds to implement staff-development programs in the area of expectations and student achievement, particularly as this topic relates to minority students.

2. *Implement early childhood education programs.* Preschool programs have been demonstrated to be effective in improving the educational achievement of minority students and students from low-income families. State-provided financial assistance to establish and maintain such programs in areas which would reach the minority and poor students who could best benefit from them is highly desirable. State departments of education should ensure that preschool programs are educationally sound, have competent staff, and are operated in a safe environment. Importantly, states should monitor and evaluate the effectiveness of these programs over time.

3. *Improve parental involvement in schools and their educational awareness.* As a condition of receiving funds for categorical programs, states should require local schools to involve parents in the school in such areas as decision making with respect to school goals and objectives and in the determination of school programs. Schools should also be required to implement a parent awareness program to enable parents to become aware of academic requirements for various educational and career options that their children might pursue and to develop plans that will assist them in financing educational options for their children.

Recommendations at the Federal Level

Educational policies and funding at the federal level can also be tremendous vehicles for school innovation and improvement. Recommendations at this level include the following:

1. *Student financial assistance for postsecondary educational opportunities.* For many black students, postsecondary educational options are restricted because of limited financial resources. College costs are substantial. By providing greater student financial assistance for college attendance, the federal government provides an investment in the future of this nation. The federal government

must provide adequate financial assistance to enable needy students to attend and remain in college.

2. *Provide funding for demonstration projects.* The reluctance of local school districts to implement new programs and practices is often due to a lack of fiscal resources. Funding provided to local school districts through grants could stimulate the implementation of, for example, heterogeneous ability classes, parent awareness training, and role model and mentoring programs. Funds should also be provided for research and the dissemination of program results through professional journals, workshops, and site visitations.

3. *Provide funding for establishing pre-school and early school year programs.* The implementation of policy at the national level requiring the establishment of preschool programs in the inner city and simultaneously providing funding for such programs are important federal functions. These must be national priorities if we are to improve the educational opportunities of students whose foundation for educational growth is weak. Funding should also be provided for innovative yet theoretically sound programs in the early elementary grades for students in greatest need—those who traditionally have been unsuccessful in the schools.

Postlude

Estimates are that by 2020 the majority of school-age children will be minorities (Hodgkinson, 1985). Unfortunately, for large numbers of the population, the public schools have not been successful. As has been discussed, for black students, school drop-out rates are high, academic achievement low, and college-going rates significantly below high school graduation rates. Several reasons have been advanced to explain why these conditions persist. The elimination of these conditions will certainly require such solutions and recommendations as have been advanced in this chapter. But most importantly, reversing the negative school experiences and poor academic performance of black students in general, and black males in particular, will require unwavering commitment on the part of school officials, parents, community agencies, and individuals.

Elementary and secondary education provides the foundation for future career and academic choices. Clearly, we cannot afford to permit educational practices to exist which restrict the nurturance and growth of students. The challenge to schools, parents, community members, policymakers, and students is to reverse those policies and practices which contribute to the school failure of black and other minority students. We must, in addition, uncover the means through which a significantly greater proportion of black and other minority students who experience failure in the schools will be successful. Unless we are able to meet these aims, the human resources needed to sustain the social, political, and economic health of this nation will be endangered, the waste of human potential tragic, and the destruction of the human spirit criminal.

References

Ashton, P. T., and Webb, R. B. (1986). *Making a difference: Teachers' sense of efficacy and student achievement*. New York: Longman.

Astin, A. S. (1982). *Minorities in American higher education*. San Francisco: Jossey-Bass.

Benson, C. S., and Lareau, A. P. (1982). The uneasy place of vocational education. *Education and Urban Society* 15 (1):104–24.

Berrueta-Clement, J. R. et al. (1984). *Changed lives: The effects of the Perry preschool program on youths through age 19*. Ypsilanti, Mich.: The High/Scope Press.

Brookover, W. et al. (1979). *School social systems and student achievement: Schools can make a difference*. New York: Praeger.

Brophy, J. E. (1983). Research on the self-fulfilling prophecy and teacher expectations. *Journal of Educational Psychology* 75 (5):631–61.

Brouder, K. (1987). *Parental attitudes toward pre-college planning*. (Research Paper). New York: College Entrance Examination Board.

Center for Education Statistics. (1986). *The condition of education. 1968 ed.* A Statistical Report. Washington, D.C.: U.S. Government Printing Office.

Children's Defense Fund. (1975). *School suspensions: Are they helping children?* Cambridge: Children's Defense Fund.

Clifford, M. M., and Walster, E. (1973). The effect of physical attractiveness on teacher expectations. *Sociology of Education* 46 (2):248–58.

College Entrance Examination Board. (1985). *Equality and excellence: The educational status of black Americans*. New York: College Entrance Examination Board.

DeMeis, D. K., and Turner, R. R. (1978). Effects of students' race, physical attractiveness, and dialect on teachers' evaluations. *Contemporary Educational Psychology* 3 (1):77–86.

Duesk, J., Hall, V., and Meyer, W., eds. (1985). *Teacher expectancies*. Hillsdale, N.J.: Erlbaum.

Fair, G. W. (1980). Coping with double-barrelled discrimination. *Journal of School Health* 50 (5):275–76.

Fleming, E. S., and Anttonen, R. J. (1971). Teacher expectancy or my fair lady. *American Educational Research Journal* 8 (2):241–52.

Gallup, A. M., and Clark, D. L. (1987). The 19th annual gallup poll of the public's attitudes toward public schools. *Phi Delta Kappa* 69 (1):17–30.

Gollub, W. L., and Sloan, E. (1978). Teacher expectations and race and socioeconomic status. *Urban Education* 13 (1):83–94.

Grant, W. V., and Eiden, L. J. (1982). *Digest of educational statistics, 1982*. Washington, D.C.: U.S. Government Printing Office.

Grant, W. V., and Snyder, T. D. (1986). *Digest of educational statistics, 1985–86*. Washington, D.C.: U.S. Government Printing Office.

Hare, B. R. (1987). Structural inequality and the endangered status of black youth. *Journal of Negro Education* 56 (1):100–10.

Harris, M., and Rosenthal, R. (1985). Mediation of interpersonal expectancy effects: 31 meta-analyses. *Psychological Bulletin* 97 (3):363–86.

Herriot, R. E., and St. John, N. H. (1967). *Social class and the urban schools*. New York: Wiley & Sons.

Hodgkinson, H. L. (1985). The changing face of tomorrow's student. *Change* 17 (3).

Kerman, S., Kimball, T., and Martin, M. (1980). *Teacher expectations and student achievement*. Bloomington, Ind.: Phi Delta Kappa.

Ladner, J. A. (1987). Black teenage pregnancy: A challenge for educators. *Journal of Negro Education* 56 (1):53–63.

Long, B. H., and Henderson, E. H. (1974). Certain determinants of academic expectancies among southern and non-southern teachers. *American Educational Research Journal* 11 (2):137–48.

Mazer, G. E. (1971). Effects of social-class stereotyping on teacher expectation. *Psychology in the Schools* 8 (4):373–78.

Murray, H. B., Herling, G. B., and Staebler, B. K. (1973). The effects of locus of control and pattern of performance on teachers' evaluation of a student. *Psychology in the Schools* 10 (3):345–50.

National Center for Education Statistics, U.S. Department of Education. (1985). *The condition of education, 1985 ed*. A Statistical Report. Washington, D.C.: U.S. Government Printing Office.

National Coalition of Advocates for Students. (1987). *A special analysis of 1984 elementary and secondary school civil rights survey data*. Boston: National Coalition of Advocates for Students.

———, Board of Inquiry. (1985). *Barriers to excellence: Our children at risk*. Boston: National Coalition of Advocates for Students.

Oakes, J. (1985). *Keeping track: How schools structure inequality*. New Haven: Yale University Press.

Reed, R. J. (1975). Ethnicity, social class, and out-of-school educational opportunity. *Journal of Negro Education* 44 (3):316–34.

Research and Policy Committee of the Committee for Economic Development. (1985). *Investing in our children, business and the public schools*. New York: Committee for Economic Development.

Rist, R. C. (1970). Student social class and teacher expectations: The self-fulfilling prophecy in ghetto education. *Harvard Educational Review* 40 (3):441–51.

Rokeach, M. (1968). *Beliefs, attitudes, and values: A theory of organization and change*. San Francisco: Jossey-Bass.

Snyder, T. D. (1987). *Digest of education statistics, 1987*. Washington, D.C.: U.S. Government Printing Office.

Trent, W. T. (1984). Equity considerations in higher education: Race and sex differences in degree attainment and major field from 1976 through 1981. *American Journal of Education* 92 (3):280–305.

U.S. Bureau of the Census. (1985). *Special demographic analysis, CD5-85-1, Education in the United States: 1940–1983*. Washington, D.C.: U.S. Government Printing Office.

——. (1987). *Statistical abstract of the United States: 1987*, 107th ed. Washington, D. C.: U.S. Government Printing Office.

Williams, J. H., and Muehl, S. (1978). Relations among student and teacher perceptions of behavior. *Journal of Negro Education* 47 (4):328–36.

Willie, C. V. (1985). The problem of standardized testing in a free and pluralistic society. *Phi Delta Kappa* 66 (9):626–28.

Woodworth, W. D., and Salzer, R. T. (1971). Black children's speech and teachers' evaluations. *Urban Education* 6 (2/3):167–73.

Yee, A. H. (1968). Interpersonal attitudes of teachers and advantaged and disadvantaged pupils. *Journal of Human Resources* 3 (3):327–45.

References: Court Cases

Goss v. *Lopez*, 419 U.S. 565, 95 S. Ct. 729, 42 L.Ed.2d 725 (1975).

Hobson v. *Hansen*, 269 F.Supp. 401 (D.C. Cir. 1967), *aff'd in part and appeal dismissed in part*, sub nom *Smuck* v. *Hobson*, 408 F.2d 175 (D.C. Cir. 1969).

Larry P. v. *Riles*, 343 F. Supp. 1306 (N.D. Cal. 1972); No. C-71-2270 RFP (Oct. 1979), Order Modifying Judgement (Sept. 1986).

McNeal v. *Tate County School District*, 508 F.2d 1017 (5th Cir. 1975).

Wood et al. v. *Strickland et al.*, 420 U.S. 308 (1975).

Chapter 3

EMPLOYMENT AND UNEMPLOYMENT OF YOUNG BLACK MALES

Tom E. Larson

> *Handicaps of race, poverty, inadequate education, and illiteracy combine to plague disadvantaged youth in the labor market and, without intervention, will continue to plague them for the rest of their working lives.*

> From "A Call to Action," speech delivered by the Hon. William E. Brock, Secretary of Labor in 1986.

Chapter 3 reports the results of recent research on the problem of falling employment rates among black male youth, focusing on teenagers aged 16–19 and young adults aged 20–24, groups at the center of the current employment crisis. At the end of 1986, the employment rate for black male teenagers was 26.8 percent, and the white male rate was 49.7 percent (*Economic Report of the President*, 1987). In the 1970s, employment rates for young black males fell in all parts of the country and generated widespread concern that these youth were experiencing an economic and social crisis and needed help. To date, however, there is no consensus on the nature and causes of the fall in employment or on the remedies.

Even though today some people believe that blacks face little or no discrimination and need only to increase their educational attainment to enjoy equal opportunity (perhaps with some financial assistance due to the poverty of many black families), there is evidence that discriminatory labor practices and racial segregation continue to have an adverse economic impact on the black population and are reducing the ability of young blacks to succeed in an economy that is switching from the production of goods to the production of services (Larson, 1986).

The Paradox of Falling Employment Among Young Blacks

During the 1970s the employment-to-population ratio of young black males fell markedly, both absolutely and relative to the employment ratio for young whites.[1] This was true for black males aged 16–19 and for those aged 20–24 (see Figures 3–1 and 3–2). In 1955 the black and white employment rates among teenagers were about equal (52 percent for each); by 1980 a 26 percentage point gap had opened up as the employment rate for blacks fell to 27 percent and the employment rate for whites rose to 53 percent. The widening of racial employment gaps among male youth appears paradoxical at a time when other economic differences between the races appear to have been converging. In the 1980s there has been relatively more deterioration in the employment of white males than among black males (white males had an employment rate of 53.4 percent in 1980 and 49.6 percent in 1986, while black male employment fell from 27.0 percent in 1980 to 26.5 percent in 1986). This small reduction of the employment gap reflects a large decline in white male teen employment that has received little comment.

The productivity characteristics of blacks and whites have become more similar over time in terms of years of education, returns to education, and quality of education. During the 1960s and most of the 1970s, the educational gap narrowed considerably; in 1980, the median education of black males was 12.3 years, and of white males, 12.7. In 1962, the medians had been 9.0 and 12.1, respectively (*Employment and Training Report of the President*, 1981). During the 1970s, the percentage of blacks and whites graduating from high school neared parity, and there had been a closing of the college gap (Farley, 1977). Several studies report that returns to education had also increased for blacks relative to whites (Welch, 1973; Harrison, 1972; Freeman, 1982; Smith and Welch, 1986). Between 1964 and 1974, income, educational attainment, and occupational status improved more rapidly among black men than among whites. In line with improvements in education and in opportunity, the black/white income ratio improved considera-

bly—among males, from .52 in 1963 to .65 in 1979, and among
families, from .53 to .61.

Continued improvement in the economic status of blacks may
depend on solving the youth employment problem. If the employment gap represents a fall in the demand for young black male
workers, then income gains for blacks are probably at an end
unless economic equality is more vigorously pursued. Indeed,
since 1974, there has been little further improvement in male
black income (for those receiving income) and since 1976 there has
been a reduction in college enrollment rates among blacks aged
18–24 (from 22.6 percent in 1976 to 20.4 percent in 1984) (U.S.
Bureau of the Census, 1985). While high school graduation rates
have continued to fall among blacks, the percentage of high school
graduates going on to college has also fallen. The importance of
race is reflected in the acceptance of the notion that the youth
employment problem has become largely a black youth employment problem (Freeman and Holtzer, 1986).

During the 1960s and early 1970s, racial economic convergence
was linked to greater opportunity stemming from civil rights
activity and legislation and from tighter Vietnam era labor markets.
A rise in the relative proportion of black workers in professional
and managerial occupations suggested increased employment opportunities for educated blacks. (This rise is frequently linked to
affirmative action and the rise in government employment during
the 1960s.)[2]

The period from 1964 to 1973 was one of apparently remarkable
economic advancement for blacks. If any part of the black population could be expected to benefit from increased opportunity, it
was those young blacks entering the labor force. Thomas Sowell
(1981) has stated that "current effects of current policies are found
in the incomes and occupations of younger members of ethnic
minorities . . ." (p. 12). Yet black youth employment slipped lower
and lower, and chronic unemployment became increasingly common among young blacks. The more like whites that blacks became
in terms of education and training, the more dissimilar became
their employment rates.

Is Unemployment a Problem?

Summarizing an extensive review of youth employment issues,
Freeman and Wise (1982) concluded that "for the vast majority of
youth, lack of employment is not a severe problem." This view is
widely accepted because for most young people, jobs are not hard

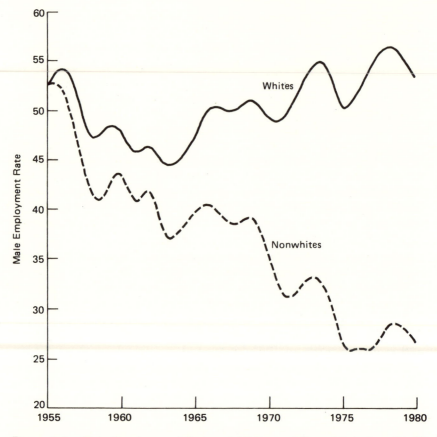

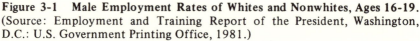

Figure 3-1   Male Employment Rates of Whites and Nonwhites, Ages 16-19.
(Source: Employment and Training Report of the President, Washington, D.C.: U.S. Government Printing Office, 1981.)

to find. Most young people go from job to job, generating high unemployment rates simply as a result of turnover, but they do not experience chronic unemployment. For most young people, high unemployment rates reflect the nature of both their labor supply and the type of jobs offered to them. Many teenagers are just looking for pocket money or only work during school vacations; they tend to place a high value on leisure or schooling rather than on holding a job. They are primarily employed in jobs with high turnover rates that require little training (such as work in fast-food restaurants) and that provide little on-the-job training. Most available jobs are part-time and temporary.

The youth employment problem represents the difficulties faced by a minority of youth. One-half of male teenage unemployment is concentrated among 7 percent of the youth population. This small

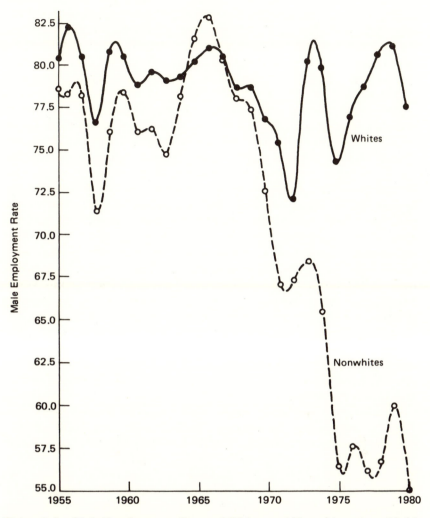

Figure 3-2   Male Employment Rates of Whites and Nonwhites, Ages 20-24.
(Source: Employment and Training Report of the President. Washington,
D.C.: U.S. Government Printing Office, 1981.)

group of chronically unemployed youth are often disadvantaged by
living in a poverty area and/or being high school dropouts (Freeman and Holtzer, 1986).

In January 1986, the *Wall Street Journal* observed that the
unemployment rate among teenage blacks had remained high
despite a general decline in national unemployment. The *Wall
Street Journal* editorialized that the problem is not due to a
shortage of jobs and is sociological rather than economic (*Wall
Street Journal*, 1986). It recommended more discipline and guid-

ance in our courts, schools, churches, and homes rather than more jobs. Although this view is fast becoming the conventional wisdom, there are compelling reasons to believe that the sociological problem remains that of discrimination and that economic solutions remain feasible but are constrained by racist institutions, customs, and practices.

One view held by labor economists is that high unemployment rates among young people are due to high turnover rates (Feldstein, 1973). Accordingly, higher unemployment could simply reflect rising turnover rates. Many experts agree with Michael Piore (1979) that young blacks are rejecting low-wage and menial employment. This claim is largely based on anecdotes and is not supported by major studies. Recent studies of young men's job histories have shown that blacks are increasingly plagued by chronic unemployment. Black teenagers appear to be simply having a harder time finding employment. Among young black men lower employment has been accompanied by lower turnover (Pollard, 1984). Young blacks appear to be less likely than young whites to quit jobs (Blau and Kahn, 1981). While many young workers do go from job to job over short periods of time, black youth are simply finding less and less work over time (Freeman, 1982). The pattern among young blacks is to have short-term employment followed by long spells of being out of work. In fact, among central city black youth, a year of nonemployment is not unusual (Freeman and Holtzer, 1986).

A major problem facing black youth has been a shortage of jobs. Black teenagers are concentrated in declining central cities where there are simply too few jobs for the local residents (Larson, 1986). With few jobs to go around, employers can be more selective. Supplyside characteristics will help determine who will get the job, just as buying more tickets improves one's chance in a lottery. Unfortunately, the "employment lottery" is rigged so that skin color and family connections help determine the outcome. High unemployment and discrimination will reduce the returns to investment in education and training.[3]

There are at least two compelling reasons for trying to get more jobs for young blacks. First, lower employment rates are contributing to the rising poverty rates of black families and have been associated with a variety of social problems such as crime, drug use, suicide, and school violence (Freeman and Wise, 1982). Second, the future is being foreclosed to blacks. Paul Osterman (1982) has found that it is important for youth from low-income families, white or black, to gain job experience as teenagers. Those who don't tend to have difficulty finding employment as adults.

Becker and Hills (1978) and Stevenson (1978) also found that youth nonemployment was associated with adult nonemployment. Ellwood (1982), in a study of male youth, found nonemployment effects to be largely short term on employment, but also found evidence of strong negative wage effects due to a lack of experience. Ballard and Freeman (1986) found that among inner-city black youth, nonemployment significantly reduced chances of future employment. Increasing numbers of blacks are entering their 20s without any job experience. By being out of the labor market, black youth become less and less employable, and aging will not solve the problem (Freeman and Holzer, 1986). Lack of experience, can be a permanent handicap for today's unemployed youth, and what will happen to the expectations and attainments of the children of these youth is an unknown. Why should these children go to school or plan for a future if the adults in their lives cannot succeed and cannot show them how to succeed. Some fear that these rising unemployment rates among black males reflect the development of a class of workers who are faced with prolonged and chronic unemployment (Freeman and Wise, 1982) and that a permanent black underclass is forming (Wilson, 1978; Glasgow, 1981; Auletta, 1982; Hout, 1984).

Black youth may be a sensitive barometer of changes in labor market conditions for all blacks. This is especially true if the vintage hypothesis, proposed by Finis Welch (Smith and Welch, 1977; Hoffman, 1979) is correct. The vintage hypothesis states that one's relative economic position is established fairly early in life. This means that success or failure during one's early years tends to be a predictor of success or failure at a later age (for a group). It is difficult to overcome a bad start. This vintage effect can be observed by comparing people's incomes as they age. In a given year, if we compare the earnings of black males to white males, the older age cohorts tend to have lower relative earnings. Among high school graduates in 1949, young black graduates 18–24 earned 74 percent as much as young white graduates (see Table 3–1). In 1949, older black workers who were high school graduates show much lower earnings relative to whites. Blacks aged 55–64 earned only 57 percent as much as their white counterparts. These lower earnings may have reflected the type of labor market that existed when these older workers entered the labor force and are not predictive of what younger workers can expect as they age. Over time, we see that the 18–24-year-old graduates of 1949 retain or slightly improve their relative position, earning 69 percent as much as the white cohort in 1959, 71 percent in 1969, and 74 percent in 1979 when they are 45–54 years old (reading diagonally). Between

Table 3–1 Male Average Nonwhite Income as Percentage of Average Income,
by Age and Education

Education and Age	1949 (median)	1959 (mean)	1969 (mean)	1979 (mean)
All levels of education				
18–24	70%	67%	85%	
25–34	59	61	70	74%
35–44	55	57	64	66
45–54	54	52	58	63
55–64	49	51	54	64
High School Graduates				
18–24	74	73	87	
25–34	72	69	76	77
35–44	67	71	71	75
45–54	63	62	70	74
55–64	63	57	66	74
College Graduates, Four Years or more				
18–24	81	80	98	
25–34	64	67	78	81*
35–44	59	59	71	68*
45–54	56	49	65	58*
55–64	52	45	57	57*

*Four years only.

SOURCES: 1949, U.S. Census of the Population (1953), Vol. 4, PC5, *Education*, Table 13;
(1959), U.S. Census of the Population, 1960, *Educational Attainment*, PC(2)-5b, Tables 6, 7
(1963); (1969), U.S. Census of the Population, 1970, *Detailed Characteristics*, Table 249
(1979) U.S. Census of the Population, 1980, *Earnings by Occupation and Education*, Tables
2, 4.

1959 and 1969, relative earnings greatly improved for young blacks
entering the labor market, while gains for older blacks were
modest. Looking at the last column, we see that young blacks have
been unable to retain the relative income gains of the 1960s. In
1969, black men aged 18–24 earned 85 percent of white men aged
18–24. Ten years later, the relative earnings of black men aged 25–
34 are only 74 percent of those of white men aged 25–34. This is a
sharp reversal of the trend from 1959 to 1969—a disturbing, but
not unpredictable, trend.

Explaining the Gap

Explaining how employment levels could worsen for blacks while
appearing stable for whites requires an understanding of how labor
markets function. Many commentators on labor issues assume

there is a single labor market that is basically competitive, meaning that anyone in the labor force can compete for any job, anywhere. Making this assumption and observing that blacks face high unemployment rates can lead one to conclude that blacks are either less interested in working or that they are less valuable to employers (less productive in some way). This is the conclusion reached by advocates of supplyside solutions, such as Smith and Welch (1986) and Charles Murray (1984). Smith and Welch (1986) see increased educational attainment and rising returns to education as central to black economic progress, which they see as continuing, albeit at a slower rate, in recent years. But, educational attainment and returns to education have greatly improved for blacks relative to whites since the 1950s, so their theory predicts success for today's young blacks.

The end of black economic progress is now becoming apparent to many (with the clear exception of Smith and Welch) and has led other supplysiders to attack government programs, alleging they have reduced black self-reliance (Murray, 1984). They argue that if blacks can't find or keep jobs after years of government programs (and the presumed end of discrimination), there must be something dysfunctional about black culture itself. But, the bulk of the evidence shows that blacks are typically paid less for given productivity attributes than are nonblack workers. This was recently confirmed in a study of the returns to CETA training, by race (Seeborg, Seeborg, and Zegeye, 1986). The presence of high unemployment rates and discrimination can reduce the economic returns to education and training. Changes in the demand for black labor must be considered as well as changes in the characteristics of the black job seeker.

How Do Labor Markets Work?

To assume that markets are competitive is to assume that the real problem—that of discrimination—does not exist. But how can discrimination affect employment? It is easy to see that racial prejudice exists and that economic inequality exists, but how does one lead to the other? Why don't Jews, Chinese, and Japanese seem to be affected today? There must be a mechanism, but it is not found in a competitive labor market.

Polls consistently report that racial attitudes are far less discriminatory today than 20 years ago. If we continue to assume that labor markets are reasonably competitive, we cannot find a role for discrimination at all in explaining economic inequality. With competitive labor markets and discrimination, employers must act as if hiring blacks of the same productivity as whites and at the same wage brings an added psychic cost. If this is the case, the discriminatory employer must pay whites more than blacks. An all-white labor force will lead to higher labor costs. Less discriminatory employers will hire blacks at the lower wage and enjoy a cost advantage over discriminatory employers. This competitive model predicts that there should be no economic inequality because the market will penalize discriminatory employers and reward nondiscriminatory employers (Arrow, 1973). The fact that discrimination continues to be associated with racial economic inequality strongly suggests that a simple competitive model of the labor market is inappropriate for understanding how discriminatory labor markets work.

Labor market analysis has long been burdened by the difficulty of analyzing noncompetitive behavior (labor is not simply allocated by prices in a free market, but neither is labor a commodity to be traded like frozen pork bellies). Dealing with this problem is part of the basis for the Keynesian revolution in economic thought. The competitive model argues that wages are the primary means of allocating labor resources and that workers should be paid according to their productivity and not according to skin color, gender, age, or religion. When we observe the wage payments actually made to people, it is hard to accept the model as credible. Are women, blacks, Hispanics, Native Americans (American Indians), and Asians all worth less than male Anglos? Efforts to explain earnings purely on the basis of productivity differences have not been successful (Treiman and Hartman, 1981).

Various theories of segmented or balkanized labor markets have been advanced based on observations of employment segregation among women and blacks and of earnings inequality (Edgeworth, 1922; Kerr, 1954; Doeringer and Piore, 1971; Gordon, 1972; Gordon, Edwards, and Reich, 1982). These theories indicate that employment segregation itself acts to reduce wages by restricting competition between groups.

Another approach to understanding employment inequality is simply to observe that the persistence of unemployment reflects a lack of competitive conditions in the labor market and then to model how jobs are rationed under conditions of less than full employment. Thurow (1975) argues that "the labor market is not primarily a bidding market for selling existing skills, but a training market where training slots must be allocated to different workers." Thurow sees productivity as associated with the job, not with the worker, since the skills are learned on the job and can be easily acquired. With this theory, the importance of going to school is only in whether you can demonstrate an ability to be trained. The content of your education may not matter at all to the employer.

Both of the above approaches are helpful. We need to understand the labor market as it really works—not as it might work under conditions of perfect competition. We do observe employment segregation and see that this acts to reduce job mobility, and we do observe involuntary unemployment and know that this leads to job rationing. With segregation and rationing, changes in the structure of the economy can contribute to the employment gap.

The Role of Structural Change in the Economy

This section examines structural and institutional causes for the increasing employment problems of young blacks and predicts that these problems will gradually, without intervention, become those of older workers (the vintage effect). There has been a major change in the nature of the black labor market, unrelated to civil rights activity, that may have effectively reduced opportunities for young blacks. Blacks may be experiencing greater impact from discriminatory labor practices as a result of structural changes in the economy even as racial attitudes are improving.

A simple explanation for the rise in unemployment among young blacks would be that discrimination increased during the 1970s. The racial convergence trends in education and income suggest that discrimination has decreased since the civil rights reforms of the mid-1960s. Reports of improvements in the return to education for blacks also indicate less discrimination. Polls consistently indicate that racial attitudes have become less discriminatory. The only evidence of increased discrimination is the fall in employment itself.

The gains of the 1960s seem to have masked structural problems that only now are becoming apparent. These structural changes are important if segregation is the mechanism that turns discrimination into economic inequality. Blacks are less mobile geographically and occupationally as a result of discriminatory practices which lead to segregated labor markets (Larson, 1986). Because of labor market segregation, blacks may be more sensitive to structural changes in labor demand. The 1970s and 1980s have been periods of rapid structural change.

Donald Harris (1983) has found that uneven development across sectors can have a negative economic effect on blacks. Looking at data for the period 1948–1978, Harris found that the single greatest cause of the rise in the black/white income ratio was the movement of blacks out of agriculture. The postwar shift toward higher-status occupations and service occupations was negatively associated with changes in the income ratio. During the 1970s there was little further shift out of agriculture, but the shift toward high-status occupations and service occupations continued.

The evidence of improving economic circumstances needs to be more carefully evaluated in light of the problems faced by many black youth in gaining employment. Through the 1960s blacks made great progress, relative to whites, in raising their incomes. The rise in the black/white income ratio had a number of sources: the shift from agriculture to urban occupations (Harris, 1983), migration north (Masters, 1972), rise in educational levels (Smith and Welch, 1986), greater occupational status (Hauser, 1976), and the tight labor markets of the Vietnam era. Part of the rise in the racial income ratio reflects the replacement of older, relatively less educated blacks, by young blacks with educations similar to young whites. Much of the rise was due to improvement of black income in the South (Reich, 1981) and some of the improvement is due to a rise in dropouts (nonincome earners) (Brown, 1984). The data reported here are for those with positive earnings. If zero income earners (a growing category) are included in the measure, the rise is smaller and ends earlier (Brown, 1984). The overall trend among black males is buoyed by improvements in the South through the 1970s but is reduced by losses in the North and West in the last few years (Reich, 1981). The improvement in the South may simply reflect the continued urbanization of southern blacks. This process appears to be at an end; by 1981 relative income was falling in the South as well as in the North and West.

Table 3–1 shows that the employment of teenage male blacks has been declining since the 1950s. For the 1950s and 1960s, part of the decline can be traced to the movement of blacks out of agriculture and into urban labor markets (Cogan, 1982). By 1970 this movement was a trickle and cannot explain much of the post-1970 decline. In a study of urban labor markets, Friedlander (1972) reported that the relative employment of young blacks had been declining in the central cities even during the 1960s. Looking at 54 major Standard Metropolitan Statistical areas (SMSAs), black male teen employment fell between 1970 and 1980, falling from 29 to 26 percent (white male employment went from 42 to 48 percent), paralleling the national trend. In 36 of these SMSAs, the black male employment rate for teenagers fell, while the white rate fell in only 6 SMSAs.[4] Black youth employment was falling in many major SMSAs even as white youth employment was rising.

The rise in unemployment in the late 1970s and early 1980s is easier to understand since this was a period of economic stagnation, if not decline, for blacks of all ages. Among males, the black/white income ratio was no longer increasing by the late 1970s. Among families, the black/white income ratio fell, reflecting the rise in labor force participation among married white women, the rapid rise in the number of black female-headed households, and the employment problems of black males. In recent years the relative earnings of young blacks compared to whites have been declining. For those age 20–24, the black/white income ratio was .82 in 1972 and .61 in 1982 (Census Bureau, 1973, 1983).

Structural changes involve both change in the industrial structure and geographic changes in investment and employment patterns. During the 1960s and 1970s, employment growth in the major industrial cities tended to lag behind national employment growth (Bradbury, Downs and Small, 1982). Employment growth in the older metropolitan areas has been concentrated in suburban growth (Bradbury, Downs, and Small, 1982). There is not enough new investment in many older cities to maintain the employment of the resident labor force (Varaiya and Wiseman, 1981).The white population has not only been exiting central cities to move to the suburbs, but has also been moving to smaller metropolitan areas and to nonmetropolitan areas (net). Meanwhile, the black population has continued to move to central cities in our largest metropolitan areas (Larson, 1986).

Current structural changes will importantly contribute to rising social inequality if, in general, racially restricted industries are expanding while more integrated industries are in decline. Employment segregation and discrimination, coupled with shifts in the industrial structure, can reduce black employment—if those sectors that tend to employ whites are growing faster than those that tend to employ blacks and if blacks enjoy little mobility. Changes in the employment patterns of youth suggest that changes in industrial structure are affecting employment opportunities.

Characteristics of the Urban Labor Market

For older generations of blacks, central city residence offered greater opportunity. For example, the jobs that opened up to blacks during World War I and World War II were in manufacturing centers such as Detroit and Chicago. The decline of smokestack industries, the suburbanization of jobs, and the general switch from blue-collar to white-collar employment are all likely to contribute to the rising unemployment of today's young blacks. While previous generations were able to escape rural poverty by moving to the industrial cities, today's young blacks are in stagnating urban economies, are typically second-generation ghetto dwellers, and have no promised land to beckon them. The white population has moved to the suburbs and to high-tech centers in the Sunbelt, while black males remain largely an industrial blue-collar labor force 20 years after the Civil Rights Act of 1964.

Employment Patterns of Black and White Male Teenagers, 1950–1980

In the post-war period, all male teenagers have come to be concentrated in retail employment. In 1950, 23 percent of employed male teenagers were in trade (mostly retail). In 1980, 46 percent were employed in wholesale and retail trade. Table 3–2 shows the distribution of the employed across occupations. Agriculture has become one of the least important employers of teenage males (dropping from 25 percent of employment in 1950 to only 6 percent in 1980). The percentage of teenage employment in manufacturing fell slightly, from 22 percent in 1950 to 17

Table 3–2   Male Teen Employment by Industry, as a Percent of Civilian Employment (for those aged 16–19)

Industry	1950	1960	1970	1980
Total Employment	100%	100%	100%	100%
Agriculture	30	15	7	6
Mining	1	1	*	1
Construction	6	5	5	7
Manufacturing	22	21	20	17
durables	11	10	10	10
nondurables	11	11	10	7
Transportation, utilities, and communications	4	3	4	3
Wholesale and retail	23	34	43	46
Finance, insurance, and real estate	1	1	1	2
Service	10	14	17	18
business	2	3	4	5
personal	3	3	3	2
entertainment	3	3	2	3
professional	2	5	8	8
Public administration	1	1	2	2

*Less than .5%.

SOURCES: U.S. Census, *Industrial Characteristics*, 1950 (Table 3); 1960 (Table 4); 1970 (Table 34); *Number of Inhabitants*, 1950, 1960, 1970, 1980; *CPS Data Book*, Tables A–2, 58; *U.S. Summary*, 1950 (Table 38); 1980 (Table 289).

percent in 1980. These declines are similar to overall employment declines in those industries. (The overall fall was from 29 percent in 1950 to 22 percent in 1980 in manufacturing, and from 14 to 4 percent in agriculture.) Offsetting the declines in agriculture and manufacturing are increases in employment in trade and services, with the increase in service employment being largely in business and professional services. Comparing Tables 3–3 and 3–4, which report employment divided by population, we see that white male teens have increased their relative employment in trade and service industries from 18 percent in 1960 to 24 percent in 1970, but black male teens saw absolutely no relative increase in employment between 1960 and 1970 and have lost ground since 1950.

The usual scenario is that manufacturing has featured less youth employment over time. Ginsberg (1982) argues that today there are relatively fewer unskilled jobs in manufacturing. However, looking at the male teen share of employment in manufacturing, there has been little change since 1950 (dropping from 8 to 7 percent). The proportion of all workers in manufacturing has

Table 3–3   Male Teen Employment by Industry, as a Percent of Population (Employment Rates)

Industry	1950 (Age 18–19)	1960 (Age 16–19)	1970	1980
Civ. Employment/Pop	.52	.39	.39	.42
Total Emp/Pop	.65	.47	.44	.44
Agriculture	13	6	3	2
Mining	1	*	*	*
Construction	3	2	2	3
Manufacturing	14	8	8	7
durables	8	4	4	4
nondurables	6	4	4	3
Transportation, utilities, and communications	3	1	1	1
Wholesale and retail	12	13	17	19
Finance, insurance, and real estate	1	1	1	1
Service	5	5	7	7
business	1	1	2	2
personal	1	1	1	1
entertainment	1	1	1	1
professional	1	2	3	3
Public administration	*	*	1	1
Armed forces	13	8	5	2

*Less than .5%.
SOURCE: see Table 3–2.

declined since 1950, so the proportion of male teenagers in manufacturing has actually risen.

Blacks lost jobs in all major sectors of the economy but one
between 1950 and 1980 (the exception was in professional services). Shifts toward service and retail employment in the general
economy work to the relative disadvantage of young blacks. During
the 1960s, young blacks did improve their position in manufacturing, from a 5 percent employment rate to 7 percent (see Table
5–3), even as the overall share of teen jobs in manufacturing was
falling. This may have reflected the added demand during the
Vietnam War that tended to preserve employment in aging central
city factories (Friedlander, 1972).

A considerable and growing difference is evident in teenage
patterns of employment by race. While nonblack youth have made
up for losses in agriculture and manufacturng by getting more
retail jobs, black youth just lost jobs as agriculture and manufactur-

Table 3–4   Black Male Teen Employment by Industry, as a Percent of
Population (Employment Rates)

Industry	1950 (nonwhite) Age 18–19	1960 (nonwhite) Age 16–19	1970 (black) Age 16–19	1980 (black) Age 16–19
Civ. Employment/Population	.56	.32	.27	.24
Agriculture	22	8	2	NA
Mining	1	*	*	NA
Construction	4	2	1	NA
Manufacturing	11	5	7	NA
durables	7	2	4	NA
nondurables	3	3	3	NA
Transportation, utilities, and				
communications	2	1	1	NA
Wholesale and retail	9	8	8	NA
Finance, insurance, and real				
estate	*	*	1	NA
Service	7	6	6	NA
business	1	1	1	NA
personal	4	2	1	NA
entertainment	1	1	*	NA
professional	2	2	4	NA
Public administration	1	*	1	NA
Armed forces	NA	NA	4	NA

*less than .5%.
SOURCE: see Table 3–2.

ing declined in employment. Indeed, blacks have experienced a relative fall in employment, even in expanding sectors of the economy.[5] This trend goes back at least to 1960 and may go back to 1950.[6] Blacks are especially underrepresented in trade, the major sector of teen employment. Young blacks were only 40 percent as likely as young whites (nonblacks) to work in wholesale and retail trade in 1970, and this is part of a worsening trend that goes back to 1950 when blacks were 80 percent as likely as whites to be employed in trade.

Potential Employment Problems for Black Youth

Structural shifts suggest several potential problems for young black job-seekers: First, in a period seeing the rapid development of new industries and the decline of old ones, those employed in traditional industries must seek out jobs in new industries. For blacks this will entail breaking color barriers—historically a slow and painful process. Employment segregation means that blacks will lag behind whites in mobility (geographic as well as occupational and industrial). Second, young workers increasingly are becoming concentrated in trade employment, a sector of little growth. This suggests that there is greater segmentation in the youth labor market today for both whites and blacks. Both the rise in service employment and the shift toward trade employment among youth will have stronger adverse effects on young blacks than on white youth, since blacks are poorly represented in retail and have become underrepresented in service. This may be aggravated by the decline in central city retail employment (most black youth live in the central cities) and the great growth of retail in the suburbs, where most white youth live (Greenwood, 1981).

A third potential problem for black job seekers is that blacks may be more concentrated than whites in areas of high unemployment. Being at the back of the labor queue, this further reduces relative employment prospects. Thus, in the central cities, blacks are being penalized both by being at the end of the labor queue and being overrepresented in a declining area.

In the 1970s, jobs were being generated for young people, but blacks were not getting the new jobs.[7] This would suggest that both races are not competing in the same labor market. It also is consistent with the argument that young whites benefit from being in the expanding suburbs. (This hypothesis is discussed in the next section.)

Determinants of Youth Employment

There has been considerable recent research on the primary determinants of youth employment. Here, these findings are summarized. A variety of different methodologies have been used to estimate the strength of various factors and no study has been able to include all factors that are important; therefore; it is not possible to compare fully the strength of each factor.

Aggregate Demand

When aggregate unemployment rates rise, youth unemployment rates rise disproportionately. Freeman (1982) and Larson (1986) both found that a 1 percent rise in the overall unemployment rate leads to about a 3 percent rise in male teenage unemployment. The major factor affecting youth employment is simply aggregate demand for goods, but this cannot explain the widening racial differential.

Education and Training

There are clear benefits for both blacks and whites who stay in school. High school graduates of both races have higher earnings and more employment than high school dropouts. However, there are also racial differentials in the economic benefits of schooling. The racial employment gap has widened for both in-school and out-of-school youth. Black high school graduates do not do as well as white high school dropouts in terms of earnings or employment rates. In 1976, blacks aged 20–24 with some college had higher unemployment rates than white high school dropouts (18.4 vs. 15.1 percent).

The type of program pursued in high school also matters. Completing an academic program (one stressing reading, writing, and arithmetic) has been found to be useful; vocational education, in contrast, has no benefit in terms of expectations of employment or better wages (Meyer and Wise, 1982). The best preparation for doing well as an adult is to work while going to high school and take academic courses (Meyer and Wise, 1982).

The best training programs for unemployed youth are those that provide prolonged and intensive assistance for the truly disadvantaged job seeker. Those needing help need lots of it. Programs targeted to the chronically unemployed are difficult and expensive, but there are examples of effective programs. One of the most respected programs is the Jobs Corps, created in 1964 by the

Economic Opportunity Act and run by the Department of Labor. In 1984, the annual cost of providing one training slot was $13,595. The cost per trainee was $5,595 (the average length of training was several months) (Dept. of Labor). Mathematica Policy Research (1982) estimated that the rate of return on this investment was about 46 percent. Participants enjoyed higher earnings as a result of the programs and quickly repaid their cost to society.

A recent study of employment and training programs observed that a "problem cited in many reports was the tendency of program operators to serve the least disadvantaged of the eligible youth, leaving the most disadvantaged and needy without services" (Betsey, Hollister, and Pagageogiou, 1985). This "creaming," as it is called, is a widespread problem and reflects the impact of providing incentives for placements as well as the difficulty of working with and locating the hard-core unemployed. Those who most need the services are hard to recruit and to place and so are ignored. In delivering services, funds are often spent to maximize the number of successful "placements." Since placements are rewarded, agencies seek to work with the most employable of their clients—thereby ensuring the appearance of success—so those who least need help get the most attention.

A government report estimated in 1978 that about one million disadvantaged youth aged 16–21 (of all races) were most in need of federal assistance (U.S. Government Accounting Office, 1982). In 1979, about 2.5 million youth (aged 14–21) were enrolled in various federal employment programs (and many more in numerous state and local programs). By targeting fewer clients, more resources could be provided for those youth in greatest need. The Job Corps has shown that training the hard-core unemployed can be very cost-effective.

School Enrollment

Mare and Winship (1984) claim to show that changes in school enrollment patterns between the races explain a large part of the widening employment gap. They observed that during the 1970s school enrollment and armed service enlistments rose (relatively) among blacks; however, they admit that this only "explains" part of the fall in employment (employment rates are lower for those in school) and may be a result rather than a cause. Since reduced employment opportunity can cause young people to stay in school, causality is difficult to establish. Freeman (1982) and Larson (1986) examined the effects of school enrollment on employment (across SMSAs) and found no clear relationship. It is likely that civilian jobs would be preferred to military jobs (if available), and for those aged 16–19, school attendance might be lower if jobs were available (it is hard to keep young people in school—that's why attendance is compulsory). Finally, changes in school enrollment patterns between the races cannot explain why the employment gap widens between blacks and whites in school.

Residence

Kain (1968) has argued that residential integration is important to black economic success. It is not clear, in general, that the jobs disappearing in the central cities are simply moving to the suburbs and being filled by whites, although there are some instances of this. Many of the central city manufacturing jobs are simply gone, due to decline in industry or movement to other regions and offshore. Larson (1986) found that employment growth in the central city benefits blacks but not employment growth in the suburbs. Also, in areas where there are relatively more blacks in the suburbs, black youth employment is not aided (Larson, 1986). This is consistent with the idea that the jobs are different (reflecting both racial and employment practices and the lack of black owner-ship in retail)—not that transportation or information are severe problems.

Industrial Structure

Studies consistently find that industrial structure has an important impact on youth employment. (Kalachek, 1969; Friedlander, 1972; Freeman, 1982; Osterman, 1982; Larson, 1986). The proportion of teenagers in manufacturing has actually increased, so it is only the absolute decline in manufacturing that has hurt youth employment (particularly black youths), not changes in skill levels. Further work should be done on youth employment in services. This growing sector has aided youth but not black youth, and racial barriers need to be examined in more detail.

Crowding

Youth employment is reduced as the proportion of youth in the population increases (Kalachek, 1969; Al-Salam, Quester, and Welch, 1981; Wachter and Kim, 1982; and Larson, 1986). This effect should have strongly improved conditions for blacks in the 1980s, as the relative size of the youth population declines, but this has not happened. Larson (1986) found no support for the argument that white or black migrants (Friedlander, 1972) or women (Iden, 1980) were taking jobs away from young blacks. In the future, the possibility of competition between young blacks and Hispanics should be examined.

Size of the Black Population

The Becker model of economic discrimination assumes that employers' utility is affected by the number of white and black workers in the firm (Becker, 1971). Arrow (1973) added that employers' utility is affected by the proportion of blacks in the firms' workplace. For the discriminatory employer, disutility increases as the percentage of blacks employed rises. It is this disutility (or psychic cost) arising from a "taste" from discrimination that is then proposed as leading to racial economic inequality.

Similarly, some sociologists have theorized that there is greater prejudice as the relative size of a minority population increases (Allport, 1954). Both of the above approaches predict greater inequality as a result of greater "distastes," as the relative size of the minority population rises.

There are opposing arguments that a larger minority population would lead to greater economic equality. Turner (1951) and Lieberson (1980) argue that a large black population may aid black employment by opening up a wider range of occupations. A large black community would provide demand for specialized skills and allow black doctors, lawyers, bankers, and others to establish themselves. As the proportion of blacks rises, the proportion of whites falls, leaving fewer whites for semi-skilled positions and enabling blacks to move upward occupationally. A large black population can support autonomous black institutions and provide a base for political power. Using data for large metropolitan areas, Larson (1986) found that black youth employment was greater (after controlling for other factors) in those areas with higher percentages of blacks in 1970 and 1980, supporting the Turner and Lieberson views. Even if there is an increase in the desire to discriminate, there may be a counterbalancing reduction in the ability to discriminate as the black population increases.

Minimum Wage

Jeffrey Zuckerman, a Reagan nominee to the Equal Employment Opportunity Commission, privately suggested that blacks should offer to work for lower wages than whites in order to get jobs (*San Francisco Chronicle*, 1986). This is just saying that blacks should be paid less than their value, which is already the case and is a major source of inequality. Some see young blacks as having lower productivity characteristics due to their greater likelihood of attendance at inferior inner-city schools and argue that blacks can only compete if paid lower wages. If productivity lies in the job and since most workers receive their training on the job, this should not matter much. It is clear, in theory, that creating a wage floor will tend to reduce the flexibility of wages and act as a restraint to employment during periods of high unemployment. However, there is a considerable body of empirical work that has consistently found that the employment effects of increases in the minimum wage are very modest (Brown, Gilroy, and Kohen, 1982). For all youth, a 10 percent cut in the minimum wage may cut unemployment by one percentage point. For black youth, the results are less certain, but appear to be smaller (Brown, Gilroy, and Kohen, 1982). These results also indicate that cutting the minimum wage will greatly reduce the wage bill to low-wage workers. Those who advocate lower wages for youth from poor households are offering the following bargain: We will cut your wages by 30 percent but increase your hours by 3 percent, for a net loss in earnings. There is no clear evidence that black youth would see any increase in their employment, but they would certainly earn less. Since 1968, the real minimum wage has fallen by more than 20 percent, yet there has been no accompanying rise in black youth employment.

High Wages

Friedlander (1972) reported that high-wage industries did not hire youth and that employment growth was lower in high-wage areas. He found a positive association between wage levels and youth unemployment (with controls) during the 1960s. Larson (1986), using data for the 1970s, found the opposite—that youth employment was higher in areas of higher income. High income may stimulate demand for goods and services produced in youth sectors and thus benefit youth even if high-wage sectors do not directly employ youth. Efforts to cut wages in areas of high unemployment may be counterproductive.

Culture of Poverty Theory

Reflecting on what appeared to be modest success in the war on poverty, Moynihan (1968) concluded that poverty partly reflected "cultural and environmental obstacles to motivation." Anthropologist Oscar Lewis (1968) argued, on the basis of his work in Mexico, that a culture of poverty tends to perpetuate itself; poor people stay poor because they lack middle-class values, aspirations, and behavior. Today, some people just agree with Piore (1979) that blacks are unwilling to take menial jobs or low wages. The widening employment gap can then be attributed to changes in expectations and attitudes among blacks, due to the civil rights movement and an increase in black pride. However, actual studies have found that blacks are more willing than whites to work. This was found in a 1970 study by Hamel, Goldberg, and Gavett and in a more recent study by Borus (1980). Borus found black youth willing to work at menial jobs at lower wages than white or Hispanic youth. This tends to refute the culture-of-poverty theory. We do not need to resort to disparaging the victims for lack of other solutions to the youth employment problem.

Discrimination

There is evidence of continued employment discrimination. In a study in which black and white applicants applied for the same jobs, the applicants were found to be treated differently, based on their race (Culp and Dunson, 1986). Statistical studies of the determinants of earnings continue to find that a large share of the earnings gap between blacks and whites reflects discrimination, and not just differences in educational and training levels. The importance today of retail employment presents several problems for blacks. Even if retailers are not discriminatory, many hire friends and relatives (typical of small firms). Such nepotism hurts blacks because so few own firms. The Reagan administration has raised the size requirement for firms required to file affirmative action plans. Again, this can only hurt young blacks who need to get jobs in smaller establishments. Teenagers are especially affected by a lack of neighborhood retail jobs.

Conclusions

Blacks are clearly affected by macro events over which they have no control—still they have followed sensible optimizing strategies, given institutional and structural constraints on their opportunities. The failure of the federal government to pursue full employment policies, the decline of the older manufacturing centers, the effects of nepotism, and the intense discrimination faced by young blacks in the retail sector are not under the control of the black community. These are not problems that can be solved by the marketplace or just through increased educational expenditures.

There is evidence of a general deterioration in the range and level of employment opportunities for young people. There are fewer jobs for young people in almost all industries except retail, which is becoming crowded with young people. In the 1980s, despite a decline in the relative size of the youth population, youth employment rates are falling. Because of continued discrimination, segregation, and nepotism, black youths have taken the brunt of these losses. The reason that blacks still have lower educational attainment than whites appears due to higher poverty rates among black families. According to the William T. Grant Foundation, in 1985 the high school drop-out rate for youth from poor families was 31.6 percent for blacks and 39.6 percent for whites. Increasing poverty rates for black youth may lead to higher drop-out rates.

Discrimination and employment segregation currently act to keep blacks out of expanding sectors of the economy. Young blacks are clearly hurt by the shift toward youth employment in retail. There are few retail jobs for teens in black neighborhoods, and blacks simply have a hard time getting jobs in white neighborhoods (Ellwood, 1983). Teenage blacks are less able to compete in suburban areas than whites and may receive little advantage in black neighborhoods where adults compete for a limited number of low-wage jobs. The shift toward service and retail work requires breaking another set of color bars.

Policy Implications and Recommendations

Only a few years ago, many economists believed we would quickly achieve racial economic equality in this country. Richard Freeman (1973), for example, thought that discrimination was virtually at an end and that racial economic equality was around the corner. In 1986, however, Freeman saw black youth facing a crisis. In recent years people in public policy have become more pessimistic about our ability to achieve racial economic equality in this century, or even in our lifetime. Even though the black middle class is larger, more affluent, better educated, and enjoys greater occupational prestige than it did 20 years ago, both absolutely and compared with whites, one segment of the black population has clearly fallen further and further behind its white counterpart—young black males. Today, Freeman is writing of the crisis of black youth employment (Freeman and Holzer, 1986).

Currently, newspapers such as the *Wall Street Journal* are

focusing on the alleged inability of government programs to end poverty and unemployment among minorities. After years of government programs to aid minority youths, former advocates are joining the far right in arguing that the programs have become the problem and have reduced the incentive of poor people to help themselves. There is compelling evidence that there is a shortage of jobs made available to blacks and that the primary sociological problem is the perpetuation of racist attitudes and practices. The important lesson to be learned is that more must be done to overcome the effects of discrimination and that we have consistently underestimated the extent of the problems facing black youth. Education and training programs and other efforts to aid minorities are not compromised by "bad attitudes," but by the presence of high unemployment rates (which create a need for job rationing) and the presence of discrimination (which becomes a basis for rationing jobs), as well as by the need for program reform.

We need to create conditions that discourage the creation and continuation of discriminatory practices. We seem to have difficulty dealing with problems that are due to "society" and not the individual, but that is what must be done. There is a new set of color bars to be broken. The evidence cited in this chapter supports the following recommendations for increasing the employment rate of young blacks.

1. Commitment to full employment is essential, since blacks are still the first to be unemployed. But even at full employment, occupational and industrial segregation will prevent full economic equality.

2. To counteract persistent discriminatory employment practices, a renewed commitment to affirmative action is needed. Jonathan Leonard (1984a) has found that affirmative action is effective in increasing black employment opportunities. Without a full employment economy this approach is endangered by white backlash—it is clear that the majority population does not want to give "their" jobs to blacks.

3. Completing high school and going on to college is important and will become even more beneficial when combined with policies to create more employment opportunities for blacks. Increased employment and higher earnings will aid blacks in investing in their own education. Greater efforts must be made to retain black males through high school graduation, and the fall in college enrollment must be reversed.

4. Placement and training programs for young blacks (and disadvantaged whites) are needed in the service sector and in retail.

But, there is also tremendous need for reforms here. Priority should be given to identifying and serving high-risk youth and not to just "creaming" the pool of program eligibles. The Jobs Corps, a cost-effective program for the hard-core unemployed, has lost much of its funding; instead, it should be expanded. Employment training programs need to emphasize skills that are appropriate for white-collar occupations. This means a concentration on basic skills and on transferable skills and less on traditional vocational education programs. David Stern (forthcoming) has found that vocational education is important for drop-out prevention, but the programs need to be reformed to emphasize analytic ability.

5. Aid to develop black neighborhoods is needed. There may be economic advantages to the "Black metropolis." Jobs must be created in the ghetto, and firms outside the ghetto must be pressured into hiring blacks. In recent years the black community has been less able to help young blacks—this may be due to rising poverty in the community. Neighborhood jobs for teenagers are clearly lacking in the ghetto.

6. A higher minimum wage may be needed to help the black community. There is little evidence that a higher minimum wage would lead to much employment loss, but there is overwhelming evidence that a higher minimum wage would greatly increase the incomes of low-wage earners. Minimum wage studies have had mixed results on the employment effects for blacks, perhaps because there is often a gain in employment in the black community due to the rise in income. Increasing the resources of the black community would be an important stimulant to local employment. Larson (1986) found that a high-income economy is associated with more youth employment.

7. Residential segregation may be part of the economic problem, but it may only represent added transportation costs due to the lessened ability of blacks to find housing near their place of work.[8] Segregation may serve to shelter some jobs for blacks. It is clear that teenage blacks are not getting jobs in the suburbs but do benefit from employment growth in the central city (however, this effect declines with age). Residential integration may reduce black employment unless there is a concomitant effort to increase employment opportunities for blacks in non-inner-city areas.

The goal must be to integrate society. This will require integrating the workplace. Since jobs are critical, this is the place to start. With the shift among youth toward retail employment it is necessary for black youth to get jobs in retail establishments with white clientele. Just as separate schools cannot provide equal education, separate societies cannot provide equal opportunity.

It has been hypothesized that blacks gain from working as a group (it is not just chain migration that leads to concentration of blacks in a few large urban areas, but a rational optimizing process). Past black success centered on employment in a narrow range of industries; today, these industries are in decline, so a new strategy is needed. What can young black males do to break into new industries during a period of excess labor supply? It is not just a question of being in the wrong city, for blacks appear barred from the expanding sectors of the urban economies where they are concentrated. Discrimination has put blacks at the end of the job queue and, with high unemployment rates in the cities, there is no market pressure to hire blacks, especially youth.

The rising unemployment of recent years under conditions of discrimination and structural change only pushes young blacks further back on the job queue, further from the threshold of employment. Since whites are preferred and available, they will do well in the job lottery. Blacks are, as has been the case historically, left with the least desirable openings, and young blacks cannot compete with whites outside their own neighborhoods. Leaving the private sector alone will only exacerbate the problem. This is a problem that urgently requires social intervention.

We cannot afford to let a generation of black males fall through the cracks. These young men will be poor marriage partners due to expected low earnings and unstable employment for years to come, contributing to the rise of female-headed households. Their low earnings will retard the development of the black community, foster dependence on other taxpayers to provide unemployment and health benefits, reduce the tax base, and help to undermine other social programs. Lack of employment may contribute to delinquent behavior, drug abuse, vandalism, and crime, as well as retard the development of good work habits and job skills that these young people will need as adults.

Endnotes

1. The data cited here are primarily from Census surveys gathered decennially or monthly through the *Current Population Survey*. Any person doing at least one hour of paid work during the survey week is counted as employed. Unemployed people are those who have not had even one hour of paid work

and are looking for work or are on layoff from a job during the prior four weeks. People who are not employed and are not looking for work or are not on layoff are not counted as part of the labor force. The employment ratio is simply the number of those employed to the civilian population. The unemployment rate excludes those who have given up looking for work and is less accurate as a gauge of employment opportunity than the employment ratio. The employment rate is simply the employment ratio expressed as a percentage.

2. Jonathan Leonard (1984a) has shown that blacks of all educational levels benefited from affirmative action.

3. Paul Ong (1986) has found evidence that returns to education, for blacks, are affected by market conditions, with returns increasing during periods of economic expansion and decreasing during periods of little growth.

4. The black male teenage employment rate increased in 15 of the 54 SMSAs and was stable in 3. Substantial increases occurred in Dallas (from .36 to .43), Oklahoma City (from .32 to .40), and Omaha (from .17 to .27) (Larson, 1986).

5. Since 1950, blacks have lost their employment advantage in service. This largely reflects a sharp decrease in personal service employment among blacks.

6. For blacks, the 1950 data are for those aged 18–19 while for other years the data are for those aged 16–19. This gives an upward bias to the 1950 employment rate, as older teens are far more likely to be employed.

7. The increase in youth employment was a surprise, given fears of the effect of the baby boom on crowding in the labor market and of the effect of the reduction in the armed forces during the 1970s. From 1960 to 1970, the proportion of employment going to male teens grew from 3.9 to 4.3 percent, nationally.

8. The Kain theory of the effect of residential segregation is that segregation affects schooling (poor neighborhood, poor school), schooling affects job placement, which in turn affects income. But, links between residence and employment are hard to find.

References

Allport, G. (1966). *The nature of prejudice*. Reading, Mass.: Addison-Wesley.

Al-Salam, N., Quester, A., and Welch, F. (1981). Some determinants of the level and racial composition of teenage employment. In *The economics of legal minimum wages*, edited by S. Rottenberg. Washington, D.C.: American Economics Institute.

Arrow, K. (1973). The theory of discrimination. In *Discrimination in labor markets*, edited by A. Pascal. Princeton, N.J.: Princeton University Press.

Auletta, K. (1982). *The underclass*. New York: Random House.

Ballard, J., and Freeman, R. (1986). Transitions between employment and nonemployment. In *The black youth employment crisis*, edited by R. Freeman and H. Holzer. Chicago: University of Chicago Press.

Becker, G. (1971). *The economics of discrimination*. Chicago: University of Chicago Press.

Becker, B., and Hills, S. (1980). Teenage unemployment: Some evidence of the long-term effects. *Journal of Human Resources* 15:354–72.

Betsey, C., Hollister, R., Jr., Pagageogiou, M. (1985). *Youth employment and training programs: The YEDPA years*. Washington, D.C.: National Academy Press.

Blau, F., and Kahn, L. (1981). Race and sex differences in quits by workers. *Industrial and Labor Relations Review* 34, 1 (July).

Borus, M. (1980). Willingness to work. In *Pathways to the future: A longitudinal study of young Americans*, edited by M. Borus. Columbus: Ohio State University, Center for Human Resources Research.

Bradbury, K., Downs, A., and Small, K. (1982). *Urban decline: And the future of American cities*. Washington, D.C.: Brookings Institution.

Brown, C. (1984). Black-white earnings ratios since the Civil Rights Act of 1964: The importance of labor market dropouts. *Quarterly Journal of Economics* 99 (February).

Brown, D., Gilroy, C., and Kohen, A. (1982). The effect of the minimum wage on unemployment. *Journal of Economic Literature* 20, 2 (June).

Cogan, J. F. (1982). The decline in black teenage employment: 1950–70. *American Economic Review* 72, 4 (September).

Culp, J., and Dunson, B. (1986). Brothers of a different color: A preliminary look at employer treatment of white and black youth. In *The black youth employment crisis*, edited by R. Freeman and H. Holzer. Chicago: University of Chicago Press.

Doeringer, P., and Piore, M. (1971). *Internal labor markets and manpower analysis*. Lexington, Mass.: Lexington Books.

Economic report of the president, 1987 (1987). Washington, D.C.: Government Printing Office.

Edgeworth, F. Y. (1922). Equal pay to men and women. *Economic Journal* (December).

Ellwood, D. (1982). Teenage unemployment: Permanent scars or temporary blemishes? In *The youth labor market problem*, edited by R. Freeman and D. Wise. Chicago: University of Chicago Press.

———. (1983). The spatial mismatch hypothesis: Are there teenage jobs missing in the ghetto: Paper presented at the Conference on Inner City Black Youth Unemployment, August 11.

Farley, R. (1977). Trends in racial inequalities. *American Sociological Review*. 42: 189–208.

Feldstein, M. S. (1973). *Lowering the permanent rate of unemployment*. Joint Economic Committee, 93d cong., 1st sess.

Freeman, R. B. (1973). Changes in the labor market for black Americans, 1948–72. *Brookings Papers on Economic Activity*, vol. i.

———. (1982). Economic determinants of geographic and individual variation in the labor market position of young persons. In *The youth labor market problem*, edited by R. Freeman and D. Wise. Chicago: University of Chicago Press.

Freeman, R. B., and Holzer, H. (1986). *The black youth employment crisis*. Chicago: University of Chicago Press.

Freeman, R. B., and Wise, D. A. (1982). *The youth labor market problem: Its nature, causes, and consequences*. Chicago: University of Chicago Press.

Friedlander, S. L. (1972). *Unemployment in the urban core*. New York: Praeger.

Ginsberg, E. (1982). The mechanization of work. *Scientific American* (September).

Glasgow, D. (1981). *The black underclass*. New York: Vintage Books.

Gordon, D. (1972). *Theories of poverty and unemployment*. Lexington, Mass.: Lexington Books.

Gordon, D., Edwards, R., and Reich, M. (1982). *Segmented work, divided workers*. Cambridge: Cambridge University Press.

Greenwood, M. J. (1981). *Migration and economic growth in the United States*. New York: Academic Press.

Hamel, H., Goldberg, M., and Gavett, T. (1970). Wage expectations. In *Youth unemployment and minimum wages*, BLS Bulletin #1657. Washington, D.C.: Bureau of Labor Statistics.

Harris, D. (1983). Economic growth, structural change, and the relative income status of blacks in the U.S. economy, 1947–78. *Review of Black Political Economy* 12, 3 (Spring).

Harrison, B. (1972). Education and unemployment in the urban ghetto. *American Economic Review* 62, 5 (December).

Hauser, R. (1976). Changes in the socioeconomic stratification of the races, 1962–73. *American Journal of Sociology* 82:621–51.

Hoffman, S. (1979). Black-white life cycle earnings differences and the vintage hypothesis: A longitudinal analysis. *American Economic Review* 69, 5 (December).

Hout, M. (1984). Occupational mobility of black men: 1962 to 1973. *American Sociological Review* 49, 3 (June).

Iden, G. (1980). The labor force experience of black youth: A review. *Monthly Labor Review* 103, 8 (August).

Kain, J. F. (1968). Housing segregation, Negro employment, and metropolitan decentralization. *Quarterly Journal of Economics* 82, 2 (May).

Kalachek, E. (1969). The youth labor market. Ph.D. diss., University of Michigan, Institute of Labor and Industrial Relations.

Kerr, C. (1954). Balkanization of labor markets. In *Labor mobility and economic opportunity*, edited by E. W. Bakke. Cambridge, Mass.: MIT Press.

Larson, T. E. (1986). Job placement of young black males: The roles of migration and structural change in urban labor markets. Ph.D. diss., University of California, Berkeley.

Leonard, J. (1984a). Splitting blacks? Affirmative action and earnings inequality within and across races. NBER Working Paper, #1327 (April).

———— (1984b). Employment and occupational advance under affirmative action. *Review of Economics and Statistics* 66:377–85.

Lewis, O. (1968). The culture of poverty. In *On understanding poverty*, edited by D. P. Moynihan. New York: Basic Books.

Lieberson, S. (1980). *A piece of the pie*. Berkeley: University of California Press.

Mare, R., and Winship, C. (1984). The paradox of lessening racial inequality and joblessness among black youth: Enrollment, enlistment and employment, 1964–1981. *American Sociological Review* 89, 7 (February).

Masters, S. (1972). Are black migrants from the south to the northern cities worse off than blacks already there? *Journal of Human Resources* 7, 4 (Fall).

Mathematica Policy Research (1982). *Evaluation of the economic impact of the jobs corps program*. Third followup report. Management summary, September 1982. Princeton, N.J.: Mathematica Policy Research.

Meyer, R., and Wise, D. (1982). The transition from school to work: The experience of blacks and whites. NBER Working Paper #1007, National Bureau of Economic Research, Cambridge, Mass.

Moynihan, D. P., ed. (1968). *On understanding poverty: Perspectives from the social sciences*. New York: Basic Books.

Murray, C. (1984). *Losing ground: American social policy 1950–1980*. New York: Basic Books.

Ong, P. (1986). Uncertain economic progress, racial inequality among California males, 1940–80. Working paper, School of Architecture and Urban Planning, University of California, Los Angeles.

Osterman, P. (1982). *Getting started*. Cambridge, Mass.: MIT Press.

Piore, M. (1979). *Birds of passage*. Cambridge: Cambridge University Press.

Pollard, T. K. (1984). Changes over the 1970s in the employment patterns of black and white young men. In *Youth and the labor market*, edited by M. E. Borus. New Brunswick, N.J.: Rutgers University, Institute of Management and Labor Relations.

Reich, M. (1981). *Racial inequality*. Princeton, N.J.: Princeton University Press.

San Francisco Chronicle (1986). A rough day for a Reagan nominee. *San Francisco Chronicle*, March 5.

Seeborg, I., Seeborg, M., and Zegeye, A. (1986). Training and labor market outcomes of disadvantaged blacks. *Industrial Relations* 25, 1 (Winter).

Smith, J., and Welch, F. (1977). Black-white male wage ratios: 1960–70. *American Economic Review* 67, 3 (June).

———— (1986). *Closing the gap: Forty years of economic progress for blacks*. Santa Monica, Calif.: Rand Corporation.

Sowell, T. (1981). *Markets and minorities*. New York: Basic Books.

Stern, D. (forthcoming). Reconstituting vocational education. *California Tomorrow* (forthcoming).

Stevenson, W. (1978). The relationship between early work experience and future employability. In *The lingering crisis of youth employment*, edited by W. E. Magnum. Kalamazoo, Mich.: Upjohn Institute for Employment Research.

Thurow, L. (1975). *Generating inequality*. New York: Basic Books.

Treiman, D., and Hartman, H. (1981). *Women, work and wages: Equal pay for jobs of equal value*. Washington, D.C.: National Academy Press.

Turner, R. (1951). The relative position of the Negro male in the labor force of large American cities. *American Sociological Review* 16, 4 (August).

U.S. Bureau of the Census (1973). *Current Population Reports*, Ser. P-60, no. 90. Washington, D.C.

————. (1983). *Current Population Reports*, Ser. P-60, no. 147. Washington, D.C.

————. (1985). School enrollment—Social and economic characteristics of students, October 1984. *Current Population Reports*, Ser. P-20. Washington, D.C.

U.S. Department of Labor. *Performance results for 107 Job Corps centers*. Washington, D.C.: Government Printing Office.

U.S. Government Accounting Office (1982). *Labor market problems of teenagers result largely from doing poorly in school*. Washington, D.C.: Government Printing Office.

Varaiya, P., and Wiseman, M. (1981). Investment and employment in manufacturing in U.S. metropolitan areas, 1960–1976. *Regional Science and Urban Economics* 11, 4 (November).

Wachter, M., and Kim, C. (1982). Time series changes in youth joblessness. In *The youth labor market problem*, edited by R. Freeman and D. Wise. Chicago: University of Chicago Press.

Wall Street Journal (1986). A troublesome syndrome. *Wall Street Journal*, January 23.

Welch, F. (1973). Black-white differences in returns to education. *American Economic review* 63, 5 (December).

William T. Grant Foundation. *American youth: A statistical snapshot*. Washington, D.C.: William T. Grant Foundation, Commission on Work, Family and Citizenship.

Wilson, W. J. (1978). *The declining significance of race*, 2d ed. Chicago: University of Chicago Press.

Chapter 4

DELINQUENCY AMONG BLACK MALE YOUTH

Richard Dembo

> *What happens to a dream deferred?*
> *Does it dry up*
> *like a raisin in the sun?*
> *Or fester like a sore—*
> *And then run?*
> *Does it stink like rotten meat?*
> *Or crust and sugar over—*
> *like a syrupy sweet?*
>
> *Maybe it just sags*
> *like a heavy load.*
>
> *Or does it explode?*

There is a deep and growing concern over substance use and crime by young black males and the overrepresentation of this group in the juvenile and adult criminal justice systems. At the same time, and incredibly, given the long-standing nature of this concern, there is a dearth of firm knowledge on this issue. Most available information is descriptive in nature and does not provide deep

NOTE: The author acknowledges the support of the Florida Department of Health and Rehabilitative Services, Northside Community Mental Health Center and administration, staff and detainees of the Hillsborough Regional Detention Center; and his associates Mark Washburn, Linda Williams, Alan Getreu, and Estrellita Berry.

insight into the causal dynamics that may be involved in these relationships. However, tentative conclusions can be drawn from the information that is currently available—conclusions that point in a rather consistent direction.

Because our knowledge of the drugs-crime relationship among young black males is limited, interpretations of this information often reflect authors' value predilections. Depending on the direction taken, this practice tends to offend liberally or conservatively oriented persons who believe their perception of the issues is not properly represented in these accounts, and they respond accordingly. Such a situation has the effect of increasing our confusion on this vital topic.

In view of these factors, no contribution to the national discussion on drug use and crime among young black males can, at this stage of our understanding, be definitive in nature. The present chapter represents a modest attempt to sift through, compare, and draw conclusions from official statistics, the National Youth Survey (NYS) (self-reported delinquency), and victimization survey data in regard to the relative rates of substance use and delinquency among young black males. On balance, this information leads to the conclusion that delinquency, especially offenses involving crimes against persons, is more prevalent and frequent among young black than white males; however, white males tend to be more involved in the use of various substances. Although we do not devote equal attention to black youth in the 18–25-year-age range in this chapter, the data we review indicate that for most youth delinquent behavior starts at a relatively early age, that most older adolescents and adults initiated law-violating activity in their early teens, and that it is uncommon for individuals to begin a life of crime in early adulthood.

Next, we discuss the major theoretical perspectives put forth to account for delinquency among black male youth and relate this literature to the currently available information on delinquency among this group. Then we review the flow of youth into the juvenile justice system, especially the key entry point of the detention center; we assess the commensurability of the flow rates of black youth into this system vis-à-vis data derived from studies involving official statistics, the NYS, and surveys of children in custody.

In addition, since November 1985, we have been involved in implementing an innovative screening-triage project at a regional juvenile detention center in Tampa, Florida. Data collected on black and white male youth during the first six months of our project have been analyzed for inclusion here. We report the results of a multivariate analysis identifying important background, social-personal history, and court-referral differences between the two groups and relate these findings to the major theories of delinquency among black youth.

The results of our review of the existing research and theoretical literature, and our analyses of data on detainees served during the first six months of our screening-triage project, lead us to conclude that the juvenile justice system has increasingly become used as a device to "handle" black youth. There are poignant social problems stressing the fabric of black social life, particularly in urban areas: high unemployment, high crime rates, a large proportion of female-headed, single-parent households with low incomes, high mortality, and high teenage pregnancy and school drop-out rates (Gibbs, 1984). These stressors, together with an increasingly reduced level of resources being directed to strengthen these communities, have led to a growing drift of troubled black adolescents into the juvenile and, ultimately, adult criminal justice systems.

Statistics on Delinquency and Substance Abuse

Official Statistics

Each year, the FBI publishes a summary volume of statistics on arrests and crimes known to the police, which is based on monthly figures sent to the agency by law enforcement agencies throughout the nation. Participating law enforcement agencies cover all but a very small proportion of the U.S. population.

The FBI *Uniform Crime Reports* (UCR) categorizes the reported data into two major categories. *Index crimes* represent more serious offenses, and are subdivided into two subgroups: (1) violent index crimes—murder and nonnegligent manslaughter, forcible rape, robbery, and aggravated assault, and (2) property index crimes—burglary, larceny-theft, motor vehicle theft, and arson. The second major category of offenses, Part II crimes, refers to a large number of so-called less serious crimes, such as public disorder offenses, embezzlement, vandalism, and violation of drug laws. Although the UCR underrepresents the actual amount of crime occurring in the United States in any given year (U.S. Department of Justice, 1981), and although the data sent to the FBI by various law enforcement agencies sometimes reflect various forms of bias (e.g., manipulation of statistics and police officer judgments regarding who to arrest), the UCR represents the largest, most extensive, and longest term set of information on delinquency-crime in our society. Given its limitations, what does the UCR indicate about this phenomenon?

A review and synthesis of information published in the UCR for 1984 and the Florida Department of Law Enforcement's *Crime in Florida: 1984 Annual Report* (CIF) highlights that persons arrested for index offenses or drug abuse violations tend, overall, to be disproportionately young males (given their representation in the U.S. population). Table 4–1, drawn from the UCR 1984 monograph, documents this point. From 41 to 74 percent of the various index crimes are accounted for by persons 24 years of age or younger, and 55 percent of the arrests for various drug law violations involve this age group. Further, for each age group, males are more highly represented in the arrest figures than females. Similar conclusions for the state of Florida emerge from an analysis of CIF 1984 data (these tables are available upon request).

Table 4–2 presents UCR 1984 data comparing index crime and drug abuse violation arrests by race for persons under 18 and 18 and over. The data document that persons 18 and over account for the majority of arrests for the listed offenses and indicate a sizable representation of persons under 18 in these arrest data. This is especially the case in regard to Index property offenses. Here, although youth under 18 account for 27 percent of the U.S. population, this age group accounts for 48 percent of the burglary arrests, 34 percent of the larceny-theft arrests, 36 percent of the arrests for motor vehicle theft, and 43 percent of the arrests for arson. CIF 1984 data reflect a similar trend for the state of Florida.

Important racial group differences are also shown in Table 4–2. American Indian, Alaskan native, Asian, or Pacific Islander persons account for an extremely small proportion of the reported arrests. Importantly, although black youth constitute 15 percent of the 1984 U.S. population under age 18, they represent 45 percent, 54 percent, 68 percent, and 39 percent of the arrests for murder/ nonnegligent manslaughter, forcible rape, robbery, and aggravated assault, respectively, among this age group. CIF 1984 data indicate a similar pattern for the state of Florida.

Unfortunately, UCR data do not include information in regard to the socioeconomic status (SES) of arrestees. However, two birth cohort studies completed in the city of Philadelphia involving 9,945 males born in 1945 and 13,610 males born in 1958, who lived in Philadelphia from their 10th to 18th birthdays, provide insight into SES differences in delinquent behavior (Wolfgang, Figlio, and Sellin, 1972; Tracy, Wolfgang, and Figlio, 1985). Records of the Juvenile Aid Division (JAD) of the Philadelphia Police

Department provided delinquency data on the youths in each birth cohort.

The 1945 cohort consisted of 71 percent white and 29 percent nonwhite (predominantly black) males, whereas the 1958 cohort was 47 percent white and 53 percent nonwhite. For both cohorts, a larger proportion of white youths (70 percent in 1945, 79 percent in 1958) compared to nonwhite youths (16 and 27 percent, respectively) were high SES.

Importantly, both cohorts found a relationship between race and delinquency, and SES and delinquency, although these differences were less pronounced in the 1958 data set. In each cohort, a larger proportion of nonwhite boys were delinquent (50 percent in 1945 and 42 percent in 1985), than white males (29 percent in 1945 vs. 23 percent in 1958); and, a similar SES differential, reflecting a greater prevalence of delinquency among low SES compared to high SES youths, was found in the 1945 and 1958 cohorts (19 and 18 percent, respectively). This issue is discussed further later in the chapter.

Incidence (or frequency) data reflected similar race and SES differences, with nonwhite and low SES youths being more delinquent and more involved in serious offenses, although these differences were more pronounced in the 1945 cohort. In particular, nonwhite boys were more likely to inflict physical harm on others than were whites.

An additional analysis of the 1958 cohort data (Tracy and Piper, 1982) provides insight into a key factor relating to the nonwhite–white male differences in delinquent behavior, particularly in regard to involvement in violent acts. In this analysis, gang membership was determined for each youth from JAD records. Analysis of these data showed clearly that gang members were more delinquent in general, and more highly involved in violent behavior, than nongang members. Significantly, nonwhite males were far more likely to be gang members than white males (231 vs. 8 youths, respectively).

Self-Report Studies—The National Youth Survey

Although self-report studies can be traced to 1958 (Short and Nye, 1958), it is only recently that data of sufficient quality and representativeness have been available to draw reasonably firm conclusions from this source of knowledge on law-violating behavior among youth. In particular, the work of Elliott and his associates (Elliott and Ageton, 1980; Elliott et al., 1983) has made the most significant contribution to the self-report literature to date.

Table 4-1 *Uniform Crime Reports, 1984* Index Crime and Drug Abuse Violation Arrests by Sex and Age Group

	Total Arrests Male/Female All Ages	Males under 18(%)	Females under 18(%)	Males 18–24 (%)	Females 18–24 (%)	Males 25–34 (%)	Females 25–34 (%)	Males 35–44 (%)	Females 35–44 (%)	Males 45–54 (%)	Females 45–54 (%)	Males 55+ (%)	Females 55+ (%)
Index Crimes													
Murder and nonnegligent manslaughter	13,676	6.6	0.7	30.1	3.8	28.5	4.7	12.3	2.3	5.2	1.1	3.8	0.6
Forcible rape	28,336	15.3	0.2	31.0	0.2	31.6	0.3	14.1	0.1	4.5	-.1	2.5	-.1
Robbery	108,614	24.0	1.6	38.6	2.7	23.0	2.2	5.5	0.5	1.3	0.1	0.5	-.1
Aggravated assault	231,620	11.2	2.2	27.2	4.0	28.2	4.2	12.2	1.8	4.9	0.7	2.9	0.3
Burglary	334,399	35.4	2.8	33.9	2.2	17.3	1.7	4.3	0.5	1.2	0.1	0.5	0.1
Larceny-theft	1,009,743	24.5	9.0	20.2	8.4	14.6	7.0	5.9	2.9	2.4	1.4	2.1	1.5
Motor vehicle theft	93,285	32.2	4.1	33.1	2.7	17.6	1.7	5.4	0.5	1.7	0.1	0.8	-.1
Arson	14,675	38.7	3.8	18.9	2.6	16.3	2.9	8.1	1.8	3.8	0.7	1.9	0.4
Drug abuse violations	562,255	10.1	1.8	37.2	5.7	28.8	4.8	7.4	1.2	1.7	0.3	0.8	0.1

SOURCE: Prepared by combining Tables 33 and 34 from Federal Bureau of Investigation, *Uniform Crime Reports, 1984*. Washington, D.C.: U.S. Government Printing Office, 1985.

134

Table 4–2 *Uniform Crime Reports, 1984 Index Crime and Drug Abuse Violation Arrests by Race, Under 18 and 18 Years of Age and Over*

			Arrests Under 18				Arrests 18 and Over			
	Total Arrests	Arrests Under 18	White (%)	Black (%)	Am. Indian or Alaskan Native (%)	Asian or Pacific Islander (%)	White (%)	Black (%)	Am. Indian or Alaskan Native (%)	Asian or Pacific Islander (%)
Index crimes										
Murder and non-negligent manslaughter	13,656	1,004	3.9	3.3	<.1	<.1	49.8	41.6	0.6	0.6
			53.7	45.2	0.7	0.4				
Forcible rape	28,297	4,394	7.0	8.3	0.1	<.1	45.7	37.6	0.6	0.5
			45.2	53.8	0.7	0.3				
Robbery	108,534	27,788	7.8	17.5	<.1	0.2	29.7	43.9	0.4	0.4
			30.3	68.5	0.2	0.9				
Aggravated assault	231,403	31,126	8.0	5.3	<.1	<.1	52.5	32.8	0.7	0.4
			59.5	39.3	0.7	0.6				
Burglary	333,854	127,521	29.0	8.6	0.3	0.3	41.2	19.9	0.5	0.2
			76.0	22.4	0.8	0.7				
Larceny-theft	1,008,105	338,235	23.9	8.9	0.4	0.4	43.7	21.5	0.7	0.5
			71.2	26.5	1.1	1.2				
Motor vehicle theft	93,187	33,795	26.1	9.4	0.4	0.4	42.0	20.8	0.5	0.4
			72.0	25.9	1.0	1.0				
Arson	14,647	6,235	36.1	5.8	0.4	0.3	41.5	15.2	0.4	0.3
			84.8	13.6	1.0	0.7				
Drug abuse Violations	560,729	66,484	9.4	2.3	<.1	0.1	60.7	26.7	0.3	0.4
			79.0	19.6	0.5	1.0				

SOURCE: Prepared by combining Table 37 Total Arrests, Distribution by Race, 1984 data on arrests under 18 and arrests 18 and over from Federal Bureau of Investigation, *Uniform Crime Reports, 1981.* Washington, D.C.: U.S. Government Printing Office, 1985.

135

The NYS was a longitudinal study involving a national probability sample of 1,725 (915 males, 804 females, and 6 cases with missing information regarding gender) youths 11–17 years of age whose self-reported, law-violating behavior was determined by confidential interviews for the five-year period, 1976–1980. Using standardized scores on the 1976 self-report data, Elliott and Ageton (1980) found black youth were significantly more likely to report committing predatory crimes against persons (sexual assault, aggravated assault, simple assault, and robbery) than white youth, and lower-class youth reported greater involvement in serious offenses against persons than youngsters from working-class or middle-class families. Further, a significant race-by-social-class interaction was uncovered for this subscale, indicating a relatively high participation of lower-class youth in serious offenses against persons.

Subsequent analyses of the self-report data for the five-year period found consistent, strong social class differences in the prevalence and incidence of all serious offenses (Elliott and Huizinga, 1983). When significant class differences were found, they almost always involved lower prevalence and incidence rates for middle-class youths compared to working- or lower-class youths.

However, the greater involvement of black youth in serious crimes against persons, which was uncovered in the 1976 self-report data, was not found in later years of the study (Elliott et al., 1983). Prevalence rate differences between black and white youth diminished over time. With the exception of the 1976 findings, no significant race differences were found in any of the violent or serious offense scales in subsequent years.

It is hard to know what to make of these race comparisons over time. Although it is possible the results are valid, one cannot be sure. As Wilson and Herrnstein (1985, 462–463) point out, the study "did not—and could not—address the question of whether high-rate offenders underreport their offenses." Evidence exists that youths who are heavily involved in delinquency tend to underreport their law-violating behavior—especially black delinquents (Hindelang, Hirschi, and Weis, 1981).

Interestingly, consistent and significant race differences were found in regard to drug use. Whites consistently reported higher hard drug use prevalence rates than blacks across the five-year period; and whites reported higher frequency of hard drug use levels than blacks in four out of the five years (Elliott et al., 1983). These findings are consistent with relevant research (Tucker, 1985).

As might be expected, substantial differences were found in the prevalence and incidence of male and female self-reported delinquency during the 1976–1980 period. Although the pattern of female delinquent behavior was much the same as that of the boys, male youths reported higher prevalence rates and incidence rates than females across a wide range of individual offenses and almost all of the offense scales. The male-to-female sex ratios were especially high with respect to serious and violent offenses (Elliott et al., 1983).

Victimization Survey Results

Victim surveys represent another major source of information on crime in our society, and they have come to occupy a valued place in the activities of the Bureau of Justice statistics (U.S. Department of Justice, 1981). The National Crime Survey (NCS) collects crime victimization information from a probability sample of 60,000 U.S. households.

NCS data consistently show that victimization rates for crimes of violence and crimes of theft are highest among persons 24 years of age or younger, especially 16–24-year-old youths (Empey, 1982; U.S. Department of Justice, 1982, 1983, 1984). Further, blacks are more likely to suffer from crimes of violence and burglary, whereas whites are more likely to report having been victimized by theft crimes; males, whether black or white, generally report higher victimization rates than females; and victimization rates are higher in metropolitan areas compared to nonmetropolitan areas (Empey, 1982; U.S. Department of Justice, 1982, 1983, 1984). In addition, victimization survey findings indicate that single-offender victimizations are predominantly intraracial in nature (U.S. Department of Justice, 1982, 1983, 1984).

The fact that blacks, particularly young black males, are at greater risk of being victimized by crimes of violence than white males is a strong indication of a racial difference in engaging in these behaviors. Not surprisingly, victimization survey data show that families with the lowest incomes are most vulnerable to violent crimes; conversely, the higher a family's income, the more likely it will suffer from a personal theft without contact (National Criminal Justice Information and Statistics Service, 1975a–1979c). However, even in this case race is an important factor. Within the black and white groups, poor people have the highest rates of violent victimizations compared to more affluent persons; and, the greater the income, the greater the personal larceny without contact. Comparing across races shows blacks to suffer more from crime, especially violent crime, than whites—regardless of their income (Empey, 1982; U.S. Department of Justice, 1982, 1983, 1984). The effects of poverty, combined with their minority status, makes blacks highly vulnerable to being victimized by crime.

The effects of victimization are most poignantly seen in regard to homicide. A majority of homicides are cleared by arrest—74 percent in 1984 (FBI, 1985); and we know that the great majority of homicide perpetrators and victims are of the same race.

Data analyzed by the Centers for Disease Control (CDC) (1985) indicate that homicide is currently the leading cause of death among young black males (15–24 years old). The 1982 homicide rate for this group was 72.0 per 100,000 population, nearly six times the rate for white males in the same age range (13.1 per 100,000); the rate for 15–19-year-old black males was approximately 45 per 100,000. Between 1970 and 1978 the homicide rate for black males 15–19 years of age ranged between 65.3 (in 1971) to 39.8 (in 1978) per 100,000 population (Mercy, Smith, and Rosenberg, 1983). The homicide rate for young black males living in standard metropolitan statistical (SMSA) areas is twice that for young black males living in non-SMSA locations. Most young black male homicide victims in 1982 were killed during or after arguments or other nonfelony circumstances by persons known to them, not by the police. Black-white racial differences in homicide victimization become much smaller or disappear when blacks are compared to whites of similar SES. However, these descriptive data do not permit insight into the mechanisms by which low SES is associated with violent behavior (CDC, 1985).

Comparing the Three Sources of Information on Delinquency

Official statistics, self-report data, and victimization data give complementary and congruent accounts of delinquency, with official statistics and victimization data showing rather close agreement. Police records indicate arrest rates are higher for the young, males, blacks, persons with low incomes, and those living in urban areas. Victimization surveys paint a very similar picture.

Self-report studies, particularly the NYS, yield results that are generally similar to those provided by arrest records and victimization studies. At the same time, the NYS stresses the importance of distinguishing between the prevalence and incidence of delinquency. Prevalence comparisons in delinquent behavior show few differences between black and white juveniles, and youths from lower-, working- and middle-class backgrounds (Elliott and Ageton, 1980). On the other hand, the incidence of delinquent behavior appears greater among low-income and black juveniles (Elliott and Ageton, 1980).

High-frequency participators in delinquent behavior, as well as youths committing offenses against persons, are more likely to be arrested (Williams and Gold, 1972). Hence, at the upper range of the frequency continuum, self-report and official record race and social class correlates of delinquent behavior appear similar (Elliott and Ageton, 1980).

Theories of Black-White Differences in Delinquent Behavior

Wilson and Herrnstein (1985) distill four major theories accounting for racial differences in crime from the literature: (1) constitutional factors, (2) economic deprivation, (3) inadequate socialization, and (4) subcultural views. This section of the chapter reflects my indebtedness to their work.

Constitutional Factors

Intelligence and temperament have been put forth as constitutional factors accounting for black-white differences in delinquent behavior. In regard to intelligence and temperament, it is important to point out that these traits may or may not be genetic. Patterns of prenatal care as well as inheritance could be responsible for their development. Further, even if a genetic influence is determined for any of these traits, it merely reflects a predisposition to engage in certain behavior and does not make it inevitable.

Osborne and McGurk's (1982) review of 16 studies assessing the IQ-crime linkage, in which at least some of the subjects were black, concluded that offenders have lower scores than nonoffenders. However, if IQ relates to crime independently of SES, and if blacks, on average, have lower IQ scores than whites, such facts might help explain some black-white differences in crime rates—if we were able to determine *why* a lowered IQ score is related to law-violating behavior. Unfortunately, there is a lack of firm evidence on these dynamics (Wilson and Herrnstein, 1985).

Some interesting work has been completed on the IQ-delinquency issue by incorporating the factor of school performance. Hirschi and Hindelang (1977) argue that IQ influences delinquency through its effect on school performance. Hirschi (1969) first suggested the use of school performance to explain differences in delinquency rates between white and black youths. His analysis of data collected in connection with his study of California youths demonstrated a strong relationship between academic competence, as measured by the Verbal Achievement Scores of the Differential Aptitude Test (DAT), and official delinquency rates for both blacks and whites. Boys with higher DAT scores had fewer officially recorded offenses.

In regard to temperament, research indicates that blacks often obtain different scores than whites on standardized personality tests. For example, on one of the most widely used of these tests, the MMPI, blacks tend to have higher (i.e., less "normal") scores on most of the scales. However, there is an absence of test norms with which to compare the blacks' scores. The MMPI was developed as a measure of psychopathology among whites. Assuming the existence of cultural differences between the two groups, it is possible the blacks' answers may not reflect disturbance at all—merely variations in cultural norms (Wilson and Herrnstein, 1985).

Even if personality inventories were developed that were equally valid for blacks and whites, and personality differences were found between the two groups, one would have to demonstrate that these traits are inherited—if they are to be considered constitutional predispositions (Wilson and Herrnstein, 1985). Much work remains to be done on this topic before any firm statements can be made regarding temperament differences between blacks and whites.

Economic Deprivation

Studies have consistently demonstrated that people—black or white—who have low incomes and poor employment records are more likely to break the law than persons from more affluent circumstances (Wilson and Herrnstein, 1985). However, the explanations for this fact are not clear.

We do know from the 1945 and 1958 Philadelphia birth cohort studies that a large majority of black youths were low SES (84 percent in 1945, 73 percent in 1958), that lower-class black youths had higher delinquency rates than lower-class white boys, and that black males had their first official contact with the police at an earlier age than white boys (Wolfgang, Figlio, and Sellin, 1972; Tracy, Wolfgang, and Figlio, 1985). The dynamics underlying these differences remain to be explicated.

At the same time, economic factors alone do not seem sufficient to explain the relatively high delinquency rates among black ghetto youths. West Indian blacks are indistinguishable, physically, from native American blacks; and West Indian immigrants have lived in the same inner-city areas as native blacks. Reid (1939) compared the crime rates among immigrant and native blacks during the early part of this century. He found West Indians to comprise a much smaller percentage share of New York State prison inmates than would be expected based on their share of the state's population. On the other hand, native blacks were overrepresented in the prison inmate population. West Indian blacks have also been found to be less involved in illicit drug use than native American blacks (Kleinman and Lukoff, 1975, 1978).

These West Indian and native American black delinquency rate differences reflect dissimilar effects of economic factors among various segments of the black community. The West Indian community has traditionally had a greater cultural coherence and higher rates of family intactness than that of native American blacks (Kleinman and Lukoff, 1975). Young persons raised in unstable households, with little feeling of economic well-being, and facing chronic unemployment could be expected to turn disproportionately to crime (Wilson and Herrnstein, 1985). However, not all youths raised in these environmental circumstances become involved in crime. Hence, this theory is not sufficient in itself to account for delinquency among native American Blacks.

These comments are not meant to imply that discrimination is less impacting on the black community today than it was in years past. Discrimination, in its various forms, continues to be a poignant factor in black communal life.

Inadequate Socialization

In their various forms, inadequate socialization views hold that, on average, black families do a poorer job of socializing their children than white families and that single-parent families (most often mother-headed), which are more common among blacks, do an even poorer job of child raising. Begging the important question of why this problem exists—and the possible value bias it reflects—much public concern, both within and outside the black community, has been addressed to this issue. It is also an area of scholarship where the effects of ideology and lack of firm research data are probably greatest (Wilson and Herrnstein, 1985).

There is evidence to indicate that the quality of family life is more important than its economic circumstances and composition in understanding how children from relatively poor families grow up to become responsible adults. Werner and Smith (1982) completed a 20-year longitudinal study of all children born in the Hawaiian Island of Kauai in 1955. Most of the approximately 600 children were Asian or Polynesian and lived in low-income families who were dependent on the agricultural industry on the island. Many of these children experienced a variety of difficulties in growing up in addition to poverty, including birth defects, serious parental discord, absent or unemployed fathers, and siblings with conduct or school problems. Most children who experienced four or more of these problems by two years of age developed serious learning or behavior problems, including delinquency, by age 18. Some "high risk" youths did not have these difficulties. Boys who, despite poverty and family crises, became responsible, healthy adults were distinguished from the problem youths in that they tended to be the first born; were active, affectionate infants who were able to elicit positive responses from adults (especially the mother); experienced few early health problems; had a close bond with the mother during the first two years of life; and grew up in a family with four or fewer children.

Aside from the matter of family composition, are there specific child-rearing practices of black families that lead to higher rates of delinquency among their offspring than those of white families—controlling for social class? Again, we are on uncertain ground (Wilson and Herrnstein, 1985). There is a lack of definitive research data from which to draw firm conclusions. That we know very little about the child-rearing practices of black families, and their consequences, is surprising, given the great concern expressed on this issue (Joint Center for Political Studies, 1983).

Subcultural Views

It has been argued that some blacks engage in delinquent behavior because they distrust or reject the values and interests of mainstream society. Silberman (1978) echoed this explanation in his much-discussed book. According to this theory, the effects of slavery, racism, and discrimination led to a growing sense of anger among blacks, which could not be expressed safely. Black rage became intense among black males, who were psychologically emasculated by white society. Unable to conceal their anger or continue to turn it inward, black crime began to increase when blacks no longer feared whites and discovered that "whites are intimidated by their very presence" (Silberman, 1978, p. 208). Young black males could express their rage directly and physically, and this expression of anger turned out to be cumulative rather than cathartic (Grier and Cobbs, 1968).

How much support exists for this theory? Silberman is not able to provide direct evidence of a link between subcultural values and criminal behavior. However, to be fair, this has been a very difficult area to research—given that culture is such a pervasive phenomenon and that its influences are often subtle and hard to track (Wilson and Herrnstein, 1985).

There is some evidence to suggest that subcultural identification is a relatively more salient feature in the delinquent behavior of black male youths than their white counterparts. Harris and Lewis (1974) found among the youthful New Jersey correctional institution inmates they studied that the self-esteem of the black inmates increased as the expected value of crime increased, whereas the self-esteem of the white inmates decreased. The more black inmates identified with the criminal class, the greater their self-esteem. This result suggests a greater acceptance of illegal activities in the areas in which the black inmates live.

McCord et al. (1969), Rosenthal et al. (1976), and Mancini (1980) pursued descriptive-exploratory efforts to identify forms of adaptation to black ghetto life, some of which are conducive to delinquent behavior. McCord et al. (1969) interviewed male youths living in the ghettos of Houston, Watts, and Oakland; Rosenthal et al. (1976) and Mancini (1980) carried out their work in the Roxbury section of Boston. A number of adaptation styles identified in both study efforts involved engaging in delinquent activities. Youths found to reflect the "exploiter" and "rebel without a cause" styles (McCord et al., 1969), "staying clean," "going under," and "getting over" styles (Rosenthal et al., 1976), and "tough guy" style (Mancini, 1980) were more delinquent than black youths enacting other modes of adjustment. The delinquency-prone adaptation styles are cultural "options" which seem attractive to young, black males who feel alienated from white society and perceive few achievable routes to conventional success being available to them.

As noted previously, Tracy and Piper (1982) found black male youths to be significantly more likely to be a member of a gang than white males and that gang membership was strongly related to engaging in delinquent behavior, particularly violent offenses. Gangs, which are more prevalent in socioeconomically deprived areas, represent an important means of affiliation in these settings.

It is important to avoid oversimplifying the subcultural perspective. While black males are disproportionately represented in delinquent behavior, many blacks do not engage in criminal activity, even though they, too, are subjected to the same influences as black delinquent youths. Deviant behavior life-styles need to be regarded as several of a number of adaptations that black male adolescents make to life in the inner city, many of which are nondeviant. McCord et al. (1969), Rosenthal et al. (1976), and

Mancini (1980) suggest several of these nondeviant adaptive styles. However, this work, although provocative, is basically descriptive in nature and limited in its generalizability. Subcultural views of delinquency among black male adolescents need to reflect the complex set of historical and sociocultural factors, together with individual differences, that are involved in their disaffiliation with mainstream society.

Comparing the Four Theories

Considering the complexity of human nature, it is probable that each theory is partially correct. We wait for further research to permit us to synthesize the key concepts of each theory into more comprehensive, casual models. Although disappointing from a policy perspective, it is premature to claim definitive knowledge in a situation where there is none. Whatever the ultimate form this theoretical development takes, it would be surprising if it did not give an important place to the adverse effects, including delinquency, which result from youths who feel deeply alienated from and perceive little or no stake in the values and activities of conventional society.

Representation of Black Youth in the Juvenile Justice System

Whatever the complex reasons accounting for delinquent behavior among black youth, there is consistent evidence that they are overrepresented in the processing activities of various juvenile justice system agencies—from point of arrest through incarceration. The 1945 Philadelphia cohort study (Wolfgang, Figlio, and Sellin, 1972) identified both race and SES effects in the decision to arrest offenders. Forty-four percent of nonwhite delinquents were officially arrested, compared to 23 percent of white offenders. The arrest rate difference was only slightly less for SES; 24 percent of high SES offenders were arrested compared to 39 percent of low SES delinquents.

The discrepancy persisted when race and SES were considered together. For high SES youths, 41 percent of nonwhites compared to 20 percent of whites were arrested. Among low SES youngsters, 44 percent of nonwhites were arrested compared to 28 percent of whites. Additional analyses showed that whether a youth was a one-time offender or a recidivist, he was more likely to be arrested if he were nonwhite.

The researchers further examined the 1945 cohort data to deter-mine whether these arrest rate differences were not due to race per se but reflected the greater likelihood that recidivists, Index offenders, and youths committing offenses with high severity fell into categories which disproportionately involved nonwhites. Anal-ysis showed these factors did not explain the race difference in arrest rates.

These race and SES arrest rate differences persisted for the 1958 Philadelphia cohort, although at a lower level. In regard to race, 51 percent of the whites compared to 60 percent of the nonwhites were arrested. In terms of SES, 53 percent of high SES delin-quents were arrested versus 60 percent of low SES offenders. The joint race and SES association with the decision to arrest was found in the 1958 cohort data, although at a lower level than in the 1945 data set. Among high SES youth, 56 percent of nonwhites versus 51 percent of whites were arrested. For low SES youngsters, 61 percent of the nonwhites were arrested compared to 53 percent of the whites. When the researchers examined for race effects, controlling for whether the youth were recidivists, Index offen-ders, or involved in committing offenses with high severity, the race differences in arrest rates remained. Additional analyses showed that whether a youth was a one-time offender or recidivist, he was more likely to be arrested if he were nonwhite (Tracy, Wolfgang, and Figlio, 1985).

In a further analysis of the NYS data set, Huizinga and Elliott (1986) have come up with similar results. In 1979–80 and 1984–85, a search of police records was done for each survey respondent in each location where he or she lived between 1976–1979 and 1976–1983, respectively.

The researchers found that only 16 percent of the self-reported offenders were arrested and that the youths who were arrested were unrepresentative of the larger group of active, self-reported offenders. Of those arrested, about 64 percent were referred to juvenile or adult court; and, of those referred to court, some 2 to 10 percent were incarcerated. Concern about the underreporting of delinquent behavior by black youths does not affect the basic conclusions we now report.

Comparison of the prevalence rates of black and white youths on measures of general delinquency, UCR Index offenses, felony assault, and felony theft offenses for the years 1976 through 1980 with the youths' arrest records led the researchers (Huizinga and Elliott, 1986, p. 8) to conclude: "It does not appear that differences in incarceration rates between racial groups can be explained by differences in the proportions of persons of each racial group that engage in delinquent behavior." Similar results emerged when the incidence (or frequency) rates of the black and white youths on these measures were studied.

In terms of arrest, and consistent with the findings of the two Philadelphia cohort studies, blacks were found to be at a much higher risk of arrest than white youngsters. Among non-Index offenders, blacks have a much higher chance of being arrested for an Index offense than whites (at a 7:1 ratio). For Index offenders, black offenders have significantly higher arrest rates for Index offenses, compared to whites (approximately 2:1). These findings suggest that the risk of being apprehended and charged with an Index offense is significantly greater among black youths who report involvement in the same kinds of offenses as white youngsters.

Huizinga and Elliott (1986) are aware that SES differences between black and white youth could affect their results. The findings of the 1945 and 1958 Philadelphia cohort studies lend support to their assertion, although they do not lead one to expect that the race differences in arrest and incarceration will be eliminated.

Huizinga and Elliott's (1986) finding that black, non-Index offenders have a greater chance of being arrested for an Index offense is striking. In this vein, Gibbs (1984, pp. 8–9) observes that black youth may be arrested more frequently for minor offenses because police patrol inner-city neighborhoods more intensively and because of police responses to the "antiauthority demeanor" of black youth.

For most youth, the detention center is the gateway into the juvenile justice system. Based on the research of Schwartz and his associates (Schwartz et al., 1986; Krisberg et al., 1986), there are disturbing indications that black male youth are being disproportionately *committed* to these facilities in increasing numbers. These researchers examined Children in Custody survey data, a biennial survey administered by the U.S. Census Bureau and involving all known publicly operated juvenile detention and correctional facilities. They found that, although the number and rate of admissions to detention centers declined between 1977 and 1982, there has been a substantial increase in the number of juveniles who are committed to detention centers on a short-term basis for violating court orders or failing to adhere to the conditions of their probation. The practice of committing juveniles to secure detention is quite popular and appears to be spreading throughout the nation. The number of states reporting the practice more than doubled between 1977 and 1982.

Most poignantly for our discussion, the data indicate a substantial increase in the number of minority youths who are being confined in detention centers. Minority youth currently constitute over half of the youth confined on any one particular day. This problem is particularly acute for black male youth. In 1977, black male youngsters comprised 31.3 percent of the youth confined on a particular day; this rate increased to 32.6 percent in 1979; and, in 1982, the rate reached 36.9 percent. During the same period, the confinement of white male youth declined from 54.9 percent in 1977 to 51.6 percent in 1979 to 45.2 percent in 1982 (Schwartz et al., 1986).

The rates per 100,000 white and black male youth incarcerated in public juvenile detention centers and training schools in 1979 and 1982 are most telling. In 1979, the incarceration rates for blacks in detention centers and training schools were 125.2 and 348.2, respectively; comparable rates for white youth were 35.2 and 85.9. For 1982, the black male incarceration rate in detention centers was 179.8 (a 43.6 percent increase over 1979); the training school incarceration rate was 479.2 (a 37.5 percent increase over 1979). On the other hand, white male youth 1982 incarceration rates in public detention centers (43.1 percent) and training schools (96.6 percent) showed much smaller increases over the 1979 rates (22.4 and 12.4 percent, respectively).

Differences Between Black and White Male Youth Entering a Juvenile Detention Center

What demographic, referral history, psychiatric history, alcohol and other drug use, sexual and physical abuse experience, special education, and substance abuse treatment experience differences exist between black and white male youth entering the juvenile detention center? Some insight into this important topic is provided by an ongoing triage-screening project we are pursuing in a regional juvenile detention center in Florida (Dembo et al., 1986).

Project Methods

Description of the Facility. Our triage-screening activities take place in a modern, regional, state-operated detention center located in Tampa. Although the center has a bed capacity of 93 detainees, it averages over 105 children each day. During times of overcrowding, youths sleep on mattresses on the dorm floors.

There are three dorms for male detainees, and one dorm for 12 girls.

The Triage-Screening Process.   The project, which is supported by general revenue funds from the Florida Legislature, seeks to identify youth who are experiencing mental/emotional or substance abuse problems and to involve these youth and their families in appropriate community-based services. The project is a collaborative effort involving the University of South Florida, Department of Criminal Justice; Northside Community Mental Health Center (NCMHC); and the Florida Department of Health and Rehabilitative Services (HRS).

Each day, the two full-time mental health counselors who are working at the detention center on this project are informed about youth who have been ordered into secure detention that day by a juvenile court judge. The counselors are employed by the NCMHC. Since there is a 3 to 1 ratio of male to female detainees who are ordered to secure detention, and we lack the resources to screen every detained youth (although this would be ideal), all girls ordered into secure detention and a 50 percent random sample of boys are evaluated.

The evaluations involve completion of a voluntary screening interview form, which gathers the following information about the youths:

1. Demographic characteristics (gender, age, ethnicity, occupations of the primary care givers in whose household the youth lives).
2. Reasons for referral to juvenile court.
3. Psychiatric/medical history.
4. The frequency and recency of alcohol and other drug use (marijuana/hashish, inhalants, LSD or other hallucinogens, cocaine, heroin, other illicit drugs such as MPTP or "China White," and the nonmedical use of sedatives, tranquilizers, stimulants, or analgesics).
5. The frequency of experiencing 9 different adverse consequences of using each claimed drug during the 12 months preceding the screening interview ((1) missed school, (2) did poorly in school work, (3) got into trouble with teachers or principal, (4) had an accident, (5) got the shakes or depressed (down) unless kept on using the drug, (6) got into trouble with one's family, (7) got into trouble with friends, (8) got into trouble with the police, and (9) got sick or ill);
6. Sexual abuse history.
7. Physical abuse history.
8. Current mental status.

In addition to this information, urinalysis is performed for each youth assigned to receive screening/triage. Urine samples are obtained as soon as possible after the youth are ordered into secure detention (usually 24 hours or less after they have entered the detention center) to identify traces of various substances before they metabolize. Participation in the urine testing is voluntary.

Referral history information is also obtained on each youth from agency records, which document all contacts he or she has had with the juvenile court. Referral reasons include physical abuse, sexual exploitation, mental injury, neglect, status offenses, misdemeanor offenses, and felony offenses.

Each screening interview takes approximately 30 minutes to complete. From the information provided, the screening staff make one of four decisions regarding each screened youth:

1. Refer for mental health follow-up;
2. Refer to an outreach worker from one of our three collaborating substance abuse treatment programs for an assessment of youth's treatment needs;
3. Refer for mental health follow-up and an evaluation of substance abuse treatment needs; or
4. No subsequent follow-up or referral indicated.

Youth who are referred for mental health follow-up are 12 years of age or younger and/or have a history of psychiatric hospitalization or are on psychotropic drugs, are sexual abusers or abused, are suicidal, and/or have a physical abuse history. Youngsters who claim to have been drunk or very high on alcohol six or more times in the 12 months preceding the screening interview and claim to have experienced two or more different adverse consequences of alcohol use during the previous 12 months are referred for substance abuse evaluation. In addition, youngsters claiming to have used any of the other drugs probed 11 or more times in their lives, and to have reached or exceeded the adverse consequence threshold just noted, are also referred for substance abuse assessment.

Placing Troubled Youth in Needed Services.   Once it has been determined that a youngster needs mental health follow-up or referral to a drug program outreach worker for further evaluation, or both, efforts are made to place the youth in needed treatment services. The project's referral and placement activities link youngsters with needed services and, to this end, seek to build accountability into the assessment process. If a youth is believed to need mental health and/or alcohol-other substance abuse treatment services, the particular counselor or outreach worker assigned to the case is expected to seek the youth's placement in this service and to inform project staff of the results. This aspect of the project's work reflects our appreciation that, in order to be beneficial, the screening-triage process has to provide troubled youth with the services they need. Attempts are made to involve youngsters' families in treatment planning.

Participation Rates.   Over 90 percent of the youth we contact each month participate in the screening process. We believe this high response rate is a result of the quality service we provide, detainees' belief in the integrity of the project staff, the perceived value of the project in providing needed services, and our efforts to protect the interests of the detainees and, when possible, the information they share.

Demographic and Offense/Referral History

Overall, 332 unduplicated male detainees were screened during the first six months of the project. Of these, 109 (32.8 percent) were black, 202 (60.8 percent) were Anglo, 17 (5.1 percent) were Hispanic, and four (1.2 percent) were of an "other" ethnic group affiliation. The proportion of black male youth in the detainee sample is greater than the 17 percent representation of this ethnic group among male youth 10–17 years of age in the county from which most of the detainees entering the center derive. However, since 30 of these youth lacked complete data on all the variables included in our analysis, the following discussion focuses on the 204 nonblack, predominantly white males (this group includes a few Hispanic youth) and 98 black males included in the main analyses we report. No significant demographic, referral history, psychiatric history, alcohol and other drug use, sexual victimization, physical abuse, special education or alcohol/other substance abuse treatment experience characteristic differences were found to exist between the 302 included and 30 excluded youth on any of these variables.

The subjects averaged 15 years of age (s.d. = 1.43). Available information documented the low to moderate socioeconomic status range of the households represented by the youth in the survey. For example, only 10 percent of the youths' primary care givers held an executive, professional, or technical-type job; 9 percent were in service occupations (e.g., cooks, waiters/waitresses), 10 percent were skilled or semiskilled workers, and 3 percent were unskilled workers. Sixteen percent of the youths' households were on public assistance/disability support.

In regard to pending charges, a majority of the youth were placed in the detention center as a result of being arrested in burglary or another nondrug felony (primarily property) offense (63 percent), and 12 percent were being detained on nondrug misdemeanor charges. Approximately 5 percent of the youths were placed in secure detention for one or another status offense reason (truancy, running away, or being ungovernable).

Referral histories are routinely obtained on the youth, which document all contacts they have had with the juvenile court. Information on the youths' referrals to juvenile court indicates that relatively few youngsters were ever referred to juvenile court for sexual abuse, mental injury (emotional abuse, emotional neglect), drug misdemeanors, or drug felony reasons. On the other hand, sizable proportions of the detainees had one or more juvenile court referrals for being physically abused or neglected; and a near majority or majority of the youth were referred to juvenile court for status offenses, nondrug misdemeanors, or nondrug felony offenses. Further, substantial proportions of the youth were referred to juvenile court on four or more occasions for nondrug misdemeanor (29 percent) or nondrug felony (38 percent) offenses. According to these data, many youth who were screened had repeated contact with the juvenile court.

Psychiatric History

Screened youth are routinely asked a number of questions regarding their psychiatric histories, including whether they have ever seen a psychiatrist or social worker, ever been hospitalized for their nerves, ever tried to hurt themselves, or ever taken medication for their nerves. These data indicate that a sizable proportion of this group has experienced psychological problems. Forty-eight percent of the 302 detainees have seen a psychiatrist or social worker at least once in their lives, 11 percent claimed to have been hospitalized for their nerves, 10 percent indicated they had tried to hurt themselves, and 10 percent noted they had taken medication for their nerves.

Sexual Victimization

Drawing upon the work of Finkelhor (1979), a number of questions were asked regarding the subjects' history of sexual victimization by adults (someone over the age of 18), including strangers, friends, or family members. Each youth was asked if he or she ever had a sexual experience with an adult. Respondents answering "yes" to this question were asked how many of these experiences they had. Youth claiming more than one such experience were asked to think back to the first time they had a sexual experience with an adult.

All youth having one or more sexual experiences with an adult were asked a number of specific questions regarding their first incident with an adult, including data about their age, the age of the adult, how they were related to the adult, whether they were threatened or forced to take part, and their reaction to the experience.

In line with Finkelhor's (1979) operational definition, all children who were 13 years of age or younger at the time of their first sexual experience with a person over the age of 18 were considered to have been sexually victimized. In addition, youths whose first sexual experience with an adult occurred between the ages of 14 and 17, and who claimed they were forced or who reacted to the experience with fear or shock or had this experience with their parent or stepparent, were also considered to have been sexually victimized.

Overall, 11 percent of the 302 youths were sexually victimized during their first sexual experience with an adult. For 76 percent of the victimized youths, this victimization first occurred at age 13 or younger. These sexual victimization rates should be regarded as conservative estimates of this experience. Our restrictive definition of sexual abuse, which we are in the process of refining, does not capture a full range of information on this experience. Youth having more than one sexual experience with an adult may not have been abused on the first occurrence. In addition, information is not collected on the youths' sexual abuse experiences involving a person 18 years of age or younger. Further, as we advise the youth, Florida state law requires that we inform appropriate officials if we learn a youngster is being sexually abused at home.

Physical Abuse

The work of Straus and his associates (Straus, 1983; Straus, Gelles, and Steinmetz, 1980; Gelles, 1979; Straus, 1979) was used to develop six items designed to determine the youths' physical abuse experiences with an adult (someone over the age of 18). In particular, the youth were asked whether they had ever (1) been beaten or *really* hurt by being hit (but not with anything), (2) been beaten or hit with a whip, strap, or belt, (3) been beaten or hit with something "hard" (like a club or stick), (4) been shot with a gun, injured with a knife, or had some other "weapon" used against them, (5) been hurt badly enough by an adult to require (need) a doctor or bandages or other medical treatment, and (6) spent time in a hospital because of being physically injured by an adult.

Results showed 17 to 33 percent of the 302 youths claimed to have had the physical abuse experiences noted in items, 1, 2, or 3 above. In addition, 15 percent of the youth claimed three or more of the six experiences.

Normative data on this behavior are difficult to obtain. However, available information from the 1976 national survey on family violence (Gelles, 1979; Straus, Gelles, and Steinmetz, 1980) found parent-to-child violence prevalence rates for being hit with something (20 percent), beaten (4 percent), threatened with a knife or gun (3 percent), or using a knife or gun (3 percent) that were lower than those reported by the youths we interviewed.

Again, the physical abuse data we obtained should be regarded as conservative estimates of this experience. Florida state law requires that we inform appropriate authorities if we learn that a youth is being physically abused at home. During the time period we collected these data, we did not routinely gather information on the youths' physical abuse experiences at the hands of a person 18 years of age or younger.

Alcohol and Other Drug Use

A number of questions on drug use were adopted from the 1979 NIDA national survey (Fishburne, Abelson, and Cisin, 1980) to determine the youths' use of ten categories of drugs: (1) alcohol, (2) marijuana/hashish, (3) inhalants, (4) hallucinogens, (5) cocaine, (6) heroin, and the nonmedical use of (7) sedatives, (8) tranquilizers, (9) stimulants, and (10) analgesics. Since we pursued separate analyses of alcohol use and illicit drug taking (categories 2 through 10), these measures are discussed individually.

Alcohol Use. Two key questions were asked about the youths' alcohol use: (1) the most recent time they used alcohol and (2) how many different days in the past 30 days they used alcohol. Comparison of the youths' answers to these questions with those obtained from the 12–17-year-old youths surveyed by NIDA in 1982 (Miller, et al., 1983) indicates a much higher level of alcohol use to exist among the detainees we studied. For example, 86 percent of the detained youths claimed they used alcohol one or more times in their lives compared to 65 percent of the NIDA survey youths; 65 percent of the detainees indicated they used alcohol within the past month compared to 27 percent of the youths surveyed by NIDA; and 20 percent of the detention center youngsters said they had used alcohol on 5 or more different days in the 30-day period preceding their interview versus 6 percent of the NIDA survey group.

Use of Other Drugs. Relatively high rates of the use of illicit drugs were uncovered. As Table 4-3 shows, 33 percent of the 302 youth claimed to have used marijuana/hashish 100 or more times in their lives; 12 percent indicated they used cocaine, and 10 percent noted they used stimulants nonmedically 11 or more times in their lives to get high.

These drug use rates are much higher than those reported by the 12–17-year-old youths interviewed in the 1982 NIDA national household survey (Miller, et al., 1983), substantially higher than those reported by New York State seventh to twelfth graders surveyed in 1983 (N.Y.S. Division of Substance Abuse Services, 1984), and higher than the usage reported by seventh- to twelfth-grade youngsters in a neighboring county who were surveyed in October 1983 (Operation Par, 1984).

Special Education and Substance Abuse Treatment Experiences

Sizable proportions of the male detainees indicated they had problems in their school work and in their use of alcohol or other drugs. Forty-four percent of the youth claimed they were currently in or had been in a special education program, such as an alternative learning or learning disabilities program (see Murray, 1976), and 20 percent of the youth noted they had received treatment for an alcohol or other substance abuse problem.

Pooling the Six Months' Screen Information

A major consideration in our preliminary study of the data focused on whether there was a statistical basis for pooling the six months'

Table 4–3   Lifetime Use of Various Illicit Drugs Claimed by Black and Nonblack Male Detainees Screened from November 1985 Through April 1986

	Never Used (%)	Used 1 or 2 times (%)	Used 3 to 10 times (%)	Used 11 to 99 times (%)	Used 100 or more times (%)	Total (n = 301 or 302) (%)
Marijuana/hashish	23.8	11.6	18.5	12.9	33.1	99.9
Inhalants	78.8	5.6	8.6	4.0	3.0	100.0
Hallucinogens	80.4	8.6	7.0	3.7	0.3	100.0
Cocaine	65.9	11.6	10.9	7.9	3.6	99.9
Heroin	98.0	1.3	0.7	—	—	100.0
Nonmedical use of:						
Stimulants	73.8	8.6	7.9	5.3	4.3	99.9
Sedatives	87.7	4.3	3.3	3.6	1.0	99.9
Tranquilizers	87.4	5.0	3.6	2.6	1.3	99.9
Analgesics	90.1	3.6	3.0	2.3	1.0	100.0

screen information for analysis purposes. Accordingly, variable comparisons of demographic, psychiatric history, alcohol and other drug use, physical abuse, sexual victimization, special education, and alcohol or other substance abuse treatment experience were made across the six-month data collection period. These analyses found few significant differences in these characteristics across the November 1985 to April 1986 period. Hence, it was decided to pool the six months' screen data into a combined data set for further analyses.

Developing Indices of Physical Abuse, Alcohol, and Other Drug Use

Attention next focused on combining the multiple measures of physical abuse, alcohol use, and other drug use into summary indices of these experiences for use in further analyses. It was recognized, however, that these variables needed to be incorporated into the analysis in a manner that respected possible ethnic group differences that might exist in their patterns of relationship.

Physical Abuse. Examination of the equality of the covariance matrices of the six physical-abuse items across black and nonblack detainee groups was pursued using LISREL VI (Jöreskog and Sörbom, 1984). This analysis tests the hypotheses that a similar factor structure underlying these variables exists in both groups.

Our initial analyses using physical-abuse items 4 to 6 encountered difficulties due to the relatively low variance of these items. Hence, the number of these three different modes of physical abuse was calculated and included as a variable in the analysis. A good fit across the two ethnic groups was obtained for the covariance matrices involving the first three physical-abuse items and the summed variable involving physical-abuse items 4 to 6 (chi-square = 11.66, *df* = 10, *p* = .308; goodness-of-fit index = 0.963). These items were combined into a regression factor score for use in further analyses. According to the manner in which this score was derived, the higher the score the larger the number of different types of physical-abuse experiences claimed.

Alcohol Use. Examination of the intercorrelation of the two-alcohol-use variables found a respectable, positive relationship to exist between the recency of alcohol use and the number of days in the past 30 days alcohol was used for black and nonblack male detainees (black males: $r = .547$, $n = 107$, $p < .001$; nonblack males: $r = .451$, $n = 219$, $p < .001$). Examination of the equality of the covariance matrices of these two variables across the male detainee groups was next pursued involving LISREL VI (Jöreskog and Sörbom, 1984). A poor fit was obtained (chi-square $=$ 31.38, $df = 3, p < .001$).

Based on these results, youths' use of alcohol in the past 30 days and their recency of alcohol use were included as separate variables in further analyses. For each variable, the higher the score the more recent and the greater number of days in the past 30 days the use of alcohol was claimed.

Use of Other Drugs. Following the work of Single, Kandel, and Faust (1974), sedatives, tranquilizers, stimulants, and analgesics were combined into a single variable called "pills," based on the maximum lifetime frequency of use claimed for any of these drugs. Heroin, cocaine, and hallucinogens, which Single, Kandel, and Faust (1974) found at the extreme of the Guttman scale but which they found differed in order for blacks and whites, were also combined into a single variable called "hard drugs." Combining these infrequently used substances (see Table 4–3) in the same manner as described for the pills variable provided greater stability to the analysis.

Inhalants were not included in the Single, Kandel, and Faust (1974) analysis. Inhalants differ from other substances in being more prevalent among younger users (Uppal, Babstrand Schmeidler, 1977; N.Y.S. Division of Substance Abuse Services, 1978, 1984). For this reason, it is relatively likely to be the first substance for young but not older initiators. This suggested separating inhalants from other substances used.

Initial correlation analysis indicated positive and moderate to high relationships to exist among the marijuana/hashish, pills, inhalants, and hard-drug variables for the black and nonblack male detainee groups. Accordingly, examination of the equality of the covariance matrices of the four drug variables for the two ethnic groups was undertaken using LISREL VI (Jöreskog and Sörbom, 1984). A poor fit was obtained for each of the analyses we pursued, which involved all four, and various combinations, of the drug-use variables. Based on these results, each of the four drug-use variables was separately included in further analyses. For each drug-use variable, the higher the score the more frequent the claimed lifetime use of the various illicit drugs.

Results

A stepwise discriminant analysis was performed to learn whether demographic, referral history, psychiatric history, alcohol and other drug use, sexual/physical abuse characteristics, and special education and alcohol/other substance abuse treatment experiences discriminated between the black and nonblack male detainee groups (Bennett and Bowers, 1976; Klecka, 1980). Determination of inclusion in further study of the data was based on each variable's Wilks' lambda value (an inverse measure of group discriminating power) and its equivalent F ratio.

The characteristics of the one discriminant function resulting from a stepwise analysis of the predictor variables were quite good. The function had a respectable canonical correlation (0.5468) and good group discriminating power (Wilks' lambda = 0.7009). The chi-square test of Wilks' lambda was used to test the significance of the discriminant function. Although the discriminant function was based only on the 12 characteristics that contributed substantially to differentiating between the black male and nonblack male detainee groups, a conservative test of significance was used, based on the 20 variables originally used in the analysis. Despite this conservative test of significance, the discriminant function remained statistically significant (chi-square = 104.47, $df = 20$, $p < .001$).

The means of the 12 predictor variables differentiating the black and nonblack male detainee groups, and their associated discriminant function structure coefficients, are presented in Table 4–4. Lifetime frequency of use of marijuana/hashish and maximum lifetime frequency of nonmedical use of pills are highly correlated with the discriminant function.

According to the results shown in Table 4–4, black male detainees, in comparison to nonblack male detainees, are younger, less likely to have ever seen a psychiatrist or social worker, less often claim they have tried to hurt themselves, have a higher rate of referral to juvenile court for neglect, have a lower rate of referral to juvenile court for status offense reasons, have a higher rate of referral for nondrug misdemeanors (see Table 4–5 for a detailed description of each of these referral categories), have not as recently used alcohol, have on average used alcohol on a fewer number of days in the 30 days prior to entering the detention center, have a lower claimed lifetime frequency of use of marijuana/hashish, have a lower maximum lifetime frequency of nonmedical use of pills, less often claim to have received treatment for an alcohol or other drug abuse problem, and a smaller proportion have been involved in a special education program.

The results of the discriminant analysis suggest that the white male detainees' greater involvement in alcohol, other drug use, and problem behavior that brought them to the attention of the juvenile justice system is related to a higher degree of emotional/psychological dysfunction than is the case for the black male

Table 4–4 Means and Discriminant Function Structure Coefficients of the 12 Predictor Variables for the Black and Nonblack Male Groups (n = 302)

Predictor Variable	Black Male Detainees	Nonblack Male Detainees	Structure Coefficients
1. Age	15.24	15.31	.0346
2. Ever seen a psychiatrist or social worker	0.31	0.56	.3733
3. Ever tried to hurt self	0.04	0.13	.2184
4. Number of referrals to juvenile court for neglect	0.97	0.65	−.1595
5. Number of referrals to juvenile court for status offenses	0.76	1.15	.1655
6. Number of referrals to juvenile court for nondrug misdemeanors	3.39	2.09	−.3625
7. Recency of alcohol use	2.85	3.97	.4278
8. Number of different days in the 30 days prior to entering the detention center alcohol was used	2.58	4.02	.1616
9. Lifetime frequency of use of marijuana/hashish	1.38	2.59	.5929
10. Maximum lifetime frequency of nonmedical use of sedatives, minor tranquilizers, stimulants or analgesics	0.13	0.93	.5184
11. Ever received treatment for an alcohol/other drug abuse problem	0.05	0.27	.4063
12. Ever involved in a special education program	0.41	0.46	.0690

Note: According to the manner in which the means were calculated, the higher the mean, the older the youths, the larger the proportion of youths claiming to have ever seen a psychiatrist or social worker, the larger the proportion of youths indicating they ever tried to hurt themselves, the greater the number of referrals to juvenile court for neglect, the greater the number of referrals to juvenile court for status offense reasons, the larger the number of referrals to juvenile court for nondrug misdemeanors, the more recent the use of alcoholic beverages, the greater the number of different days in the 30 days preceding entry into the detention center alcohol was used, the higher the lifetime frequency of use of marijuana/hashish, the higher the maximum lifetime frequency of nonmedical use of sedatives, minor tranquilizers, stimulants or analgesics, the larger the proportion of youths claiming they ever received treatment for an alcohol/other drug abuse problem, and the larger the proportion of youths indicating they were involved in a special education program.

Means (Centroids) of the black and nonblack male detainee groups on the discriminant function: black males = 0.9393; nonblack males = 0.4512.

youths. On the other hand, the black male detainees' problem behavior appears related to impoverished home and family conditions that led to their affiliation with a delinquent life-style. Our findings are consistent with those of Harris and Lewis's (1974) research which was discussed earlier. The white male youth who engaged in delinquent behavior in degree and type sufficient to bring them to the attention of juvenile justice agencies appear to have moved a greater psychological and ethical distance than the black youth, who, perhaps, come from environmental settings in which delinquency is more prevalent and, hence, regarded as less unacceptable by their peers.

Conclusions

The above discussion leads to a number of important conclusions that can inform research, policy formulation, and program development. First, it is critical that more systematic research information of high quality be obtained on delinquency and drug use among black males. Ideally, these data should be gathered from long-term, longitudinal studies involving black and white male youths growing up in a large urban area (where delinquency rates are highest). This work should gather information on the factors relating to delinquent behavior among black male youth posited by the constitutional factors, economic deprivation, inadequate socialization, and subcultural theories reviewed earlier. These research efforts should be interdisciplinary in nature and work toward the development of comprehensive causal models. Joint undertakings by federal agencies are needed to provide the kind of research base from which to create more effective delinquency reduction and prevention programs than have characterized our efforts to date.

Second, the issue of bias in the juvenile justice system, reflected in the disproportionate rates of arrest for black male youth, their placement in detention centers, and commitment to public juvenile correctional facilities, requires immediate action. Public awareness needs to be raised about this disgraceful situation. Individual states, especially those permitting commitment to detention centers, need to review their policies and the working practices and decision-making activities that produce this deplorable outcome. We need to identify and study those jurisdictions which have lower rates of black male youth represented in various stages of the operation of the juvenile justice system to learn what

Table 4–5 Juvenile Court Referral Reasons by Category

Nondrug Felonies	Nondrug Misdemeanors
murder/manslaughter	assault and/or battery (not aggravated)
attempted murder/manslaughter	prostitution
sexual battery	sex offenses not included in felony category and
other felonious sex offenses	excluding prostitution
armed robbery	petty larceny (excluding retail theft)
other robbery	retail theft (shoplifting)
arson	receiving stolen property—under $100
burglary (breaking and entering)	concealed weapon (except firearms)
auto theft	disorderly conduct
grand larceny (excluding auto theft)	criminal mischief (vandalism)
receiving stolen property	trespassing
concealed firearm	loitering and prowling
aggravated assault and/or battery	violation of hunting, fishing, and boating laws
forgery	resisting arrest without violence
escape from training school, secure detention, or community-based residential program	unauthorized use of motor vehicle
resisting arrest with violence	other misdemeanor
shooting/throwing a deadly missile into an occupied dwelling/vehicle	
other felony	

Physical Abuse	Neglect	Status Offenses
skull fracture/brain damage/ subdural hematoma	malnutrition/deprived of food	local (intra-county) runaway
internal injuries	failure to thrive	runaway from other Florida
bone fracture	deprived of clothing	county
sprain/dislocation	deprived of shelter	out-of-state runaway
bruises/welts	medical neglect	truancy
cuts/punctures/bites	failure to provide medical care (religious reasons)	beyond control
burns/scalds	unattended/unsupervised	
asphyxiation/suffocation/drowning	conditions hazardous to health	
intentional poisoning	abandonment	
confinement/bizarre punishment	other neglect	
excessive corporal punishment/ beatings (injury unknown)		
other physical abuse		

Sexual Abuse/Exploitation	Mental Injury	Misdemeanor Drug Offense
sexual battery (incest)	emotional abuse	misdemeanor violation of drug laws (excluding marijuana)
sexual battery (not incest)	emotional neglect	misdemeanor marijuana offense
fondling/other sexual abuse		possession of alcoholic beverages
sexual exploitation—child pornography		other alcohol offenses
other sexual exploitation (including prostitution)		

Felony Drug Offenses
felony violation of drug laws (excluding marijuana)
felony marijuana offense

SOURCE: From the HRS, Children, Youth and Families, Client Information System: Selected Elements and Codes for Intake Staff.

ameliorating factors can be applied in high-rate states (Krisberg et al., 1986). In addition, the training of personnel in the juvenile justice system needs to include exposure to information on the nature and long-term consequences of this problem. Policies guiding the use of the broad discretionary powers often given to these personnel should also be established. Further, the activities of various agencies within the juvenile justice system need to be monitored to ensure compliance with these policies. The social injustice reflected in current practices threatens great societal turmoil in the future.

The third conclusion we draw is that efforts are needed to identify youth at high risk of future delinquency and drug use and to involve them and their families in meaningful intervention programs. The detention center represents an important gateway into the juvenile justice system where these activities can take place. This line of work, such as that being pursued in Florida (Dembo et al., 1986) and in California (Feltman, 1986), urges that the purposes of detention be redefined to include diagnostic-assessment activities and the linking of troubled youth to relevant community service agencies. Involving these youth, and their families, in meaningful intervention programs is cost-effective and increases the likelihood that many of these youth will redirect their lives to socially constructive goals. In particular, efforts should be made in specific communities to identify respected individuals who can serve as role models for high-risk youth. These persons should be action-oriented and have the social and interpersonal skills necessary to work with these youth and various community agencies in developing ethnographically focused intervention programs. Strategies for pursuing these efforts are detailed elsewhere (Dembo and Burgos, 1976; Dembo et al., 1978).

Our fourth and final conclusion is that whatever the ultimate causes of delinquent behavior—particularly violence against persons—among black male youth it would be contrary to experience if an important place were not given to the factors which result in these youth having little stake in conventional society, thus increasing the perceived net benefit of engaging in crime (Wilson and Herrnstein, 1985). Evidence abounds that there are great stressors in the lives of black youth and their families in urban areas. As Gibbs (1984) persuasively documents, these stressors include poverty; educational difficulties, including poor performance in school and lack of communication with educational authorities; high rates of unemployment, particularly among youth; large percentages of babies born out of wedlock; high infant mortality rates; and an alarming increase in suicide rates among black teenagers. This nexus of problems presents a very serious threat to an important part of our social fabric. In a time of declining federal funds for desperately needed community support programs, there is an increased need for coalition building, joint efforts by various constituency groups to press legislators for needed programs, and collaborative undertakings involving civic groups, churches, community agencies, the helping professions, universities, and individually concerned citizens to develop and implement services targeted to the needs of black youth that are reflected in these problems.

These issues are not local concerns; they belong on the national agenda. Delinquency among black youth is deeply connected with the variety of stressors affecting them, their families, and their community. Failure to respond creatively to these problems is as inhumane as it is socially destructive.

References

Bennett, S., and Bowers, D. (1976). *An introduction to multivariate techniques for social and behavior sciences*. New York: Wiley & Sons.

Centers for Disease Control. (1985). Homicide among young black males—United States, 1970–1982. *Morbidity and Mortality Weekly Report* 34: 629–33.

Dembo, R., and Burgos, W. (1976). A framework for developing drug abuse prevention strategies for young people in ghetto areas. *Journal of Drug Education* 6:313–25.

Dembo, R., Burgos, W., Babst, D. V., Schmeidler, J., and La Grand, L. E. (1978). Neighborhood relationships and drug involvement among inner-city junior high school youths: Implications for drug education and prevention programming. *Journal of Drug Education* 8:231–52.

Dembo, R., Washburn, M., Broskowski, A., Getreu, A., and Berry, E. (1986). Development and evaluation of an innovative approach to identify and engage troubled youths in mental health and substance abuse treatment services at entry into secure detention. Paper presented at the Annual Meeting of the Academy of Criminal Justice Sciences, March, Orlando.

Elliott, D. S., and Ageton, S. S. (1980). Reconciling race and class differences in self-reported and official estimates of delinquency. *American Sociological Review* 45:95–110.

Elliott, D. S., and Huizinga, D. (1983). Social class and delinquent behavior in a national youth panel: 1976–1980. *Criminology* 21:149–77.

Elliott, D. S., Ageton, S. S., Huizinga, D., Knowles, B. A., and Canter, R. J. (1983). *The prevalence and incidence of delinquent behavior: 1976–1980*. Boulder, Colo.: Behavioral Research Institute.

Empey, L. T. (1982). *American delinquency: Its meaning and construction*, rev. ed. Homewood, Ill.: Dorsey Press.

Federal Bureau of Investigation. (1985). *Uniform crime reports, 1984*. Washington, D.C.: U.S. Government Printing Office.

Feltman, R. (1986). The Ventura project. Paper presented at the Annual Meeting of the American College of Mental Health Administrators, San Diego.

Finkelhor, D. (1979). *Sexually victimized children*. New York: Free Press.

Fishburne, P. M., Abelson, H. I., and Cisin, I. (1980). *National survey on drug abuse: Main findings—1979*. Rockville, Md.: National Institute on Drug Abuse.

Florida Department of Law Enforcement. (1985). *Crime in Florida: 1984 annual report*. Tallahassee: FDLE.

Gelles, R. J. (1979). *Family violence*. Beverly Hills, Calif.: Sage Publications.

Gibbs, J. T. (1984). *Black adolescents and youth: An endangered species*. *American Journal of Orthopsychiatry* 54:6–21.

Grier, W. H., and Cobbs, P. M. (1968). *Black rage*. New York: Bantam Books.

Harris, A. R., and Lewis, M. (1974). Race and criminal deviance: A study of youthful offenders. Paper presented at the Annual Meeting of the American Sociological Association.

Hindelang, M. J., Hirschi, T., and Weis, J. G. (1981). *Measuring delinquency*. Beverly Hills, Calif.: Sage Publications.

Hirschi, T. (1969). *Causes of delinquency*. Berkeley: University of California Press.

Hirschi, T., and Hindelang, M. J. (1977). Intelligence and delinquency: A revisionist view. *American Sociological Review* 42:571–87.

Huizinga, D., and Elliott, D. S. (1986). Juvenile offenders: Prevalence, offender incidence and arrest rates by race. Boulder, Colo.: Institute of Behavioral Science. Paper presented for the Meeting on Race and the Incarceration of Juveniles, Racine, Wisconsin.

Joint Center for Political Studies. (1983). *A policy framework for racial justice*. Washington, D.C.: Joint Center for Political Studies.

Jöreskog, K. G., and Sörbom, D. (1984). *LISREL VI: Analysis of linear structural relationships by the method of maximum likelihood*. Mooresville, Ind.: Scientific Software, Inc.

Klecka, W. R. (1980). *Discriminant analysis*. Beverly Hills, Calif.: Sage Publications.

Kleinman, P. H., and Lukoff, I. F. (1975). *Generational status, ethnic group and friendship networks: Antecedents of drug use in a ghetto community*. Washington, D.C.: U.S. Department of Justice, Law Enforcement Assistance Administration.

———. (1978). Ethnic differences in factors related to drug use. *Journal of Health and Social Behavior* 19:190–99.

Krisberg, B., Schwartz, I., Fishman, G., Eisikovits, Z., and Guttman, E. (1986). *The incarceration of minority youth*. Minneapolis: Hubert H. Humphrey Institute of Public Affairs, Center for the Study of Youth Policy.

Mancini, J. (1980). *Strategic styles: Coping in the inner city*. Hanover, N.H.: University Press of New England.

McCord, W., Howard J., Friedberg, B., and Harwood, E. (1969). *Life styles in the black ghetto*. New York: Norton.

Mercy, J.A., Smith, J. C., and Rosenberg, M. L. (1983). Homicide among young black males: A descriptive assessment. Paper presented at the Annual Meeting of the American Society of Criminology, Denver.

Miller, J. D., Cisin, I. H., Gardner-Keaton, H., Harrell, A. V., Wirtz, P. W.,

Abelson, H. I.,and Fishburne, P. M. (1983). *National survey on drug abuse: Main findings, 1982*. Rockville, Md.: National Institute on Drug Abuse.

Murray, C. A. (1976). *The link between learning disabilities and juvenile delinquency: Current theory and knowledge*. Washington, D.C.: U.S. Government Printing Office.

National Criminal Justice Information and Statistics Service. (1975a). *Criminal victimization in the United States: 1973*. Advance Report 1 (May). Washington, D.C.: Law Enforcement Assistance Administration.

———. (1975b). *Criminal victimization*. Surveys in the Nation's Five Largest Cities. Washington, D.C.: U.S. Government Printing Office.

———. (1976a). *Criminal victimization in the United States: A comparison of 1973 and 1974 findings*. Washington, D.C.: Law Enforcement Assistance Administration.

———.(1976b). *Criminal victimization in the United States, 1974*. Washington, D.C.: U.S. Government Printing Office.

———. (1977). *Criminal victimization in the United States, 1975*. Washington, D.C.: U.S. Government Printing Office.

———. (1978). *Criminal victimization in the United States, 1976*. Washington, D.C.: U.S. Government Printing Office.

———. (1979a). *Criminal victimization in the United States, 1977*. Washington, D.C.: U.S. Government Printing Office.

———. (1979b). *Criminal victimization in the United States: A description of trends from 1973 to 1977*. Washington, D.C.: U.S. Government Printing Office.

———. (1979c). *Criminal victimization in the United States: Summary of findings 1977–78, changes in crime and trends in 1973*. Washington, D.C.: U.S. Government Printing Office.

New York State Division of Substance Abuse Services. (1978). *Substance use among New York State public and parochial school students in grades 7 through 12*. Albany: N.Y.S. Division of Substance Abuse Services.

———. (1984). *Substance use among New York State public and private school students in grades 7 through 12, 1983*. Albany: N.Y.S. Division of Substance Abuse Services.

Operation Par. (1984). *Substance use among Pinellas County Youth: A summary of findings*. Pinellas Park, Fla.: Operation Par, Inc.

Osborne, R. T., and McGurk, F. C. J. (1982). *The testing of Negro intelligence*, vol. 2. Athens, Ga.: Foundation for Human Understanding.

Reid, I. D. A. (1939). *The Negro immigrant: His background, characteristics, and social adjustment, 1899–1937*. New York: Columbia University Press.

Rosenthal, R., Bruce, B., Dunne, F., and Ladd, F. (1976). *Different strokes: Pathways to maturity in the Boston ghetto*. Boulder, Col.: Westview.

Schwartz, I. M., Fishman, G., Hatfield, R. R., Krisberg, B. A., and Eiskovits, Z. (1985). Juvenile detention: A new prison for kids? Paper presented at the Annual Meeting of the American Society of Criminology, San Diego.

Short, J. F., Jr., and Nye, F. I. (1958). Extent of unrecorded delinquency, tentative conclusions. *Journal of Criminal Law, Criminology and Police Science* 49:296–302.

Silberman, C. E. (1978). *Criminal violence, criminal justice*. New York: Vintage Books.

Single, E., Kandel, D. B., and Faust, R. (1974). Patterns of multiple drug use in high school. *Journal of Health and Social Behavior* 15:344–57.

Straus, M. A. (1979). Measuring intrafamily conflict and violence: The conflict tactics (CT) scales. *Journal of Marriage and the Family* 41: 75–88.

———. (1983). Ordinary violence, child abuse, and wife-beating: What do they have in common? In *The dark side of families: Current family violence research*, edited by D. Finkelhor, R. J. Gelles, G. T. Hotaling, and M. A. Straus. Beverly Hills, Calif.: Sage Publications.

Straus, M. A., Gelles, R. J., and Steinmetz, S. K. (1980). *Behind closed doors: Violence in the American family*. New York: Doubleday/Anchor.

Tracy, P. E., and Piper, E. S. (1982). Gang membership and violent offending: Preliminary results from the 1958 cohort study. Paper presented at the 1982 Annual Meeting of the American Society of Criminology, Toronto.

Tracy, P. W., Wolfgang, M. E., and Figlio, R. M. (1985). *Delinquency in two birth cohorts*. Washington, D.C.: U.S. Department of Justice.

Tucker, M. B. (1985). U.S. ethnic minorities and drug abuse: An assessment of the science and practice. *The International Journal of the Addictions* 20:1021–47.

U.S. Department of Justice. (1981). *Measuring crime*. Washington, D.C.: U.S. Department of Justice, Bureau of Justice Statistics.

———. (1982). *Criminal victimization in the United States, 1980*. Washington, D.C.: U.S. Department of Justice, Bureau of Justice Statistics.

———. (1983). *Criminal victimization in the United States, 1981*. Washington, D.C.: U.S. Department of Justice, Bureau of Justice Statistics.

———. (1984) *Criminal victimization in the United States, 1982*. Washington, D.C.: U.S. Department of Justice, Bureau of Justice Statistics.

Uppal, G. S., Babst, D. V., Schmeidler, J. (1977). Assessing age-of-onset data on substance use among New York State public secondary school students. *American Journal of Drug and Alcohol Abuse* 4:505–15.

Werner, E. E., and Smith, R. S. (1982). *Vulnerable but invincible: A study of resilient children*. New York: McGraw-Hill.

William, J. R., and Gold, M. (1972). From delinquent behavior to official delinquency. *Social Problems* 20:209–29.

Wilson, J. Q., and Herrnstein, R. J. (1985). *Crime and human nature*. New York: Simon & Schuster.

Wolfgang, M., Figlio, R. F., and Sellin, T. (1972). *Delinquency in a birth cohort*. Chicago: University of Chicago Press.

Chapter 5

YOUNG BLACK MALES AND SUBSTANCE USE

Ann F. Brunswick

> *There is still so much drug activity on the streets of the nation's capitol that a casual cruise . . . through the Shaw, Cardozo, and Columbia Heights sections, just north of the White House, made it clear that operation Clean Sweep was far from complete. . . . In this part of the city streets are littered with broken bottles, broken-down automobiles, and broken spirits. . . . old men sit on stoops nursing bottles of cheap wine and young people hang out on street corners, selling just about any kind of illegal substance a body could want.*

> From "On the Drug Patrol: Hands Tell It All,"
> *New York Times* (Aug. 31, 1987).

This chapter is concerned with still another strand in the web of circumstances and behavior that is identified with the special segment of young black males called "underclass" (e.g., Glasgow, 1980) and/or "endangered" (Gibbs, 1984). Perhaps it is more obvious in the case of substance use than in some of the other behaviors with which this book is concerned that the risk is more one of degree than of kind. That is to say that at the ages of concern—adolescence and the early adult transition—some degree

NOTE: The longitudinal research reported in this chapter was supported by the National Institute on Drug Abuse (NIDA), Alcohol, Drug Abuse and Mental Health Administration, U.S. Department of Health and Human Services, Research Grants, #5 R01-DA-00952 and #R18-DA-03287.

of substance use is normative, meaning that substantial proportions of the population report this behavior. This at least is the case with alcohol and marijuana. Nor need we restrict the normativity of substance use to this population subgroup only. Clearly, drugs and alcohol need some further definition to obtain an appropriate perspective on their use as part of the syndrome of conditions identifying the endangered young black male.

In the first pages of this chapter, a theoretical orientation and conceptual model suggested so as to enlighten the subsequent discussion of young black males' patterns of substance use, their life-style and health concomitants, and finally, their treatment experiences. Given the policy interests of this book, this introductory discussion is especially important for achieving an integrated perspective on the issues that place the young urban black male at risk. If we are to develop meaningful prevention and intervention programs, more attention needs to be given to the processes that influence the acts of initiating and continuing drug use *to a problematic degree*—that is, where substance use adds to the burden that the young black male's age and societal position already impose.

Four tenets are basic to the discussion that follows:

1. Both drugs used and the drug user defy easy explanation. Multiple influences, including time, place, social position, and age, to name the more obvious, are involved. Problem substance use is neither random nor idiosyncratic. How else can the unequal distribution in rates and types of substances used across different population subgroups be explained?

2. Explanations that emphasize individual attributes of personality, which have ranged from depression to rebelliousness (see Hawkins, Lishner, and Catalano Jr., 1985), are inadequate in the case of the young urban black male's substance use. Instead, a social-situational or ecological model is required, which can account for responsiveness to different norms and values; differential access to, and success in, the "opportunity structure"; influences channeled through alternative interpersonal networks; and developmental needs specially linked to the adolescent and early adult life stage.

3. Drug-use behavior among young black males is part and parcel with other domains of youthful activity described elsewhere in this book. Although its understanding requires separate analysis, programmatically it must be seen as part of a broader set of issues. Remember, for example, the following linkages: the onset of illicit drug use precedes school dropout, but poor school attain-

ment precedes drug use; delinquency also precedes drug use (Elliot, Huizinga, and Ageton, 1982; Hawkins, Lishner, and Catalano, Jr., 1985; Johnston, O'Malley, and Evelard, 1978); and the unemployed among urban black males have higher rates of hard drug use (Brunswick, 1980a).

4. An often overlooked cornerstone of hard drug use among urban young black males is that it is not only, and perhaps even not primarily, a consumption and/or recreational behavior. It also serves economic functions of occupation and career for this group (Johnson et al., 1985; Preble and Casey, 1969; Williams and Kornblum, 1986). In a population subgroup where employment opportunities are severely constrained, and at a life stage when economic independence is expected and required, the drug economy is one of relatively few options available. For this and other reasons, Simon's (1957) theory of the rational man is a starting point for understanding young black males' problematic involvement in drugs (Boyle and Brunswick, 1980). It is also suggestive of what may be needed for intervening in it. People select from among the options available to them those they perceive as having positive rewards. In this regard, urban young black males are no exception.

Winick (1980) has identified three factors that are critical to our understanding of problem substance use among 15–24-year-old black males. The first and obvious condition is availability—that individuals have access to the requisite substances. The black ghetto has long been a recognized hub of the drug trade, prompting Waldorf's (1973) reference to Harlem as "the heroin capital of the world." The requirement of availability—for consuming and/or for trading—is readily met in the circumstances of the urban young black male. Availability by itself, of course, is not a sufficient explanation of drug use (Boyle and Brunswick, 1980; Messeri and Brunswick, 1987). The second of Winick's necessary conditions is disengagement from proscriptions against substance use. Young black males' estrangement from the dominant opportunity structure engenders weaker ties to traditional social norms, resulting in shifting adherence to alternative subcultural norms, values, and interpersonal linkages (Brunswick, 1980a; Brunswick and Messeri, 1984; Johnson, 1980). The adolescent life stage, furthermore, is itself a time when ties to the earlier authority figures of childhood are modified if not broken.

The third condition in Winick's (1980) theory even more explicitly explains the linkage between onset of drug use and adolescence. That posits the necessary precondition of role strain and/or role deprivation. Role strain and role deprivation are characteristic of transitional periods, such as leaving school and assuming adult roles of economic and social independence. It is no accident that the timing of drug use onset coincides with a developmental period that is marked by transiency, lack of role commitment, and low status both in social and economic terms (Riley and Waring, 1978). These conditions become more exaggerated when added to the experiences of a racial group whose identity, regardless of age, carries its own role strains and deprivation.

Definition of Problem Substance Use

This chapter, like others in the book, is concerned primarily with the plight of a minority within the young urban black male population—too large a group to be sure, but a minority nonetheless—who will be distinguished from the larger group from which they are drawn who do *not* become problem drug users. In distinguishing the substance user of concern, the concept "addict" is rejected. That term commonly implicates three specific states: physical *and* psychological dependency and the need for increasing dosage to achieve effect. These criteria are not easy to discern in a general population and seem unnecessarily limiting. Just as important, they refer only to the drug user. The concept of "problem drug use" seems a more appropriate one, just as investigators in the so-called field of drinking and alcoholism have suggested that "problem drinker" is a more suitable term than "alcoholic" (Cahalan, 1970). The idea of "problem drug use," furthermore, is sufficiently expansive to refer to the problematic effects of committed drug use which extend beyond the user himself, to its impact on younger black males who are at risk of becoming problem users, and to the impact on the quality of life for the community more generally (Brunswick, 1986).

Black and White Substance Use Rates Compared

Reliable comparisons of patterns of substance involvement in carefully matched black and white youth groups are needed to demonstrate young black males' higher drug use rates implied by the theoretical position outlined above. But valid comparative data are difficult to come by and, indeed, do not exist. Most of what we know about national trends in drug use, for example, comes from periodic national household surveys and the annual surveys of high school seniors (in addition to surveillance systems covering emergency room admissions and treatment facilities), all supported by the National Institute on Drug Abuse (United States Dept. Health and Human Services). These do not, however, accommodate the specific comparisons we need to make (Brunswick 1979, 1980a; Kozel and Adams, 1986). The reasons for the difficulty are germane to this discussion. Geographically, the young black males of interest are concentrated in defined large inner-city areas, while national samples are drawn to reflect the census distribution of the total population. Thus they yield too small a representation of the geographically concentrated groups. Furthermore, despite compensatory attempts at "oversampling" in a statistically reliable way, the young men of interest are more likely than others their ages to be living outside of households. In my research, for example, I found that 3 percent of a community representative sample of black males who had been identified for study at younger ages, by 18–23 years of age had no locatable residence; I dubbed them "nomads" (Brunswick, 1979). But it is in just such a subgroup that higher rates of the behavior of interest will be found.

A third difficulty in performing the needed comparisons stems from the practice of combining, for purposes of analysis, southern and substantially rural black people, who evidence lower drug-use rates, with inner-city black people, whose prevalence is high. The single average rate for the black population obtained this way conceals more than it reveals and cannot be used as a guide to understanding variations in drug-use rates.

Different difficulties arise when data are based on school samples. They have become increasingly recognized as underestimating behavior linked to school dropout and to high rates of absenteeism, a situation which obviously characterizes substance use (Brunswick, 1979, 1980a). The national high school survey mentioned earlier, for example, does not report separate rates by race for just this reason (Johnston, Bachman, and O'Malley, 1982).

Notwithstanding all these good arguments against interracial comparison, some comparative estimates will be attempted, noting the margin of error with which they must be interpreted. These particular comparisons have been selected because of their comparability in historic period (date), in developmental period (age), and gender specificity (male). The database for these estimates of inner-city black male drug use (and the other attributes reported in this chapter) come from my longitudinal study of a homogeneously non-Hispanic black community sample, initially numbering 668 black adolescents (351 males and 317 females). They constituted all adolescents living in a 4 percent (1 in 25) sample of households in central Harlem in 1967–68. Those aged 12–15 were studied over two years; 16–17-year-olds were studied over a single year. For the most part, therefore, they were drawn into study prior to age 16 and consequently circumvent the risks in sampling households which were suggested earlier.

Comparing rates of use for *males* in this inner-city sample at ages 18–23 (N = 277) with a national study of selective service registrants aged 20–30, which was also conducted in the mid-1970s (O'Donnell et al., 1976), showed that black youth use rates exceeded white use rates for all substances except tranquilizers/sedatives and stimulant pills. (The lower black use rates of "pills" have been a consistent finding in all comparisons of black and white youth substance-use patterns.) Even in the mid-1970s, when attention was riveted on young whites' use of marijuana, young black males in the inner-city community sample reported half again as high rates of lifetime experience with marijuana (86 percent) as the 55 percent rate in the slightly older national panel of selective service registrants ages 20–30 (Brunswick, 1979; O'Donnell et al., 1976). Parenthetically, at subsequent interview ages 26–31, in 1983–84, males in the inner-city community sample (N = 211) reported lifetime marijuana experience rates of 92 percent. As a comparison, a New York statewide sample of males aged 24–25 studied in the mid-1980s, reported lifetime rates of 77 percent (Kandel, Murphy, and Karus, 1985). In the mid-1970s, heroin and cocaine use rates in the inner-city black sample both were three times higher than among the national sample of selective service registrants (Brunswick, 1979, 1980a).

Thus, with few exceptions, higher black rates of nonmedical or recreational substance use have been established in population representative urban samples in the postadolescent or early adult years.

Drug Use: Life Histories and Patterns

In the second wave of the just-cited inner-city study (1975–76), when young black men were ages 18–23, reported lifetime prevalence of alcohol (86 percent) was no greater than marijuana (88 percent).Current (past month) use of alcohol (63 percent), marijuana (56 percent), and tobacco cigarettes (57 percent) were all within comparable ranges—the latter referring to daily cigarette use. Cocaine, psychedelics, and heroin were next most frequent in total lifetime prevalence, but were markedly lower than marijuana rates. While overall experience with psychedelics slightly exceeded that with heroin, this excess was due to substantially greater experimentation. Not much regular use of psychedelics (particularly, phencyclidine or PCP) was reported by the black sample in the mid-1970s. Heroin exceeded psychedelics in patterns of regular use. Barbiturates and amphetamines showed the already-noted low rates of use. Overall, 81 percent of men used at least one illicit substance, and 37 percent used an illicit substance "harder" than marijuana on more than an experimental basis (Brunswick and Boyle, 1979).

Other descriptors of drug use, beyond prevalence, are important: age at onset, frequency or heaviness of use, and duration of use. Data from the inner-city study showed that 20 percent of all males reported having taken alcohol by 10 years of age; 10 percent had taken marijuana by age 11, with use of other illicit substances beginning by age 13. Risk of initiation to various substances peaked by age 18 (Brunswick, 1979; Brunswick and Boyle, 1979). According to the mean age of reported onset, the chronological sequence for beginning use of individual substances was alcohol, inhalants, marijuana, heroin, cocaine, and psychedelics. At time of onset these youths were usually attending school.

Not unexpectedly, the substance used with greatest frequency when it was used was heroin. After heroin, alcohol, and then marijuana, showed greatest frequency of use. Length of time used was correlated with earliness of onset, for obvious reasons. Alcohol and marijuana, consequently, were the longest used substances. When comparing rates of lifetime experience and current use, the most sizable decrease in users was observed for heroin. This phenomenon was not explained by the age or the aging of the study group (Brunswick, 1979; Brunswick, Merzel, and Messeri, 1985).

Understanding changing patterns of drug use requires attention to two situational influences: historic time (which is a marker of changing availability of, or access to, particular substances) and cohort (a marker of changing norms of tolerance for use of particular substances—a change that can occur with or without changes in availability). Both of these influences were apparent in the inner-city community study. The influence of historic time was demonstrated in use patterns of phencyclidine (PCP). In the inner-city study group, PCP use began at an older age and was less regular or frequent in the mid-1970s than was reported for other substances. This happened because phencyclidine as a drug of choice was just making its entry into the inner city (Brunswick and Boyle, 1979). On the subsequent third-wave study, parenthetically, both the prevalence and frequency of PCP use had increased (Brunswick, Merzel, and Messeri, 1985).

Of all the patterns of substance use which were observed in the inner-city study group, perhaps the most striking was the dramatic decline in onset and prevalence of heroin use. Even within the narrow span of six birth years which were included in the study's sample, prevalence consistently declined from a high of 24 percent (for males and females combined) among the oldest cohort, who had been born in 1952, down to 3 percent in the youngest birth cohorts, born in 1956 and 1957 (Boyle and Brunswick, 1980). Nor was this a temporary aberration. The absence of new onset of cases among the younger cohorts upon subsequent investigation in the third study wave confirmed that the change persisted (Brunswick, Merzel, and Messeri, 1985; Messeri and Brunswick, 1987). Subsequent reports from heroin treatment facilities similarly confirmed the increasing age of heroin users, an indication of the reduction in onset of new young heroin users within the black inner-city community (DeLeon, 1986; Frank, Hopkins, and Lipton, 1986). Sharp cohort effects such as were observed in the inner-city study group are evidence of the important role of social, structural, and situational factors in black males' drug use.

The following regularities in substance use appeared in the inner-city black sample's pattern of drug use, which have been reported for white youth samples as well:

1. The earlier the onset of a substance's use (relative to the average age at onset), the longer and more heavily that substance will be used and the more likely that harder substances also will be used (Brunswick, 1979; Clayton and Voss, 1981; Kandel, 1978).

2. The harder the drugs that are used, the more heavily individuals are likely to use even "lighter" substances. For example, when the black sample was stratified into four groups representing progressive degrees of drug involvement (satisfying Guttman scale criteria for scalability and reproducibility), rates of daily cigarette smoking increased from 26 percent among black males who had used no illicit substance, to 56 percent among users of marijuana but nothing stronger, to 62 percent of males who had used cocaine but not heroin, and reached 84 percent among heroin users. Heavy drinkers (defined as those taking five or more drinks in a single day at least once a week) increased from 2 percent of males who had used no illicit substances, to 9 percent heavy drinkers among

those who used marijuana but nothing harder, 14 percent among those who had used cocaine but not heroin, and 36 percent among heroin users.

3. The harder the substance used, the greater the number of substances used. In the inner-city community study, 82 percent of males who had used heroin had used at least *five* substances, compared with 25 percent of cocaine users who had used that many substances. No males who used substances "softer" than these used more than three recreational substances. Thus, harder substances do not appear to be substituted for "softer" substances; rather, they are added to them.

4. Other regularities noted in analyzing the black community data suggest imperviousness in a substance's age of onset of use to changing prevalence, once availability has been established (Brunswick and Boyle, 1979). Consequently, despite the dramatic decline in proportions taking up heroin use, the age when its use began tended to remain constant. (Median age of heroin onset for the studied black males was 15.4 years.)

5. Age of onset was influenced by availability only when the substance was newly introduced, as was the case in the older age observed for phencyclidine onset.

6. It goes without saying that, despite the substantial numbers who continue using "recreational" or nonmedical substances, others stop after a period of experimentation, lending support to Johnson's (1976) refutation of "the myth of irreversibility."

In concluding this discussion of substance-use patterns, an impression of the magnitude of the problem of committed or problem drug users can be obtained from the population distribution rates of the four drug involvement groups described above. The proportion of males in the community representative sample who had not used any illicit substance, even marijuana, amounted to but 20 percent of the 277 males reporting; those who had used marijuana but nothing stronger comprised 44 percent of the sample; slightly better than a third had used one of the so-called "hard" drugs on more than an experimental basis: 20 percent had used cocaine but not heroin and 16 percent had used heroin. Within these groups, the extent of use of softer drugs progressively increased as harder drugs were used. All heroin users, for example, also had used marijuana, and 80 percent also had used cocaine. This provides further documentation of the pyramidal or hierarchical nature of substance-use involvement. This fact has obvious and important implications for policy and programs: They need to be directed at general processes governing drug use—not at separate or individual substances. And they need to be directed at the *early* and *heavy* users of widely used substances—the bottom of the pyramid, so to speak (Brunswick, 1979, p. 468).

Concomitants of Drug Use in Life Roles

The four progressive drug involvement groups from the inner-city sample will now be used to examine life and health conditions associated with substance use. The community representative nature of the study group provides the opportunity to compare a range of life experiences across different levels of substance involvement—an opportunity that is missing when data are obtained from special samples of young black men such as those who are incarcerated or in drug treatment programs.

We are reminded that the four drug involvement groups represent lifetime experience and may or may not identify current involvement with a substance. Also, these data are correlational and, unless otherwise noted, were collected at a single point in time. Causal inference might well be spurious without controlling for the interrelationship among drug use, life-style, psychosocial outlooks, and social attainment. Later in the chapter, therefore, certain health analyses will be reported, which were conducted specifically to control the temporal sequence in these matters.

Mortality

Between ages 18–23 and 26–31 (the subsequent follow-up of the inner-city sample), young men who had used heroin had quadruple the death rate of nonheroin users, 8 percent and 2 percent, respectively. Numbers are too small for a meaningful analysis of cause of death separately by drug use status. Experiences in the total group conform to the well-established association with violent causes. For the group as a whole, from adolescence on, there were 22 deaths, amounting to 6 percent of the initial adolescent male sample. Examination of death certificates revealed the following distribution by cause: 9 were victims of homicide, 3 were narcotics deaths, 3 were suicides, 3 resulted from other accidents, 2 were attributed to convulsive disorder, and 2 were unspecified. Thus, all but 4 of 22 deaths were known to have resulted from violent causes. Involvement in narcotics increased the risk of death from any violent cause.

Background Demographics

Two items of information were examined here: birthplace (own and mother's) and maternal education. The sample of urban black non-Hispanic males was approximately 23 percent southern born and 77 percent with mothers who had been born in the South. Generations of residence in the North made no difference in rates of drug involvement. Maternal education, on the other hand, was inversely related to drug involvement. Specifically, the mothers of young men who had used heroin had lower educational attainment than mothers of less involved drug users; mothers or maternal guardians with no more than grade school education amounted to 46 percent among heroin-using males compared to 24 percent of the full male sample. Thus, prior social status does play a role in drug involvement.

Living Arrangements

The four substance involvement groups were compared on current household composition (who was household head and the number of people living in that household), sources of household income, and residential mobility. Household composition showed no variability by drug involvement. Sources of income did vary: Hard drug users, both the cocaine and heroin groups, reported more "hustling" (42 and 41 percent, respectively) than those who used no illicit substances (5 percent) or users only of marijuana (17 percent). Some past-year household income from job earnings ranged from 57 percent among heroin users and among those who used no illicit substance (who were in school, see below) to a high of 73 percent among marijuana-only users. As to residential mobility, those with modest involvement, marijuana-only users, were more likely to have moved away from Harlem than the more drug involved (and also the nonillicit users). Thus, drug involvement evidenced linkages to current social status as well as prior social status.

Social Role and Drug Involvement

Educational and social handicaps linked to hard drug involvement, specifically in the heroin-using group, were both in evidence by ages 18–23. *Both educational attainment* and *current school enrollment* showed an inverse relationship to degree of drug involvement: the *less* drug involved, the *more* likely currently to be in school, to have completed and to aspire to higher educational levels. Half of those who had not used an illicit substance (51 percent) were in school, either as their sole activity or in combination with working/looking for work. Rates currently in school comprised 35 percent of marijuana-only users, 25 percent of cocaine, and 18 percent of heroin users.

While on the basis of their ages almost the entire sample would have been expected to have completed high school, in reality, one-third of all males (35 percent) had *not* (yet) done so. Among heroin users, the rate was 55 percent for those who had not completed high school. Nearly half of those who reported no use of illicit substances (46 percent) had education *beyond high school,* as did about a third of users of marijuana only and of those who had used cocaine but not heroin. The proportion dropped to a fifth going beyond high school among those who reported heroin use.

Working was the most frequently reported activity among both the marijuana and cocaine groups (50 and 48 percent, respectively), either as a sole activity or in combination with attending school. Among men who had used heroin, however, almost as many were looking for work (31 percent) as were working (33 percent). Heroin users were the only group among whom a majority (55 percent) reported no meaningful current activity. When they did work, however, there was little difference in the types of formal jobs held or in salary; most were in clerical, sales, or service work.

Not unexpectedly, heroin users reported higher rates of incarceration than others. Almost a third (30 percent) had been in prison at some time compared to a rate of 3 or 4 percent among lesser drug-involved groups.

With respect to *marriage* and *family formation,* by ages 18–23 only 5 percent of the total male sample reported having ever been married, with inconsequential variation by drug involvement. Neither did they vary much when asked at what age they would *like* to marry. ("Never" marrying was the choice of 10 percent of marijuana-only users, 7 percent of heroin users, and 2 percent of the other groups.) While proportions *having a child* varied considerably among different drug involvement groups, here the older age of the heroin users has to be reckoned with. (Four in five of the heroin group were ages 21–23 compared to about half as many who were these ages in the other drug involvement groups.) Half of the heroin users had fathered a child; this rate declined consistently with decreasing drug involvement. Only 13 percent of those who had not used any illicit substances reported having a child.

When asked for their *preferences* regarding the number of *children they wanted,* however, heroin users reported a smaller desired number (mean of 2.8 children) than the others (cocaine users' average 4.7, 3.1 among marijuana-only users, and 3.6 among those not using any illicit substances).

Health and Drug Involvement

A major reason for undertaking the longitudinal inner-city study was to examine relationships between drug use and health. A substantial number of different measures were included to reveal how the inner-city black sample perceived their general health status and to identify their particular symptoms and health problems. The latter included 47 somatic problems and eight mood and self-concept questions. These were formulated into three scales: physical health (38 items, .67 reliability), psychophysical (9 items, .73 reliability), and affective well-being (8 items, .62 reliability). In this section we examine drug involvement in relationship to both the general health status measures and to the symptom scales.

General Health Status

The following relationships were observed among the four drug involvement groups:

1. With increasing drug involvement, perceived quality of health declined. Fewer than half as many young men who had used heroin rated their health "very good" (24 percent) compared to those who had not used any illicit substance (57 percent).
2. Reports that health limited the capacity of drug users to engage in chosen activities increased with increasing drug involvement. Six in seven (83 percent) of heroin users compared to about half (53 percent) of those who used no illicit substances reported such limitations.
3. Disability days (days when health prevented the individual from carrying on usual activities) increased from a mean average of 4.7 among those who did not use any illicit substances to a mean of 13.8 days among those who had used heroin.

Nature of Health Problems

When health problems were stratified into physical, psychophysical, and affective domains, heroin users scored more problems on each, with the strongest and statistically higher increase observed on the physical health index.

The predominant somatic symptoms and conditions reported by

these young men have been analyzed and reported elsewhere (Brunswick, 1980b). Briefly, they include: dental (45 percent), skin (27 percent), musculoskeletal (26 percent), frequent colds (21 percent), vision impairment (19 percent), serious accident or injury (18 percent), and gonorrhea (17 percent). Except for vision problems, heroin users reported higher rates of each, with the most noticeable excesses in skin problems (37 percent compared with 17 percent in the group with no illicit substance use), serious accident or injury (27 percent among the heroin group compared with 12 percent among nonillicit users), and gonorrhea (45 percent in the heavy or heroin group compared with 3 percent in the nonillicit group).

Although the heroin user scores were also higher on the other two scales, they were not statistically so. Reportable differences did appear for chest pains (31 to 18 percent) among the symptoms classified as psychophysical and "not having a good time these days" (47 vs. 28 percent) among symptoms of affective dysfunction.

In interpreting these differences, it is important to recall that the drug-user groups represented cumulative and increasing poly-drug involvement. As reported earlier, the heaviest group was distinguished not only by having used heroin, but also by having used a greater number of other substances, by having begun using these substances at an earlier age, and by using them more heavily. In examining the health differences reported above, therefore, we are dealing with differences linked to heavier drug involvement generally, without implicating any one substance. Furthermore, we could not yet assert that, even in a temporal sense, drug use caused or preceded poor health. Before being able to do this, the competing hypothesis that sicker people selected into drug use needed to be discounted. Further analyses were performed, therefore, to attempt to specify particular substance linkages and to clarify the temporal linkages between drug involvement and poorer health among the young men who had used heroin.

First, male heroin users were subdivided into two groups: those who retrospectively reported already using heroin by the first interview at ages 12–17—that is, by the time their first health measurements had been taken; and those whose use of heroin began after the adolescent interview and whose first set of health measurements, therefore, could not be affected by use. These two groups were then compared for their change in health between interviews. If the group we called *onsetters*—those whose use began after the adolescent interview—showed a greater difference than the change recorded for those who were already using, that would support the temporal linkage of drug use preceding decline in health. This is what the results showed. Health change was significant in all three health domains (physical, psychophysical, and affective) for the "onsetters," but not for those who had been using heroin earlier.

Taking a further step to clarify the linkage between drugs and health, multivariate analyses were then performed. Health (somatic and affective, separately) in young adulthood (ages 18–23) was regressed on individual substance used; life-style indicators were added in after that. If a significant linkage between substance involvement and health persisted after the life-style controls were added, it would support the specific linkage of drug use to poor health. While supporting this hypothesis, the results also give evidence of the complexity of arriving at simple answers regarding drug-use effects on health.

The results of the analysis of somatic health, regressed simultaneously on all substances used, no longer demonstrated that heroin had a significant health effect. Instead, what captured the health effect—that is, the change in health between the two study times—were inhalants and methadone. Introducing the life-style indicators showed that they also had significant effects on health. But they did not diminish the relationship of inhalants and methadone to health decline. Almost a quarter of the differences in young men's somatic health between the two interviews (23 percent) was associated with their substance use. (See Brunswick and Messeri, 1986a, for a more complete report of this analysis.)

It bears repeating that even with this refinement in the drug measures, the polydrug nature of all substance use prevents us from asserting with certainty that the particular identified substances—and *not* their close interconnections with another substance—was the cause of the health decline. Nor, when it comes to programmatic issues, is that an especially compelling concern. Even if the interwoven strands of polydrug use cannot be disentangled as to the individual or combined role of specific substances, policy needs to be concerned with the user and with intervening in the complex behavior of substance use.

The use of methadone is a good example of the difficulty in attempting to separate individual substance effects from some underlying attributes of the person who uses that substance—when it is a substance whose use is not normative in the population—and in separating that substance's effects from another with whose use it is closely correlated. Methadone was used by only 9 percent of the sample. All methadone users had also used heroin. This is not to say that all of this was therapeutic methadone use. On their last use, at least 60 percent of users had *not* used it in connection with treatment. This reflects another dynamic of problem drug use: any mood-altering substance, regardless of whether its original function was therapeutic, can be subverted to illicit or street use. This is not just because of its mood-altering effects but because it is marketable, reminding us of one of the basic tenets stated in the beginning of the chapter: Substance involvement frequently serves economic functions for young black men.

For these and perhaps other reasons, methadone use captured the most seriously drug-involved young men in the sample. Note, for example, that methadone use and heavy drinking were almost perfectly correlated (Pearson $r = .91$). Methadone-using men uniformly had high levels of alcohol drinking. The observed effect of methadone, we must assume, is capturing the complexities of these associations as well.

These remarks bear also on what was observed in the multivariate analysis of change in *affective distress* in relation to specific substances used. When tested simultaneously against all drugs used, methadone was identified as the substance with significant effects on males' affective distress. As before, analysis then proceeded to identify whether associated life-style and/or psychosocial attitudes might explain the apparent linkage between methadone use and distress. In this case it did indeed—just about all of the methadone relationship was mediated. It was explained by methadone's association with role dysfunction (unemployment, school dropout, prison experience) and the association of these dysfunctional roles with feelings of demoralization—chiefly feelings of powerlessness and perceived life stress, and even anticipation of death (Brunswick, 1987). (As we saw earlier, the latter is not without a base in reality, given the quadrupling of the death rate among men who had used heroin.)

Drug Treatment and Cessation of Drug Use

This section, like prior ones, will take advantage of the comparative mode to enlighten perspectives on young black men's treatment experiences for problem drug use, comparing them to young men from the same community sample who have used hard drugs, specifically heroin, but have not been treated.

By ages 18–23, 9 percent of the entire sample of 277 urban black males had been in treatment for substance use (including detoxification) at least once. This constituted 51 percent of the group who had used heroin more than experimentally (once or twice). Compared with females from the same community representative sample, males started treatment at younger ages (half reported their first treatment experience by age 18); males had briefer treatment episodes (reflecting their greater likelihood than females to go in for detoxification only); and males reported a larger number of treatment episodes (Brunswick, 1979; Brunswick and Messeri, 1985). Of particular interest, males were more likely to enter treatment earlier in their heroin-use careers than females. About two in ten of the males who entered treatment did so within the first year that they were using heroin; another quarter entered within their second year of use. Black males reported greater use of residential facilities than females. A third of the treatment experiences reported by the 18–23-year-old men were in residential facilities (32 percent); a quarter were in methadone clinics (23 percent).

Notwithstanding this distribution of treatment modalities, methadone was administered in half of the treatment episodes (including episodes of detoxification only). According to their interview reports, personal therapy was available in a similar proportion of treatment episodes; job help had been offered in a mere 3 percent of treatment episodes. (Note that although these data were collected a decade ago, 1975–76, judging from the study's more recently collected data the dominant trends are intact.)

When those who did and did not enter treatment were compared, only minimal differences were observed in relation to age when use started, in relation to frequency and to recency of use. The sole difference of note between the two groups was the length of time heroin had been used. (O'Donnell, et al., 1976, obtained a similar finding in their national study of selective service registrants.) The lack of contrast in major parameters of use can be explained by a truism often overlooked because of its simplicity: Treatment is a choice for, and only for, those who cannot terminate substance use without it. Those who can stop, do; those who cannot, enter into treatment.

The comparison of social role attainment between treated and untreated heroin users also supports this inference: Rates of school dropout and current unemployment were notably higher among treated than untreated users. Generally, the disadvantage in heroin users' social roles reported earlier in this chapter were disadvantages of the treated, not of the untreated. The latter group, for the most part, is comprised of those who had terminated heroin use on their own.

Men in this black inner-city community sample who entered treatment for their substance use were different *before* their treatment experience from those users who were not treated. Our analysis, furthermore, indicated that male relapse was widespread after first treatment (Brunswick and Messeri, 1986b). Comparing treated males with females, treatment was a more attractive alternative for females—judging by their lengths of stay in treatment, by lower posttreatment relapse rates, and by the relative rates with which men and women achieved cessation with and without treatment. Even controlling for frequency of use, age, and length of time heroin was used, the effects of treatment measured in the inner-city study only marginally improved a man's chances of ceasing to use drugs.

This cannot be interpreted as an indication that treatment was ineffective. Referring to the general proposition that some people need treatment to abstain while others can terminate use without it, obviously individuals who entered treatment had more barriers to overcome in order to stop drug use.

To quote from a more detailed analysis of these issues reported elsewhere:

When analysis centers on comparison of treated and untreated users, entry into treatment clearly represents a choice point: a problematic juncture in a heroin career. Treatment intervention is but one variable component in a longer sequence of events describing alternative pathways out of heroin use. Not all heroin users enter treatment to kick their habit. Those who do, enter at varying stages in their heroin careers. They may experience numerous treatment episodes during the course of drug use. When viewed as part of a natural history of heroin use, treatment entry—whether self- or externally imposed—represents an opportunity for individuals to acquire resources and skills needed for ending drug dependency. For those among whom drug use does not cease without treatment, their entry into treatment ipso facto signifies that the resources and supports needed for abstinence were lacking in their natural environment.

Conceptualized in these terms, treatment becomes an issue of behavior change and of the imparting and acquisition of skills and resources needed to overcome inadequate interpersonal and role supports. Heroin treatment is not unlike other programs for behavior change. Hunt et al. (1979) reported that smoking cessation and alcohol programs succeed only 25 percent of the time in producing behavior change sustained for at least one year. Given the magnitude of the task, it may be inappropriate to judge the success of treatment on the basis of any single episode. Instead, treatment intervention might better be viewed as a possible sequence of exposures of varying lengths, depending on what different individuals require (Brunswick and Messeri, 1986b, 129–131).

Conclusions

Early in this chapter, we emphasized that an adequate theory and set of guidelines for understanding young black men's substance-use behavior would have to recognize the importance of external and situational factors intersecting with developmental ones—that is, emergence into manhood—to explain high rates of drug use in the population of interest to us. Among external conditions, we have emphasized not only *place*—upon which availability may be contingent—but also *time*—which brings with it changing norms of tolerance for particular substances of choice. Thus, different drug markers than extended heroin involvement may well be needed today to identify the most socially disadvantaged among young black men. Yet the substantive associations with social roles, health, and appropriate treatment services we believe would still apply.

An essential point which was made at the outset of the chapter and repeated subsequently concerns the linkage between substance involvement and economic activities in the lives of young black men—drug use as drug trade. Although high rates of young black male unemployment have been with us for a long time, these analyses of experiences in drug treatment indicated all too clearly that job training and job counseling were essentially absent. So, too, the link is often overlooked in discussing "the drug problem" among young black men. Yet, if anything is to produce change in drug-use behavior and correlated conditions discussed elsewhere in this book, it is preparing young black men for, and providing meaningful access to, gainful employment opportunities. Otherwise, they must continue to listen to the beat of a different drummer and to look for alternative activities and experiences to attempt to satisfy what they share with all young people—needs for growth and self-realization, for affiliation, for respect from others, for social belonging, and basic to all of these, for a source of material sustenance.

Finally, substance use by young black males has to be recognized as a symptom of social neglect—a neglect that begins long before drinking and drug problems appear. It is identifiable by academic failure in the elementary school years. As early as ages 6, 7, and 8, community and school programs need to be in place to engage children in activities purposeful to them, that also will foster attitudes and skills needed for later meaningful employment. Such programs might be viewed as early components of a comprehensive school drop-out prevention program—supported by public funds—that would be maintained up through the final high school years. They then should be followed by specific youth employment and training opportunities, appropriately supervised to ensure a future role for these young men in the mainstream of society.

References

Boyle, J., and Brunswick, A. F. (1980). What happened in Harlem? Analysis of a decline in heroin use among a generation unit of urban black youth. *Jounal of Drug Issues* 10(1):109–30.

Brunswick, A. F. (1979). Black youths and drug-use behavior. In *Youth and drug abuse: Problems, issues and treatment*, edited by G. Beschner and A. Friedman. Lexington, Mass.: Lexington Books.

———. (1980a). Social meanings and developmental needs: Perspectives on black youths' drug use. *Youth and Society* 11(4):449–73.

———. (1980b). Health stability and change. *American Journal of Public Health* 70(5):504–13.

———. (1986). Dealing with drugs: Heroin abuse as a social problem. *International Journal of Addictions* 20(12):1733–91.

———. (1987). Drug use and affective distress. In *Advances in Adolescent Mental Health*, vol. III, *Depression and suicide*, edited by R. A. Feldman and A. R. Stiffman. Greenwich, Conn.: JAI Press.

Brunswick, A. F., and Boyle, J. (1979). Patterns of drug involvement: Developmental and secular influences on age at initiation. *Youth and Society* 11(2):139–62.

Brunswick, A. F., Merzel, C., and Messeri, P. (1985). Drug use initiation among urban black youth: A seven-year follow-up of developmental and secular influences. *Youth and Society* 17(2):189–216.

Brunswick, A. F., and Messeri, P. (1984). Gender differences in processes of smoking initiation. *Journal of Psychosocial Oncology* 2(1):49–69.

———. (1985). Timing of first drug treatment: A longitudinal study of urban black youth. *Contemporary Drug Problems* 2(3):401–18.

———. (1986a). Drugs, life style and health. *American Journal of Public Health* 76(1):52–57.

———. (1986b). Pathways to heroin abstinence. *Advances in Alcohol and Substance Abuse* 5(3):103–22.

Cahalan, D. (1970). *Problem drinkers*. San Francisco: Jossey-Bass.

Clayton, R., and Voss, H. (1981). *Young men and drugs in Manhattan: A causal analysis*. NIDA Research Monograph No. 39. Washington, D.C.: U.S. Government Printing Office.

DeLeon, G. (1986). *The therapeutic community: Enhancing retention in treatment*. Progress Report on Grant No. 1-R01-DA-03617-02, National Institute on Drug Abuse, June.

Elliot, D. S., Huizinga, D., and Ageton, S. S. (1982). *Explaining delinquency and drug use*. Boulder, Colo.: Behavioral Research Institute.

Frank, B., Hopkins, W., and Lipton, D. (1986). Current drug use trends in New York City. In *Proceeding of the Community Epidemiology Work Group's Meeting*. San Diego, National Institute on Drug Abuse, December.

Gibbs, J. T. (1984). Black adolescents and youth: An endangered species. *American Journal of Orthopsychiatry* 54(1):6–21.

Glasgow, D. (1980). *The black underclass*. San Francisco: Jossey-Bass.

Hawkins, J. D., Lishner, D., and Catalano, R. F., Jr. (1985). Childhood predictors and the prevention of adolescent substance abuse. In *Etiology of drug abuse*, edited by C. L. R. Jones and R. J. Battjes. NIDA Drug Research Monograph No. 56. Rockville, Md.: National Institute on Drug Abuse.

Johnson, B. D. (1976). The race, class and irreversibility hypothesis. In *The epidemiology of heroin and other narcotics*, edited by J. D. Rittenhouse. Rockville, Md.: National Institute on Drug Abuse.

———. (1980). Towards a theory of drug subcultures. In *Theories on drug abuse*, edited by D. J. Lettieri, M. Sayers, and H. W. Pearson. NIDA Research Monograph No. 30. Rockville, Md.: National Institute on Drug Abuse.

Johnson, B. D., Goldstein, P. J., Preble, E., Schmeidler, J., Lipton, D. S., Spunt, B., and Miller, T. (1985). *Taking care of business: The economics of crime by heroin abusers*. Lexington, Mass.: D. C. Heath.

Johnston, L., Bachman, J., and O'Malley, P. (1982). *Student drug use, attitudes and beliefs, national trends 1975–1982*. DHHS Publication No. (ADM)83-1200. Washington, D.C.: U.S. Government Printing Office.

Johnston, L., O'Malley, P., and Evelard, L. (1978). Drugs and delinquency: A search for causal connections. In *Longitudinal research on drug use*, edited by D. B. Kandel. Washington, D.C.: Hemisphere Press.

Kandel, D. B. (1978). Convergences in prospective longitudinal surveys of drug use in normal populations. In *Longitudinal research on drug use*, edited by D. B. Kandel. Washington, D.C.: Hemisphere Press.

Kandel, D. B., Murphy, D., and Karus, D. (1985). Cocaine use in young adulthood: Patterns of use and psychosocial correlates. In *Cocaine use in America: Epidemiologic and clinical perspectives*, edited by N. J. Kozel and E. H. Adams. NIDA Research Monograph No. 61. Rockville, Md.: National Institute on Drug Abuse.

Kozel, N. J., and Adams, E. H. (1986). Epidemiology of drug abuse: An overview. *Science* 234:970–74.

Messeri, P., and Brunswick, A. F. (1987). Heroin availability and aggregate levels of use: Secular trends in an urban black cohort. *American Journal of Drug and Alcohol Abuse* 13(1 & 2):105–29.

O'Donnell, J. A., Voss, H. L., Clayton, R. R., Slatin, G. T., and Room, R. G. W. (1976). *Young men and drugs*. NIDA Research Monograph No. 5. Washington, D.C.: U.S. Government Printing Office.

Preble, E. A., and Casey, J. J., Jr. (1969). Taking care of business—The heroin user's life on the street. *International Journal of Addictions* 4:1–24.

Riley, M. W., and Waring, J. (1978). Age, cohorts and drug use. In *Longitudinal research on drug use*, edited by D. B. Kandel. Washington, D.C.: Hemisphere Press.

Simon, H. (1957). *Models of man*. New York: Wiley & Sons.

Waldorf, D. (1973). *Careers in dope*. Englewood Cliffs, N. J.: Prentice-Hall.

Williams, T. M., and Kornblum, W. (1985). *Growing up poor*. Lexington, Mass.: Lexington Books.

Winick, C. (1980). A theory of drug dependence based on role, access to and attitudes toward drugs. In *Theories on drug abuse*, edited by D. J. Lettieri, M. Sayers, and H. W. Pearson. NIDA Research Monograph No. 30. Rockville, Md.: National Institute on Drug Abuse.

Chapter 6

TEENAGE FATHERHOOD: ISSUES CONFRONTING YOUNG BLACK MALES

Michael E. Connor

> *When jobless figures among black men are combined with their relatively high rates of incarceration . . . and premature mortality . . . it becomes clear that the ability of black men to provide economic support is even lower than official employment statistics convey . . . black women, particularly younger black women, are confronting a shrinking pool of economically stable, or "marriageable" men.*
>
> R. APONTE, K. NECKERMAN, and W. WILSON in
> "Race, family structure, and social policy,"
> *Working Paper 7: Race and Policy* (Washington,
> D.C.: Project on the Federal Role, National
> Conference on Social Welfare, 1985).

Introduction

Issues relating to teen sex and teen sexuality have concerned parents for generations. What are our children doing? With whom? Why are they doing it? What do they know and where did they learn it? These are variations of questions that have bothered parents over the years. Related to these questions regarding teenage sexuality are concerns about problems of teenage pregnancy and childbirth.

The purpose of this chapter is to review the literature regarding black teenage parents; the focus is on males. Because the literature on black fathers in general and black teenage fathers in particular is so sparse, information extrapolated from a variety of sources (including historical writings about black men, from black women, from those studies which do deal with black teenagers, and from inferences in the literature) will be used. Questions about black teenage fathers include: Who are they? How do they feel about their child or children? How do they feel about their child's mother? What are their goals and aspirations? What problems do they encounter? What is being done to help them? What can and should be done to help them?

In addition to presenting a brief historical overview of black men in families and reviewing the literature about black teenage fathers, the chapter also discusses selected programs that serve this population and offers suggestions for policy changes and implications for programs.

Although teenagers are sexually active, apparently few are sexually responsible. Gallas (1980) claims that 50 percent of teenagers between 15 and 19 are sexually involved, and few use any form of contraception. Stark (1986) found that 50 percent of teenagers between 15 and 17 were sexually involved and "only 14 percent of teenage girls use contraceptives the first time they have intercourse" (p. 28). These teenagers are sexually active almost one year *prior* to obtaining information regarding birth control!

Since 1960, the total number of unmarried teen births has risen from 91,700 to 199,900 in 1970 to 269,346 in 1982. Among black females 15–19, the out-of-wedlock birth rate has actually decreased from 96.9 per 1,000 in 1970 to 86.4 per 1,000 in 1983, while the rate for white females has increased from 10.9 to 18.5 per 1,000 in that same period (CDF, 1986). In spite of the decreasing rate for blacks, nearly nine of every ten babies born to black teens are out of wedlock. In 1980, the estimated intended fertility rate (EIFR) for black females 15–19 was 1.8 times higher than the rate for whites, while the estimated unintended fertility rate (EUFR) was also higher for black females (Spitz et al., 1987). In 1983 only 16,000 of 137,000 babies born to black teenagers were born to married teens, which partially reflects a negative attitude toward abortion (CDF, 1986).

American teens also have a higher rate of abortion than any other Western nation. The number of teen abortions has risen from 244,070 in 1973 to 448,570 in 1981 (Moore, 1985). Research indicates that teen mothers (as compared to older mothers) are more likely to have birth complications, not to receive quality prenatal care, and to have more premature babies and low birth weight babies. These babies are more likely to experience abuse and neglect. Teen mothers are more likely to drop out of high school, go on welfare, and to be less competent as parents (Chilman, 1983; Furstenberg, 1980; Gibbs, 1984; Stark, 1986). Unfortunately, little is known about teen fathers, because researchers tend to focus on females.

Although teen pregnancy and childbirth are *not* exclusively a black problem, they are a problem which seriously impacts the black and other low-income communities. These communities are already beset by the interrelated problems of racism, political and social oppression, powerlessness, unemployment and poverty, substandard housing and education, crime, and deteriorating neighborhoods. In addition, the low-income black family is experiencing growing disintegration. The number of intact black families has steadily declined since the 1960s. Additionally, Chilman reports that the parents of black youngsters, as compared to white parents, have less education, less money, and more unemployment. Black youth, particularly males, have significantly higher unemployment rates than white teens (34 percent compared to 17 percent in 1987), and many of these black teens live in female-headed homes with a higher rate of poverty than male-headed homes. Chilman's (1983) data indicate that 67 percent of female-headed families are poor.

Although the birth rate for black teenagers is declining, in 1983, 40 percent of births to white teenagers and 86 percent of births to black teenagers were "out of wedlock." By age 20, 19 percent of white teens and 41 percent of black teens are mothers. Gibbs (1986) found that black and low socioeconomic status (SES) teenage girls are more likely to be sexually active than other girls. Her sexually active sample was also experiencing school problems and delinquency, and were abusing substances. Chilman (1983) found that black teenagers tend to engage in less petting than whites; they tend to have fewer sexual partners, and there tends to be less of a double standard about one's sexuality—that is, girls feel less guilty about being sexually active. Chilman also found that black teenage males were more permissive regarding premarital intercourse than white males and females and black females. Religiosity is not related to sexual activity for black teenagers. Ladner (1971) found that black females were fearful of contraception, because they thought it might contribute to birth deformities.

Social Science and Black Men in Families

In reviewing the literature regarding black males in the United States, one is hard-pressed to find information that is not negatively oriented. Researchers usually emphasize father absenteeism and other perceived deficits, such as low aspirations/low self-esteem, language deficits, sensory deprivation (or overstimulation), unemployment/under employment, educational handicaps, school dropout, alcohol and substance abuse, violence and aggression, genetic inferiority, and family disorganization (including the matriarchy), the unstable family, juvenile delinquency, and illegitimacy (Hetherington and Parke, 1975; Lamb, 1981; Lynn, 1974). Seemingly few "positives" happen within the black family. Petras (1975), in an otherwise serious and scholarly book, deals with black males from a "humorous" perspective. When looking more directly at black fathers, the situation is even more bleak—the usual discussion deals with illegitimate children and/or father absenteeism. (The "other side" of absenteeism is single-parent households: the matriarchy.) Absenteeism of males, combined with matrifocal homes, is suggested by the literature and accepted by society at large as the primary type of black family household in the United States today. In 1983, 48 percent of black families with children under 18 were female-headed (Aponte, Neckerman, and Wilson, 1985).

Dodson (1981) suggests the two major social science approaches for dealing with the black family are the pathological and dysfunctional approach and the cultural relativistic approach. The former focuses on disorganized, unstable households, and the latter focuses on family strengths, often controlling for socioeconomic status. The pathological orientation was so pervasive during the 1960s that an entire literature was devoted to it.

Johnson (1981), in reviewing the family studies literature, found this negative orientation to be the most pervasive approach utilized by (dominant culture) social scientists. McAdoo (1981) writes that researchers "generally studied . . . most economically deficient, socially vulnerable, problematic black families and inferred negative interaction patterns" (p. 115). Gray (1981) says the research tends "to be social problem oriented" (p. 10) with a focus on social position, role-enactment issues, and absenteeism. Not much data exist for father-present households. Jackson (1978) notes that the focus on the pathology of black males is so severe that she describes "ordinary black husbands/fathers" as the truly hidden men from the perpetrators of the "culture of investigative poverty" (p. 139). Cazenave (1981) found no research on father-present households.

Certainly, issues and problems confront the contemporary black community. No serious scholar can downplay or ignore the impact of black-on-black crime, of black unemployment, of black children having children, and of fathers (at any age) who are not providing for their children—emotionally or financially. However, one may ask if the images presented and accepted by society at large (black, white, others) regarding black males as fathers are or were accurate.

Historical Overview

Some researchers argue that during slavery there was evidence suggesting that black men were actively and directly involved in family life. Genovese (1978), for example, notes that slaves were willing to risk punishment in order to keep families together. He says that the slaveowners were cognizant of this and often argued against separation of families because slaves worked better when kept together. He also indicates in studying runaway slaves that the importance of family life was second only to the resentment of punishment as a reason for running away. Gutman (1976) writes that large numbers of slave couples lived in long marriages, and most lived in double-headed households.

During the years following the Civil War, Harris (1976) found two-parent households to be dominant in the black community. Migration to the North, especially from the Deep South, was minimal at this time. The movement that did occur was primarily from border states to Boston or New York and primarily for work (cooks, maids, servants). Many blacks returned to the South after a few years due to unanticipated problems as "freed" people. Hostilities from recent immigrants arriving from Europe regarding adequate work and/or housing were the major causes of this return (Johnson and Campbell, 1981).

The Exodus of 1879 (the "Kansas Exodus") was a planned and organized migration of freed people to the Kansas Territory. Blacks migrated in large numbers for social, political, and economical gains. Many bought farms or homesteaded. However, most were ill-prepared for the harsh Kansas winters or for the hostilities encountered from whites, who passed laws making land ownership difficult, staying overnight in communities without a residence or a job a punishable offense ("Sundowner" laws), and limiting the political powers of blacks to govern themselves.

During the early 1900s, black men, women, and children came North in large numbers seeking "a better way of life." This was the Great Migration, which led to the urbanization and industrialization of masses of blacks. Data suggest that single men, women, families, and married men without their families participated in this move. Some families were forever torn apart as a result of this movement. Promises and dreams of an independent life off the farm and in the city were enticing. Unfortunately, the dreams became nightmares; even though black women were permitted domestic work, there were no jobs for the masses of black men (Genovese, 1978).

The years following World War I were harsh ones for black Americans. Systematic exclusion from all facets of life was pervasive. "Jim Crowism" was alive, well, and thriving. Political, economical, educational, and social advances were slow in coming and painfully gained. The country which fought a great war to "make the world safe for democracy" made few and feeble attempts to include people of color in the democratic processes.

By the 1930s, the country was in the midst of the Great Depression—unemployment of white Americans was at an all-time high at 24.9 percent in 1933. Examples abound regarding the impact of this unemployment on family life in white America. Families broke up, men were despondent, newspapers wrote about hobos and soup lines, and suicide and suicide attempts were not uncommon. White America came to understand the impact of poverty, the lack of work and despair—on white males. Underemployment and unemployment among "freed" black males in the United States have never been lower than 24.9 percent and white America continues to show little understanding, compassion, or concern for this issue.

By 1940, the United States was moving toward a second great War to make the world "safe for democracy." During the early years of World War II there was little migration of blacks due to the lack of employment possibilities. The situation was so bad that in 1943 riots broke out in Harlem, Detroit, and Los Angeles. These uprisings were in response to the frustrations of whites getting work over blacks. As the war intensified and white males went off to fight and die in a segregated armed forces, the demand for black laborers increased. By 1944, hiring practices changed, and blacks in large numbers migrated to large industrial areas in search of employment and opportunity. Usually, black males were involved in this migration; thus, they created an uneven sex ratio in the communities to which they moved and in the communities from which they came. Often, this displacement was permanent and led to numerous social problems, including the disruption of families and family life when married males migrated.

When family units migrated, an entirely new set of social problems evolved. In racially segregated America, there was a shortage of housing (single-family homes) for these newly arriving families. To "solve" this problem, existing single-family houses were converted to tenements; overcrowding and public health problems followed. (Housing projects were designed and developed to solve these problems!) Prostitution, homicide, drug addiction, juvenile delinquency, and violence ensued (Johnson and Campbell, 1981).

The 1950s were a time of heightened tension between the races. Jobs, housing, adequate educational opportunities, and the lack of political strength continued to frustrate the masses of blacks who desired to alter the status quo. In 1950, 9 percent of black homes in America were one-parent. By 1970, the number had grown to 33.3 percent, and by 1980, black single-parent homes swelled to 45.8 percent (Glick, 1981). The cumulative effects of poverty, racism, and segregation had exacted an enormous toll. It can be argued that the direct attempts to control and to destroy black families in general and black males in particular, which began during slavery with emasculation, continued into "freedom" through widespread discrimination in education, employment, and housing. This procedure has had devastating psychological, social, political, and economic effects on the U.S. citizens—both black and white.

Billingsley (1970) wrote that the majority of black families were headed by men (at that time), most of whom were married to their original wives and were employed full time, but were unable to pull themselves from poverty.

Pinkney (1969) wrote that in 1965, 72 percent of all black families were composed of both husband and wife. He then went on to state that "the economic and social conditions under which black Americans have lived have led to a disorganized family life, . . . characterized by instability" (pp. 94–95). Pinkney's figures represent about one-fourth of all the black families, yet this "one-fourth" is presented as being typical.

Moynihan (1965), who analyzed and compared blacks and whites primarily from the 1960 census data on items such as illegitimacy, unemployment, father-absent homes, welfare dependency, and so forth, tended to find blacks lacking and proceeded to conclude that the problems facing blacks were due to family disorganization. Staples (1978) declared the Moynihan report hypocritical, because it made the victim the criminal. Billingsley (1970), too, was critical of Moynihan, saying that the report perpetuates the racism, ignorance, and arrogance of social science. In a more recent study, Moynihan (1986) notes that family life among the poor of all races continues to deteriorate. He espouses a national policy which would increase the financial resources of the poor who have children. Moynihan's viewpoint is diametrically opposed to the controversial views of Charles Murray (1984), who suggests that financial assistance for the poor is part of the problem, because it reinforces dependency and decreases the desire and motivation to work. Wilson and Neckerman (1984) believe that the lack of adequate employment of black males and the resulting inability to provide for one's family is directly related to the rising number of black female-headed homes. They argue that there is a declining "pool" of marriageable black males—that is, those who can economically support a family. These researchers believe that the problems this "pool" of black men encounter must be considered in any serious discussion about the rise in single-parent homes.

Father-Absent Homes

As noted earlier, much of the research about black males deals with father absenteeism. Parker and Kleiner (1966) suggested that many problems such as delinquency, homosexuality, and mental disorder are attributed to a father-absent family environment, and that "mothers in the broken home situation have poorer psychological adjustment and lower goal-striving for themselves and for their children than mothers in the intact family situation" (p. 100).

Hess and Shipman (1965) found a "lack of cognitive meaning" between the mother and child in deprived families. "Deprived" mothers do not attend to the "individual characteristics" of a given situation and respond appropriately, thus creating a child who responds to authority and status rather than rationale. Bee et al. (1969) agreed with Hess and Shipman that the mother of the deprived child is the source of learning difficulties which the child later experiences in school. If Bee et al. and Hess et al. were correct, it seems logical that these children would respond well in the authoritarian organization of the school environment. However, the number of studies reporting disciplinary problems of black children in school belies this point. Lynn (1974) suggests that children reared in father-absent homes are more likely to exhibit delinquency, experience poor masculine development, and demonstrate compensatory masculine development in their teens. He also says that father absenteeism is associated with drug addiction, alcoholism, suicide attempts, and lower scholastic performance. Biller (1971) notes that boys reared in father-absent homes gravitate to gangs and gang activities. In another article, Biller (1981) writes that lower-class black males in father-absent homes suffer in terms of sex-role orientation. These males and black males in general are downgraded by black females (mothers, sisters, aunts, grandmothers, etc.), a situation that contributes to potential problems in future male-female relationships. Apparently, neither black males nor females feel good about black males. In these homes, there is much family instability and many financial problems. Lamb (1986), in summarizing the research on males in father-absent homes, concludes that they have problems with sex role and gender identification, problems in their school performance, problems in their psychosocial adjustment, and problems learning to control aggression.

Schulz (1969), in writing about black men growing up in a midwestern inner-city ghetto, suggested that black fathers have problems providing effective role models for their sons due to their marginal participation in the society at large. He believes that black teenage males seek out peers "on the street" with whom to identify. Status on the street is important if there is no status at home. Liebow (1967), observing the plight of unemployed inner-city black men (many of whom had fathered children), addressed the issue of lack of employment opportunities for black men. In his view they experience problems getting work; the work is too hard; without cars, getting to job sites is impossible; and the jobs that are available are "dead end." Scanzoni (1971) acknowledged that one-third of black families were headed by women in 1968. He says that many stereotypes exist regarding the black family due to social scientists' focus on this population and then generalizing findings to the population as a whole. Scanzoni attempts to shed light on the remaining two-thirds (the "intact," male-female headed) families. However, he tends to focus on perceived deficiencies. For example, he notes that the literature "is replete with the alleged 'inability' of the [black] father to move his sons towards goals" (p. 96). He claims that black men came to believe they were inferior after being told they were for so many years and after being systematically excluded from opportunity.

Each of these works contains some accuracies regarding the specific black populations that were studied. However, Liebow and Schulz focused on the problems of low-income black males, generalized their findings to black males across SES, tended not to study mother-father-present black families, tended to look at those males where pathology was present, tended to ignore inherent strengths in black families and in black men, and tended not to deal with the issues of white racism which these men were facing on a daily basis. This failure to deal with white racism and discrimination is most apparent in Scanzoni's work in that he acknowledges it as a problem but ignores any meaningful attempt to study, comprehend, or deal with the magnitude of white racism on his intact black families. It is important to attempt to understand how these "intact" families experienced the successes they did in spite of racism, prejudice, and discrimination.

Teen Fathers

The research on adolescent fathers is very limited. Seemingly little is known about this population and few services are available for them. Barret and Robinson (1985) suggest there are several myths regarding adolescents who father children. These myths include the following:

1. They are worldly wise and know more about sex and sexuality than most teenage boys.
2. They usually have fleeting, casual relationships with the young mother and experience little emotional reaction to the pregnancy.
3. They are rarely involved in the support and rearing of their children.
4. They complete school and enter high-paying jobs, leaving their partners to fend for themselves.
5. They are psychologically different from teenage boys who do not become fathers during adolescence.

Hendricks (1981), in his study of adolescent fathers, found that they came from large families, their fathers were present, they became fathers at 17.8 years, about half had unwed sisters with children, about a third had brothers who were unwed fathers, and a fourth were born to single-parent homes. He also found the majority were not involved with church, were working, and had completed high school. They also saw nothing wrong with what they had done and were concerned about their children's and the mother's future. However, he found that they were "unrealistic" about parenthood. In another paper, Hendricks and Montgomery (1983) found that teenage fathers were accepting of fatherhood, expressed love for the mother and child, and were concerned about the child's future. They were not concerned about having had a child "out of wedlock." Robinson, Barret, and Skeen (1983) found no difference in locus of control between unwed adolescent fathers and nonfathers. Redmond (1985) found teenage fathers and fathers-to-be want to know and understand what's going on in their girlfriend's life. These teens indicated a willingness to help with physical care and finances, and demonstrated affection for their child. This sample was also supportive of abortion and adoption.

Furstenberg (1980) found that teen males expressed an interest and desire to help with their children. Barret and Robinson (1985) found that teenage dads maintained a positive relationship with their girlfriend and her family and that they planned to meet certain social, educational, and financial expectations for the mother and child. Brown (1983) found black adolescent fathers to be primarily concerned about financial support for their child, continuing their own schooling, problems with their girlfriend's parents, and their own future. These males were not perceived as being exploitative of their girlfriends. While the above studies may be indicative of one aspect of adolescent fathers, they certainly contradict the established stereotype of this population. Obviously, more research is needed.

Parke, Power, and Fisher (1980) suggest that more studies are needed to understand the father as caregiver and playmate, including teenage fathers. They found teens to be involved with their children after birth and many teenage fathers to be living with their children after having been separated one to two years.

Research does not support the popular notion that these teenagers father children with several different females. They tend to express love, affection, and caring for their girlfriend and their child.

As noted, studies about teen fathers are sparse, but certain trends are present. In attempting to predict at-risk teens, Robbins, Kaplan, and Martin (1985) found that low-income males who were experiencing school problems and who were popular were vulnerable. Their sample of minority youth was not low on powerlessness or self-esteem as Lewis (1961) formulates in his "culture of poverty" conception.

In reviewing the literature, one is struck with the paucity of studies dealing with the male role in teen pregnancy in general and with black male teenagers in particular. Little is known about this population. The studies which do exist indicate that black teens are more pessimistic about the future and are more dissatisfied with society in general as compared to white teens. Young blacks tend to doubt the validity of marriage, accept children born "out of wedlock," and espouse more sexual freedom; white teens tend to have more sexual partners and engage in more frequent sexual activities (Chilman, 1983; Gibbs, 1984; Furstenberg, 1976).

Unemployment and the Black Family

An ongoing problem in social science research is the establishment of criterion reference points by which or to which something is to be measured. In relating to the black community, social scientists traditionally measure blacks against whites, with whites as the reference group. Social scientists tend to focus on the most problematic of the black population and generalize their findings to the population as a whole; furthermore, they tend to identify problems while often ignoring meaningful solutions. These procedures are as old as social science and continue today. Dreger and Miller (1968), Hetherington and Parke (1975), Ladner (1973), Lamb (1981), Lynn (1974), and Aponte, Neckerman, and Wilson (1985) are a few of the numerous examples of these approaches. While there is some value to these procedures, they also are lacking, perhaps because using any "out-group" criteria to study "in-group" phenomenon would be lacking. It does appear that the black family has not been well studied by social scientists and that the few studies which have taken place are poorly controlled and tend to emphasize "negatives." However, there does seem to be a trend of black social scientists beginning to study and analyze the family much as Billingsley suggested. It is important not merely to study what black families *do not do*, but what they *do*.

Perhaps the "outculture" social scientist who is interested in studying the black family might take a lead from anthropology. In studying black family structure in the Caribbean, several anthropologists found a large percentage of female-headed households (R. Smith, 1956; M. G. Smith, 1963; Cumper, 1958; Otterbein, 1965; and Clarke, 1957), the percentage ranging from 17 percent in British Guyana to 59 percent in Carriacori. Some researchers concluded that these people were immoral, promiscuous, and possessed a loose, disorganized family life. However, upon closer scrutiny it was determined that certain economic-demographic factors characterized the Caribbean family system. These factors included the opportunity to earn and save money and the male-female sex ratio. More specifically, many men prior to 25 years of age left their villages to join a migratory wage labor force and worked until they had saved enough money to purchase a house. For marriage to take place, it was important that the man owned a home. Because many of the younger men left their villages to work, the male-female sex ratio remaining in the village was unbalanced. Since some of the younger men never returned to the village, the sex ratio was permanently imbalanced; thus, some women were not able to find spouses. The women seemed to adapt to these situations by either leaving the village to seek work, or by seeking married male members of the village with whom to have ongoing "relationships." The married men helped these women set up and maintain a household, and the behavior was acceptable to the villagers. Clarke's data (1957) indicated that the greater the economic well-being of an area, the greater the percentage of marriage and the lower the percentage of consensual unions. It thus appeared that the black family in the Caribbean had adapted to the economic and family demands characterizing life there.

We are not suggesting that black families in the United States are exactly like those in the Caribbean. However, social scientists can and should learn from the above example. For survival purposes, a reasonable assumption is that the black family in the United States, regardless of its socioeconomic status, has also adapted to its situation (i.e., discrimination, segregation, prejudice, poor economic and educational opportunities, etc.), but this adaptation has not been adequately researched or studied. Certainly, this adaptation can be perceived as a strength. Several researchers, including Aponte, Neckerman, and Wilson (1985), Malson (1984), Sklar (1986), and Wilson and Neckerman (1984) report that unemployment is related to marital instability or the lack of marriage altogether. Family life during the depression deteriorated following unemployment. The above-mentioned researchers indicate that during the 1960s employment decreased rapidly among black males, and at the same time the number of father-absent families increased dramatically. The authors suggest a correlation which merits further investigation. They go on to say that combining joblessness with rates of incarceration plus early mortality (drugs, violence, combat-deaths, and suicide) lowers the pool from which appropriate black husbands might be selected (Wilson's Male Marriageable Pool Index). Wilson and Neckerman (1984) claim that the ratio of employed black men to black women has declined substantially since 1960—especially among younger black men. This decline is especially true in northern industrial areas and in the South. It is in these areas of the country where most blacks reside. If one adds to this shrinking pool those males who never marry or who marry nonblacks, the pool is further reduced. Thus, the number of black males who are not "marriageable" is rather large. It can be argued that adolescents, regardless of their intent, are generally ill-equipped to handle the demands of marriage and are therefore part of this pool.

Correlates of Teenage Parenthood

Many researchers are finding relationships between teenage pregnancy, school dropout, vocational unemployment, and crime and delinquency. Gibbs (1984) found unemployment among black youth was 48.3 percent in 1983, the rate of delinquency was 21.4 percent in 1979, drinking and substance abuse were increasing, 44 percent of black children under the age of 18 were living in female-headed homes in 1980, and 15.4 percent of black youth in the 16–24 age group were high school dropouts. Gibbs is not discussing separate and distinct populations. Rather, these figures relate to low-income black youths in the United States who are experiencing a multitude and variety of serious problems. Sklar (1986) believes that unemployment is a major contributor to teen pregnancy, especially for low-income and minority males. Sullivan (1986) claims that the lack of employment is related to teenage childbirth, leaving school, criminal activity, drug and substance abuse, suicide, and poor mental health. He also found that for inner-city youth, the lack of work is a fact of life. Bumpass, Rindfuss, and Janosik (1978) note that early parenthood and "illegitimacy" are associated with lower educational and vocational attainment, marital instability, larger families, and poor mental and physical health. Malson (1984) believes the situation is so bleak that many black males have given up looking for work and thus will never be able to provide financial care for their children. Additionally, children born in black female-headed homes are likely to be reared in poverty. Chilman (1983) claims that 67 percent of black single mothers between the ages of 14 and 24 are poor.

Involved Black Fathers

Cazenave (1981) indicates that black men believe responsibility is the key to manhood. His sample (54 black fathers employed as letter carriers) also indicated that ambition, firm guiding principles, and being an economic provider—that is, taking care of one's family—are important. Interestingly, Sullivan (1986) found that the black community expected teenage fathers to participate in caring for their children. In fact, he found that local standards exist for judging young fathers who do and do not attempt to provide care for their children; those who do not incur disrespect in their neighborhoods. Glick (1981) notes that "as the income level of men increases, the proportion of men with intact first marriages tend to increase" (p. 117). He observes that stability seems not to depend on being well-to-do, but rather on not being poor.

In a study conducted in 1983, Connor (1986) surveyed the attitudes toward children and mates of 136 working-class black men in an urban southern California area. The sample ranged in age from 20 to 45. The mean age was 32.8. This research looked at four issues:

1. The black male's perception of his role as father.
2. The black male's perception of his role as mate.
3. The black male's perception of other black men's role as father.

4. The black male's perception of gender-related child-rearing differences.

Connor advanced five hypotheses;

1. Black men see themselves as actively involved with their children.
2. Black men see themselves as actively involved with their mates.
3. Black men see other black men as actively involved with their children.
4. Black men see other black men as actively involved with their mate.
5. Black men believe in treating male and female children alike.

Hypotheses 1, 2, and 5 were supported; hypotheses 3 and 4 were not. The black men in Connor's study tended to see other black men lacking as relates to both children and mate. They perceived other men having problems getting along and being meaningfully involved with both children and mate, although they reported they themselves were meaningfully involved with their children and mate. Among other explanations, this finding might suggest this population was not involved themselves and were projecting this lack of involvement onto others—a defensive posture. This was the dominant view accepted by those reviewing the paper for publication, and they requested an elaboration, as if everyone knows and accepts as fact that black men are not involved with their families. However, an equally plausible explanation is that these men (perhaps the black community in general) have accepted the popular and widespread notion that black males are not involved with their families and therefore do not perceive any meaningful interaction. Psychologically, this implicit acceptance has dire consequences for the community at large in terms of acceptance of the stereotype and behaviors that might follow. The impact of this acceptance on young black males in search of and in need of positive role models is immense. (This point is discussed more fully later.)

A primary weakness of the Connor's study (other than general problems using self-report inventories) was that only males were sampled. In an unpublished follow-up study conducted in 1983, black male ($N = 277$) and female ($N = 138$) respondents were asked to complete an expanded questionnaire regarding black male attitudes toward children and mate. Interestingly, the results were much the same as the previous study: Black men see themselves meaningfully involved with their children and mates but see other black men as lacking meaningful involvement. Black women perceive black men to be meaningfully involved with children and mate. The support from females seemingly casts doubt on the notion of pathological projection as a defense for black men. It also supports the notion that black males are not seeing other black men as meaningfully involved and adds credence to the notion that the pervasive stereotype has been accepted by males.

Teenage Sexuality

It seems clear from the data that problems in mature sexual behavior, marriage, and child rearing need to be confronted by adults (who already have enough difficulty in these areas). Children of any ethnic group having and attempting to rear children seems doomed to failure. The toll on the individuals and the community at large is too great (see Chilman, 1983). According to a 1986 California Department of Mental Health newsletter, children begin to express an interest in sexuality by the fourth grade. By the sixth grade pregnancy becomes an issue, and by high school family relationship issues are a major concern. Clearly, many of our children are interested in, want information about, are usually ignorant of, and are participating in sexual activities. Wanting this problem to go away or pretending it doesn't exist often perpetuates and exaggerates the problem. Estimates are that if the present rate of adolescent pregnancy continues, 40 percent of our 14-year-old children will become pregnant by the time they are 20. This translates into one million teenage pregnancies each year! Our teenagers have a higher pregnancy and abortion rate than any other Western society (California Department of Mental Health, (1986).

Some lessons learned from involved teenage dads suggest that they work, are willing and able to communicate with their children and mate, share household and child-rearing responsibilities, are committed to the relationship, and put time and energy into their adult responsibilities (Harrison, 1981; McAdoo, 1986).

Clinical observations of and interactions with some of the fathers who have participated in my Involved Fathers Workshops,* classes, counseling sessions, and parent meetings suggest that fathers who

---

*These workshops are open to any father on a first-come basis. Most of the participants are working men who are married. The workshops meet one night a week for four weeks on the school grounds. These programs are geared toward involved fathers who wish to learn strategies to help them increase their level of meaningful participation with their children. Many of these men want to be involved with their children but indicate they don't know how or what to do. Fathers are "recruited" via notices sent home with their children, by posters placed at strategic places on the school ground, by notices placed in local newspapers, by "word of mouth" from fathers who have participated in previous workshops or who are planning to attend a future program, and by mothers who want their spouses to become more involved. Men from a cross-section of ages, socioeconomic status, and ethnic backgrounds attend.

are involved and care take time to be with and learn about their children. Some of these men have attended prepared childbirthing classes and were present in the labor and delivery rooms. Most of them participate routinely in the care of their children—albeit generally with play and recreation. A few are involved with child-care activities—nurturing, bathing, dressing, cooking for/feeding, changing diapers, taking children to school, participating with the teacher in the child's education, and so forth. Many of these fathers allow for quiet time with their children—talking with, listening to, and sharing with them. Some of them take their children to work in order for the children to see and experience the variety of moods they experience—the ups and downs in life, allowing themselves to be honest, to make mistakes, to apologize. These fathers want to learn about parenting (thus, their attendance at the workshops, classes, etc.). They care and therefore consider taking time for their families to be a high priority. They seem to be in a partnership with their mate and do things together. Church tends to occupy an important aspect of these men's lives, and they attend with their families on a regular basis. These men also tend to be active in sports and recreation, often with family or friends. They take an active part in family decision making. Those who are most successful in their family relationships tend to understand, accept, and encourage active decision making with their spouses. Most of these fathers participate in the discipline of their children; they tend to use a variety of techniques, ranging from corporal punishment to discussion to time out to loss of privilege. They also are encouraged and do participate in bedtime activities, taking the initiative to make going to bed a relaxed and mellow time. During this time, fathers talk with their children, read to them, listen to them. These fathers allow themselves to be tender, although primarily with their daughters—hugging, kissing, holding them.

Younger fathers (23–27 years) and fathers of first-borns tend to be more anxious. They are concerned about being financially able to support their young family adequately, concerned about the effect the child will have on their adult lives (being tied down and less able to participate in many of the activities they used to do), concerned about having enough time for themselves and their spouse, and worried about the enormity of the responsibilities hovering over them and for which they were so poorly prepared. These younger fathers tend to take their lead from their spouse in terms of interacting with their child. All of the fathers in these programs have demonstrated an active participation and interest in their children, their spouses, and their future.

Attempts at reeducation, including contraception, anatomy and physiology, responsibility, and child development, have been lacking. Many parents, children, churches, and politicians object—yet the problem escalates. Gordon (1986) says that fewer than 10 percent of the schools in the United States offer meaningful sex and sexuality information to students. This includes information which students want and need to hear—information about male and female genitalia, masturbation, female orgasm, homosexuality, oral and anal sex, feelings of love, contraception, and venereal disease prevention. Gordon suggests that most of the opposition to educating teens is based on the premise that knowledge is harmful—that is, arming teenagers with facts will somehow entice them to become even more sexually active. Gordon further claims that teens do not receive adequate information from their parents, who may be uncomfortable with their own and their teenager's sexuality. Parents basically tell teenagers not to have sex, but this is an unrealistic and unenlightened approach.

Other researchers report that parents are interested and support sex education for their teens, but these parents have several concerns. For example, Marsman and Herold (1986) report that parents want schools to teach sex education classes, but want clarification over what *values* are being taught. Arcus (1986) notes that support for sex education is found among students, parents, teachers, administrators, and the general public, but it is unclear if these programs should be required or elective courses. Arcus believes programs should go beyond sex education to family life education. Alexander (1984) reports that parents of junior high school teenagers want to be the primary sex educators of their children and desire the school to support them. These parents want schools to introduce programs by the ninth grade in an effort to reduce pregnancy and venereal disease, and they want a course for themselves to help them communicate with their children. The parents in Alexander's sample want their teens to learn about sex-related issues, personal values, the meaning of love and relationships, contraception, homosexuality, abortion, and masturbation.

Gordon (1986) notes that teens receive negative sexual material from television, which tends to project antisexual information (rape, violence, and infidelity). Churches have not been at the forefront in educating teens about their sexuality, and it is unlikely that teens are reading materials that will adequately inform them in this area. Thus, the primary purveyors of information (home, school, church, the media) are not purveying accurate and relevant sex information. Inadequate education and information are likely to be related to our high teenage pregnancy rate. Few teens use any form of contraception when they first become sexually active (less than one in seven according to Gordon), and many report they are embarrassed to get information about contraception (Stark, 1986). Others report they did not think they could get pregnant (Chilman, 1983).

Policy Suggestions for Decreasing Teenage Pregnancy

Three interrelated areas of intervention are needed at the local, state, and federal levels to attempt to decrease the incidence of teenage pregnancy. These areas are education, employment, and social programming. Programs must be comprehensive and be geared toward males and females—toward those who are parents as well as those who are nonparents—thus a remedial *and* prevention orientation. Services must be developed for those who are most in need and difficult to reach, as well as for those who desire the services.

Family Life Education

Family life education which deals with contraception, responsible decision making, reproductive physiology, values clarification, communication, and mature relationship development should be implemented in the junior high school years and continued throughout high school. Parents of teenagers must be apprised of these courses (perhaps they can be encouraged to enroll in the courses themselves), and these parents can encourage uninvolved parents of teenagers to participate.

Competent, knowledgeable, and culturally sensitive teachers must be recruited and trained to work with parents and adolescents in achieving the goals of the family life education programs. Male and female teachers who are in "successful" marriages themselves would be useful role models.

Peer counselors, rap groups (with trained and sensitive adults facilitating), and informal discussions that focus on responsible behavior are needed. Teenagers can be shown how to make responsible decisions and must be reinforced when they do make "good" decisions.

Teen parenting programs must be expanded. Extended child care is needed on or near the school grounds so that young mothers can continue their education and graduate, thus potentially becoming marketable. Young fathers can learn effective techniques of infant child care, including diapering, bathing, feeding, and so forth. Labor and birthing classes can be offered. The goal is to encourage these young men to accept and fulfill their obligations to their young.

Academic programs in the public schools must be reevaluated and redesigned to determine why so many black children are dropping out or being pushed out. The relationship between early pregnancies and school-related problems (including dropping out) is clear for both black and white youth. Remedial education focusing on basic skills (reading, writing, and math) is a must and should be implemented during the elementary years. Compensatory educational programs must be restored and expanded to include the parents of elementary-aged children, who are often children themselves. These young parents must be trained and motivated so they can help teach their children.

Vocational education which teaches marketable skills, job attitudes, and performance competencies are needed so that black children can be competitive in the labor force when they seek employment.

In order to accomplish these goals, teachers and teacher training programs must be reassessed to ensure that competent and sensitive professionals are working with black children. These professionals must be paid at a competitive level so they are not lost to business and industry. The school curriculum must be revamped so that black children have equal access to the information, techniques, procedures, and knowledge (including computer literacy) available to white children. Efforts must be first directed toward understanding why black children drop out of school at such high rates and then toward keeping these children from dropping out and reenrolling those who have left school.

Employment Training

Obviously, if young men are to provide for their children and to position themselves so that they can support future children, they need relevant work. This work must compensate them at a level whereby they feel good about themselves and believe they have a stake in the future. Marginal, meaningless, dead-end jobs are not the answer. Thus, concerted efforts to train young black males for the technical jobs of tomorrow are required. School-to-work transition programs which facilitate the progression from the educational environment to the work environment are needed at all high schools serving black youth. The Job Corps should be expanded to include adolescents at age 16; this is also true of the Job Training Partnership program (Gibbs, 1985).

Once these low-income young people are placed on a job,

relevant follow-up is needed to help them continue to work, to help them resolve unanticipated problems, and to reinforce any attempts for self-improvement.

Social Programs

Efforts are needed to advise, inform, and educate the public regarding problems confronting young people who are sexually active. Currently, attempts are being made to inform the public of AIDS and the potential tragic consequences for our youth. These efforts must be expanded to include prevention of teenage pregnancy.

Programs providing low-cost, quality child care are needed for women and families who desire to work or further their education. These services should be based on the "ability to pay" and/or in-kind contributions so that participants might feel good about "earning" the services. Additionally, young parents can learn about organizing their time, prioritizing, and assuming personal responsibility in these programs. It is important that these young people return to school after the birth of their child so they might develop their skills, including vocational attainment. An aspect of this training must be on positive social roles.

Young females and males need help adjusting to the pregnancy and the birth of their child. Thus, programs servicing pregnant teenagers should be expanded to include males. Additionally, these young people and their children need medical care, access to contraception, family counseling, personal counseling, knowledge about child development, information regarding proper nutrition for themselves and their children, and help in establishing and maintaining a household and transportation.

Society as a whole must acknowledge, reinforce, and perhaps fund the natural helpers whom these teenage parents utilize, usually their mothers. It is important that this support system be recognized for the service it provides and encouraged to continue.

Finally, the society must come to grips with the impact of racism, poverty, youth unemployment, poor family relations, and inadequate human services, especially for those most in need. The cost of these problems is great, but ignoring the need they create is greater.

Programs for Teenage Fathers

Efforts to curtail repeat pregnancies must focus on education and training aimed toward self-sufficiency. People must be reinforced to avoid the dependent "welfare mentality." These efforts must be expanded to include males as well as females. We need to redefine our values and take a stand to save our children. We must understand what we want from our children in the future, and use this standard to guide our present activities. The role and impact of church, family, parents, education, work, contraception, responsibility toward self and others, the government, and the dominant culture must be assessed. We can no longer afford the luxury of blaming others, as this does not solve our problem. Rather, we must be willing to take direct action, be it popular or unpopular, to deal with adolescent pregnancy. We must assess the programs that exist and support those that are working, regardless of our pet theories and projects. We must be willing to alter or discard those programs that are not successful.

Several successful programs which offer services to teenage fathers and/or fathers-to-be exist across the country. Efforts are needed to expand the scope of these programs so they might exist in other communities, so that they may service more youths, and so that responsible sexual behavior might begin to resolve this serious problem.

The Teen Father Collaboration, which was coordinated by Bank Street College in New York City, is one such program. The goal was to develop strategies to reach young males (who are sexually active) and to provide services to them, including personal counseling, vocational and educational counseling, parenting skills classes, job training, and prenatal classes. Programs were developed and placed in hospitals, schools, and social service agencies in eight cities. According to Sander (1986), 395 youth from a variety of backgrounds were served. Most of these teenagers were unemployed, and many had dropped out of school. These youth tended to report positive feelings for the mother of their child (their "girlfriend"); they offered money (when they had it) and child care. Most of these males were 17 and 18 years old. One hundred forty-eight (67 percent) found jobs after participating in the program, and approximately 50 percent of those who were nongraduates returned to school.

Some communities have developed school-based clinics which provide comprehensive services to teenagers on school grounds. Services often include reproductive health services, with some clinics prescribing and distributing contraceptive methods. Many of these clinics, such as those in Houston and St. Paul, reach males through physical examinations for sports programs and other novel ways of getting males to visit the clinic. These programs are interested in helping males to become independent, healthy, and socially responsible.

Still other communities have found older teens and men to serve as positive role models for younger teens. Some use the services of popular sports and entertainment figures; others use video equipment to tape the teenagers at parks, playing ball, etc. and invite them to the clinic to see themselves on tape. Some communities are establishing networks among agencies which serve youth in attempting to develop comprehensive services. Finally, some communities espouse a "will power–won't power" approach, teaching teens to say no to sex.

Joy Dryfoss (1985) believes that teenage males must be offered a "package" that includes eight objectives: (1) helping them understand the need for shared responsibility, (2) providing them with knowledge, (3) providing access to contraception, (4) advertising the need for responsibility, (5) teaching them to communicate, (6) providing family planning with comprehensive health services, (7) altering the environment of family planning clinics so that males are comfortable and welcome, and (8) expanding the "life options" for all young people.

Unfortunately, most programs tend to offer services to pregnant teenagers or to teenage mothers only (Campbell, Breitmayer, and Ramey, 1986; Adler, Bates, and Merdinger, 1985; Vukelich and Kilman, 1985). Often these programs are not geared to male needs, usually do not have male co-workers, and are not oriented to offer services to males (Center for Population Options, 1986). Roosa (1986) notes that many school-based programs for teen mothers tend to serve only those who are easiest to reach and ignore teenagers most in need. Underserved/nonserved females include those who drop out of school prior to pregnancy, those who drop out shortly after birth, and those who experience a second pregnancy.

Research Suggestions for Decreasing Teenage Pregnancy

One research approach might be to study those adolescent males and females who do not become pregnant. Who are they? What are their goals and attitudes? What do they feel about teenage pregnancy? How did they avoid the trap which many of their friends fell into? Who are their parents? Culturally sensitive researchers might look at a large segment of this population across the country—in large cities and small towns, in rural and urban areas, across socioeconomic lines. Perhaps these young people will provide us with the direction we so desperately need and seek. Focus on the "successes"—but do not ignore the "failures" who continue to need help. In relating to those children who have had children, we must redirect their energies and actions to curtail repeat pregnancies.

Strategies must be developed that make children having babies "unfashionable." The National Urban League's Adolescent Male Responsibility Project represents a beginning. This is a national public awareness campaign to encourage responsible male involvement in parenting and involves posters, print ads, and radio public service announcements admonishing black adolescent males not to make a baby if they're not prepared to be a father. We must get the message across that making a baby is not a sign of manhood (or adulthood), that making a baby doesn't take any special talent or skill, that not taking care of one's children is both irresponsible and reprehensible, that sex is for adults who understand the consequences and accept the responsibilities, and that a measure of an adult is not simply having children but adequately rearing them. The media is in the position to convey this message directly, forceably, and competently. Popular commercial television programs, which shape so many of our perceptions, attitudes, and beliefs, and to which so many of our children attend, must take a lead. They can portray the changes and problems with teenage pregnancy. The programs our children watch and companies whose products sponsor them must be subjected to pressure geared toward helping us save our children. "Soul" radio stations are also in a position to convey this message regarding responsible behavior. Discussions in between songs, with guest artists and teenagers themselves talking about reducing teenage pregnancy, can have an impact. There is also a need to convince young rappers/song writers, who are often rapping/writing/singing irresponsibly about sexuality, to modify their message. Parents, who are the primary educators of their children, must learn to pay attention to lyrics which our young children hear and demonstrate judgment and maturity by turning off the radio when they do not approve of the message. These same parents must also object to the management of these stations (and protest if necessary) about songs that contain unsuitable messages. Popular magazines can also serve as a vehicle for alerting our children about the extent and magnitude of the problem through articles written at a variety of levels which can be understood by all.

Coaches need to discuss responsible sexuality and teenage pregnancy with their players (male and female) in the gym, in the locker room, and on the field. The message of responsible parenthood can be discussed at school, on the playground, at concerts, in pool halls and barber shops, on the job, at social service agencies, at church, in the home, at family gatherings, and so on. In short, we must begin to modify the image that kids having kids is okay. We need to have men discuss with men that having babies which they cannot or do not want to support is unacceptable. The media, at all levels, can present positive and appropriate role models for our young people. If our males have bought the stereotype that black men don't care, that they are irresponsible, that they are not involved, we must be cognizant of the psychological damage done and take strident measures to overcome it. We must acknowledge appropriate role models when and wherever we encounter them. We must consistently point out and praise black fathers who are involved. We must take the initiative to offer a contrary view of every negative stereotype about black men to which our children are subjected. Black fathers who are involved with their children and families must remain involved and take the lead in eradicating these negative stereotypes.

Churches and other visible community organizations must be encouraged and reinforced to get involved with this pressing matter. Black clergymen must be made aware of the intent of the problem and the economic, educational, medical, social, political, and psychological consequences of children having children. They are in the position to offer space for programs, to help with school and home visits to potential participants, to counsel those parents of teens and teen parents-to-be who may be in need, to lead their congregation toward acceptance of programs designed to combat the problem, to help spread the word regarding the availability of such programs, and to support the goals and objectives of teen pregnancy reduction, sex education, family life education, and parenting programs.

Conclusions

Parenting in today's technological, fast-paced, shrunken, and ever-changing world is a very complex, frustrating, demanding, expensive, and (often) rewarding experience. Potential parents might decrease the probability of problems if they are adults, educated with "good" jobs, in stable relationships, and healthy. However, even these ideal parents are not immune from the problems that confront today's children. Then, if under the best of circumstances, parents are confronted with daily issues and concerns about their children and child rearing, parents whose circumstances are suspect or lacking might confront more severe, overwhelming problems. Parents in poverty, overcrowded conditions, oppressed and depressed neighborhoods, those with no marketable skills, with marginal reading and writing skills and with little hope to improve their position in the society have many problems. Additionally, parents with poor relationships (or no relationships), those who are abusing substances (alcohol, prescribed medications, street drugs, etc.), and those who are unable or unwilling to care for their children are facing problems.

Estimates are that it costs $250,000 to rear a child to the age of 18 in a "middle-class" situation. This constitutes a major investment, which society must be willing to make. In fact, much of American society is ready, able, and willing to make such a commitment. Historically, children of educated people receive education. Children of those who control the technical, entrepreneurial, and professional places in America are able to find jobs, and their parents are often in positions to help get jobs for their friends. America loves a "rags to riches" story and America takes great pride in advertising that in the "Land of the Free," any one with initiative can succeed.

Unfortunately, much of America's black inner-city underclass is permanently and systematically barred from such lofty ambitions. The few who do "make it" do so through the only avenues open to them, mainly entertainment, sports, or street crime.

The black family trying to stay together confronts daily obstacles relating to racism manifested in discrimination, the lack of educational facilities and opportunities, ceilings on vocational attainment, economic instability, inadequate services available to help address these problems, and inadequate housing (to name a few). Social science would do well to try and understand how the number of black children who do progress do so in such dire circumstances. Obviously, as Hill (1971) wrote years ago, there are strengths in the black family which must be considered. Although there have been gains in the progress of "middle-class" blacks, the process has not been without problems. Unfortunately, the masses of blacks have not achieved "middle-class" status. If problems are evident for "so-called educated blacks," it is not surprising that blacks from less advantaged backgrounds would have even more problems. One in seven children in the United States is officially poor, and one of five children under 18 lives in poverty—children are the largest group living in poverty in America, and most of these children live in female-headed homes (Children's Defense Fund, 1984). As of March 1984, 11 percent of America's children had one parent not working, with black children three times more likely to be poor than white children. The unemployment rate in the black community reached 15 percent (4 percent is what the government considers "acceptable") (Children's Defense Fund, 1985).

A major problem confronting American society in general and the black community specifically is the dramatic increase in the number of single-parent households, especially among teenagers. This is an expensive problem that we cannot afford to ignore. Teen pregnancies cost the United States $16.65 billion in 1985 alone (Center for Population Options, 1986). It is reasonable that some, if not most, of that money should be redirected to comprehensive programs aimed at preventing and/or reducing teenage pregnancy. As noted, these programs must be culturally sensitive and should include educational and vocational retraining, parenting skills, family life education, personal counseling, and sex education; they must include both males and females.

Glenn Loury (1986) writes that the "Moynihan Report" in 1965 warned us about the crisis confronting black America. He notes that many social scientists—black and white—were offended by the report; although much controversy developed, little was done to stem the tide. Commenting on the Moynihan report, Professor Loury suggests that we have "lived to see history prove him right in his original assessment" (p. 23). While not convinced that Moynihan's assessment was correct, because I believe in a "self-fulfilling prophecy," I do agree that nothing was done to deal with black family strengths and to reinforce parental responsibility. It is clear that we are facing a serious problem which will impact us for generations if we do not take action. It may be too pessimistic to say the problem can never be completely eradicated, but it is not too optimistic to believe that the tide can be turned. In developing solutions to this very complex problem, it is imperative that we avoid the crisis-oriented, short-sighted, band-aid approaches that are so pervasive in our attempts at problem solving.

References

Adler, E. S., Bates, M., and Merdinger, J. M. (1985). Educational policies and programs for teenage parents and pregnant teenagers. *Family Relations* 34(2):183–89.

Alexander, S. J. (1984). Improving sex education programs for young adolescents: Parents' views. *Family Relations* 33(2):251–59.

Aponte, R., Neckerman, K., and Wilson, W. (1985). Race, family structure and social policy. Working Paper 7: *Race and policy*. Washington, D.C.: National Conference on Social Welfare.

Arcus, M. (1986). Should family life education be required for high school students? *Family Relations* 35(3):347–57.

Barret, R. L. and Robinson, B. E. (1982). A descriptive study of teenage expectant fathers. *Family Relations* 31(3):349–52.

———. (1985) The adolescent father in *Dimensions of Fatherhood,* edited by S. M. H. Hanson and F. W. Bozett, pp. 353–69. Beverly Hills, Calif.: Sage Publications.

Bee, H. L., Van Egeren, L. F., Streissguth, A. P., Nyman, B. A., and Leckie, M. S. (1969). Social class differences in maternal teaching strategies and speech patterns. *Developmental Psychology* 6(1):726–34.

Biller, H. B. (1971). Father, child and sex role. Lexington, Mass.: D. C. Heath.

———. (1981). The father and sex role development. In *The role of the father in child development,* edited by M. Lamb. New York: Wiley and Sons.

Billingsley, A. (1970). Black families and white social science. *Journal of Social Issues* 26(3):127–42.

Brown, S. V. (1983). The commitment and concerns of black adolescent parents. *Social Work Research and Abstracts* 19(4):27–34.

Bumpass, L. L., Rindfuss, R. R., and Janosik, R. B. (1978). Age and marital status at first births and the pace of subsequent fertility. *Demography* 15:75–86.

California Department of Mental Health. (1986). *California Staying Well News* 3(1).

Campbell, F. A., Breitmayer, B., and Ramey, C. T. (1986). Disadvantaged teenage mothers and their children: Consequences of educational daycare. *Family Relations* 35(1):63–69.

Cazenave, N. A. (1981). Black men in America: The quest for manhood. In *Black Families,* edited by H. P. McAdoo. Beverly Hills: Sage Publications.

Center for Population Options. (1986). Conference report. Washington, D.C.

Children's Defense Fund. (1984). *American children in poverty.* Washington, D.C.: CDF.

———. (1985). *A children's defense budget: An analysis of the president's FY 1986 budget and children.* Washington, D.C.: CDF.

———. (1986). *Welfare and teen pregnancy: What do we know? What do we do?* Washington, D.C.: CDF.

Chilman, D. (1983). *Adolescent sexuality in a changing American society.* New York: Wiley & Sons.

Clarke, E. (1957). *My mother who fathered me: A study of the family in three selected communities in Jamaica.* Ruskin House.

Connor, M. E. (1983). *Black male attitudes towards fathering: A follow up report.* Presented at the Western Psychological Association Annual Conference, San Francisco.

———. (1986). Some parenting attitudes of young black fathers. In *Men in Families,* edited by R. A. Lewis and R. E. Salt. Beverly Hills, Calif: Sage Publications.

Cumper, G. E. (1958). The Jamaican family: Village and estate. *Social and Economic Studies* 7:76–108.

Dodson, J. (1981). Conceptualizations of black families. In *Black Families,* edited by H. T. McAdoo. Beverly Hills, Calif.: Sage Publications.

Dreger, R. M., and Miller, K. S. (1968). Comparative psychological studies of negroes and whites in the United States: 1959–1965. *Psychology Bulletin Monograph Supplement* 70(3)2:1–58.

Dryfoos, J. (1985). School based clinics: A new approach to preventing adolescent pregnancy? *Family Planning Perspectives* 17(2).

Furstenberg, F. F. (1976). *Unplanned parenthood—The social consequence of teenage child bearing*. New York: Free Press.

———. (1980). Burdens and benefits: The impact on the family. *Journal of Social Issues* 36(1):45–64.

Gallas, H. B. (1980). Introduction, Teenage parenting: Social determinants and consequences. *Journal of Social Issues* 36(1):1–7.

Gary, L. E. (1981). *Black men*. Beverly Hills, Calif.: Sage Publications.

Genovese, E. D. (1978). The myth of the absent family. In *The black family: Essays and studies*, edited by R. Staples. Belmont, Calif.: Wadsworth Publishing.

Gibbs, J. T. (1984). Black adolescents and youth: An endangered species. *American Journal of Orthopsychiatry* 54(1):6–21.

———. (1985). The current endangered status of young black males: Implications for the black family in America. Paper presented at the Annual Civil Rights Institute, NAACP-Legal Defense and Educational Fund, New York.

———. (1986). Psychosocial correlates of sexual attitudes and behaviors in urban early adolescent females: Implications for intervention. *Journal of Social Work and Human Sexuality* 5:81–97.

Glick, P. C. (1981). A demographic picture of black families. In *Black Families*, edited by H. P. McAdoo. Beverly Hills, Calif.: Sage Publications.

Gordon, S. (1986). What kids need to know. *Psychology Today* 20 (October):22–28.

Gutman, H. (1976). *The black family in slavery and freedom, 1750–1925*. New York: Pantheon Books.

Harris, W. (1976). Work and family in black America, 1880. *Journal of Social History* 9(3):319–30.

Harrison, A. (1981). Attitudes towards procreation among black adults. In *Black families*, edited by H. P. McAdoo. Beverly Hills, Calif.: Sage Publications.

Hendricks, L. E. (1981). Black unwed adolescent fathers. In *Black men*, edited by L. E. Gary. Beverly Hills, Calif.: Sage Publications.

Hendricks, L. E., and Montgomery, T. (1983). A limited population of unmarried adolescent fathers: A preliminary report of their views on fatherhood and the relationship with the mothers of their children. *Adolescence* 18(69): 201–10.

Hess, R. D., and Shipman, V. (1965). Early experience and the socialization of cognitive modes in children. *Child development* 36:869–88.

Hetherington, E. M., and Parke, R. D. (1975). *Child psychology*. New York: McGraw-Hill.

Hill, R. B. (1971). *The strengths of black families*. New York: Independent Publisher's Group.

Jackson, J. (1978). But where are the men? In *The black family: Essays and studies*, edited by R. Staples. Belmont, Calif.: Wadsworth Publishing.

Johnson, D. M., and Campbell, R. V. (1981). *Black migration in America*. Durham, N.C.: Duke University Press.

Johnson, L. B. (1981). Perspectives on black family empirical research: 1965–1978. In *Black families*, edited by H. P. McAdoo. Beverly Hills, Calif.: Sage Publications.

Ladner, J. A. (1971). *Tomorrow's tomorrow*. Garden City, N.Y.: Anchor Books, Doubleday & Company.

———. (1973). *The death of white sociology*. New York: Vintage Books.

Lamb, M. (1981). *The role of fathers in child development*. New York: Wiley Interscience.

———. (1986). *The father's role: Applied perspectives*. New York: Wiley Interscience.

Lewis, O. (1961). *The children of Sanchez*. New York: Random House.

Liebow, E. (1967). *Tally's corner*. Boston: Little, Brown.

Loury, G. C. (1986). The family, the nation and Senator Moynihan. *Commentary* (June), pp. 21–26.

Lynn, D. B. (1974). *The father: His role in child development*. Monterey, Calif.: Brooks Cole.

Malson, M. (1984). *The flip side of black families headed by women: The economic status of black men*. Washington, D.C.: Center for Social Policy.

Marsman, J. C., and Herold, E. S. (1986). Attitudes toward sex education and values in sex education. *Family Relations* 35(3):357–63.

McAdoo, J. L. (1981). Black father and child interactions. In *Black men*, edited by L. E. Gary. Beverly Hills, Calif.: Sage Publications.

———. Black fathers' relationships with their preschool children and the children's development of ethnic identity. In *Men in families*, edited by R. A. Lewis and R. E. Salt. Beverly Hills, Calif.: Sage Publications.

Moynihan, D. P. (1965). *The Negro family: The case for national action*. Washington, D.C.: U.S. Department of Labor.

———. (1986). *Family and nation*. New York: Harcourt Brace Janovich.

Moore, K. A. (1985). Facts at a glance. (Newsletter, January). Washington, D.C.: Child Trends, Inc.

Murray, C. (1984). *Losing ground, American social policy, 1950–1980*. New York: Basic Books.

Otterbein, K. F. (1965). Caribbean family organization: A comparative analysis. *American Anthropology* 67:66–79.

Parke, R. D., Power, T. G., and Fisher, T. (1980). The adolescent father's impact on the mother and child. *Journal of Social Issues* 36(1):88–107.

Parker, S., and Kleiner, R. J. (1966). *Mental illness in the urban Negro community*. New York: Free Press.

Petras, J. W. (1975). *Sex male. Gender masculine*. Sherman Oaks, Calif.: Alfred Publishing.

Pinkney, A. (1969). *Black Americans*. Englewood Cliffs, N.J.: Prentice-Hall.

Redmon, M. A. (1985). Attitudes of adolescent males toward adolescent pregnancy and fatherhood. *Family Relations* 34(3):337–43.

Robbins, C., Kaplan, H. B., and Martin, S. S. (1985). Antecedents of pregnancy among unmarried adolescents. *Journal of Marriage and the Family* 47(3):567–85.

Robinson, B. E., Barret, R. L., and Skeen, P. (1983). Locus of control of unwed adolescent fathers versus adolescent non-fathers. *Perceptual and Motor Skills* 56(2):397–98.

Roosa, M. W. (1986). Adolescent mothers, school drop-outs and school based intervention programs. *Family Relations* 35(2):313–19.

Sander, J. (1986). Teen father collaborative. Paper presented at Young Unwed Fatherhood Symposium, Washington, D.C.

Scanzoni, J. H. (1971). *The black family in modern society.* Boston: Allyn & Bacon.

Schulz, D. A. (1969). *Coming up black.* Englewood Cliffs, N.J. Prentice-Hall.

Sklar, M. H. (1986). Employment and training for unwed fathers: An unmet and unrecognized need. Paper presented at Young Unwed Fatherhood Symposium, Washington, D.C.

Smith, M. G. (1963). West Indian family structure. *American Social Review* 28:304–05.

Smith, R. T. (1956). *The Negro family in British Guiana.* London: Routledge and Paul, Ltd.

Spitz, A., Strauss, L., Maciak, B., and Morris, L. (1987). Teenage pregnancy and fertility in the United States, 1970, 1974, and 1980. *Mortality and Morbidity Weekly Report 36* (Supplement, No. 188): 1SS–10S8.

Staples, R. (1978). *The black family: Essays and studies.* Belmont, Calif.: Wadsworth Publishing.

Stark, E. (1986). Young, innocent and pregnant. *Psychology Today* 20 (October):28–35.

Sullivan, M. L. (1986). *Ethnographic research on young fathers and parenting.* New York: Vera Institute.

Vukelich, C., and Kilman, D. S. (1985). Mature and teenage mothers' infant growth expectations and use of child development information sources. *Family Relations* 34(2)189–97.

Wilson, W. J., and Neckerman, K. M. (1984). Poverty and family structure: The widening gap between evidence and public policy issues. Paper presented at Conference on Poverty and Policy: Retrospect and Prospects, 6–8 December, Williamsburg, Virginia.

Chapter 7

HEALTH AND MENTAL HEALTH OF YOUNG BLACK MALES

Jewelle Taylor Gibbs

> *Thus the black boy in growing up encounters some strange impediments. Schools discourage his ambitions, training for valued skills is not available to him, and when he does triumph in some youthful competition he receives compromised praise, not the glory he might expect. In time he comes to see that society has locked arms against him, that rather than help he can expect opposition to his development, and that he lives not in a benign community but in a society that views his growth with hostility. . . . throughout his life, at each critical point of development, the black boy is told to hold back, to constrict, to subvert, and camouflage his normal masculinity.*

> From *Black Rage*, by William H. Grier and Price M. Cobbs. © 1968 by William H. Grier and Price M. Cobbs. Reprinted by permission of Basic Books, Inc., Publishers.

Introduction

In American society today no single group is more vulnerable, more victimized, and more violated than young black males in the 15–24 age range (Gibbs, 1984). While this statement may seem overdramatic and deliberately provocative, the social indicators and social problems that support such a strong statement are documented in this chapter. The goals of Chapter 7 are threefold:

(1) to paint a picture of the deteriorating health and mental health status of black male youth; (2) to analyze the forces and social context in which these problems have developed; and (3) to suggest implications for policies and programs that will reverse the downward trends and promote positive health and mental health outcomes for this group.

Black males are endangered even before they are born, since male fetuses are more likely to spontaneously abort; this vulnerability characterizes their health and mental health for the rest of their lives, particularly during adolescence and young adulthood. If black males survive the high infant mortality rates, which are nearly double the rates for white infants, they are still more likely to experience problems associated with low birth weight and lack of preventive health care. They are less likely to be immunized against infectious childhood diseases such as diptheria, polio, measles, rubella, and mumps. They are more likely to have chronic illnesses and higher rates of psychological or behavioral problems. They are less likely to have access to regular medical and dental care. They are more likely to suffer from poor nutrition and related health problems. And most tragic of all statistics, they are more likely to die before age 20 than any other sex-race group (CDF, 1985b; DHHS, 1985; Kovar, 1982).

The public is only dimly aware of the most disturbing trends in the health and mental health of this group, partly due to recent publicity about the "new morbidity" among all American youth. Recent startling statistics indicate that the three major causes of death among all youth are accidents, homicide, and suicide, accounting for over three-fourths of the fatalities in the 15–24 age group (DHHS, 1985). However, homicide is the leading cause of death for black youth, followed by accidents and suicide. In the past 25 years, the suicide rate has nearly tripled among black males, while the homicide rate has actually declined since 1968. The causes and consequences of this "new morbidity" and changing patterns in the mortality rates for young black males have such important social implications that they are discussed separately in Chapter 8.

The newest and most invidious threat to the health of young black males has been the spectre of AIDS (acquired immunodeficiency syndrome), which is now one of the leading causes of death in this group in several metropolitan areas such as New York, San Francisco, and Miami (NCHS, 1986). This phenomenon has occurred primarily because of the spread of AIDS among black drug addicts who use contaminated needles. Yet this group has been seriously neglected both in research and treatment because of the perception of the government and much of the medical community that AIDS is primarily a "gay" white male disease, transmitted through homosexual contacts.

Psychiatric disorders have increased among young black males, as evidenced both in the rates of outpatient treatment and admissions to inpatient treatment facilities. As more black youth join the ranks of the homeless, they become more vulnerable to severe health and mental health problems stemming from lack of housing, inadequate health care, and the vicissitudes of survival on the streets (Jones, 1986).

The Children's Defense Fund recently reported that in 1983 nearly half of the nation's foster children were teenagers; about one-third of this group were black (CDF, 1986a). Many of these teens in out-of-home placements will never be adopted or have a permanent foster home. Not only do many of these youth experience frequent physical, sexual, and psychological abuse in these placements, but they are also usually released from the protection of the welfare system at age 18 and left to fend for themselves, often without adequate education, employable skills, or material resources. Thus, they enter young adulthood ill-equipped to cope with the daily challenges of life and are at risk for subsequent decompensation or dysfunction in society.

It is essential to emphasize the close relationship between health and mental health, which is particularly relevant in understanding this population. As will be demonstrated later in this chapter, the health risks associated with poverty (e.g., poor nutrition, substandard housing, lack of adequate health care) are exacerbated in this group by behavioral risks associated with the subculture of the inner city (e.g., delinquency, substance abuse, family and community violence). Thus, for low-income urban black youth, the health risks are multiplied exponentially by their exposure to and/or involvement in self-destructive behavioral patterns which, in turn, make them extremely vulnerable to negative health outcomes such as psychiatric disorders, venereal diseases, drug addiction, and physical disabilities.

This chapter is organized as follows: First, the major health problems of young black males, 15–24, and the mental health problems of this group are summarized. Next, the relationship between psychosocial factors and health outcomes in this group is analyzed. Finally, the implications for policies and programs that address the deteriorating health and mental health status of black male youth are discussed.

Health Problems

Young black males are the victims of the cumulative effect of not-so-benign neglect of their health and mental health needs. In order to comprehend fully the health status of these youth in adolescence and young adulthood, it is important to document the health problems experienced by them in infancy and early childhood. First, many black children are born out of wedlock, to teenage mothers, and in low-income families—circumstances documented in Chapters 1 and 6. They enter life with the triple disadvantage of being black, poor, and illegitimate in a society that idealizes people who are white, rich, and legitimate. Their mothers are more likely to experience prenatal, perinatal, and postnatal complications associated with their pregnancies, and thus many of these children are born with a health disadvantage (CDF, 1986a). Many are born prematurely or are low birth weight babies, conditions that are further exacerbated by poor nutrition and lack of vitamin supplements in their diets. The unmarried teenage mothers of many of these babies rarely are mature enough to have adequate maternal skills; nor do they have the emotional and financial support of a spouse with whom to share the child-rearing tasks.

These are "childen having children" trying to deal with their own adolescent developmental issues while simultaneously trying to cope with the difficulties of caring for babies who are often unplanned and unwanted. Is it any wonder that many of these youthful mothers abuse, neglect, or reject their children? Even under the most optimal circumstances—that is, if they live with supportive parents and complete high school—these young mothers are still more likely to experience adverse social, physical, and psychological outcomes as adults. Their offspring are also more likely than children born to older mothers in intact marriages to experience long-term negative outcomes in health, education, and income (CDF, 1986a).

Substandard housing makes these children vulnerable to chronic respiratory problems from insufficient heat, infestation from lice and other vermin, bites from rats and insects, and lead poisoning from peeling paint. Because they are often reared in single-parent families and may not receive consistent supervision, they are also prone to more household and street accidents, traumas, and other noxious events (CDF, 1986a; Kovar, 1982). The following scenario is typical:

And by burned-out buildings in the Bronx, 15-year-old Ronald Richardson patiently fills plastic jugs from a dripping fire hydrant.

Although his mother works as a New York City welfare clerk, they
live in a condemned tenement in a dimly lit apartment with no
water, gas or heat. The bathroom ceiling has collapsed. Rats roam
the dark, rubble-strewn halls.

"Every day, I go to the fire hydrant to get water for cooking, to
clean dishes and to wash up for school," the shy eighth-grade
student said as the pop song "We Are the World" blasted through a
broken window. "I got no choice." [APWA, 1986, p. 9]

Access to Medical Care

As children in low-income families, many of these youth grow up
without access to the basic requirements for a healthy mind and a
healthy body. They do not receive what every middle-class child
in America takes for granted—annual checkups with a pediatrician
and a dentist, early detection of infectious and chronic diseases,
and adequate treatment for minor and major illnesses. Inner-city
neighborhoods have the highest ratio of patients to doctors, all of
whom are overworked and underpaid compared with doctors in
middle-class areas (CDF, 1986a).

Hospitals that serve inner-city neighborhoods are generally
housed in older, poorly maintained buildings. They are under-
staffed, often with foreign-born health professionals who are less
well trained than American-educated professionals. They are un-
derfinanced and constantly threatened with closure, and they are
equipped with outdated, technologically inefficient equipment. In
addition, the emergency services of these inner-city hospitals are
overwhelmed by people who use the services as the first line for
medical care, as well as increasing numbers of long-term patients
with life-threatening illnesses who cannot afford private hospitalization or convalescent care (DHHS, 1985). These conditions result
in constant political and professional conflicts over "turf" issues,
service delivery, revenue sources, and accreditation, diverting the
energies of the professional staff from providing quality health care
to inner-city families and, thus, further eroding the confidence of
these families who often have no other accessible facilities to serve
them.

Childhood Health Conditions: Precursors to Later Problems

The poor health status of inner-city black males begins in infancy,
primarily because of the poverty status of their families, as noted
in Chapter 1. In her 1982 review of the health status of American
children under age 18, Kovar pointed out that, while the majority

were in excellent health, black children and poor children were among the two out of five who had a health deficit. Her analysis of the results of the National Health Interview Survey in 1975–76 showed that 58 percent of black children reported a health deficit, nearly 20 percent had not had any contact with a physician within a specified "adequate" interval, and 57 percent had not seen a dentist in that same time period. Even though more black than white children were rated as having "fair or poor" health by their parents, fewer of them reported any limitation on their activity or days of disability, which suggests that they continued with their regular activities in spite of poor health. Kovar concludes from these data: "Children with poor or poorly educated parents, black children, and children in large families are significantly less likely than other children to have received [medical and dental] care within an adequate interval. . . . Thus equity—equal access according to need—has not been achieved" (Kovar, 1982, p. 14).

Nutrition.   The poor nutrition of low-income black children has been well documented in a number of studies. In the government's 1976–1980 study of children's health, over one-fifth of black males in the 3–14 age group fell below the median hemoglobin level in comparable white youth (CDF, 1986a). This low hemoglobin count is often an indicator of malnutrition and also related to stunted growth, anemia, low energy, and a host of physical and psychological problems. In her review of studies showing the high incidence of iron deficiency anemia in low-income black children, Carter (1983) points out that "low iron stores have been correlated with increased illness, feeding difficulties, fatigue, listlessness, anorexia, impaired weight gain, decreased attentiveness, impaired cardiorespiratory function and impaired muscular activity during exercise" (p. 19).

Recent studies in the state of Massachusetts, Chicago, and New York City indicated that 20 to 30 percent of all low-income children suffered from health problems related to inadequate diets or chronic malnutrition (CDF, 1985b). Since these samples included a high proportion of black children, they lend additional support to the highly publicized reports on hunger in America, particularly among low-income black families in the South and the urban North (Physician Task Force, 1985; Select Committee on Hunger, 1985).

Chronic malnutrition not only stunts physical growth and impairs mental health; scientists have also documented that it damages brain cells and may cause permanent intellectual deficits. Thus, one-fifth to one-third of young black males are at risk for physical, emotional, and intellectual problems due to a legacy of poor nutrition in their formative years.

Vision and Hearing Problems. Data from the National Health Examination Survey (NCHS, 1979) revealed that poor children and adolescents, 6–17 years of age, reported more frequent symptoms of hearing loss and earaches. Vision problems are also more frequent among poor black children (Egbuonu and Starfield, 1982; CDF, 1986a). This includes myopia, the most common childhood visual defect, which is easily corrected with eyeglasses. Since many of these children do not have regular pediatric examinations, these visual abnormalities are not likely to be detected and treated.

It is obvious that hearing and vision problems will impair learning ability, regardless of a child's intellectual capacity. Children who do not see and hear well not only will develop problems in reading and oral communication; they will also have problems in social interactions and recreational and sports activities and will be more vulnerable to accidents and injuries.

Lead Poisoning. The National Center for Health Statistics reported that nearly one out of five (18.5 percent) of low-SES black children had elevated lead levels in their blood, which equaled the rate found in black children who lived in central cities with a population of one million or more residents (Public Health Reports, 1985). Noting that socioeconomic factors are related to household and environmental sources of lead exposure which place poorer children at higher risk for lead poisoning, the report warns: "The toxic effects of lead can be especially critical among children during certain periods of physical growth and neurological development. Children with extremely high blood lead levels can suffer permanent kidney and neurological damage. In severe cases, lead poisoning causes encephalopathy, convulsions, coma and death" (Public Health Reports, 1985, p. 246).

In a four-year study in Newark, New Jersey, of a sample of 525 children under age 7 who were treated for lead poisoning, 88 percent were black and 55 percent were male (Schneider et al., 1981). Many of these children were found to have neurological problems resulting from the toxic levels of lead in their blood. High proportions of low SES minority children with lead poisoning were also reported in St. Louis (19 percent), Boston (12 percent), Milwaukee (12 percent), Baltimore (11 percent), Philadelphia (10 percent), and New York City (9 percent).

A study by Needleman and his colleagues (1979) further indicated that dentine lead levels were higher among children in low-income neighborhoods and these higher levels were significantly correlated to psychological and academic problems in these children. In general, as Carter (1983) emphasizes, poor black children are exposed to higher levels of lead and other toxic substances which pollute their environments and create multiple health hazards for them. Moreover, she notes: "Lead is a highly toxic substance without known function in normal human physiology. Its demonstrated deleterious effects on renal function, central nervous system metabolism, and hemoglobin synthesis result in chronic debilitating sequelae—severe life-threatening encephalopathy, anemia, renal failure, seizures, cerebral palsy, psychosocial behavioral deficits, mental retardation, and long-term disabilities" (p. 18).

Sickle-Cell Anemia. Sickle-cell anemia affects one in 600 blacks in America. While 1 of every 12 blacks is a carrier of the sickle-cell trait, it is a recessive gene which may become dominant only in the children of two carriers. Black children with this disease have a variety of chronic and painful symptoms, including fevers, respiratory infections, arthritic pains, eye problems, and progressive organ damage. Carter (1983) describes the multiple side effects and medical complications of sickle cell disease:

> *Neurological complications have been reported in 26 percent of all patients. Cerebral vascular accidents occur in 4–17 percent of all patients (mean age of onset by 10 years) and are responsible for 16 percent of the deaths in these children. . . . Strokes tend to recur in over 50 percent of cases and lead to progressive neurological deterioration. Warning may be as mild as dizzy spells, fainting or recurrent headache. [p. 21]*

Because it is so rare and found primarily among blacks, it is often misdiagnosed, inappropriately treated, and can result in premature death for its victims (Carter, 1983).

Accidents and Injuries. A final indicator of childhood health status which has particularly negative implications for later development is the category of accidents and injuries. Black children have higher rates of nonfatal and fatal accidents and injuries than any other group. These include nonvehicular accidents, injuries from fires and burns, household injuries from poorly maintained housing, and drowning accidents (Berger, 1985; Kovar, 1982; Centers for Disease Control, 1983; 1985a). Many of these accidents are directly or indirectly related to their low economic status, which often denies these children access to adequate and safe housing, recreation, and even school facilities. A typical vignette illustrates the plight of these black children:

> *He chipped his front tooth when he slipped and fell on an icy metal railing near the high-rise housing project where he used to live. His right eye is slightly cockeyed from the time a cousin jabbed him in*

*the face with a stick. Cuts and scratches from street fights criss-
cross his arms and legs so frequently that he has difficulty recalling
how they got there.*

*Sean Austin lives in a makeshift world where a child born into the
underclass must provide for himself. The scars on his face and body
are a testament to the harsh conditions of his life in North Lawndale,
a poor, black community on Chicago's West Side.*

*Here an empty milk crate, its bottom carved out with a butcher
knife, doubles as a basketball hoop. A hot iron and a pot of steaming
water over a hotplate in the morning help him dry the school clothes
he washed by hand the night before.*

*To get to class each morning, Sean walks down a flight of rickety
stairs; across three vacant lots strewn with broken bottles, discarded
hypodermic syringes and weeds; past a Cadillac and a group of men
already drinking in front of a bar.*

*In school, he towers over his 5th grade classmates, older than the
rest because he failed 2d and 5th grades. [APWA, 1986, p. 11]*

Further, as children and adolescents, these youth are vulnerable
to physical abuse and sexual abuse or assault both at home and in
their neighborhoods—physical abuse partly due to the stresses
experienced by their families, and sexual abuse partly because of
overcrowded households, stranger assaults, and unsupervised leisure time in neighborhoods where youth become sexually active at
earlier ages.

In his review of studies on child abuse, Hampton (1986) notes
that blacks were overrepresented in confirmed physical abuse in
the National Study of the Incidence and Severity of Child Abuse
and Neglect, but underrepresented in a national probability sample of family violence. However, he concludes from several studies
that blacks have an overall higher rate of physical abuse due to
socioeconomic and family structural differences. Summarizing the
NIS findings, Hampton states: "Compared to others, Black victims
of assaultive child maltreatment were more likely to be in the 6 to
12 age group, live in urban areas, have mothers who had completed
high school, and suffer more serious injuries. . . . Black victims of
assaultive violence were more likely to be in households receiving
public assistance. Caseworkers report that caretaker stress was
highly associated with physical abuse among these families"
(Hampton, 1986, p. 73).

Mortality rates are also higher for black children than for white
children. Black preschool and elementary-school children died of
accidents, poisoning, or violence in 1976 at nearly twice the rate
of white children (Kovar, 1982). At each age level, black boys had

higher mortality rates than black girls, a trend that persists into adulthood.

Homelessness and Health.   Estimates are that 22 percent of the homeless population are children under age 18, many of whom are black adolescents (CDF, 1986a). Chicago's mayor, the late Harold Washington, described the homeless population in his city as follows: "We are also seeing increasing numbers of women and children among the homeless as the unemployment crisis in our cities, especially among black families, continues. We find thousands of teenagers . . . who have been thrown out of their homes or fled because of family problems, and some who have been evicted by their institutional parents—the state" (CDF, 1985a). The longer these youth are without permanent homes, the greater their exposure to physical and psychological stress, which can result in depression, psychiatric disorder, disease, and even death (Jones, 1986). For example, an alarming increase in tuberculosis has been noted in homeless shelters in Boston, New York, and other large cities, all of which have more low-income black families with children housed for longer periods in such shelters (Centers for Disease Control, 1985b).

In a recent newspaper interview, Dr. Steven Himmelstein, a psychologist who works with some of the 10,000 homeless children who are housed in New York City welfare hotels, made the following pessimistic observations about these youth: "Their needs are not being met. They simply don't trust from a very early age. . . . They aren't nurtured very much and that is why you see thumb-sucking as old as 8 or 9 years old. They are the future, as all kids are, and it's scary." He predicted that these children, most of whom are black and Hispanic, "would also be alienated adults, unable to forge relationships and tending toward anger, criminality and poor educational achievement" (*New York Times*, 1987b).

By the time these children enter adolescence, they have already experienced more infectious diseases, more accidents, more injuries, and higher death rates than their white peers. Many have been subjected to multiple traumas in multiproblem families—experiences that have made their childhood years a period of chronic psychological and physical stress rather than a time of parental nurturance and positive growth. Thus, as they enter puberty, many of these youth face the most challenging phase of their development with less than optimal personal resources to cope with the substantial physical, emotional, and social changes of adolescence. Early adolescence is a particularly crucial phase of development because children must adapt to new school environments, new peer groups, and new social and academic demands.

To the extent that black males have physical or psychological deficits resulting from earlier developmental traumas, they will have greater difficulties in negotiating these situations. Unfortunately, their childhood health experiences have often produced the kinds of personality characteristics and behaviors that are considered reliable predictors of maladjustment and dysfunction in adolescents, including low self-esteem, lack of competence, low tolerance for frustration, high impulsivity, irritability, fatigability, poor concentration, negative attitudes to authority, hyperactive behaviors, anti-social behaviors, and explosive temperaments (Knopf, 1984). As Meyers and King (1983) concluded from their study of the influence of the social context on the mental health of black children, "to be black in America is difficult; to be black and poor is disastrous. . . . Illness, dysfunction and incompetence are the natural and legitimate by-products of the concrete reality of the urban black child" (p. 295).

Adolescent and Young Adult Health Problems

Health problems that are neglected in childhood do not simply fade away. In fact, they either become chronic health problems or lead to other more serious and potentially fatal diseases or disabilities.

In its report on adolescent health programs, the Children's Defense Fund pointed out that black children and teenagers in the United States are less likely than white children to receive any form of preventive health care or dental care (CDF, 1986b). In her longitudinal study of health stability of urban black youth, Brunswick (1980) found that the increase in the number of self-reported health problems in the six- to eight-year period between adolescence and young adulthood was significantly greater for males than for females. Moreover, the deterioration in health occurred nearly two years later for males (17–18) than for females (15–16), suggesting that the transition period from adolescence to young adulthood may be especially stressful for black males.

Nutrition. In the nutritional study cited earlier, 26 percent of 15–24-year-old black males fell below the median hemoglobin level of white youth, with a level lower than any other group except black females (CDF, 1985b). Although this was a cross-sectional study, it suggests that the negative effects of early malnutrition are not counteracted in adolescence and young adulthood. In fact, as Carter (1983) notes: "Scores of iron-deficient adolescents record impaired performance on intellectual tests, and decrements in latency and associative reaction time. Webb and Oski (1974) re-

ported complaints of irritability, restlessness, and impaired attentiveness leveled against iron-deficient adolescents in the academic
milieu. Symptoms of shortness of breath, palpitations, dizziness,
and poor psychological function mimic cardiovascular and psychiatric disorders, and must be distinguished from anemia-related
illnesses" (p. 19). A recent study of 2,203 low-income youth
entering the Job Corps found that black male recruits had high
rates of iron deficiency anemia, with 18.9 percent registering
hematocrit values less than the 5th percentile of a national sample
and 11.1 percent with hemoglobin values less than the 5th percentile (Hayman and Probst, 1983). These levels of anemia are often
indicative of poor nutrition over a long period of time, suggesting
that many low-income youth enter adulthood with inadequate
levels of energy, impaired cognitive abilities, and increased risk of
physical, psychological, and behavioral problems.

Vision and Hearing. The study of Job Corps recruits also found
that one out of six had defective vision and only one-third of the
males had adequate corrective glasses (Hayman and Probst, 1983).
Although these data were not analyzed by race, black males
constituted 35 percent of the total sample, so it can be assumed
that defective vision was a major problem for them. As the study
authors point out, uncorrected defective vision "can have serious
educational and occupational consequences" (p. 372). For disadvantaged minority males who are school dropouts, poor eyesight is
both a symptom of inadequate medical care and an impediment to
learning.

Chronic/Infectious Diseases. Young black males are particularly at risk for three severe and debilitating medical conditions,
which may first appear or become considerably more incapacitating
during adolescence. Two of these are chronic conditions—sickle-
cell anemia and hypertension; the third is an infectious disease—
tuberculosis.

As noted earlier, sickle-cell anemia is a genetic disorder which
begins in early childhood. If the child survives until adolescence,
the symptoms worsen and the crises tend to become more frequent
and more severe. Carter (1983) describes this process as follows:

*Adolescents suffer repeated hardship when affected by sickle hemo-
globinopathies. Biologically prone to iron deficiency anemia, affected black adolescents face dual hemoglobin reductions from sickle
cells' reduced longevity and reduction in cell volume via repeated
crises. Each severe episode means days and weeks of missed classroom activities, and may result in loss of academic competence.*

Immature appearance, delayed puberty, and altered psychosocial function are handicapping factors. [p. 22]

Hypertension is one of the major chronic illnesses among adult black males, yet its roots can be found in adolescence. While experts may debate the exact definition and measurement of hypertension in adolescents, they do agree that a high proportion of 17- and 18-year-old black males show elevated levels of blood pressure, at least two years before this problem emerges among white youth (Carter, 1983). The long-range prognosis for adolescents with hypertension is not optimistic, since many of them will eventually develop cardiovascular problems, heart attacks, and strokes. In fact, the fifth leading cause of death for black males 15–24 is cerebrovascular disease, which is often caused by underlying hypertension (DHHS, 1986). Hypertension is often called "the silent killer" since it is frequently not detected until a person suffers from a major heart attack or stroke. For young black males who rarely have regular medical checkups or periodic health screenings, these symptoms are likely to remain undetected and untreated until it is too late.

Tuberculosis is a disease that is generally equated with poverty, poor housing conditions, and inadequate health care. It is also an infectious disease, which was widely believed to be nearly eradicated in America decades ago. Quite the contrary is true, as recently reported by the Centers for Disease Control (1987c). In 1985 over 22,000 cases of tuberculosis were recorded in the United States, over one-third (34.8 percent) of which were among blacks. Both the morbidity and mortality rates were four to five times greater for blacks than for whites, with 36 percent of the tuberculosis-related deaths occurring among blacks. This pattern continued through 1986, with only a slight decline anticipated for 1987.

As with other health problems, young black males bore the brunt of this disease, with one out of three black patients under 33 years of age. In fact, black males, 15–24, were four times more likely to contract tuberculosis than their white male age peers (at a rate of 10.8 versus 2.6 per 100,000). This higher infection rate was matched by an excess mortality rate of 227 for black males—also four times higher than white males—in this age group.

Although the incidence of tuberculosis has recently increased among whites as a disease among the elderly, it has unfortunately increased among blacks most dramatically in the young adult age group. Moreover, the most troubling trend in the upsurge of this infectious disease is that there appears to be a relationship between the risk of tuberculosis and the risk of AIDS among black youth. In four areas where the correlation of tuberculosis and AIDS has been investigated, the majority of both patients have been black young adults. For example, these rates have ranged from 93 percent in Newark, New Jersey, 79 percent in Florida, 56 percent in New York City to 16 percent in San Francisco (Centers for Disease Control, 1987c). While AIDS may weaken the immune system and make it more susceptible to the tuberculosis bacillus, it is important to identify the common risk factors in both diseases for this highly vulnerable group. It may very well be demonstrated that the underlying risk factors are similar for both diseases and that primary prevention should be directed toward the elimination of poverty, poor housing, and the prevention of drug abuse, as well as the promotion of preventive health and sanitary practices.

Thus, race and poverty are both powerful predictors of poor health status for black children, who become less healthy adolescents and young adults. This translates into days lost from school and absenteeism at work due to minor or major illnesses, into lowered resistance to chronic and infectious diseases, and into pervasive feelings of fatigue, listlessness, and lack of energy to cope with the daily challenges of life. Since 48 percent of black youth are poor, it follows that nearly half of all black youth are at risk for poverty-related health conditions, lack of access to adequate health care, and the debilitating consequences of poor or marginal health status.

Sexually Transmitted Diseases

Young black males also have slightly higher rates of sexually transmitted diseases than their white counterparts (Hayman and Probst, 1983). Several factors may account for this higher incidence of venereal diseases. First, on the average, black males begin sexual activity at an earlier age than white males; by their mid-20s they have thus had a longer period of sexual activity in which to be exposed to infection. Second, inner-city black males are reared in a subculture that has very negative attitudes toward contraception, and men, particularly, associate unprotected intercourse with "real manhood" (Schulz, 1969; Staples, 1982). Third, young black women are also less likely than whites to use contraception and are also less likely to practice preventive health care to detect early signs of venereal disease (Gibbs, 1986). In the Job Corps sample, black females actually had higher rates of venereal disease than black males (Hayman and Probst, 1983).

In July of 1987, the Centers for Disease Control reported that the incidence of new syphilis cases had increased by 23 percent in the first quarter of 1987—the first increase of this venereal disease in five years (Centers for Disease Control, 1987b). Most of the new cases were found among black heterosexual males, concentrated in three major geographical areas: New York City, Florida, and California. Further, this increase in syphilis was related to higher rates of infection of the HIV virus that causes AIDS, which also occurs at high rates in these same geographical areas. The report concluded that "having had syphilis or another sexually transmitted disease puts you at greater risk of AIDS" and that the increase in the incidence of syphilis "may be the forerunner of future increases in HIV-related morbidity and mortality" (Centers for Disease Control, 1987b, p. 386).

While the national report did not target any specific age group that was particularly at risk for syphilis, an earlier report of syphilis cases in Broward County, Florida found that the incidence had tripled between 1980 and 1986 and that the highest rate was found among 20–24-year-old black male heterosexuals (Centers for Disease Control, 1987a). In this county the incidence of syphilis was 35 times higher among blacks than whites, with 80 percent of new cases occurring among blacks. Seventy percent of these syphilis patients were concentrated in just 11 census tracts with a median income of $15,000 per year, just slightly above the poverty line. Again, the question must be raised if there is a set of underlying sociodemographic factors, common to venereal diseases, tuberculosis, and AIDS, which create a much higher likelihood that young black males will be vulnerable to contracting one or more of these diseases. Indeed, one of the earliest cases of AIDS occurred in a young black male:

In 1969, Robert, age 14, a poor black teenager was admitted to the Washington University Clinic in St. Louis with multiple illnesses and mysterious symptoms, with swelling of his lymph nodes, legs, lower torso and genitalia. Although a team of doctors tried valiantly to cure him for 15 months, his symptoms worsened and his immune system completely broke down. He lost weight, developed a severe infection of chlamydia, and eventually died of bronchial pneumonia. An autopsy revealed that Robert had Kaposi's sarcoma, rectal lesions and hemorrhoids, but doctors were baffled by his illness. In 1987, Robert's frozen tissues were subjected to a new series of tests and doctors concluded that he had contracted AIDS, one of the earliest known cases in the United States. [New York Times, 1987c]

Since 1981 when the acquired immunodeficiency syndrome (AIDS) opportunistic diseases were first reported in the United

States, there has been an alarming increase of these conditions among young black males. AIDS occurs 2.6 times more often among black men than it does among whites. Between 1981 and 1986, 25 percent of the reported cases of AIDS were among blacks and black males accounted for 23 percent of all male cases (Centers for Disease Control, 1986a, 1986b). Among blacks, homosexual and bisexual men represented 46.3 percent of the cases and heterosexual intravenous drug users, 35.4 percent. A 1986 Public Health Service report noted the following trends: "The cumulative incidence of AIDS among blacks and Hispanics is over three times the rate for whites. Seroprevalence studies of military recruit applicants and of potential blood donors also indicate a higher prevalence of infection (of HILV-III/LAV) among blacks than whites" (Centers for Disease Control, 1986a, p. 658). This trend was more recently confirmed in a report to the International AIDS Conference, held in Washington, D.C., in June 1987, by Dr. Donald S. Burke of the Walter Reed Army Institute. He reported that the infection rate among all army recruits appeared to be doubling every 10 years, but it is doubling every 3 years for blacks (*Washington Post*, 1987). Due to their tendency to postpone medical care and the higher incidence of the more lethal pneumocystis pneumonia among blacks, black AIDS patients have an average survival rate of only 8 months, compared to the 18- to 24-month rate for whites (Houston-Hamilton, 1986).

In San Francisco, blacks diagnosed with AIDS comprised 4.3 percent of the new cases reported in the city in 1984, but this rate increased to 7.1 percent by September 1987 (*San Francisco Chronicle*, 1987a). The age group most at risk for the disease is 18 to 30, the peak age both for sexual activity and for drug use among black males. The incidence of AIDS in this group has increased fastest among intravenous drug users who share dirty needles. Public health officials are particularly concerned about these AIDS carriers because of the unknown period of incubation, as well as the difficulties of reaching these addicts through traditional channels of education and preventive health care. It has been estimated that by the year 1991 in the United States, approximately 200,000 persons will be infected with the AIDS virus and a high proportion of that group will be young black males (Mays and Cochran, 1987). Younger black males, who were also drug abusers, were found to have one of the poorest prognoses of all AIDS patients in a New York City study of survival rates from 1981–1985 (*New York Times*, 1987c).

An additional population at very high risk for AIDS is the prison population, where young black males are significantly overrepresented. In June 1987, the California State Department of Corrections announced that 83 prisoners with AIDS, AIDS-related complex (ARC), or the AIDS virus were incarcerated in one cell block at the Vacaville prison (*San Francisco Chronicle*, 1987b). Forty percent of those AIDS patients were black inmates, with an average age of 33, but many were in their early 20s. Three out of five had contracted AIDS from intravenous drug use and 40 percent from homosexual activity. The report further predicted an increase of AIDS cases in the state prison system to 300 by the end of 1987.

The most alarming issue in the spread of AIDS among young black inner-city males is that their risk is probably significantly increased by two sociocultural factors: their negative attitudes toward using any kind of male contraceptives in sexual activity and their higher rates of intravenous drug use. These two factors, combined with the drug use of their female partners, have resulted in a growing population of black infants with the AIDS virus, so that by late 1986 three out of five cases of pediatric AIDS were black (*San Francisco Chronicle*, 1987c). Both of these factors are further exacerbated by the low educational level and social isolation of young black men from mainstream health care, which creates major difficulties in conducting effective programs of education and prevention in inner-city communities.

AIDS has raised a number of ethical, legal, social, psychological, and political issues which have already created much controversy and exposed deep ideological divisions within this society. There is an urgent need for more funds for research and treatment, yet those who are the primary victims of AIDS—homosexuals, non-white intravenous drug users, and infected children—have the least leverage to lobby Congress for these appropriations. As an example of the complex issues raised by AIDS, the Vacaville inmates have instituted a lawsuit to protest their inadequate treatment facilities. In essence, they complained that they had been segregated from the other prisoners and left to die without the basic necessities of medical care and adequate housing, not to mention the humane concerns which address the psychological issues of premature death in as dignified a manner as possible.

Miscellaneous Health Conditions

Black male youth also have higher rates of a number of other infectious diseases, drug-related conditions, alcoholism and trauma—conditions all related to poverty. In a three-year-study of hospitalization rates of navy enlisted men, it was found that the

15,695 blacks, with an average age of 23, had higher overall admission rates than four other ethnic groups (whites, Asian-Americans, American Indians, and Malaysians) (Hoiberg, Berard, and Ernst, 1981). Blacks had the highest or second-highest rates for diseases of the respiratory, digestive, musculoskeletal, genito-urinary, and circulatory systems, as well as the highest rate for venereal diseases. A partial explanation by the authors to explain the racial difference in utilization rates is the presence of long-term health problems of black sailors for which they had not received adequate medical care prior to their military service, particularly considering that the majority came from lower socio-economic backgrounds.

The two large-scale studies of young black males in the Job Corps and in the navy provide powerful evidence that unrecognized and untreated health problems of these low-income youth will ultimately worsen and require more expensive and prolonged intervention in young adulthood.

Finally, those young adult black males who are fortunate enough to be employed often face occupational health and safety risks because they are concentrated in low-paying, physically demanding, and inherently more dangerous jobs (Lawrence and Guess, 1986; Taylor, 1974). In their analysis of the data from the Health Promotion and Disease Questionnaire, part of the government's 1985 National Health Interview Survey, Shilling and Brackbill (1987) found that black male workers perceived a number of health and safety risks in their current jobs. In the 18–29-year-old age group, 42 percent of black males reported that they worked with health-endangering toxic substances, 35 percent reported work conditions injurious to their health, and 43 percent felt that they risked accidents or injuries on their jobs. Higher risks of injuries were reported by occupational groups who used motor vehicles— for example, driver-sales workers, taxi cab drivers, chauffeurs, bus drivers, and truck drivers, job categories which all have a dispro-portionate share of black males. This relationship between occupation and health status was also demonstrated in the study of navy enlisted men, where black sailors had the highest overall hospitalization rate, as well as the highest proportion of unskilled and "miscellaneous" jobs of the large multiracial sample (Hoiberg, Berard, and Ernst, 1981). One could conceivably conclude from these studies that, for a poor, unskilled black youth, *having* a job might just pose a danger to his physical health, while *not having* a job might prove detrimental to his mental health. This is a perfect example of Hobson's choice.

Mental Health Problems

Several indicators can be used to illustrate the scope and severity of psychological and behavioral problems among young black males (Gibbs, 1984). Studies have shown that, as early as elementary school, black males report more psychological symptoms and display more behavioral problems than black females (CDF, 1986b). As they progress through adolescence to adulthood, black males appear to be more vulnerable than black females to problems in their families, their schools, and their communities, as evidenced by rates of behavioral and learning disorders in schools, incidence of emotional disturbances in delinquents, and rates of inpatient and outpatient psychiatric treatment among this group (Myers and King, 1983).

Studies of self-esteem among black youth have shown mixed results, primarily because of the differences in methodology, measurement and sampling. However, in spite of early theoretical assumptions that black children must necessarily have damaged self-esteem because of their disadvantaged minority status, recent findings from well-designed surveys suggest that the level of self-esteem in black children and adolescents is equal to or higher than in comparable white youth (Gibbs, 1985; Powell, 1973; Taylor, 1976). However, sex differences in self-esteem indicate that young black females generally report higher levels of self-esteem than young black males and this effect increases with age through young adulthood (Rosenberg and Simmons, 1971; Smith, 1982).

Since studies also suggest that black male children, as compared to females, are given less nurturance by their parents, treated more harshly by their teachers, discriminated against more by employers, and treated less favorably by nearly every other institution in American society, it is reasonable to infer that their lowered self-esteem is the inevitable outcome of their persistent differential and demeaning treatment. The links between low self-esteem, psychological disorder and behavioral dysfunction have been extensively documented in the social science literature. The complex interrelationship among these three dimensions are of paramount importance in analyzing and understanding the psychological and behavioral problems of young black males.

Behavioral and Learning Problems in School-Aged Adolescents

Several studies by educators and civil rights organizations have found that low-income black youth, especially males, are disproportionately represented among junior and senior high school students who are suspended or expelled from public schools. While these figures may vary from state to state and within school districts, the overall pattern is quite striking. Data from an Urban League Study showed that many black male teenagers leave school because of family economic problems, academic difficulties, or disciplinary problems, while females often drop out due to pregnancy (Williams, 1982). More recent figures from the Children's Defense Fund indicated that black students were almost twice as likely as white students to be suspended from public schools (9.9 versus 5.2 percent) and about 50 percent more likely to receive corporal punishment (7.0 versus 4.7 percent). The majority of blacks who were suspended or punished were males (CDF, 1985b). Black children and adolescents were also three times more likely than whites to be placed in classes for the educable mentally retarded (3.3 versus 1.0 percent) and slightly more likely to be assigned to classes for the learning disabled (4.1 versus 3.8 percent) or severely emotionally disturbed (0.7 versus 0.6 percent) (CDF, 1985b).

In 1981, nearly half of all black male 17-year-olds were either behind grade level in high school or had dropped out. In 1978 black males reported four major reasons for dropping out of school: "did not like school" (28.9 percent); "expelled or suspended" (13.5 percent); "chose to work" (13.5 percent); and "poor grades" (8.1 percent) (CDF, 1986a). Unfortunately, over half of these dropouts will not be able to find employment, further contributing to their psychological and social dysfunction.

These figures clearly suggest differential treatment for black youth in our public schools, but it is not clear whether or not the punishment fits the crime. The statistical reports are not designed to evaluate the fairness of the suspensions or expulsions; nor do they shed any light on alternative disciplinary practices for white students accused of similar infractions of school rules. The infractions for which blacks are suspended or expelled include excessive truancy, incorrigible and disruptive behavior, assaultive behavior, extortion and theft, vandalism, using or selling illicit drugs, sexual misconduct, gang violence, and cheating. While some of these behaviors obviously represent immature socialization and minor delinquency, others probably reflect deeper psychological disturbances.

For many of these youth, school is a haven from a chaotic home, dangerous streets, and an alienated community, yet they find it difficult to set aside their street survival skills when they enter the school milieu. The very skills they have honed to "make it" on the streets are counterproductive in the schools, for example, playing the dozens, hustling money and goods, fighting for turf, and "playing it cool" (Hannerz, 1969; Mancini, 1980; Schulz, 1969). By the time many have reached junior high school, these youth are two or more years beyond grade level, are barely passing or failing in most of their courses, and are potential dropouts. In such circumstances, school becomes simply another experience of failure and frustration, another arena of conflict with unsympathetic and judgmental adults, and another institution of oppression and exploitation. From the vantage point of these young black males, it may make perfect sense to act out their rage and frustrations on educational institutions which have essentially failed them since kindergarten; to test the limits of a school system that has not been able to develop effective educational programs to train them for productive social roles; and to assault persons and property as they have themselves been assaulted—physically, sexually, or psychologically (Tolmach, 1985). To expect these inner-city youth to love learning in inhospitable classrooms with burned-out teachers is to deny the bleak reality of their lives, the depth of their disillusionment with the system, and the depression and despair just beneath the surface of their hostility and anger.

Delinquency and Psychopathology

In Chapter 4, Richard Dembo pointed out the high incidence of emotional disorders in his sample of younger delinquents. A number of other investigators have described a subpopulation of delinquents who are psychiatrically disturbed, neurologically impaired, or have a combination of mental and physical disabilities (Lewis and Balla, 1976; Offer, Marohn, and Ostrov, 1975; Tolmach, 1985). In several of these studies, black youth were overrepresented among the most disturbed and most dysfunctional of the delinquent samples.

Although it is undoubtedly true that many delinquents can be appropriately described as socialized in that their behaviors are normative within a particular subcultural milieu, there are also many who display moderate to severe psychological problems. In the case of black youth, symptoms of psychological disorder are less likely to be detected early; thus, early intervention approaches to interrupt the downward spiral of behaviors are not initiated. Moreover, black youth who are most likely to develop symptomatology are those who have grown up in chaotic homes with disturbed or dysfunctional parents, where they have been subjected to parental deprivation or neglect, experienced various forms of abuse, and been exposed to drugs and antisocial behavior (Lewis and Shanok, 1977; Offer, Marohn, and Ostrov, 1975).

Delinquent and criminal behavior for this group of psychologically disturbed black youth can be viewed as serving two functions. First, these youngsters have not developed inner controls which enable them to moderate their impulses, to delay gratification of their immediate needs, and to anticipate the consequences of their actions. Second, they are displacing their anger and rage over their own victimization, built up from long years of frustration, onto the society which has been unable to protect and nurture them. Statistics on robberies, assaultive burglaries, and rapes only present numbers, which are concrete and objective indicators of the extent of criminal behavior in this group, but they do not provide any insights into the dynamic meaning or subjective aspects of these behaviors. Vignettes of black youth who commit serious crimes (or Index offenses, as described in Chapter 1) almost invariably portray them as victims themselves of poverty, parental neglect, abuse, school failure, and societal discrimination:

> . . . *Reggie Brown spent most of his short life in foster homes, jails, and on the streets of New York City. The [diabetic] son of a young welfare mother and an absent father, Reggie began his journey in the foster care system in a body cast at age 13, when he was severely injured from being thrown out of a second-story apartment window by his mother's boyfriend. At 18 he was discharged from foster care with a 9th grade education, no job skills, and no home. Unsuccessful as a minor thief and a minor drug dealer, Reggie slept mainly in abandoned buildings and on the subways, but always managed to take his daily doses of insulin. On August 25, 1985, just three months before his 22nd birthday, Reggie was shot trying to sell valium tablets to three young men. Ten days later his luck finally ran out and he died at Harlem Hospital, mourned by only a few relatives and friends who did not hear the news on the street until weeks later.* [New York Times, 1987d]

> . . . *At age 13 Michael Hagan was viciously attacked by a dozen members of a South Central Los Angeles gang. He defended himself so aggressively that he was recruited on the spot as a "homeboy." The oldest child in a poor fatherless family, Michael was arrested for the first time in 1979. Because of his gang activity, he was assigned to five different high schools before finally graduating while serving a 4-year jail term for mugging an off-duty policeman. A dedicated gang member, Michael particularly enjoyed drinking, doing drugs, fighting, and stealing. In the summer of 1986, while high on PCP, Michael and four of his "homeboys" drove into enemy*

gang territory looking for some action. Without provocation, he took a semiautomatic rifle and shot Kellie Mosier, a 17-year-old high school junior, six times in the back. A year later, Michael, age 23, was convicted of first-degree murder. While in jail awaiting sentence, he showed no remorse and explained to a reporter, "The gang is your family. If you're my homeboy, I fight for you, no matter what the odds. . . . If you're in a war, you just accept that the only thing you can do is stay alive." [Time Magazine, 1987]

Such cases are not atypical of the thousands of black youth who are arrested and incarcerated each year, usually without benefit of any psychological or psychiatric evaluation (Lewis and Balla, 1976). Without an assessment of underlying psychological problems, these youth do not receive any therapeutic treatment, and the opportunity to help them to resolve long-standing emotional conflicts is lost.

As several authors have noted, a two-tier system has developed whereby troubled white youth are processed through the mental health system and troubled minority youth through the juvenile criminal justice system (Krisberg et al., 1986; Lewis and Balla, 1976; Myers and King, 1983). This phenomenon is particularly true for low-income black youth whose families cannot afford to refer them to private mental health facilities or to hire lawyers to defend them when they are charged with criminal offenses. Thus, for similar acting-out behaviors the white youth might be referred for counseling while the black youth is charged with a delinquent offense.

The inevitable outcome of this institutional discrimination is the denial of mental health services to acting-out black youth and the perpetuation of a group of severely disturbed antisocial youth who have no investment in the social contract and no compunctions about violence. As long as juvenile and adult penal institutions are oriented toward punishment rather than rehabilitation and treatment, this group will continue to increase, with negative long-term consequences for themselves, their families, and society.

Psychiatric Admission Rates

Dr. Chester Pierce's (1970) concept of "micro-aggression" is very useful in understanding the level of psychic stress experienced by young black males in our society. Not only are these inner-city youth reared in extremely inhospitable environments; they are also subjected daily to reminders of their disadvantaged status in American society. These daily reminders are expressed in a variety of subtle and blatant ways to a young black male—a teacher calls him stupid; a white stranger gets up and walks away when he sits next to him on a crowded bus or subway; a bank teller reacts suspiciously when he tries to cash a check; an employer refuses to interview him for a job; a clerk ignores him in a department store; a cab driver ignores him or refuses to take him to a "black" neighborhood; a police officer stops to question him in a white neighborhood. These micro-assaults are so common that most black youth (as well as most black adults) learn unconsciously to anticipate such incidents, to ignore their rudeness, or to discount them with humor and sarcasm. However, a considerable (and growing) number of black youth have neither the self-control nor the motivation to tolerate such incidents. Many of these youth have such fragile egos and such low tolerance for frustration that they are unwilling to deny these constant assaults on their dignity or to delay their reactions to such behaviors. It is a question of Hobson's choice again: If they do not respond to the assaults and insults, they may internalize their anger and become depressed, develop psychosomatic symptoms like hypertension and ulcers, or drown their frustrations in alcohol and drugs; if they do react in a confrontational way to these assaults, their response might easily turn into uncontrolled aggression and lead to assaults and invite counterviolence from the very people who insulted them in the first place. Regardless of the choice, these daily interactions take an enormous toll on the mental health of black youth in America, driving many of them to the depths of despair and the brink of madness.

Accurate rates of psychiatric disorder among young black males are difficult to obtain and to interpret for many reasons. First, help-seeking patterns among blacks for psychological problems vary considerably according to socioeconomic status and, in general, differ from those of whites (Neighbors and Jackson, 1984; Snowden, 1982). When blacks experience emotional distress, they are initially less likely than whites to seek psychiatric treatment and more likely to discuss their problems with a minister, family doctor, or close relative. Second, blacks have a greater tendency to use hospital emergency rooms for medical and psychological symptoms, so these latter cases would not usually be counted in outpatient-psychiatric statistics. Third, blacks may have a greater tendency to somatize when they are anxious or depressed, so they seek medical rather than psychiatric treatment for these symptoms. Finally, the statistics represent only those who seek treatment in public and private psychiatric facilities and do not indicate the true prevalence of psychiatric disability among black youth.

Given the limitations of the data, it is useful to view the incidence of psychiatric disorders in this population as only a fraction of all those who may be emotionally disturbed and a very rough estimate of those who either seek some type of treatment to alleviate their distress or are hospitalized involuntarily.

Admission rates of nonwhite males 18–24 to state and county mental hospital inpatient services in 1980 were over 2.5 times the rate for white males in the same age group (Taube and Barrett, 1985). This ratio also held true for admissions to psychiatric inpatient facilities at Veterans Administration Hospitals, but the rate was only slightly higher for nonwhites in private psychiatric inpatient services. Similarly, for children under 18, nonwhite males had higher admission rates than whites to state and county inpatient psychiatric facilities but lower rates to private inpatient services. A recent utilization study of inpatient psychiatric services for adolescents, 10–17, indicated that while state, county, and public general hospitals accounted for 20 to 40 percent of nonwhite admissions, private psychiatric facilities accounted for less than 15 percent of nonwhite patients (Thompson et al., 1986). The category of "nonwhite" usually includes 90 to 95 percent blacks. The authors concluded:

> *Private psychiatric hospitals and private general hospitals have increasingly become the sites for treatment of adolescents. . . . Demographically, the data seem to support the idea that the specialty sector is in actuality a dual system of care, at least as far as race is concerned. Private facilities largely treat white patients in the adolescent age groups, while public facilities take more responsibility for nonwhite patients. [Thompson et al., 1986, p. 589]*

These figures also indicate that a higher proportion of nonwhite psychiatric patients are in the 18–24 age group than among white patients, suggesting that nonwhite males may find this period of life more stressful than do white males (Taube and Barrett, 1985). Moreover, the admission rate of nonwhite males 18–24 is over three times the rate of nonwhite females to state and county facilities and 1.5 times their admission rate to private psychiatric facilities. Thus, nonwhite males appear to be at much higher risk of being hospitalized for psychological disorders than nonwhite females or whites of either sex.

These statistics represent the opposite side of the phenomenon of high rates of incarceration of black youth—that is, they are overrepresented in the juvenile justice system and underrepresented in private psychiatric facilities in the mental health system. As Myers and King (1983) document, these differential rates of hospitalization and treatment facilities for young black males have persisted for many years.

In the study of hospitalization rates of navy enlisted men earlier cited, blacks also had the highest rates of nonalcoholic mental disorders (Hoiberg, Berard, and Ernst, 1981). These researchers attributed the high rate of psychiatric disorders among black sailors to their low socioeconomic status and lack of access to mental health care in their prior civilian lives. Community surveys have also found that younger black males had higher rates of depression than white males or black females; this pattern was particularly true of low-income black males, but is the opposite pattern for white males and females (Comstock and Helsing, 1976; Neighbors et al., 1983; Roberts, Stevenson, and Breslow, 1981).

A closely related issue is the type of treatment black youth receive in psychiatric facilities. Several studies have indicated that young black males are significantly less likely to receive insight-oriented, long-term, or short-term psychotherapy than almost any other group of patients (see Jenkins, 1982; Jones and Korchin, 1982; Sue, 1977). They are more likely to be referred for crisis intervention, supportive treatment, and medication than similar groups of patients. Thus, even though they tend to receive more severe psychiatric diagnoses, the treatment offered to them reflects a long-standing and persistent attitude that these patients are not motivated, not capable of insight, and not appropriate candidates for psychotherapy.

Mortality and Morbidity

The short-range and long-range health outcomes for black males are very poor, since their mortality rates exceed all other sex-race groups in the ten leading causes of death. Among black males in the 15–24 age group, the five leading causes of death are homicide, accidents, suicide, cancer, and heart disease (DHHS, 1985). Black males in this age group have the highest incidence of death from cancer and heart disease as compared to the other three sex-race groups, yet causes for this discrepancy are not clear. Recent studies indicate that black males are more likely than white males to smoke, so this may increase their risks for certain types of cancer and heart disease. Higher rates of these diseases may also be related to other risk factors to which many black males are chronically exposed, such as poor nutrition, carcinogenic substances in their environments, high levels of stress, substance abuse, and other risk factors associated with poverty.

The three major causes of death for this group—homicide, drug-related accidents, and suicide—have such significant implications that they will be discussed in Chapter 8. Suffice it to say that young black males are in an unenviable position in our society: They are less healthy, suffer more accidents and injuries, have more psychological disorders, and are more likely to face death at a very early age.

Policy and Program Recommendations

The recent government report on the health status of blacks and other minority groups clearly stated: "The poor health status observed in many minority groups and differences remaining between minorities and nonminorities in types of care and financing, suggest that minorities still have poorer access to and use of comprehensive and high quality health care" (DHHS, 1985, p. 187). While there is general agreement among policymakers that current federal and state policies do not provide adequate health coverage for low-income families and children, there is no widespread consensus on the most effective and efficient ways to change these policies.

The following discussion will focus on a limited number of health policy options that have been proposed to address the inequities of the current system, particularly those which would have a direct and substantial impact on the health status of black youth and their families. The emphasis will be on those policies that primarily address the problems of adolescents and young adults rather than on those concerned with maternal and child health, the focus of several recent books (Edelman, 1987; Rodgers, 1986). Specific programs to address the major health problems of black youth will also be discussed briefly as they relate to the proposed policy changes.

Access to Health Care

The major problem for low-income black families is that few have any form of health insurance and most of these are underinsured for comprehensive health care. Approximately half of those families who are eligible for Medicaid are not covered, for a variety of reasons. Yet, health care for poor children and their families has greatly improved since the Medicaid legislation went into effect, increasing their access to medical and dental services, particularly in states with liberal eligibility requirements and generous matching funds. Thus, the most important recommendation proposed by several advocacy groups is that Medicaid should be extended to provide coverage for all low-income children and youth in both single-parent and two-parent families (Edelman, 1987). A corollary to this recommendation is that the income eligibility level of families should be raised so that the "working poor" would be eligible for Medicaid even if they are not eligible for AFDC benefits. A second corollary would require states to extend benefits to all children and youth up to age 21, which is now a policy in only 26 of the states. These three changes would provide health coverage for nearly all poor and minority youth in this country.

A more radical proposal is advocated by Schorr (1986), who proposes a national health insurance program that would be a universal system for all citizens similar to the national insurance system in Canada. Although less controversial than a nationalized health service based on the British model, such a system would have no eligibility requirements, would provide comprehensive services, would emphasize prevention and early intervention, and would provide high-quality health care for everyone. Schorr believes that the time has come to develop a national consensus on the financing of a comprehensive system of health care which would meet the criteria of a just society for equity and equality for all citizens.

Providing universal health coverage is only one component of an effective health policy for underserved black youth and their families. Major changes are also needed in the health service delivery system so that services will be available and accessible in inner-city neighborhoods. The federal government must be convinced to allocate more funds for community health centers, which have actually proven to be more cost-effective than Medicaid in providing health care to low-income families, who have shifted from private doctors to hospital emergency rooms and public clinics for their primary care since many neighborhood health centers were phased out (Schorr, 1986).

In addition, the Children's Defense Fund (1986a) makes two important recommendations: (1) comprehensive health clinics for school-aged children, authorized under Title V of the Maternal and Child Health Block Grant, should receive additional funding for child-health projects in low-income areas, and (2) school-based health clinics for teenagers should be established in all states. These clinics offer comprehensive health and mental health services for children and youth and have demonstrated their effectiveness in providing prevention and early intervention services in terms of screening for early detection of vision, hearing, and dental problems, early treatment of health problems, and prevention of dysfunctional or self-destructive adolescent behaviors such as pregnancy, substance abuse, and suicide (CDF, 1986b).

In addition to increased federal support for community health centers and school-based clinics for children and adolescents, the federal government should also provide leadership in improving the coordination among the many systems which deliver health services to emotionally disturbed, institutionalized, and delinquent youth, including the child welfare, juvenile justice, special education, and mental health systems, in order to improve the quality of care, to reduce duplication, and to prevent neglect of the many low-income black youth in these systems. An important vehicle for accomplishing this goal is the Child and Adolescent Service System Program (CASSP), currently funded through the Adult Community Support Program (Stroul and Friedman, 1986).

The third major component of adequate health care for these youth is the availability of well-trained health professionals who are sensitive to the sociocultural aspects of health care. As Schorr (1986) points out, the much-publicized oversupply of physicians is not applicable to urban ghettos and rural areas. In 1980, the ratio of physicians to population in Manhattan was 1:164; but in Harlem, one of the nation's largest black communities, it was 1:4,500.

Although the *Report on Black and Minority Health* (DHHS, 1985) recommended that more minority doctors should be recruited and trained, the situation is far more complex than that. Minority doctors who are trained in major medical schools have assimilated many of the same attitudes and values as their white peers. As the inner cities have deteriorated, they have not been able to attract younger black doctors, who now have a greater range of practice options and opportunities than their predecessors. Radical changes in the health care field, such as group practices, health maintenance organizations, limitations on fees from Medicaid and Medicare, and high premiums for liability insurance, have made individual practice in low-income areas much less profitable and desirable to black physicians. Moreover, the percentage of black medical students actually declined from 6.3 percent in 1974–75 to 5.5 percent in 1983–84 (DHHS, 1985). Thus, special incentives, such as those initiated in the 1960s, should be reevaluated and revamped to recruit more black doctors. For example, medical schools could forgive partial or full payment on loans underwritten by the government for physicians who will commit an equivalent number of years to practice in inner-city areas. The Public Health Service could also recruit black physicians to work for a two- to four-year period in the ghetto in return for scholarships to finance medical school or residency training, similar to the model now used to provide doctors for Indian reservations. If a national health insurance plan were instituted, doctors could be assigned to inner-city hospitals or clinics on a rotation basis. Many other innovative suggestions have been made to increase the supply of health professionals, including dentists, nurses, and medical technicians, to health facilities in the inner cities; but all these programs require federal or state funding, coordination, monitoring, and penalties for noncompliance of contracts, none of which has been effectively implemented in the earlier efforts (see Schorr, 1986; DHHS, 1985).

Nutrition

As the poverty rate has increased in this society in the last decade, so has the incidence of hunger and malnutrition, with a particularly heavy impact on black youth and their families (Select Committee on Hunger, 1985). Yet the Reagan administration has drastically cut funds and restricted eligibility for the food stamp program and the nutrition program for Women, Infants and Children (WIC), although Rodgers (1986) notes that the total cost of all federally funded food programs in fiscal 1985 was less than $20 billion. It has been estimated that approximately one-third of the poor who are eligible for food stamps do not receive them (CDF, 1986a).

Two different approaches to improving nutrition for low-income youth and their families have been proposed. Some policymakers advocate an increase in benefit levels of food stamps to reflect the average cost of a "thrifty food plan" and an extension of food stamps for all those who are eligible (CDF, 1986a). Others recommend that food stamps be eliminated altogether and a food allotment be incorporated into a minimum guaranteed family income plan (APWA, 1986). While the latter proposal is more politically controversial, it is also more humane and less demeaning for poor families, many of whom currently are not enrolled in food stamp programs because of the stigma of receiving any form of government assistance.

In addition to changes in the food stamp program, it is essential to restore the cuts in the school lunch program, to extend the program to all public schools in low-income areas, and to provide nourishing meals for youth who often receive only one well-balanced meal a day. The relationship between good nutrition, health, and factors which promote learning has been well documented, yet the federal government spends more funds annually to store surplus farm products, purchased from well-to-do farmers, than it does to support food stamps and school lunch programs for vulnerable families and children (Rodgers, 1986).

Housing

Many of the health conditions of black youth are related to poverty and their substandard housing and sanitation conditions, particularly conditions such as lead poisoning, household accidents and injuries, respiratory diseases, and tuberculosis. As has been documented, homeless youth are particularly at risk for the development of physical and mental health problems due to their transient housing in large armories, abandoned warehouses, or cheap hotels.

The major recommendations to alleviate these problems are for the federal government to increase funds to make more low-cost housing available to families with children, to increase rent subsidies to families in subsidized housing, and to increase housing assistance for low-income families by decreasing the allowable tax deductions on interest and taxes paid by middle- and upper-income families on their homes (see Rodgers, 1986; Schorr, 1986; CDF, 1986a).

State and local governments must also subsidize low-income housing and convince building contractors and the real estate industry that integrated, mixed-income dispersed housing is not only good social policy, but will contribute to the economic revitalization of urban areas by attracting service industries, young professionals, and retail trade (Peterson, 1985). The state of Massachusetts, which has a booming economy and a shortage of affordable housing for low- and middle-income families, recently allocated $404.6 million for a package of housing programs to assist these groups and the elderly (*New York Times*, 1987a).

In July 1987, Congress belatedly passed an appropriations bill for $1 billion for emergency shelters, some permanent low-cost housing, and additional food stamps for the estimated 2 million homeless people, but that was only a piecemeal solution to an escalating social crisis in urban America. Unfortunately, the growing number of black homeless families cannot wait for the wheels of bureaucracy to grind out new comprehensive long-range housing policies. It is imperative that all levels of government cooperate to provide temporary housing which meets adequate standards of safety and sanitation for homeless families with children. It is also important that irrelevant eligibility criteria (e.g., a "permanent address") should be waived so that these families can obtain needed housing, food, medical care, and other essential services in order to maintain their health and mental health.

Housing assistance, however, is not the only problem for low-income black families. Urban planners and social scientists are increasingly aware of the noxious environment created in inner cities through a combination of deteriorating high-rise apartments, chronic unemployment, and social isolation. Thus, many now advocate that low-rent housing should be dispersed throughout cities and their suburban areas, that there should be a mix of high-rise and low-rise structures, that there should be easy access to services and transportation, and that new housing developments should be located near businesses and industrial sites with job opportunities (Peterson, 1985; Schorr, 1986).

Finally, county and local governments should intensify their enforcement of fire and safety regulations and building standards through regular inspections, as well as maintenance and repair of streets, lights, and sanitation facilities that are located in inner-city neighborhoods. Regular building inspections and improved maintenance of county and city-owned roads and facilities would probably result in substantial reductions of accidents and injuries to black youth in these neighborhoods.

Sexually Transmitted Diseases

In order to check the spread of sexually transmitted diseases, including AIDS, federal, state, and local governments must cooperate in launching massive community-based health education campaigns, particularly geared to black youth who are at high risk for these diseases. In New York City alone, where nearly half of the AIDS patients are black intravenous drug users, a total of $334 million in funds for AIDS-related programs had been spent by June of 1987 by federal, state, city, and other sources. In spite of these efforts, which threaten to bankrupt the nation's health care budget by the year 2000, the disease continues to spread, particularly within the black and Hispanic communities (*San Francisco Chronicle,* 1987c). Since AIDS is a fatal disease and there is so much misinformation about it, federal, state, and local health departments should make concerted efforts to disseminate information as widely as possible in minority communities through schools, health care facilities, small businesses, utility company bills, public transportation services, and service organizations.

Community health centers should identify popular gathering places in black communities (e.g., barber shops, beauty parlors, restaurants, bars, pool halls, youth recreation centers, fraternal lodges) at which information about AIDS could be posted. Promotion of "safe sex" practices recommended to avoid AIDS will also help to prevent the spread of other sexually transmitted diseases such as syphilis and gonorrhea. These efforts should be linked to drug education/prevention programs, since intravenous drug use is one of the major causes of AIDS among blacks.

School-based clinics should also offer information and education to adolescents about AIDS and other sexually transmitted diseases. If these clinics are not authorized to provide contraceptive services to their clients, they should have a list of referral sources at which these services are available. Not only will this information reduce the susceptibility of these youth to sexually transmitted diseases, but it may have the additional benefit of reducing the rates of teenage pregnancy in these communities. If young black males alter their negative attitudes toward contraception in order to prevent AIDS or syphilis, they will also be less likely to join the ranks of unwed teenage fathers, which has its own set of negative sequelae.

In a recent promising development, the Center for Disease Control allocated $7 million to distribute to minority groups for AIDS education and prevention, but blacks fear that these funds are too little and too late (*New York Times*, 1987d).

Mental Health

In addition to the federal programs mentioned earlier, states are granted federal funds for periodic health screening of children and youth up to age 18 (CDF, 1986a). All states need to implement these programs to provide regular checkups for youth in order to detect health and mental health problems in their early stages, particularly among poor and minority youth who have less frequent medical and dental checkups.

Several federal programs include funds for emotionally disturbed and delinquent teens in block grants to the states (e.g., Mental Health Block Grant from ADAMHA), but these funds are not always used effectively. Since black youth are disproportionately represented in both of these problem categories, they would be prime beneficiaries of any efforts to increase the utilization of these funds and to improve their program implementation. Funds for the Child and Adolescent Service System Program (CASSP) should be increased in order to improve the coordination of existing programs.

Community psychiatric treatment facilities, both public and private, are woefully inadequate for emotionally disturbed black youth. Funds must be allocated to expand the mental health components of community health facilities located in inner cities.

Emergency psychiatric services in publically funded hospitals, the source of primary care for many low-income black youth, should be improved and better coordinated with other community services.

Finally, continued federal support is necessary to train black mental health professionals (psychiatrists, psychologists, clinical social workers) in order to increase the supply of professionals who are sensitive to sociocultural issues in the treatment of psychological disorders. Training programs in general should be modified to include courses and clinical experiences which will prepare all mental health professionals to serve black youth more effectively (Gibbs, 1985; Franklin, 1982).

As is the case with community health clinics and school-based clinics, all health and mental health services for black youth should be affordable, accessible, and appropriate (CDF, 1986b). Only then will this very vulnerable group have an equal opportunity to grow and develop with healthy minds and healthy bodies.

Conclusions

An overview of the health and mental health of young black males, as presented in this chapter, indicates that they are a very high risk group for a host of debilitating and dysfunctional physical and psychological problems. It is clear that these negative outcomes are related to a number of demographic and social factors which contribute to a pathogenic environment for these youth. These factors include poverty or low socioeconomic status, deteriorating housing and neighborhoods, unstable families, high rates of unemployment, crime and delinquency, substance abuse, teen pregnancy, school dropouts, and homicide. Moreover, the prejudice and discrimination of the wider society have direct and indirect effects on the health of young black males in terms of the barriers to health care, the increased levels of stress, their occupational environments, and the limitations on their mobility and life options.

A review of the major causes of illness in this age group reveals that the incidence of morbidity is higher for nearly every disease for young black males than for any other race/sex/age group. The only exceptions are motor vehicle accidents and suicide, which occur more frequently among white youth.

There is also a vicious cycle involved in the relationship between social factors and health outcomes. On the one hand, social and economic factors contribute significantly to poor health in black youth. On the other hand, the consequences of their poor health further reduce their opportunities, their social mobility, and result in many negative sequelae over their life course.

The poor health status of this large group of youth also has negative effects on the broader society in terms of increased health care costs for chronic illnesses and disabilities, lowered productivity in their jobs, and increased costs for related social problems. For example, the high incidence of AIDS and AIDS-related complex (ARC) in this population group will eventually cost the health care system millions of dollars by the end of this century, but the effects of AIDS will also proliferate in other areas, such as the schools, the criminal justice system, housing (the real estate market), and the employment sector; all of this will require additional screening, special facilities, legal challenges concerning discrimination, and unanticipated social costs.

Policy and program recommendations were proposed to address the issues of improved access to quality health care, adequate nutrition, and decent housing. Policies and programs were also proposed to address the specific problems of sexually transmitted diseases and mental health. In the final chapter, these recommendations will be examined in the context of a comprehensive health policy for all low-income youth and families.

The need for a comprehensive health and mental health policy that would benefit black youth as well as all youth is critical. As Schorr (1986) has noted, the health care system in the United States needs massive reform if it is not to splinter into a two-tiered system for the "haves" (mostly white and middle class) and the "have-nots" (mostly nonwhite and poor). If these reforms are delayed much longer, another generation of black youth will be disabled, diseased, and decimated in the most medically advanced nation in the world.

References

American Public Welfare Association (APWA). (1986). *One child in four*. New York: APWA.

Berger, L. (1985). Childhood injuries. *Public Health Reports* 100: 572–74.

Brunswick, A. (1980). Health stability and change: A study of urban black youth. *American Journal of Public Health* 70: 504–13.

Carter, J. H. (1983). Vision or sight: Health concerns for Afro-American children. In *The psychosocial development of minority group children*, edited by G. Powell, J. Yamamoto, A. Romero, and A. Morales. New York: Brunner/Mazel.

CDF. See Children's Defense Fund.

Centers for Disease Control. (1983). Fire and burn-associated deaths—Georgia, 1979–1981. *Morbidity and Mortality Weekly Report* 32 (Dec. 9): 625–34.

————. (1985a). Drownings—Georgia, 1981–1983. *Morbidity and Mortality Weekly Report* 34 (May 24): 281–83.

————. (1985b). Drug-resistant tuberculosis among the homeless—Boston. *Morbidity and Mortality Weekly Report* 34 (July 19): 429–31.

————. (1986a). Acquired immunodeficiency syndrome (AIDS) among Blacks and Hispanics—United States. *Morbidity and Mortality Weekly Report* 35 (Oct. 24): 655–66.

————. (1986b). Update—Acquired immunodeficiency syndrome—United States. *Morbidity and Mortality Weekly Report* 35 (Dec. 12): 757–66.

————. (1987a). Early syphilis—Broward County, Florida. *Morbidity and Mortality Weekly Report* 36 (April 17): 221–23.

————. (1987b). Increases in primary and secondary syphilis—United States. *Morbidity and Mortality Weekly Report* 36 (July 3): 393–97.

————. (1987c). Tuberculosis in Blacks—United States. *Morbidity and Mortality Weekly Report,* 36 (April 17): 212–20.

Children's Defense Fund (CDF). (1985a). *A children's defense budget.* Washington, D.C.: CDF.

————. (1985b). *Black and white children in America.* Washington, D.C.: CDF.

————. (1986a). *A children's defense budget.* Washington, D.C.: CDF.

————. (1986b). *Building health programs for teenagers.* Washington, D.C.: CDF.

Comstock, G. W., and Helsing, K. J. (1976). Symptoms of depression in two communities. *Psychological Medicine* 6: 551–63.

Department of Health and Human Services (DHHS). (1985). *Report of the secretary's task force on black and minority health,* Vol. I. Washington, D.C.: DHHS.

————. (1986). *Report of the secretary's task force on black and minority health,* Vol. V. Washington, D.C.: DHHS.

Edelman, M. W. (1987). *Families in peril: An agenda for social change.* Cambridge, Mass.: Harvard University Press.

Egbuono, L., and Starfield, G. (1982). Child health and social status. *Pediatrics* 69: 550–56.

Franklin, A. J. (1982). Therapeutic interventions with urban black adolescents. In *Minority mental health,* edited by E. E. Jones and S. J. Korchin. New York: Praeger.

Gibbs, J. T. (1984). Black adolescents and youth: An endangered species. *American Journal of Orthopsychiatry* 54: 6–21.

————. (1985). Can we continue to be color-blind and class-bound? *The Counseling Psychologist,* 13: 426–35.

————. (1986). Psychosocial correlates of sexual attitudes and behaviors in urban early adolescent females: Implications for intervention. *Journal of Social Work and Human Sexuality* 5: 81–97.

Hampton, R. L. (1986). Family violence and homicide in the black community: Are they linked? In *Report of the secretary's task force on black and minority health,* Vol. V. Washington, D.C.: Department of Health and Human Services.

Hannerz, U. (1969). *Soulside: Inquiries into ghetto culture and community.* New York: Columbia University Press.

Hayman, C. R., and Probst, J. C. (1983). Health status of disadvantaged adolescents entering the Job Corps program. *Public Health Reports* 98: 369–76.

Hoiberg, A., Berard, S., and Ernst, J. (1981). Racial differences in hospitalization rates among navy enlisted men. *Public Health Reports* 96: 121–27.

Houston-Hamilton, A. (1986). A constant increase: AIDS in ethnic communities. *Focus* 1:1–2.

Jenkins, A. (1982). *The psychology of the Afro-American*. New York: Pergamon Press.

Jones, B., ed. (1986). *Treating the homeless: Urban psychiatry's challenge*. Washington, D.C.: American Psychiatry Press.

Jones, E. E., and Korchin, S. J., eds. (1982). *Minority mental health*. New York: Praeger.

Knopf, I. (1984). *Childhood psychopathology*, 2d ed. Englewood Cliffs, N.J.: Prentice-Hall.

Kovar, M. G. (1982). Health status of U.S. children and use of medical care. *Public Health Reports* 97: 3–15.

Krisberg, B., Schwartz, I., Fishman, G., Eiskovits, Z., and Guttman, E. (1986). *The incarceration of minority youth*. Minneapolis: H. H. Humphrey Institute of Public Affairs, University of Minnesota.

Lawrence, M. A., and Guess, J. M. (1986). Discrimination, occupations, and income. *The Crisis* 93: 17–18.

Lewis, D., and Balla, D. (1976). *Delinquency and psychopathology*. New York: Grune & Stratton.

Lewis, D., and Shanok, S. (1977). Medical histories of delinquent and nondelinquent children. *American Journal of Psychiatry* 134: 1020–25.

Mancini, J. K. (1980). *Strategic styles: Coping in the inner city*. Hanover, N.H.: University Press of New England.

Mays, V., and Cochran, S. (1987). Acquired immunodeficiency syndrome and black Americans: Special psychosocial issues. *Public Health Reports* 102: 221–31.

Myers, H. F., and King, L. M. (1983). Mental health issues in the development of the black American child. In *The psychosocial development of minority group children*, edited by G. Powell, J. Yamamoto, A. Roberto, and A. Morales. New York: Brunner/Mazel.

National Center for Health Statistics (NCHS). (1986). *Health—United States—1986*. Washington, D.C.: U.S. Dept. of Health, Education and Welfare.

———. (1979). *Health—United States—1979*. Washington, D.C.: U.S. Dept. of Health, Education and Welfare.

National Institute of Drug Abuse (NIDA). (1980). *Current trends and issues in drug abuse*. Rockville, Md: Alcohol, Drugs, and Mental Health Administration.

Needleman, H. L., Gunnoe, C., Leviton, A., et al. (1979). Deficits in psychological and classroom performance of children with elevated dentine lead levels. *New England Journal of Medicine* 300: 689.

Neighbors, H. W., and Jackson, J. S. (1984). The use of informal and formal help: Four patterns of illness behavior in the black community. *American Journal of Community Psychology* 12: 629–44.

Neighbors, H. W., Jackson, J. S., Bowman, P. J., and Gurin, G. (1983). Stress, coping, and black mental health: Preliminary findings from a national study. *Prevention in Human Services* 2(3): 5–29.

New York Times, National Edition (1987a). "Strong economy is no blessing for Boston house hunters," July 27, A-8.

———. (1987b). "Welfare hotel children: Tomorrow's poor," July 18, p. B-1.

———. (1987c). "Earlier U.S. AIDS incursions hinted," Oct. 28, p. 5.

———. (1987d). "High AIDs rate spurring efforts for minorities," Aug. 2, p. 1.

Offer, D., Marohn, R. C., and Ostrov, E. (1979). *The psychological world of the juvenile delinquent*. New York: Basic Books.

Peterson, P. E. (1985). *The new urban reality*. Washington, D.C.: The Brookings Institution.

Physician Task Force on Hunger. (1985). Hunger in America: The growing epidemic. Boston: Harvard University School of Public Health.

Pierce, C. M. (1970). Offense mechanisms. In *The Black 70s*, edited by F. Barbour. Boston: Porter Sargent Publications.

Public Health Reports. (1985). Blood lead levels in children exceed previous estimates. *Public Health Reports* 100: 246.

Roberts, R. E., Stevenson, J. M., and Breslow, L. (1981). Symptoms of depression among blacks and whites in an urban community. *The Journal of Nervous and Mental Disease* 169: 774–79.

Rodgers, H. R. (1986). *Poor women, poor families*. Armonk, N.Y.: M. E. Sharpe.

San Francisco Chronicle. (1987a). "67 AIDS deaths in S. F. in last month," March 4, p. 5.

———. (1987b). "Death row: Inmates with AIDS," June 28, p. 1.

———. (1987c). "AIDS in America/A special report: New York wasn't prepared," July 28, p. 1.

Schneider, J., Aurori, B., Armentis, L., and Soltanoff, D. (1981). Impact of community screening and diagnosis, treatment and medical findings of lead poisoning in children. *Public Health Reports* 96: 143–49.

Schorr, A. (1986). *Common decency: Domestic policies after Reagan*. New Haven: Yale University Press.

Schulz, D. (1969). *Coming up black: Patterns of ghetto socialization*. Englewood Cliffs, N.J.: Prentice-Hall.

Select Committee on Hunger. (1985). Hearings on poverty and hunger in the black family. Washington, D.C.: 99th U.S. Congress, September.

Shilling, S., and Brackbill, R. M. (1987). Occupational health and safety risks and potential health consequences perceived by U.S. workers, 1985. *Public Health Reports* 102: 36–46.

Staples, R. (1982). *Black masculinity: The black man's role in American society*. San Francisco: The Black Scholar Press.

Stroul, B., and Friedman, R. (1986). *A system of care for severely emotionally disturbed children and youth*. Washington, D.C.: CASSP Technical Assistance Center, Georgetown University.

Sue, S. (1977). Community mental health services to minority groups. *American Psychologist* 32: 616–24.

Taube, C. A., and Barrett, S. A. (1985). *Mental Health, United States–1985*. Rockville, Md: U.S. Department of Health and Human Services.

Taylor, R. L. (1977). The black worker in "post-industrial" society. In *The Black male in America*, edited by D. Y. Wilkinson and R. L. Taylor. Chicago: Nelson-Hall.

Thompson, J., Rosenstein, M., Milazzo-Sayre, L., and MacAskill, R. (1986). Psychiatric services to adolescents: 1970–1980. *Hospital and Community Psychiatry*, 37: 584–90.

Time. (1987). Life and death with the gangs, August 24, p. 22.

Tolmach, J. (1985). "There ain't nobody on my side": A new day treatment program for black urban youth. *Journal of Clinical Child Psychology* 14: 214–19.

U.S. Department of Labor. (1987). *Youth 2000: Challenge and Opportunity* (mimeo). Washington, D.C.

Washington Post. (1987). Aggressive prevention efforts proliferate, June 5, p. D-1.

Williams, J., ed. (1982). *The state of black America*. New York: National Urban League.

Chapter 8

THE NEW MORBIDITY: HOMICIDE, SUICIDE, ACCIDENTS, AND LIFE-THREATENING BEHAVIORS

Jewelle Taylor Gibbs

> *The neighborhood prophets began making prophecies about my life span. They all had me dead, buried, and forgotten before my 21st birthday. . . . There was much justification for these prophecies. By the time I was nine years old, I had been hit by a bus, thrown into the Harlem River (intentionally), hit by a car, severely beaten with a chain. And I had set the house on fire.*

> CLAUDE BROWN, in *Manchild in the Promised Land* (New York: Signet Books, 1966).

Introduction

In 1977, more young black men (5,734) died from homicide than were killed from 1963–1972 in the Vietnam War (5,640). Suicide rates among black males 15–24 have tripled since 1960. Nearly 2,000 black youth die or are severely disabled in accidents and injuries every year. Young black males are particularly overrepresented among the youth whose deaths are caused by accidents, homicide, and suicide. Called "the new morbidity," these three categories account for over 75 percent of the fatalities in the 15–24 age group (Centers for Disease Control, 1983c). The common thread connecting all of these phenomena is the use and abuse of drugs and alcohol, which is endemic in urban ghettos. The *new morbidity* is a term coined to describe the interrelationship of these self-destructive and life-threatening behaviors among American youth; it is particularly applicable to young black males (Gibbs, 1984, 1985).

The new morbidity refers to life-threatening diseases or disabilities which are primarily caused by social rather than biological factors. In contrast to infectious and chronic diseases which have a known organic etiology, these conditions stem from social, cultural, and economic forces that foster high-risk activities, self-destructive behaviors, and deviant life-styles. Although this chapter focuses on just four manifestations of this phenomenon in young black males, some public health experts would also include teen pregnancy in this category because of its high potential for serious physical complications to mother and child (CDF, 1986c; Chilman, 1983).

Examples of the new morbidity are frequently reported in the mass media: drive-by shootings in Oakland, California, where a pregnant teenager is fatally wounded one month and a teenage basketball star another month; gang wars in the Bronx, where black teenagers kill each other over "turf" or the right to peddle drugs on streets that resemble war zones; homeless young drug addicts in Los Angeles who share dirty needles in a downtown public park; two celebrity college athletes at the University of Maryland and in Seattle, Washington, who die of overdoses of cocaine; two brothers in Harlem who try to "roll" a plain clothes detective, with one getting killed in the attempt; a high school football hero in Chicago, who is gunned down because he accidentally jostled an unemployed school dropout; a black teenager in San Francisco who commits suicide because he was detained in juvenile hall for a weekend on a minor charge.

Many factors have been advanced to explain the increasing rates of death and disability in this group from these avoidable causes. As has been amply documented in earlier chapters, the most significant factors contributing to the new morbidity for black youth are poverty, discrimination, family breakdown, and community disorganization. Poverty and racism notwithstanding, the levels of interpersonal violence and self-destructive behaviors in black youth cannot be adequately explained simply by a sociological analysis. The influence of societal and subcultural attitudes toward violence, the impact of the mass media's glamorization of violence and drugs, the easy availability of hand guns, and the black community's attitudes toward the police are also factors. An interdisciplinary perspective is necessary to analyze the complex forces which generate and reinforce violence and life-threatening behaviors in our inner-city neighborhoods, to identify points of intervention, and to propose strategies of prevention and remediation of these forces.

This chapter examines each example of the new morbidity—homicide, suicide, accidents, and substance abuse—and concludes with a discussion of policies and programs to address the symptomatic behaviors as well as their underlying causes.

Homicide

Numerous examples are reported daily in the mass media of the casual and cold-blooded violence in our urban ghettos, where life is valued so cheaply that it is a commodity to be bartered for goods and services. Young black males kill each other over drugs, women, money, or simply to avenge a real or imaginary insult.

> *In 1986 an 18-year-old high school senior, a star athlete and school leader in Chicago, was walking down the street with a friend, excitedly discussing his many offers from college recruiters. He accidentally bumped into another young black male walking with a friend, both unemployed school dropouts. Offended by the perceived insult to his manhood, the latter young man exchanged a few hostile words with the athlete, then suddenly pulled out his gun and fatally wounded him.*

> *Marc and Andre, both students at an inner-city Oakland, California high school, had been feuding for weeks over some minor differences. In December of 1985 their feud finally erupted into a fistfight in the crowded school corridor. After the fight had been broken up by fellow students, Marc borrowed a gun from his cousin, chased Andre down the hall, and shot him twice in the back before dozens of witnesses. Andre died just two weeks before Christmas.*

These are just two examples of the senseless killings played out in macabre scenes of violence daily in urban ghettos, on the streets, in the schools, in the bars, in the projects, and even on the playgrounds.

Incidence and Risk of Homicide

The Centers for Disease Control measure the rate of premature mortality by estimating the years of potential life lost (YPLL) for various subgroups in the population. In 1982, the last year for which these rates were calculated, the YPLL rate for blacks from all causes of mortality was 99.2 per 1,000, nearly twice the white rate of 53.6 per 1,000 (Centers for Disease Control, 1986b). Blacks as a group had higher YPLL rates for ten leading causes of death, but black males had the highest rate of YPLL from these causes of all sex-race groups, followed by black women, white men, and white women. The report further notes:

> *Intentional injuries, particularly homicide, are identified as predominantly a condition affecting black males, with white males having the second highest rate. . . . Black men have now been clearly identified as the group most at risk of premature death and, consequently, most in need of interventions to lower this risk.* [p. 98]

The leading cause of death for black males 15–24 is homicide, a fact that seems so unlikely that it has lost its shock value. It has been estimated that a young black male has a 1 in 21 lifetime chance of being killed, most likely by one of his contemporaries (DHHS, 1986). Black males in this age group had a rate of 61.5 per 100,000 for homicides and legal intervention in 1984 (Table 8–1). Contrary to popular mythology, most of these young men are *not* murdered by police officers or by an adult in the commission of a crime; rather they are more often murdered by each other for reasons including street holdups, drug trade, sexual jealousy, and gang fights. In fact, 44 percent of black victims were killed by black offenders in 1980 (Hawkins, 1986).

As the recent special report on black and minority health, prepared by the Department of Health and Human Services, points out:

Table 8–1 Black and White Youth Homicide Rates, 15–24 Age Group (per 100,000 residents)

15–24 Years	1960	1970	1980	1982	1984
Black females	11.9	17.7	18.4	15.3	14.8
Black males	46.4	102.5	84.3	72.0	61.5
White females	1.5	2.7	4.7	4.4	4.3
White males	4.4	7.9	15.5	13.1	11.1

Source: *Health, United States, 1986*. U.S. Department of Health and Human Services, National Center for Health Statistics, Hyattsville, Md., Dec. 1986, DHHS Pub. No. (PHS) 87-1232.

In 1983, blacks constituted 11.5 percent of the United States popu-
lation but accounted for 43 percent of all homicide deaths. Black
men, women and children all have rates of death from homicide that
are far in excess of the rates for their fellow citizens of the same age
and gender. . . . Homicide accounts for more excess mortality among
Black Americans under age 45 than any other cause of death.
[DHHS, 1986, p. 5]

Based on 1983 rates, the National Centers for Disease Control
(1986a) recently estimated that the years of potential life lost from
homicide were highest for all black males, nearly seven times the
rate of white males (1,604 versus 252 per 100,000). Although black
males represented only 7 percent of the total population in 1983,
homicide in this group accounted for 35 percent of the total YPLL
rate attributed to homicide that year.

It has also been estimated that the life expectancy of a white
male born in 1975 was six years longer than a nonwhite male born
in the same year, with about one-fifth of the difference attributed
to higher homicide rates among nonwhites (Farley, 1980). Thus, if
homicide were eliminated, nonwhite males would gain approximately 1.5 years of longevity.

The risk of homicide for blacks in the United States is more
similar to the high levels of risk in developing countries than to the
much lower levels in industrialized countries. In fact, as Rose
(1986) points out, the homicide risk level for young black males
20–24 increased 105 percent between 1960 and 1974. While the
risk level for the 15–19 age group was increasing at a lower rate
during this same period, it was still in the second-highest risk
category for homicide of any other race-sex-age group.

Homicidal risk for black youth also increases if they reside in
substantially high-risk neighborhoods, if they use drugs, if they
are school dropouts, if they engage in criminal behavior, and if
they live in the North Central region, which has homicide rates
nearly twice as high as those in all other regions of the United
States. Urban areas which ranked highest in terms of rates of black
homicide in 1980 were St. Louis (91.6 per 100,000), Los Angeles
(87.3), Cleveland (76.8), Detroit (59.3), and New Orleans (56.8)
(Rose, 1986).

Blacks use firearms much more frequently than whites to commit both homicide and suicide. In their study of trends in suicidal
methods, McIntosh and Santos (1982) noted that the use of firearms
increased for blacks from 50 percent in the 1920s to 60 percent in
the 1970s and was the most frequent method used by black males
throughout this period. In addition, black males are much more
likely to be victims of police brutality or killed in confrontations

with police than whites (Pierce, 1986). A California study of all black homicides during the five-year period 1978–1982 found that the leading cause of death for black males was from firearms-related fatalities, including homicides, suicides, and accidents. The chilling conclusion of that study was that "if the death rate remained unchanged, one in 20 of the black males born in California during 1978–1982 would eventually have a firearms-related death" (DHHS, 1986, p. 13).

Types of Homicide

In a comprehensive article on strategies to lower the homicide risk among black youth, Rose (1986) identifies two basic types of homicide: conflict motivated and nonconflict motivated, also labeled expressive or instrumental. The major distinction is between those homicides that result from interpersonal/intrafamily conflicts in which the murderer and victim know each other, and those homicides that are motivated by criminal intent in which a felony is usually committed. From 1976 to 1982, 46 percent of black youth homicide victims were killed by acquaintances, 20 percent by strangers, and nearly 8 percent by family members. The rates of acquaintance and family homicide have remained stable since the 1970s, while the rate of stranger homicide has increased by almost one-third. Nonfelony-motivated homicides in this group decreased very slightly between 1979 and 1982 (from 66.4 percent to 65 percent), as did felony homicides (from 15.6 percent to 11.2 percent). However, the number of "undetermined" homicides also increased during this period.

The increase in the incidence of stranger felony homicides has been attributed to many factors, including the depersonalization of inner-city urban environments, the weakening of traditional value systems, the loss of social supports, the greater availability of hand guns, and the increase in the drug trade (Rose, 1986; Dennis, 1977).

The characteristics of young black male homicide offenders and their victims are remarkably similar. Offenders and their victims are typically younger than the general black population, come from lower socioeconomic backgrounds, live in large metropolitan areas, and have previous arrest records for aggravated assaults or other felonies (Farrington, 1982; Hawkins, 1986).

A third type of homicide is from "legal intervention," which includes all black youth killed by police officers and those legally executed, and accounts for a much smaller proportion of youth homicide. The term "death by legal intervention" is an antiseptic way of describing police killings and executions that contribute to the high homicide rates of black males. From 1960 to 1968, 1,188 black males versus 1,253 white males were killed by police, a number that had increased over prior years but at a rate consistently about nine times higher for blacks than for whites since 1950 (Pierce, 1986). A more recent report by the National Minority Advisory Council of the Justice Department concluded that "deaths by legal intervention of the police are increasing and . . . death rates for blacks and Hispanics remain disproportionate to the number of blacks and Hispanics in the general population. They generally acknowledge that most police shootings occur at night in urban ghetto areas and involve white, on-duty patrol officers and minority male civilians between the ages of 19 and 29" (cited in Pierce, 1986). Thus, a small but significant proportion of black youth homicides can be attributed to the police who are sworn to protect the public against violence.

Some of these killings occur in the context of "victim-precipitated homicide"—that is, police officers are frequently involved in fatal encounters with black youth who expose themselves unnecessarily to confrontations and dare the police to retaliate. The changing patterns of homicide among black youth have significant implications for planning appropriate policies and programs of prevention and early intervention.

Conceptual Perspectives on Black Youth Homicide

Theories of homicidal behavior in black youth can be grouped into three basic categories: sociological, psychological, and environmental. While it is not possible to discuss these approaches in depth here, it is important to summarize them briefly and to comment on their heuristic value in furthering our understanding of black youth homicide.

The sociological theory of homicide, advocated by social scientists like Loftin and Hill (1974) and Parker and Smith (1979), focuses on social-structural variables such as poverty, dysfunctional families, and limited economic opportunities to explain higher homicide rates in inner-city communities. This theory proposes that the interaction of these factors fosters a subculture of violence in which aggressive behaviors, frequent interpersonal confrontations, and high-risk, self-destructive activities are tolerated and positively reinforced (Wolfgang and Ferracuti, 1967).

Psychological theories proposed by black psychiatrists such as Poussaint (1983), Grier and Cobbs (1968), and Pierce (1970) stress the chronic and severe frustrations black males experience in American society; these frustrations engender feelings of aggression and rage which are displaced on convenient targets in their immediate environments. The high incidence of black-on-black homicide reflects this process of displacement by black youth who are presumed to have low levels of self-esteem, high levels of hostility, and poorly developed mechanisms for coping with their angry impulses or defending their fragile egos. This combination of unsublimated anger and low impulse control, with easy availability of hand guns and drugs, creates potentially violent situations for countless black youth who are primed to explode at the least provocation.

A third theory of homicide is proposed by social ecologists such as Rose (1986), Farley (1980), and Farrington (1982), who examine the multiple factors in the environment which interact with social, structural, demographic, situational, and psychological factors to produce differential rates of homicide. These behavioral scientists suggest that many aspects of the ghetto environment are intrinsically pathogenic for black youth—that is, they produce high levels of stress, depression, and social pathology. Such factors as excessive crowding, high levels of crime and violence, social isolation from mainstream society, and high levels of social disorganization contribute to feelings of powerlessness, despair, and social alienation.

As with all hypotheses about human behavior, these unidimensional theories are very limited in their explanatory power with regard to black youth homicide. Although each theory is a model of economy and efficiency, each also ignores critical variables in the life experiences of these youth. A multifactor theory which accounts for individual motives and personality traits, family factors, environmental factors, cultural factors, broader social policies, and situational events would have far more heuristic power in explaining and predicting homicidal behavior in this group. For example, Rose (1986) emphasizes the need to identify and analyze target environments with different levels of homicide risk, the importance of integrating individual and environmental explanations of risk, and the need to examine economic, political, cultural, demographic, and structural factors that are related to differential risk levels of homicidal behavior and victimization rates. This type of sophisticated analysis of homicidal risk factors not only contributes to more elegant theoretical development, but also generates a series of hypotheses that can be empirically tested in order to advance knowledge of this phenomenon.

Empirical Studies of Black Youth Homicide

Studies of homicidal behavior and victimization in black youth are sparse and often poorly conceived and implemented. Some major limitations of these studies in advancing our understanding of the phenomenon are that they are cross-sectional rather than longitudinal, descriptive rather than analytical, and usually based on small samples in specific geographical areas. Many of the studies are clinical and retroactively based on completed homicides rather than on experimental efforts to identify a particular high-risk cohort of black youth and to evaluate their outcomes prospectively over a specific time period. A very brief review of some of the major research findings reveals that there is not strong support for any of the single-factor theories, although there are conflicting results on several important points.

The sociological proposition that poverty alone is a major cause of crime or violence is essentially rejected by two recent analyses of homicide rates in large samples drawn from major metropolitan areas with high poverty rates (Blau and Blau, 1982; Messner, 1982). Both of these studies, using multivariate statistical techniques, found that poverty alone was not a significant predictor of homicide rates in a community. However, Messner's study of 204 cities did lend support to the concept of a "subculture of violence," since southern cities with large percentages of blacks had significantly higher homicide rates than nonsouthern cities and those with smaller proportions of black residents. In contrast, Blau and Blau (1982), in their study of 125 cities, did not find any support for the relationship of homicide rates to southern location and only minimal support for the percentage of blacks in a city's population; rather, they concluded that socioeconomic inequality between blacks and whites was significantly related to increased acts of criminal violence. Their interpretation is that the *relative* economic deprivation of blacks, particularly in urban areas, may contribute to higher levels of frustration and hostility, thus resulting in more violence and homicidal behavior; this interpretation helps to reconcile the conflicting findings about poverty and its relation to homicide. Since several other rigorously designed studies have replicated the finding that income inequality rather than poverty itself is a stronger predictor of homicide rates in black communities, this variable as a precursor of violence certainly merits further research (Messner, 1982; Ehrlich, 1973; Danziger and Wheeler, 1975).

Psychological theories of homicide are more difficult to investigate experimentally, since it is rarely possible to evaluate a person's state of mind either just before that person commits murder or is murdered. However, a number of psychological symptoms and personality traits have been linked to homicidal behavior for both offenders and victims. In a study of black males at risk for lowered life expectancy, researchers at Meharry Medical College in Nashville, Tennessee, used questionnaires and psychological tests to develop a profile of assaulters and assault victims (Dennis, 1980). Both groups had high rates of antisocial behavior, were significantly depressed, and were frequently involved in fights, but the assaulters were more likely than the assaulted to justify their behavior and to externalize the blame for the assaultive act.

Other researchers have found that homicidal youth are likely to be impulsive, rebellious toward adult authority, aggressive, and involved in high-risk behaviors such as drinking and drug use (Waldron and Eyer, 1975; Dennis, 1977). In addition, these youth are characterized as highly vulnerable to stress and lacking effective coping mechanisms to moderate their stress.

The relationship of ecological factors to black youth homicide has been investigated, and several environmental characteristics are strongly related to high rates of homicide in inner-city areas. Three of the most important factors are the availability of hand guns, the social disorganization of the neighborhood, and the declining economic base of the city (Rose, 1986). It has been estimated that 75 percent of all black homicides involve hand guns, and blacks are seven times as likely as whites to be shot to death (Centers for Disease Control, 1983b; Farley, 1980). In Oakland, California, young black men 25–35 were killed by guns at a rate of 120 per 100,000 in 1980 (Meredith, 1984). Moreover, cities in the Northeast and Midwest which have experienced considerable economic decline have higher rates of black homicide than those which have had a stable or vital economy (Rose, 1986). For example, the homicide rates of Cleveland and Detroit are much higher than those of Atlanta and Baltimore.

In summary, the results of these studies challenge some common assumptions about black youth homicide while supporting other assumptions. Clearly, environmental and socioeconomic factors interact with personality and situational factors to produce high levels of interpersonal violence among black youth. Yet, poverty or cultural attitudes, alone or in combination, do not appear to be reliable predictors of homicidal behavior.

Suicide

Suicide among blacks is a youthful phenomenon.[1] At a time when they should be developing an identity, exploring career options, or beginning a family, too many young blacks are destroying themselves. In all other ethnic groups except American Indians, suicide rates increase with age, yet the suicide rate among blacks peaks during the young adult years (25–34) and decreases with age. Suicide is the *third* leading cause of death among black youth in the 15–24 age group, after homicides and accidents; 47 percent of all black suicides occur in the 20–34 age group (U.S. Census Bureau, 1986).

Over the past 25 years, the overall suicide rate of black youth (15–24) has more than doubled, with males between 20 and 24 accounting for most of that increase. From 1960 to 1984, the suicide rate for black youth in the 15–24 age group doubled for black females (from 1.3 to 2.4 per 100,000) and nearly tripled for black males (from 4.1 to 11.2 per 100,000), following almost identical trends in the pattern of white male–white female suicide rates (see Table 8–2). Black male suicide rates in this age group are over four times the rate for black females, a ratio that has increased since 1960. However, a closer look at the data reveals peak rates in 1970, 1972, and 1979 for black males, compared with peak rates for black females in 1967, 1971–72, and 1976–77 (DHHS, 1986).

It is important to disaggregate this data to note that patterns and rates for the 15–19 and 20–24 age groups differ (see Table 8–3). First, males and females in the 20–24-year-old group have higher rates than in the 15–19 group. Second, the rates for black males 20–24 account for most of the increase in the overall black youth suicide rate, while the other three groups have increased at a much slower rate. Third, the ratio of male to female rates is much higher in the 20–24 age group than in the 15–19 group (U.S. Census Bureau, 1986).

In spite of much propaganda to the contrary, black youth suicide rates appear to be leveling off and are not converging on white youth suicide rates; instead they have maintained a fairly predictable relationship to white rates since 1958 with only a few exceptions—that is, white male rates averaged 1.8 times higher and

Table 8–2   Black and White Youth Suicide Rates, 15–24 Age Group (per 100,000 residents)

15–24 Years	1960	1970	1980	1982	1984
Black females	1.3	2.8	2.3	2.2	2.4
Black males	4.1	10.5	12.3	11.0	11.2
White females	2.3	4.2	4.6	4.5	4.7
White males	8.6	13.9	21.4	21.2	22.0

SOURCE: *Health, United States, 1986*. U.S. Dept. of Health and Human Services. Public Health Service, National Center for Health Statistics, Hyattsville, Md. Dec. 1986, DHHS Pub. No. (PHS) 87-1232.

Table 8–3   Black Youth Suicide Rates by Sub-Groups (per 100,000 residents)

	1960	1965	1970	1971	1975	1980	1982
15–19 Years							
Black females	1.1	2.2	2.9	3.4	1.5	1.6	1.5
Black males	2.9	5.1	4.7	5.0	6.1	5.6	6.2
20–24 Years							
Black females	1.5	3.5	4.9	6.5	5.2	3.1	2.9
Black males	5.8	12.3	18.7	16.1	21.1	20.0	16.0

*Source: U.S. Bureau of the Census. (1986). *Statistical Abstract of the United States, 1986* (106th Ed.). Washington, D.C.

white female rates averaged 2.5 times higher than black males and females, respectively (see Table 8–2). The rates have also remained remarkably stable since 1978, with only slight annual variations among blacks in the 15–24 age group.

If these suicide rates of black youth are so much lower than white rates and appear to be leveling off, why should we be concerned about the problem at all? Suicide is a significant problem for black youth not only because it is one of the leading causes of mortality in this age group, but also because it impacts disproportionately on the black population, which is a youthful population with a median age of 25.8 years (U.S. Census Bureau, 1986). As the proportion of nonwhites in the total youth population age 18–24 is expected to increase to approximately 30 percent by the year 2,000, at present rates the actual number of suicides will increase substantially, with negative consequences for the black community and the general economy (CDF, 1987).

Two case examples illustrate the human tragedy behind the statistics as well as the difficulty of making generalizations about black youth suicide.

Case I: *"Robert: No Place to be Somebody"*

Robert, abused and abandoned by his alcoholic mother as a child, had been reared in foster homes since the age of 3. By age 16, he had a police record, was failing in school, and was known as a "loner." When Robert's working-class foster parents felt they could no longer tolerate his increasingly aggressive behavior, he was transferred to a "group home" where he became sullen and withdrawn. After he attacked one of the counselors for saying no one really cared about him, Robert was sent to juvenile hall. On his third morning in detention, the attendant discovered Robert hanging in his room. He left a note on his pillow which said, "I haven't got

*nobody and I ain't ever going to be nothing. Tell my mom good-bye,
if you ever find her."*

Case II: *"Frank: Now I Lay Me Down to Sleep"*

*By age 23, Frank had been helping to support his widowed mother
and two younger sisters for 4 years. After his girlfriend terminated
her pregnancy soon after he said he couldn't afford to marry her,
Frank began to drink heavily, especially on weekends. He lost his
job and his girlfriend broke off their relationship in the same week.
One Sunday he told his mother he was going to take a drive in the
country "to get some peace and quiet." The highway patrol found
his car late that night on the shoulder of a rural highway. Frank
was slumped over the steering wheel with a single bullet through his
forehead.*

Methodological Issues

Some social scientists and criminologists have proposed that suicidal behavior is simply one form of violent behavior which characterizes the self-destructive life-styles of low-income, inner-city
black youth (Hendin, 1969; Seiden, 1972). Vulnerability to suicide
may reflect the same underlying risk factors as vulnerability to
homicide or to fatal accidents in this group.

In evaluating the pattern of black youth involvement in suicide,
homicide, and accidental deaths, it is important not only to note
the relationship among these three types of violent deaths, but
also to raise questions about the validity and reliability of the data,
particularly with regard to the statistics on homicide and "unintentional" accidental deaths in this group. It has been suggested that
some black males deliberately set up violent confrontations with
the police in order to provoke lethal retaliatory action or "victim-
precipitated homicide" (Seiden, 1972; Breed, 1970). Examples of
this phenomenon are seen in the aggressive anti-authority behavior
of the Black Panthers (several of whom were killed in gun battles
with the police); the revolutionary rhetoric of the Symbionese
Liberation Army (whose leaders died in a fire after a gun battle
with police); and the escalation of community conflict by members
of MOVE in the summer of 1986 in Philadelphia (who also met a
similar fate). Some experts would argue that many young ghetto
males subconsciously set up similar situations when they engage
in gang fights, high-risk burglaries, and other explosive situations
that combine the use of lethal weapons, alcohol or drugs, and
confrontational behaviors. Are some of these youth consciously or

unconsciously flirting with death, even inviting destruction, so they can remove themselves from an intolerable existence without actually taking responsibility for the ultimate act of self-annihilation? Indeed, some of these apparent homicides can be classified as forms of "revolutionary" or "fatalistic" suicide in Durkheim's (1951) terms.

Another question of validity is the categorization of "unintentional" accidents. Black males have a high rate of fatal automobile accidents, 69 percent of which involve alcohol (DHHS, 1986). Even though no age breakdown was available for these data, it is also known that about three-fourths of all youth fatal accidents involve alcohol, although the rate for black youth may be lower since black youth have lower drinking rates than white youth (DHHS, 1986). However, many of these single-car accidents, whether or not liquor is involved, may in fact be "autocides," another way of disguising suicidal behavior, perhaps to ease the pain of surviving family members. Other forms of "accidental" deaths, such as drownings, falls from high buildings, and industrial accidents, may also be disguised suicides in this group.

Some researchers have suggested that many deaths from drug overdoses can be viewed as a form of suicide (Smart, 1980). Black youth are three times more likely than white youth to be in treatment programs for drug abuse problems (NIDA, 1985) and more likely to report a primary problem with heroin, cocaine, and PCP—all addictive drugs with serious health consequences. Heroin, cocaine, and PCP were the three most frequent causes of drug-related deaths among black youth in 1980, with 45 percent of these deaths heroin-related. From 1982 to 1984 alone, cocaine-related deaths among black youth tripled, and the percentage of PCP-related deaths involving all blacks increased from 50 to 58 percent between 1983 and 1984 (NIDA, 1985).

There are also problems with the reliability of youth suicide statistics, including the previously mentioned tendency to under-report or misreport suicides as accidental or "undetermined" deaths, state and regional variations in reporting, and cultural attitudes of family members that often result in the suicidal act being "covered up" (Shaffer and Fisher, 1981; Warshauer and Monk, 1978). Several authors have proposed that the true suicide rate, particularly for blacks, would be much higher if the "unqualified" suicides were combined with the category "undetermined deaths" (Shaffer and Fisher, 1981; Warshauer and Monk, 1978; Smith and Carter, 1986). This would be particularly true for black youth, many of whom come from religious families in which suicide is culturally and spiritually alien, and thus viewed as an intolerable social stigma. These cultural factors also may partially account for generally lower rates for blacks in the South and rural areas, where religion and traditional values are more deeply entrenched (Bush, 1976).

Thus, black youth suicide rates would probably be much higher, particularly among males, if intentional accidental deaths, deliberate drug overdoses, and even "victim-precipitated" homicides were included as methods of voluntary self-annihilation. Further, improved case finding and consistency in classification across local jurisdictions and by medical examiners or coroners would undoubtedly produce more valid and reliable rates of black youth suicide (Warshauer and Monk, 1978; Shaffer and Fisher, 1981).

In addition to the more obvious methodological issues, the two very disparate case examples described above raise some significant conceptual and sociocultural issues about black youth suicide—that is, what theoretical perspectives and sociocultural factors are useful in advancing our understanding of the dimensions of suicide in this heterogeneous group?

Conceptual Perspectives on Black Youth Suicide

Three major conceptual perspectives have also been used to explain suicide among black youth: sociological, psychological, and ecological perspectives.

The Sociological Perspective. The sociological perspective was developed by Emile Durkheim (1951), the 19th-century French sociologist. He proposed that there were three types of suicide, all related to the lack of fit between the individual and society. Particularly relevant to black youth are his concepts of *anomic suicide*, which increases as the social integration of individuals decreases, resulting in weaker social bonds and group norms; and *fatalistic suicide*, which occurs among individuals who cannot tolerate excessive social restrictions and oppressive regulations. Durkheim's classic views are reflected in the more contemporary theory of status integration of Gibbs and Martin (1964) and the external constraint theory of Maris (1969).

While the concepts of anomie, social isolation, and normlessness may be applicable to all blacks who have been uprooted from stable southern rural to mobile northern urban or suburban communities, they should predict higher suicide rates for older blacks for whom the impact of moving to a new environment is arguably even more traumatic than for younger people; yet this is not the case. Further, these sociological theories fail to explain the differential suicide rates of black males and females, who presumably experience similar environmental changes and stressors and yet respond to them very differently.

The Psychological Perspective. The psychological perspective can be traced from Freud's psychoanalytic concept that suicide represents anger over the loss of a loved object, turned against the self (Freud, 1925). His followers extended this concept to depression from any kind of major loss or disappointment as represented in the contemporary theories of youth suicide by Toolan (1975) and Glaser (1978).

Hendin (1969) asserted that Freud's notion was not supported in clinical treatment of young blacks, who alternately exhibit conscious overt violence and self-destructive behavior as ways of dealing with their underlying feelings of rage and despair. Further, Freudian theory emphasizes the intrapsychic and interpersonal aspects of suicidal behavior at the expense of structural and environmental aspects, which may be even more significant as etiological factors for black youth. For example, Maris (1969) views suicide in black males, who have a history of confrontation with authority and/or police records, as a response to "retroflexed anger" toward external constraints rather than a sign of hopelessness or depression.

The Ecological Perspective. The ecological perspective, which overlaps the other two perspectives, is advanced by Holinger and Offer (1982), who demonstrated statistically that youth suicide rates increase as the proportion of the 15–24 age group increases in the population. They propose that increased competition for scarcer resources and fewer opportunities results in a cycle of loss of self-esteem, failure, and eventual suicide. However, this model predicts suicide in white youth better than in black youth, suggesting that other factors besides population density and competition for limited resources drive black youth to suicide.

The ecological approach also can be extended to include the theory of urban stress—that is, black youth are particularly vulnerable to suicide because of high rates of unemployment, dysfunctional families, police brutality, racism, and chaotic environments (Seiden, 1972; Breed, 1970; Bush, 1976). These conditions produce high levels of frustration and hostility that result either in suicide or homicidal behavior through self-destructive, risk-taking, or criminal activities (Grier and Cobbs, 1968).

Ecological factors alone do not seem to account for the suicide rates in black youth. For example, even though the black youth unemployment rate for 16–19-year-olds quadrupled between 1960 and 1983 (from 12.1 to 48.5 percent), the suicide rate for females in that age group is nearly the same, and the rate for males has only slightly more than doubled in that same time period. However, the peak suicide rates for black youth in the past 25 years occurred in 1967, two years after the passage of major civil rights legislation and urban riots; in 1971–72, two years after the demise of the poverty program and the beginning of the Nixon administration; and in 1976–77 at the end of the Nixon-Ford era. Thus, *relative deprivation* may be a moderating factor in black youth suicide—as the gap widens between young black males' rising aspirations and their opportunities to achieve them, they become more angry and frustrated, internalizing their rage and directing it back on themselves.

This brief critique of three conceptual perspectives on black youth suicide suggests the need for a multifactor interdisciplinary theory to explain and predict suicidal behavior in black youth. As in the case of homicidal behavior, such a theory should include societal factors (e.g., status integration, norms, etc.), psychological factors (e.g., self-esteem, impulse control, coping mechanisms, etc.), social-psychological factors (e.g., aspirations, risk-taking attitudes, etc.), and ecological factors (e.g., demographic trends, opportunity structures, social supports, etc.). No single-factor theory can explain why suicide rates among black youth are so much lower than among whites; why male rates are so much higher than female rates; or why black suicide decreases with age, while white suicide increases. However, more complex theories, such as those proposed by Maris (1985) and Bush (1976), would take into account the factors which foster suicidal behavior (such as lack of social integration, unsublimated anger, unfulfilled aspirations and limited opportunities), as well as the factors which mitigate against it (such as extended family networks, strong religious beliefs, alternative value systems, and alternative opportunity structures).

Sociocultural Factors in Differential Suicide Rates

As noted earlier, suicide rates of black youth have traditionally been much lower than those of white youth in spite of blacks' obvious exposure to greater external stresses of discrimination, poverty, and marginal minority status in American society. However, as the suicide rates of black youth have gradually increased in the past 25 years, it is critical that the sociocultural factors which contributed to low rates and, conversely, those which may have fostered increased rates of suicidal behavior in this group be identified.

Factors which immunized black youth against suicide can be characterized, in Rutter's (1985) term, as "protective factors." Such factors were provided by the five major institutions which characterized the traditionally segregated black community: the strong family, the church, fraternal and social organizations, community schools, and extended kin and social support networks (Allen, 1978; Billingsley, 1968; Martin and Martin, 1978; McAdoo, 1981; Stack, 1974). These institutions promoted a sense of social cohesion, shared values, and mutual support, all of which mitigated against high suicide rates.

Since blacks migrated from the South in the 1930s and 1940s and left those traditional communities, these institutions have been significantly weakened through urbanization, integration, and massive social and economic change. These changes have been accompanied by an increase in the "risk factors" for black youth (and blacks in general), which make them more vulnerable to suicide. These factors include (1) the breakdown in family structure, so that 42 percent of all black families are now female-headed (48 percent of those households with children under 18 are female-headed); (2) the decreased influence of the church and religious values among urban blacks, especially the youth; (3) the declining impact of fraternal and social organizations as middle-class blacks have moved out of the central cities; (4) the deterioration of inner-city schools as they have lost resources, personnel, and middle-class students; and (5) the weakening of social support systems as unemployment and welfare dependency have sapped the dignity, initiative, and aspirations of inner-city residents (Clark, 1965; Schulz, 1969; Glasgow, 1981; Wilson and Aponte, 1985).

Black males are at much greater risk for suicide than black females, by a ratio of 4 to 1. Not only are black males more likely than females to be involved in deviant and self-destructive behaviors (e.g., truancy, drugs, delinquency); they are also less likely to complete high school and to be employed. All these factors increase suicidal risk among youth (Gibbs (in press); Deiden, 1972).

Accidents

The second leading cause of death for young black males is accidents, of which motor vehicle fatalities accounted for 31.9 per 100,000 fatalities in this age group in 1984 (National Center for Health Statistics, 1986) (see Table 8–4). The contrast with the high rate of motor vehicle accidents among white male youth (59.1 per 100,000) is both interesting and ironic. Since the majority of these accidents are automobile accidents, the disparity is primarily caused by a basic economic reality—most young white males own

Table 8–4   Black and White Youth Death Rates from Motor Vehicle Accidents
(per 100,000 residents)

15–24 Years	1960	1970	1980	1982	1984
Black females	9.9	13.4	8.0	7.8	8.4
Black males	46.4	58.1	34.9	29.2	31.9
White females	15.6	22.7	23.0	18.9	20.1
White males	62.7	75.2	73.8	60.8	59.1

SOURCE: *Health, United States, 1986*. U.S. Dept. of Health and Human Services. Public
Health Service. National Center for Health Statistics. Hyattsville, Md, Dec. 1986 (DHHS
Pub. No. (PHS) 87-1232).

cars or motorcycles, and most young black males do not. Thus,
fewer black youth are killed in car accidents because, quite simply,
they cannot afford the monthly payments for a car or a motorcycle.
For example, in 1980 no car or truck was owned or available in 69
percent of black central-city-households in New York, and 51
percent in both Boston and Philadelphia (Kasarda, 1985). One can
speculate that, if employment rates for black males were to improve substantially, these youth would buy more cars and motorcycles and would thus increase their death and injury rates in this
category. Simultaneously, black male death rates from homicide
would probably decrease because income inequality and its consequences would be reduced. So, for every social benefit gained
by black youth, there would seem to be an offsetting cost.

The accident rate among black youth is also highly related to
two other factors: socioeconomic status and high-risk behaviors.
Socioeconomic status is particularly relevant to nonvehicular accidents such as household accidents, injuries, and drownings. Most
inner-city youth live in substandard housing, often high-rise projects that are poorly maintained, poorly lit, and often do not meet
minimal safety and sanitation standards. Growing up under these
circumstances makes these youth particularly vulnerable to injuries from broken windows, missing stairs, falling plaster, defective
elevators, and dangerous playground equipment. Bites from rats
and vermin are common among younger children.

The major correlates of childhood injuries are low economic
status, minority ethnicity, and unsafe environmental conditions.
Death rates of children from household fires are twice as high in
low-income areas; such fires are often caused by faulty heating and
wiring (Berger, 1985). A study of fire- and burn-related mortality
in the state of Georgia, 1979–1981, found that blacks accounted for
51 percent of the deaths and that 62 percent of the black victims
were males (Centers for Disease Control, 1983a). The highest rates

of burn deaths of all sex-race-age groups occurred among black males in the 10–19 and 20–29 age groups. Studies of fire- and burn-related injuries and fatalities in national and New York state samples indicate that blacks, males, young children, and the elderly are in high-risk groups. These data, as well as data from local studies in New York City and Baltimore, suggest that low socioeconomic status is related to higher risks for blacks for these injuries, particularly injuries from house fires.

Streets in inner-city neighborhoods are notoriously unsafe. In addition to abandoned buildings where unsavory activities take place, the streets themselves tend to be poorly maintained, street lights are often out of commission, and sidewalks are often crumbling. Since inner-city children use the streets as their playgrounds, they are at risk for bicycle accidents from potholes and ridges, cuts from broken glass, and injuries from the games they play. Since they play in the streets, they also are easy targets for cars, particularly at night when street lighting may be inadequate. Abandoned buildings present a number of dangers to these youth, including potential assault by drug addicts, gamblers, and prostitutes.

Drownings pose a particularly poignant problem for inner-city black youth, not because they cannot swim (as suggested by Al Campanis, vice-president of the Los Angeles Dodgers, in a highly controversial television interview on "Nightline" in April 1987), but because they usually swim in unsafe situations such as in overcrowded pools and at beaches without lifeguards. This situation is particularly true in sections of the United States where blacks still do not feel welcome at publicly owned swimming pools and beaches, especially in the deep South and smaller communities throughout the country. For example, in an analysis of drownings in Georgia from 1981–1983, black males had the highest drowning fatality rates for all sex-race-age groups, except for children under five (Centers for Disease Control, 1985b). While all 15–24-year-old males had the highest overall drowning rates, 44 percent of all swimming-related fatalities were among black males in this age group. The rate of drowning for black males is about double the rate for white males, both in Georgia and the nation. Moreover, alcohol is related to drownings among 50 percent of all teenagers and adults. The combination of swimming while intoxicated, in unsupervised swimming areas, makes black youth particularly vulnerable to drowning (Centers for Disease Control, 1985b).

Even when these facilities are completely integrated, poor black youth do not usually have access to swimming lessons in their public schools or in summer camps where many white youth take lessons in swimming, water safety, and lifesaving techniques. Thus, black youth are not only at risk for swimming accidents; they are also at greater risk than whites for boating accidents. For example, in Oakland, California, three black children from the same family, two of them teenagers, drowned in the summer of 1986 after their homemade raft was capsized by a motorboat in the city-owned lake. None of these siblings knew how to swim or how to build a seaworthy raft which would float in case of an accident.

In addition to socioeconomic status, high-risk behaviors of young black males also make them prime candidates for both vehicular and nonvehicular accidents. As noted earlier, some of the single-car fatalities may be the result of suicidal intent; other motor vehicle accidents probably occur because of the aggressive, "macho," one-arm driving style affected by many of these youth. The temptation to engage in drag racing on city streets is not limited to black youth, but they may be more likely than white youth to incur injuries or fatalities because of the more dangerous condition of the streets in their neighborhoods. Chicago's South Side, for example, does not have the wide open Western streets of Marin County, California, where the filming of "American Graffitti" elevated drag racing to a new art form for American teenagers.

Other examples of high-risk behaviors which contribute to accidents and injuries in this group are "dare devil" behaviors—that is, physically demanding and occasionally dangerous activities such as one-on-one basketball games, subway and bus hopping, aggressive interactions with each other which lead to frequent fights (e.g., "playing the dozens"), and confrontational behaviors with parents, teachers, police, and other adult authority figures that invite physical retaliation by testing the limits, breaking rules, and displaying threatening physical mannerisms (Mancini, 1980). As pointed out earlier, these kinds of aggressive confrontations with the police often lead to victim-precipitated homicide. In the Goetz case, discussed in Chapter 1, the white engineer felt threatened by the demeanor of four black teenagers who were allegedly panhandling him for $5. His response was to shoot four of them, permanently paralyzing one and wounding the others. His major defense was that he had shot them in self-defense, fearful that he would be mugged as he had been a few years before that incident. One wonders how those black males would have fared had they not picked Mr. Goetz as their target to harass. Perhaps a more important question is how they came to be in that place at that time. Would they have been planning any illegal activities if they had been able to find jobs? Such speculation is, of course, fruitless, because what happened in the Goetz case is not the coincidence of a particular encounter but the almost predictable outcome of an interdependent chain of events which can and does happen all too frequently to black ghetto youth. In the words of the old Elvis Presley song, "In the Ghetto":

> Then one night in desperation
> the young man breaks away
> He buys a gun, steals a car,
> tries to run
> but he don't get far
>
> And his mama cries
> . . . as a crowd gathers round
> an angry young man
> face down in the street
> with a gun in his hand
> in the ghetto
>
> And as her young man dies
> on a cold and gray Chicago morn
> another baby child is born
> in the ghetto
>
> And his mama cries . . .
>   [Mac Davis, 1969]*

What is also predictable is that all three of the leading causes of mortality among black youth are exacerbated by their use of alcohol and drugs, which not only lowers their inhibitions and reduces their control over their feelings of frustration and anger, but also increases their potential for aggressive and self-destructive behaviors, sometimes directed at others, sometimes at themselves, and sometimes resulting in disabling or fatal injuries to innocent bystanders.

Alcohol and Drug Abuse

Young black males in inner cities are not just at risk for sexually transmitted diseases due to their sexual behaviors and drug-use patterns as described in Chapter 7; they are also at risk for a number of health-related problems due to their patterns of alcohol consumption and illicit drug use, as described in Chapters 1 and 5.

---

*Printed with the permission of Screen Gems-EMI Music, Inc. © 1969 Screen Gems-EMI Music Inc. and Elvis Presley Music Inc. All rights administered by Screen Gems-EMI Music Inc.

Black male drinking patterns are strikingly different from those of their white peers. Although most surveys show that white youth drink more alcoholic beverages in adolescence than blacks, black youth begin to consume more alcohol in young adulthood (DHHS, 1985; Skager, 1986). By their 20s, black males begin to consume larger quantities of alcohol, and by the time they reach middle age, a higher proportion of black males are diagnosed with alcohol-related disorders than whites. In 1985 the National Center for Health Statistics estimated that the years of potential life lost (YPLL rate per 100,000) by all black males due to alcohol-related causes of mortality were 131.5 (per 100,000) for alcohol abuse, 459.1 for alcohol dependence, 253.3 for alcoholic cirrhosis, and 468.9 for other types of cirrhosis (Centers for Disease Control, 1985a). Except for American Indian males, black men had the highest YPLL rate of any sex-race group from mortalities caused by alcohol abuse, alcohol dependence, or other cirrhosis, for a staggering total of 150,998 total years of potential life lost.

In their longitudinal study of a sample of low-income black youth in Harlem, Brunswick and her colleagues (1980, 1986) found that cumulative exposure to heroin was correlated with an increased decline in health for male subjects between two interviews, spaced six to eight years apart. The use of inhalants and methadone (controlling for heroin use) was also related to a health decline for males in terms of nine items on a psychophysical scale.

In addition to the higher incidence of chronic health problems among substance abusers, the incidence of deaths from drug overdoses has also increased among young black males. The mortality rate from drug-related deaths has increased dramatically in nine major metropolitan areas since 1973, with about one-third of those fatalities occurring among black youth in the 15–24 age group (NIDA, 1980b). During a three-year period from January 1980 to December 1982, 266 fatalities from intravenous heroin use were recorded in Washington, D.C. (Centers for Disease Control, 1983a). Of these drug-related deaths, 93 percent were black and 82 percent were male, with an average age of 30. However, the average age of initiating heroin use for this group was 19. Risk factors associated with these deaths included concurrent high levels of alcohol intake, and sporadic and/or recreational use of heroin. For black males who are polydrug abusers, alcohol has a potentiating effect on other drugs, creating a higher risk for toxic or fatal effects, and a higher incidence of premature mortality (Centers for Disease Control, 1985a).

Drug abuse among black youth has not only increased in the past 25 years; it has also spread from the inner cities into the suburbs, and the users have become progressively involved in the use of "hard drugs" such as heroin and cocaine or "crack," which are inextricably tied to street crime (*New York Times*, 1987a). Moreover, an NIDA study predicted an increase in drug abuse among black and Hispanic youth through 1995 because they constitute the fastest-growing segment of the population and because of their current usage patterns (NIDA, 1980a). In 1980, 27 percent of the clients admitted to federally funded drug-abuse treatment centers were black, and approximately 12 percent of these addicts were under age 18. Three out of five of this group were addicted to heroin, and nearly 50 percent had been arrested at least once, graphically illustrating the relationship between drug abuse and delinquency (DHHS, 1980).

Gary (1980) found that more black males 15–30 are victims of alcohol-related homicides than in any other race-sex-age group. He also points out the need to examine the offenders for blood-alcohol levels as well as the victims in order to understand the mutual effects of alcohol in homicidal situations.

There have been recent efforts to educate black youth about the health dangers of drinking alcohol and using drugs, including cigarette smoking. These efforts are a response to the growing concern that manufacturers of alcoholic drinks and cigarettes are aiming expensive advertising campaigns at black young adults to expand their markets and to replace the loss of white customers in this age group. Since excessive alcohol use and cigarette smoking are both correlated to chronic and fatal diseases, increased use of these substances by black youth will further impair their health and place them at risk for long-term chronic diseases such as lung cancer and cirrhosis of the liver (DHHS, 1985).

Alcohol and drug use not only has long-term harmful effects on the health of black males; it also has serious social consequences in terms of higher mortality rates, greater burdens on health care facilities, increased costs for police and emergency services, decreased productivity, and destabilizing effects on the black community.

Policies and Programs to Reduce Life-Threatening Behaviors

Long before the concept of "the new morbidity" was introduced, the self-destructive and life-threatening behaviors just described have slowly but insidiously destroyed several generations of black youth. Young black males are continuing to kill, maim, or narcotize themselves faster than they could be annihilated through wars or natural disasters. They not only destroy themselves, but also jeopardize their families and friends, restrict family formation for young black women, threaten the stability of the black community, and endanger the health and welfare of the entire society.

Not surprisingly, a growing concern for young black women is the ratio of marriageable men available to them in the prime years of family formation and childrearing, which sociologist William Wilson has estimated as 47 employed black males for every 100 marriageable black females in the 20–24-year-old age group (Aponte, Neckerman, and Wilson, 1985). Of course, any increase in male mortality rates in this age group would further reduce the available pool of marriageable males for young black women. This male marriageable pool index (MMPI) ratio not only has negative implications for black family formation, but also suggests the possibility of increased stress, depression, and other suicidal "risk" factors for young black women.

We cannot and must not wait for more comprehensive theories, more elegant research designs, or more clinical or epidemiological data to illuminate the causes of these self-destructive behaviors. The evidence is overwhelming that young black men are truly endangered—not only indirectly from society's neglect and abuse, but quite directly by their own actions and activities. They have been neglected too long and their situation is now terminal—both literally and figuratively. We suggest that these self-destructive behaviors are symptoms of a deeper and pervasive malaise and disaffection from the society. Policies and programs need to be instituted to reverse this epidemic of life-threatening behaviors in young black males.

Black youth are alienated and angry because they do not view themselves, and are not viewed by others, as productive members of society. In a society in which persons are valued for their economic worth and occupational achievements, black youth can meet neither criterion. It is thus difficult, if not impossible, for them to develop a sense of their own value when they do not have the currency and do not even know the exchange rate. Given their isolation from the economy, they need—more than any single solution—meaningful jobs and adequate income in order to move into the mainstream. Specific proposals for employment and training opportunities are advanced in Chapters 3 and 9. Suffice it to say here that we propose a full employment policy, not only to provide job opportunities for these youth, but also to give them an incentive to participate fully in the society and to have a future to anticipate (Sum, Harrington, and Goedicke, 1987). A full-time job is in itself a preventive remedy, since employed youth are less likely to become involved in drugs and delinquency, are less likely to commit suicide or homicide, and are more likely to get married and develop a stable family life (CDF, 1987; Glasgow, 1981; Wilson and Aponte, 1985).

Federal, state, and local governments must make a coordinated effort to improve the overall environment of inner-city areas through increasing employment opportunities for male and female heads of families, increasing the supply of new and rehabilitated low- and moderate-income housing, providing access to comprehensive health care services, improving transportation services, and developing safe and inexpensive recreational facilities (CDF, 1986a). The creation of more humane and healthy environments will reduce frustrations, minimize stress, and provide a more nurturant environment for these black youth and their families. Growing up in such environments will ultimately remove many of the root causes of the self-destructive behaviors of black males.

In addition to general improvements in their social and economic environments, specific policies should be adopted to reduce the incidence of suicide and homicide in this population. First and foremost, a strong and enforceable gun control policy must be adopted by all levels of government. Since the easy availability of hand guns is one of the major causes of the high homicide and suicide rates among all American youth, this is the most important external factor which can be dealt with legislatively (Farley, 1980; Prothrow-Stith, 1986; Rose, 1986). The slogan of the National Rifle Association—"Guns don't kill people, people do"—may be technically accurate, but the slogan distorts the reality for black youth, who are mainly killing each other. It has been estimated that an effective gun control policy, including monitoring and strong penalties against noncompliant merchants, would substantially reduce the mortality rates of black youth.

Also, in conjunction with gun control legislation, local school districts should establish clear policies and guidelines banning all weapons from school grounds. Violence in schools has escalated greatly in the two decades since the movie *Blackboard Jungle* made its dramatic debut. Many of today's ghetto schools would make that high school look like a Montessori preschool. Incidents of shootings, knifings, and beatings on the school grounds are so common in the news media that they rarely evoke surprise or outrage. In a 1987 survey of public secondary school teachers, one-third of teachers in cities of 100,000 or more and in schools with 1,000 or more pupils reported that violence against students was a major problem (*San Francisco Chronicle*, 1987). Inner-city schools, in fact, can be very dangerous to a student's health. Yet civil libertarians are quick to threaten court action whenever school boards or individual principals try to control the flow of weapons and drugs by searching students' lockers or inspecting their school bags. This legalistic response may preserve the constitutional rights of some students at the expense of promoting a safe and sane learning environment for all students. A balance needs to be achieved between the privacy rights of some students and the safety rights of all students, since learning cannot flourish in an unsafe and uncivil environment.

Schools should introduce conflict-resolution programs, as pioneered in the Boston school system, to teach students how to resolve their differences without resorting to verbal or physical assaults (Prothrow-Stith, 1986). Local communities can also establish community mediation boards to negotiate neighborhood conflicts before they escalate into individual or group violence. These citizens' committees would be especially useful in defusing conflict in newly integrated residential areas, in neighborhoods rapidly changing with influxes of immigrants, and in neighborhoods experiencing gentrification with young professional whites replacing low-income blacks. Black families who move out of the inner cities often have to defend themselves against vicious assaults from whites in working-class neighborhoods. Conversely, blacks have been accused of harassing Southeast Asian immigrants who are gradually moving into formerly segregated ghettos. In all of these situations, the potential for violence is quite high, so mechanisms are necessary to reduce these conflicts before they escalate.

Another proposal is that childhood advocacy groups continue to pressure the television industry to reduce violence and aggressive behavior on prime-time programming, as well as in Saturday morning cartoons. The Surgeon General's updated 1982 report, which reviews over 2,500 studies of the effect of televised violence on aggression in children and adolescents, draws this conclusion: ". . . a causal link between televised violence and aggressive behavior now seems obvious. . . . In magnitude, television violence is as strongly correlated with aggressive behavior as any other behavioral variable that has been measured" (*Public Health Reports*, 1982, p. 492). Since several studies have found that black children spend more time than whites watching television, they are constantly barraged with images of violence glamorized and legitimized as the principal strategy for solving interpersonal conflicts (Word, 1977). Thus, if they become frustrated and angry, they have learned that violence is socially approved and socially reinforced, not only on TV but also in motion pictures, newspapers and magazines, and rock videos, where the tough guys usually win the fights and the women. As long as television consumes so much of the leisure time of black youth, stronger efforts must be made to regulate the programming through economic pressures on advertisers, political pressures on legislators, and legal appeals to regulatory commissions to minimize violence and to replace it with educationally oriented content.

Suicide prevention services should develop outreach programs for the black community, particularly targeting black youth. These services are generally tailored to middle-class whites, so they are not generally viewed as a significant resource by blacks who may feel severely depressed. These programs should also recruit and train black volunteers, set up auxiliary services in black neighborhoods, and establish good working relationships with the schools and with the "gate-keepers" of the black community—doctors, ministers, lawyers, social workers, other health and mental health professionals. An excellent school-based suicide prevention program has been developed in several rural Minnesota high schools, which includes a comprehensive and well-coordinated approach by the schools, the families, the juvenile courts, the social welfare system, and the business community (Garfinkel, 1986).

In a related area, while many of these recommendations are geared to reducing the incidence of black-on-black homicide, police brutality cannot be ignored as a factor in societal violence against young black males. Several black males are killed each week in America in lethal encounters with police officers, sometimes in the commission of a felony, but more often as the result of a noncriminal confrontation (Pierce, 1986; Smith, 1981). Local police departments can initiate several steps to reduce the unwarranted assaults and murders of black males who are not committing any crime. First, all police officers in heavily populated black communities should participate in ongoing human relations programs in which they learn to understand the culture and behaviors of inner-city blacks, how to interact with them in nonconfrontational ways, and how to intervene effectively in situations of family conflict and community violence. Since 20 percent of police officers are themselves killed in the investigation of family violence, these strategies would be of mutual benefit to them. Second, police departments should outlaw the "choke-hold" and the use of guns except in extraordinary circumstances (e.g., apprehending a suspect in the act of or leaving a felony crime). Countless numbers of black youth have been seriously injured or killed simply because the police thought that they "looked guilty" or suspected they might be carrying a "concealed weapon." These police hunches and suspicions are much more likely to occur with young blacks in the ghetto than with young whites in the suburbs. Very few white middle-class youth die from police choke-holds or from police who are too quick on the trigger. Third, police can improve their relations with inner-city communities by establishing "buddy patrols," getting to know the residents and small shop owners personally, and sponsoring youth athletic activities. In areas where so many young men are without fathers, male police officers could serve as very positive role models and could deter some youngsters from a life of delinquency and crime.

Cultural attitudes toward aggression and violence—the most resistant to change—must be openly discussed, challenged, and modified in the black community. Civil rights organizations (e.g., National Urban League, NAACP, NAACP Legal Defense and Educational Fund), churches, and civic associations have taken this issue out of the closet and have begun to develop programs to effect long-range attitudinal and behavioral changes. Black churches can play a particularly significant role in this campaign since they reach the broadest spectrum of the black community. Black clergymen are acknowledged community leaders and are in a pivotal position to work with health care professionals, social service agencies, the criminal justice system, and the schools to develop a coordinated set of strategies that will ultimately reduce levels of family and community violence by presenting and reinforcing alternative nonviolent and nonaggressive values and behaviors (see DHHS, 1986; Public Health Reports, 1980).

In the area of substance abuse, drug and alcohol abuse prevention programs have been oversold and underfunded (see Beschner and Friedman, 1986; Dembo, 1979). In spite of all the political propaganda about reducing drug use among American youth, programs have not been adequately funded or successfully implemented for a number of reasons. To stem the tide of drugs, the federal government must replace rhetoric with action and increase appropriations for the Drug Enforcement Agency (DEA) to prevent the entry of drugs to the United States, to monitor the drug trade within the country, and to prosecute major drug importers and drug suppliers. More funds must be allocated to reduce the supply of cocaine and heroin, the two drugs that are particularly destructive for young black males, both in terms of their health and in terms of their criminal life-styles.

At the state and local levels, more funds need to be allocated to assist local law enforcement agencies in the investigation, arrest, and prosecution of drug dealers, many of whom operate with impunity in public places in many inner-city areas. Unfortunately, however, too much emphasis is placed on arresting the street dealers, who are minor functionaries in the drug trade, and not enough emphasis is placed on identifying and apprehending the principal sources and suppliers of drugs. There have even been charges (during the Iran-Contra investigation in the summer of 1987) that the United States government tolerates a certain level of clandestine drug trade with certain Central American and Middle Eastern countries in order to preserve good relations with friendly governments. Whether these charges have any merit or not, drugs will continue to flourish in the ghetto as long as they are a lucrative source of income for black youth and as long as the federal, state, and local governments do not move very aggressively to stem the supply of drugs and to prosecute the powerful and prominent leaders of the international drug trade (who are, parenthetically, not black and not poor). Although such efforts will not wholly stop the total flow of drugs, they will serve to diminish the attractiveness of the drug industry to black youth, who find this an alternative route to economic self-sufficiency when other jobs are not available.

School districts must design drug and alcohol education programs which are geared to students' cognitive levels, psychological motivation, and cultural attitudes. Most approaches have not proven very effective because they have "preached" rather than educated students. The most effective approaches have involved peers as teachers and role models, group discussions, and value clarifications.

School-based clinics can play a very significant role in early detection of students who are abusing drugs, as well as providing counselors to help students to discuss their underlying problems and to explore healthier behavioral alternatives. These clinics can also promote nonsmoking campaigns and educate students about the long-range health risks of cigarette smoking (CDF, 1986b).

A range of community treatment facilities should be available so that beginning drug users do not have to associate with chronic abusers, in order for them to avoid both the stigma of participating in tertiary drug rehabilitation programs and the seductive appeal of adopting the life-style of the habitual drug addict. Counseling services should include vocational counseling and job referral for unskilled and unemployed youth.

Finally, comprehensive school-based clinics should be set up in junior high and high schools to provide all students with counseling and treatment of mental health problems such as anxiety, depression, and psychosomatic disorders. As noted in Chapter 7, these on-site clinics can and do play an important role in the early detection of psychological problems, which are amenable to early intervention. By providing this resource in the schools, many students will have access to professional help in time to prevent them from hurting themselves or others. In schools where clinics have operated, the "new morbidity" has declined with lowered rates of suicide, drug abuse, teen pregnancy, and venereal diseases (CDF, 1986b).

Conclusions

This chapter has presented an overview of the three leading causes of mortality for black youth—homicide, accidents, and suicide—and shown their relationship to alcohol and drug abuse. This "new morbidity" is the consequence of a pervasive pattern of high-risk, self-destructive, and life-threatening behaviors of young black men. The theoretical explanations for these behaviors, the empirical, clinical, and epidemiological studies of these behaviors, and the factors related to these behaviors have been discussed. Single-factor theories are not usually confirmed by empirical research, but the studies themselves are often inadequate and make unsubstantiated generalizations from unrepresentative samples. Without a doubt more research is needed to illuminate the causes and the correlates of the new morbidity among black youth. There is also little doubt that the black community is undergoing a crisis and cannot continue to wait for scholars to debate the etiology of violence, but rather must marshall its energies to generate policies and programs that can at least attack the symptoms and, perhaps, address the presumptive causes—poverty, inequality, discrimination, cultural attitudes, availability of guns and drugs—which have been identified, analyzed, and discussed for many years.

To progress toward that goal, this chapter proposes policies and programs aimed at both the symptoms and their underlying causes. Countless other proposals could be effective with these problems, but we have tried not to duplicate all previous works in this area. The selected policies and programs proposed here are intended to dramatize the problems and to underscore the many facets of the society and the environment which need to be modified if these youth are ever going to become productive citizens. The time for all persons of goodwill to address these problems is now; to delay action any longer is to court disaster for black youth and our entire society.

Endnote

1. Portions of this discussion were presented previously in a paper on "Conceptual, Methodological, and Sociological Issues in Black Youth Suicide: Implications for Assessment and Early Intervention." McCormick Award paper presented at the Annual Meeting of the American Association of Suicidology, San Francisco, May 1987.

References

Allen, W. R. (1978). Black family research in the United States: A review, assessment and extension. *Journal of Comparative Family Studies* 9: 168–89.

Aponte, R., Neckerman, K. M., and Wilson, W. J. (1985). Race, family structure and social policy. *Working Paper 7: Race and Policy*. Washington, D.C.: National Conference on Social Welfare.

Berger, L. (1985). Childhood injuries. *Public Health Reports* 100: 572–74.

Billingsley, A. (1968). *Black families in white America*. Englewood Cliffs, N.J.: Prentice-Hall.

Blau, J. R., and Blau, P. M. (1982). The cost of inequality: Metropolitan structure and violent crime. *American Sociological Review* 47: 114–29.

Breed, W. (1970). The Negro and fatalistic suicide. *Pacific Sociological Review* 13: 156–62.

Beschner, G., and Friedman, A., eds. (1986). *Teen drug use*. Lexington, Mass.: Lexington Books.

Brunswick, A. (1980). Health stability and change: A study of urban black youth. *American Journal of Public Health* 70: 504–13.

Brunswick, A., and Messeri, P. (1986). Drugs, life style and health. *American Journal of Public Health* 76: 52–57.

Bush, J. A. (1976). Suicide and blacks: A conceptual framework. *Suicide and life-threatening behavior* 6: 216–22.

CDF. See Children's Defense Fund.

Centers for Disease Control. (1983a). Fire and burn-associated deaths—Georgia, 1979–1981. *Morbidity and Mortality Weekly Report* 32 (Dec. 9): 625–34.

———. (1983b). Heroin-related deaths—District of Columbia, 1980–1982. *Morbidity and Mortality Weekly Report* 32 (July 1): 321–24.

———. (1983c). Violent deaths among persons 15–24 years of age—United States, 1970–1978. *Morbidity and Mortality Weekly Report*, 32 (Sept. 9): 453–57.

———. (1985a). Alcohol-associated premature mortality—United States, 1980. *Morbidity and Mortality Weekly Report* 34 (July 16): 493–94.

———. (1985b). Drownings—Georgia, 1981–1983. *Morbidity and Mortality Weekly Report* 34 (May 24): 281–83.

———. (1985c). Homicide among young black males—United States, 1970–1982. *Morbidity and Mortality Weekly Report* 34 (Oct. 18): 629–33.

———. (1986a). Premature mortality due to suicide and homicide—United States, 1983. *Morbidity and Mortality Weekly Report* 35 (June 6): 357–67.

——. (1986b). Premature mortality in the United States. *Morbidity and Mortality Weekly Report* 35 (Dec. 19): 15–115.

Children's Defense Fund (CDF). (1986a). *A children's defense budget*. Washington, D.C.: CDF.

——. (1986b). *Building health programs for teenagers*. Washington, D.C.: CDF.

——. (1986c). *Model programs: Preventing adolescent pregnancy and building youth self-sufficiency*. Washington, D.C.: CDF.

——. (1987). *Declining earnings of young men: Their relation to poverty, teen pregnancy and family formation*. Washington, D.C.: CDF.

Chilman, C. (1983). *Adolescent sexuality in a changing American society*. New York: Wiley & Sons.

Clark, K. (1965). *Dark ghetto*. New York: Harper & Row.

Danziger S., and Wheeler, D. (1975). The economics of crime: Punishment or income redistribution. *Review of Social Economy* 33: 113–31.

Dembo, R. (1979). Substance abuse prevention, programming and research: A partnership in need of improvement. *Journal of Drug Education* 9: 189–208.

Dennis, R. E. (1977). Social stress and mortality among nonwhite males. *Phylon* 38: 315–28.

Dennis, R. E. (1980). Homicide among black males. *Public Health Reports* 95: 549–61.

Department of Health and Human Services (DHHS). (1985). *Report of the secretary's task force on black and minority health*, Vol. I. Washington, D.C.: DHHS.

——. (1986). *Report of the secretary's task force on black and minority health*, Vol. V. Washington, D.C.: DHHS.

——. (1980). *Statistical Series. Annual data*, ser. E, no. 21. Washington, D.C.: DHHS.

Durkheim, E. (1951). *Suicide*. New York: The Free Press.

Ehrlich, I. (1973). Participation in illegitimate activities: A theoretical and empirical investigation. *Journal of Political Economy* 81: 521–65.

Farley, R. (1980). Homicide trends in the United States. *Demography* 17: 177–88.

Farrington, D. P. (1982). Longitudinal analyses of criminal violence. In *Criminal Violence*, edited by M. E. Wolfgang and N. A. Weiner. Beverly Hills, Calif.: Sage Publications.

Freud, S. (1925). *Mourning and melancholia, Collected Papers*, Vol. IV. London: The Hogarth Press.

Garfinkel, B. (1986). School based prevention programs. Paper presented at the National Conference on Prevention and Interventions in Youth Suicide. Oakland, California, June 11–13.

Gary, L. E. (1980). The role of alcohol and drug abuse in homicide. *Public Health Reports* 95: 553–54.

Gibbs, J. P., and Martin, W. T. (1964). *Status integration and suicide*. Eugene: University of Oregon Press.

Gibbs, J. T. (1984). Black adolescents and youth: An endangered species. *American Journal of Orthopsychiatry* 54: 6–21.

Gibbs, J. T. (In press). Conceptual, methodological and sociocultural issues in black youth suicide: Implications for assessment and early intervention. In *Suicide and life-threatening behavior* (in press, 1988).

Gibbs, J. T. (1985). Young black males: An endangered species. Invited lecture at Annual Civil Rights Institute, NAACP Legal Defense and Educational Fund, Inc., New York, May.

Glaser, K. (1978). The treatment of depressed and suicidal adolescents. *American Journal of Psychotherapy* 32: 252–69.

Glasgow, D. (1981). *The black underclass*. New York: Vintage Books.

Grier, W., and Cobbs, P. (1968). *Black rage*. New York: Basic Books.

Hawkins, D. F. (1986). Longitudinal-situational approaches to understanding black-on-black homicide. In *Report of the secretary's task force on black and minority health*, Vol. V. Washington, D.C.: Department of Health and Human Services.

Hendin, H. (1969). Black suicide. *Archives of General Psychiatry* 21: 407–22.

Holinger, P. C., and Offer, D. (1982). Prediction of adolescent suicide: A population model. *American Journal of Psychiatry* 139: 302–07.

Kasarda, J. D. (1985). Urban change and minority opportunities. In *The new urban reality*, edited by R. E. Peterson. Washington, D.C.: The Brookings Institution.

Loftin, C., and Hill, R. H. (1974). Regional subculture and homicide: An examination of the Gastil-Hackney thesis. *American Sociological Review* 39: 714–24.

Mancini, J. K. (1980). *Strategic styles: Coping in the inner city*. Hanover, N.H.: University Press of New England.

Maris, R. W. (1969). *Social forces in urban suicide*. Homewood, Ill.: The Dorsey Press.

———. (1985). The adolescent suicide problem. *Suicide and Life-Threatening Behavior* 15: 91–109.

Martin, E., and Martin, J. (1978). *The black extended family*. Chicago: University of Chicago Press.

McAdoo, H., ed. (1981). *Black families*. Beverly Hills, Calif.: Sage Publications.

McIntosh, J. L., and Santos, J. F. (1982). Changing patterns in methods of suicide by race and sex. *Suicide and Life-Threatening Behavior* 12: 221–33.

Meredith, N. (1984). The murder epidemic. *Science* 84 (5): 42–48.

Messner, S. F. (1982). Poverty, inequality and the urban homicide rate. *Criminology* 20: 103–14.

National Center for Health Statistics (NCHS). (1986). *Health—United States 1986*. DHHS Pub. No. (PHS) 87-1232. Hyattsville, Md.: U.S. Dept. of Health and Human Services.

National Institute of Drug Abuse (NIDA). (1980a). *Current trends and issues in drug abuse*. Rockville, Md.: ADAMHA.

———. (1980b). *Drug abuse deaths in nine cities: A survey report*. Res. Mon. 29. Rockville, Md.: ADAMHA.

———. (1985). *Drug abuse among minorities*. Rockville, Md.: ADAMHA.

New York Times, National Edition. (1987a). Crack brings violence to areas of New York. October 19, p. 13.

———. (1987b). What it's like to be in hell. December 4, 1987, p. 35.

Parker, R., and Smith, M. (1979). Deterrence, poverty and type of homicide. *American Journal of Sociology* 85: 621–29.

Peters, M. F. (1981). Parenting in black families with young children: A historical perspective. In *Black families*, edited by H. McAdoo. Beverly Hills, Calif.: Sage Publications.

Pierce, C. M. (1970). Offense mechanisms. In *The black 70s*, edited by F. Barbour. Boston: Porter Sargent Publications.

Pierce, H. B. (1986). Blacks and law enforcement: Towards police brutality reduction. *The Black Scholar* 17: 49–54.

Poussaint, A. (1983). Black-on-black homicide: A psychological-political perspective. *Victimology* 8: 161–69.

Prothrow-Stith, D. B. (1986). Interdisciplinary interventions applicable to prevention of interpersonal violence and homicide in black youth. In *Report of the secretary's task force on black and minority health*, Vol. V. Washington, D.C.: Department of Health and Human Services.

Public Health Reports. (1980). Homicide among black males. *Public Health Reports* 95: 549–61.

———. (1982). Study links TV violence to aggressive behavior. *Public Health Reports* 97: 492–93.

———. (1985). Prevention briefs. *Public Health Reports* 100: 283–84.

Rose, H. M. (1986). Can we substantially lower homicide risk in the nation's larger black communities? In *Report of the secretary's task force on black and minority health*, Vol. V. Washington, D.C.: Department of Health and Human Services.

Rutter, M. (1985). Resilience in the face of adversity. *British Journal of Psychiatry* 147: 598–611.

San Francisco Chronicle. (1987). "Urban teachers say violence is big problem." Sept. 8, p. 7.

Schulz, D. A. (1969). *Coming up black: Patterns of ghetto socialization*. Englewood Cliffs, N.J.: Prentice-Hall.

Seiden, R. H. (1972). Why are suicides of young blacks increasing? *H.S.M.H.S. Health Reports* 87: 3–8.

Shaffer, D., and Fisher, P. (1981). The epidemiology of suicide in children and young adolescents. *Journal of the American Academy of Child Psychiatry* 20: 545–65.

Skager, R. (1986). *A statewide survey of drug and alcohol use among California students in grades 7, 9, and 11*. Office of the Attorney General, State of California, Sacramento.

Smart, R. G. (1980). Drug abuse among adolescents and self-destructive behavior. In *The many faces of suicide*, edited by N. L. Farberow. New York: McGraw-Hill.

Smith, D. (1981). The upsurge of police repression: An analysis. *The Black Scholar* 12: 35–57.

Smith, J. A., and Carter, J. H. (1986). Suicide and black adolescents: A medical dilemma. *Journal of the National Medical Association* 78: 1061–64.

Stack, C. (1974). *All our kin*. New York: Harper & Row.

Sum, A., Harrington, P. E., and Goedicke, W. (1987). One-fifth of the nation's teenagers: Employment problems of poor youth in America, 1981–1985. *Youth and Society* 18: 195–237.

Toolan, J. M. (1975). Suicide in children and adolescents. *American Journal of Psychotherapy* 29: 339–44.

U.S. Census Bureau. (1986). *Statistical abstract of the United States*, 106th ed. Washington, D.C.: U.S. Department of Commerce.

Waldron, I., and Eyer, J. (1975). Socioeconomic causes of the recent rise in death rates for 15–24-year-olds. *Social Science and Medicine* 17: 1107–23.

Warshauer, M., and Monk, M. (1978). Problems in suicide statistics for whites and blacks. *American Journal of Public Health* 68: 383–88.

Wilson, W. J., and Aponte, R. (1985). Urban poverty. *Annual Review of Sociology* 11: 231–58.

Word, C. (1977). Television in the lives of black people. In *Third Conference on Empirical Research in Black Psychology*, pp. 99–106. Washington, D.C.: U.S. Dept. of Health, Education and Welfare.

Wolfgang, M. E., and Ferracuti, F. (1967). *The subculture of violence: Toward an integrated theory of criminology*. London: Tavistock Publications.

Chapter 9

THE IMPACT OF PUBLIC POLICY ON THE STATUS OF YOUNG BLACK MALES

Barbara Solomon

> *The United States is creating a permanent underclass of young people for whom poverty and despair are life's daily companions. These are youth who cannot hold jobs because they lack fundamental literacy skills and work habits. They feel alienated from mainstream society, and they seldom participate in the democratic process. They cannot attain the living standard of most Americans because they are trapped in a web of dependency and failure.*

Committee for Economic Development,
*Children in Need: Investment Strategies for the
Educationally Disadvantaged* (New York:
C.E.D., 1987).

The Black Male: A National Concern

Public policy is the outcome of a decision-making process whereby principles generated at various levels of government guide the provision of a wide range of programs aimed at meeting the needs of the public (or some segment thereof). The American public includes some 12,000,000 black males, who at times have been singled out as having special needs that have been created, exacerbated, or ignored by past or present public policy (Gary, 1981; Gibbs, 1984; Staples, 1975). The category "black male" encompasses a large number of individuals who despite their common color and gender may vary widely in regard to numerous other variables such as age, occupation, marital status, educational level, and health. As Gary has written:

> Given . . . the data available, it becomes clear that Black men are not like white men on many significant institutional measures, and that race, rather than sexism or classism, is a more powerful variable for understanding the behavior of Black men in the American society. [1981, p. 14]

Despite considerable intragroup heterogeneity, black males as a group differ significantly from white males as a group. White males are more likely to be married, while black males are more likely to be unwed fathers. White males are more likely to own their own businesses, while black males are more likely to be unemployed. Black males are more likely to be involved in the criminal justice system, while white males are more likely to serve on agency boards as directors. Previous chapters in this book have provided documentation that such differences are often related to institutionalized racial biases that are expressed in public policy. However, unlike many societies in which minorities are oppressed by a powerful majority, the basic ideologies of American society reject racial bias. Therefore, public policy has also reflected efforts to bring practice into conformity with ideology. This chapter examines past strategies and those that have been proposed for the future to eliminate public policy support of racial discrimination and to reduce the effects of past discrimination that is responsible for the disadvantaged position held by young black males in our society.

The Nature of Racial Public Policy

Almost since its inception, this country has made public policy that intensely and differentially affected its black citizens. Article I, section 2, paragraph 3 of the U.S. Constitution declared that the electorate "shall be determined by adding the whole Number of free Persons, including those bound to Service for a Term of Years, and excluding Indians not taxed, to three-fifths of all other persons." Thus, a slave was considered only three-fifths of a human being. Yet, the abolition of slavery did not end discrimination against blacks. By the start of the 20th century, a legally codified system of racial segregation in the South and a dominant laissez-faire ideology in the North, which assumed that equal rights produces equal opportunities, insured continuing discrimination against blacks in education, employment, housing, and almost every aspect of social life (Turner, Singleton, and Musick, 1984, p. 25).

The desperate economic problems brought on by the Great Depression led blacks to give almost total support to Franklin Delano Roosevelt's New Deal. However, most of the New Deal programs did little to reduce inequities between white and black citizens (Barker and McCorry, 1976, pp. 17–18). For example, New Deal housing policies gave formal recognition to residential segregation, its economic policies gave official sanction to local patterns of discrimination in employment, and its agricultural policy allowed farmers to collect money for not planting or plowing crops, thereby causing the unemployment of large numbers of black farm hands.

Several authors have described particular types of racial public policy—that is, public policy aimed at dealing with characteristic problems of racial minority subgroups in the "body politic" (Burkey, 1971; Barnett, 1976; Hill, 1986). These include policies related directly to the protection of traditional civil rights and to affirmative action as well as indirectly to racial discrimination.

Traditional civil rights policy has been concerned with guaranteeing the civil rights of minority groups by eliminating legal and illegal barriers that historically have served to maintain their inequality. Often, the result has been a redefinition and restructuring of fundamental constitutional relationships between racial groups; thus, instead of merely extending rights of the majority to minorities, new rights for both groups are created. For example, even though the Fourteenth Amendment to the Constitution was passed for the specific purpose of protecting the newly freed slaves, it created new rights for all Americans and became the basis for far-reaching constitutional change.

More recently, less sweeping redefinitions of constitutional relationships between racial groups have emanated from the Supreme Court of the United States. In the case of *Brown* v. *Board of Education*, 1954, the Court found that racial segregation in public schools was unconstitutional. Similarly, in *Reitman* v. *Mulkey*, 1967, the Court declared unconstitutional California's attempt to incorporate a policy in its state constitution that would permit racial segregation in the sale or rental of housing. The record indicates that strong and persistent support from the Court can prove crucial and even determinative in gaining policy objectives (Barker and McCorry, 1976, pp. 165–204). However, during the 1980s a change in the substance and the tone of the Court indicates that there is less interest on the part of the Court in applying or expanding judicial policies supporting the rights of minorities, less support for the use of the Court by blacks and other minorities to achieve objectives unattainable in other political forums, and less judicial support for individual or group claims that dispute governmental authority.

The 1960s have been referred to as the civil rights decade. Certainly, it was a span of years marked by the passage of an unprecedented amount of legislation to eliminate discrimination that had been legally sanctioned against blacks since the Reconstruction era. The Civil Rights Act of 1964, probably the high point of the civil rights movement, formally recognized legal rights of blacks and other minorities. A broad coalition of groups, black and white, worked to achieve this recognition. However, difficulties arose in the next decade when policies were sought to insure that these rights were actually implemented.

Affirmative action policy essentially began with the passage of the Civil Rights Act of 1965, which declared employment discrimination against blacks and other minorities illegal. Title VII established the Equal Employment Opportunity Commission (EEOC), which was given the authority to monitor compliance with provisions prohibiting discrimination in pay, promotion, hiring, training, or termination. In 1965, an executive order established the Office of Federal Contract Compliance, which prohibited discrimination by race among government contractors. Three years later, this agency required federal contractors with deficiencies in the area of nondiscriminatory practices to present a written "affirmative action" plan that included goals and timetables (Smith and Welch, 1984).

Affirmative action policy established at federal, state, and local levels has put pressure on employers to take positive action to reduce barriers to employment of blacks and other minorities. It rejects the notion that cessation of discrimination is sufficient to reduce cumulative effects from the past. Although a nondiscrimination policy may exist, its existence alone may not constitute affirmative action if minority employment in the workplace does not increase.

The persistence of underemployment of minorities may be due to minority persons' lack of conviction about the seriousness with which the nondiscrimination policy is to be implemented or to inadequate dissemination of information regarding either the changed policy or job openings. More directly, employers may have imposed qualifications not directly related to ability to perform the job—qualifications less likely to be held by blacks, such as college education or scores on unvalidated employment tests. In such instances, persons with equal probabilities of success on the job have unequal probabilities of being hired for the job (Guion, 1969).

Sowell (1984) contends that the goal of equality of opportunity should be differentiated from the goal of equality of results. The goal of equal opportunity requires that individuals be judged on their qualifications as individuals without regard to race, sex, or age, and so forth. In contrast, affirmative action policies seek to achieve some equality of results—that is, individuals are judged with regard to their group membership and receive preferential or compensatory treatment in some cases in order to achieve a more proportional representation in various institutions and occupations. Sowell condemns equality of results as a goal because it utilizes an all-purpose explanation—racism and discrimination—for the existing inequality of socioeconomic status among blacks and whites. However, these statistical differences may not mean discrimination at all but rather the effect of innumerable demographic, cultural, and geographic differences. From this perspective, an equitable society is only concerned with equality of opportunity rather than equality of results.

Proponents of affirmative action policies argue that the only way in which equality of opportunity is confirmed is through results— that is, in the reduction of group differences that have resulted primarily from discrimination. Ryan (1981) is most specific:

> *It is impossible to discriminate against individuals as individuals; it can be done only against individuals as members of a group. Racial discrimination does not consist of an unrelated series of discrete actions directed against a random group of individuals who happen to be black; it is directed against blacks in general, as a group. . . . If I don't like you for some specific reason—you're a loudmouth, you're ugly, you're hostile, or you don't laugh at my jokes—and if I treat you badly because I don't like you, that's not discrimination, unpleasant as it might be. When I decide that all women are loudmouths, all blacks are hostile, and all Jews lack a sense of humor and when I treat members of these groups unfairly, that's discrimination. By the same token, antidiscriminatory efforts and actions must be formulated in group terms. The abandonment of discriminatory practices can be documented and measured only by the observation of changes in the distribution of members of different subgroups. [pp. 155–156]*

Perhaps a more troublesome question is whether affirmative action policies have actually led to improved access to employment for blacks and other racial minorities. Utilizing the 1980 microdata file as well as newly released microdata files for the 1940 and 1950 censuses, researchers assessed the extent of economic progress made by black Americans over the 40-year period between 1940 and 1980. The findings were decidedly mixed. On the one hand, affirmative action did have a significant positive effect on the wages of young black workers. For example, wages of young black workers increased dramatically from 1967 to 1972. However, these wage gains were eroded by 1977. There was also a pro-skill bias apparent, as the permanent positive wage effects of affirmative action on black males appear to be limited to young black college graduates.

Revolutionary public policy has rarely been seriously proposed, and even when it is proposed, it has never gained support from more than a minuscule segment of the black population. Such policy would involve the restructuring of the entire society, including the political, economic, and social systems in ways that would improve the quality of life for the most disadvantaged subgroups. An example of such a movement that captured the commitment of young black males was the emergence of the Black Panther Party in Oakland, California, in 1966. The Panthers adopted a Marxist-Leninist ideology and proposed that blacks mount a revolution to remove the capitalist leadership of the United States. Barnett (1976) points out that although this type of policy has never been implemented, it is included in the spectrum of public policy debate in the black community, and therefore competes with other incremental public policies for black political attention (p. 29).

Policy indirectly related to racial discrimination generally focuses on social problems that have been experienced disproportionately by blacks, often as a consequence of racial discrimination. For example, in the Panel Study of Income Dynamics, conducted each year since 1968 by the Survey Research Center of the University of Michigan, researchers have concluded that very few white men under 45 are persistently poor—that is, poor for at least eight of the ten prior years. In contrast, black men under 45 account for a substantial portion of the persistently poor. The difference in the experience of the two groups presumably reflects the more favorable labor market opportunities available to white nonelderly men. It has been proposed that in order to resolve the problem of intransigent poverty, we need federal economic policies which increase the number of jobs and raise wage rates. Evidence suggests that most poor individuals will work if jobs are available and if they can earn wages that are normal for persons with similar skills. Duncan (1984), for example, contends that "wage subsidy programs or other programs aimed at increasing their wages, including programs to eliminate racial discrimination in the labor market, appear to be desirable approaches to eliminating the persistent poverty of this group" (p. 64).

Some social programs that successfully assisted blacks to reduce the consequences of past discrimination have in the process become targets for criticism. Food Stamps, Head Start, and Job Corps were specifically identified by Vernon Jordan, former director of the Urban League, as some of the more successful endeavors of government (Jordan, 1984). Despite the impact of these programs in the black community, and the contention of some that they have been designed to help only blacks, the big lie is defeated by statistics. For example, the majority of people on welfare are white, as are half of food stamp recipients and the majority of those placed in jobs under the major federal vocational training program (Jordan, p. 244)

Racial Public Policy and Black Males

In consideration of the problems faced by black individuals and families in this country, there have been periods when the black male was made a particular focus. In fact, a spotlight has been placed on the problems of black males during at least three periods in our history, and in each period proposals were made for the establishment of public policy that could alleviate or at least reduce the extent of the problems.

The Civil Rights Period

In 1950, E. Franklin Frazier wrote:

> Since the widespread family disorganization among Negroes has resulted from the failure of the father to play the role in family life required by American society, the mitigation of this problem must await those changes in the Negro and American society which will enable the Negro father to play the role required of him. [pp. 276–277]

The change most intensely sought by the black community was in the segregation laws, which gave powerful support to racist notions of white superiority and concomitantly to black inferiority. The status of young black males under segregation laws was no place more riddled with contradiction than in the armed forces of this country. During World War II, for example, most black soldiers were confined to menial service and supply positions where they were subjected to the subtle, day-to-day pressure of racial discrimination (Turner, Singleton, and Musick, 1984). More significantly, they returned from fighting an enemy who was white to the realization that with the ending of the war, the former enemy could be more free in parts of the United States than they themselves. The underlying rage and frustration of thousands of these black former servicemen have been identified as the fuel that ignited the civil rights movement.

There was an underlying assumption that once these barriers were eliminated, blacks would have every opportunity to realize their potential. Equal opportunity would inevitably give the lie to notions of black inferiority, as black achievement closed gaps between blacks and whites in regard to education, income, and other determinants of the quality of life. The next 15 years were characterized by efforts to adopt policies insuring that segregation laws, as well as other laws and administrative policies that institutionalized racial discrimination, would be eliminated. The passage of the Civil Rights Act of 1964 represents the culmination of much of the effort expended during this period.

Great Society Policies and Programs

When Lyndon Johnson became President in 1963 after the assassination of John Kennedy, he promised that his administration would seek the "Great Society," with a "War on Poverty" as its central mission. In his controversial report on the black family, Moynihan (1965) pointed out that because many black fathers are either not present or unemployed, or make such a low wage that they cannot support their families, women in the families have to become breadwinners. This dependence on the mother's income undermines the position of the father and deprives the children of the kind of socialization to norms and roles that are a standard feature of successful adult life. Moynihan further wrote that the President had committed the nation to a national effort to eliminate poverty, which could be stated thus:

> The policy of the United States is to bring the Negro American to full and equal sharing in the responsibilities and rewards of citizenship. To this end, the programs of the Federal government bearing on this objective shall be designed to have the effect, directly or indirectly, of enhancing the stability and resources of the Negro American family. [p. 48]

Although the Johnson administration had successfully passed multifaceted legislation in the 1964 act creating the Office of

Economic Opportunity and during the next three years implemented other social programs designed to address the needs of
inner-city and rural poor people, never did a completely accessible
opportunity system for blacks in general or black males in particular develop. Despite the criticisms of conservatives that too much
money was being poured into an effort to expand the role of the
federal government in the provision of social welfare services, the
fact is that the disparity between the lofty intentions of many of
these programs and the funds allocated to achieve them was great.
The programs often lacked adequate funding or the skillful administrative direction required to make them effective. With the
advent of the Nixon administration in 1969, the Office of Economic
Opportunity was incrementally dismantled.

The New Conservatism

Fifteen years after the Moynihan report, with a Republican administration and a prevailing conservative mood in government, the
problems of young black males were still a concern of policymakers. However, perceptions regarding the etiology of the problems
and the nature of the proposed solutions differed substantially
from the views espoused by the previous Democratic and more
liberal Republican administrations. For example, much of the
sociopolitical philosophy of the administration was reflected in
Gilder's *Wealth and Poverty* (1980), which presented a specific
position regarding the consequences for the black community
when young black males are unattached and unemployed:

> *Men, most fundamentally, are measured by their performance of
> the role of provider and if they fail in it, there are few easy appeals
> to other criteria of success. . . . The key to the intractable poverty
> of the hard-core American poor is the dominance of single and
> separated men in poor communities. . . . The problem is neither
> race nor matriarchy in any meaningful sense. It is familial anarchy
> among the concentrated poor of the inner city. . . . Boys are brought
> up without authoritative fathers in the home to instill in them the
> values of responsible paternity: the discipline and love of children
> and the dependable performance of the provider role. . . .
> [pp. 90–91]*
>
> *The problem of black male poverty arises at those income levels
> where AFDC is more than competitive with work. At those levels
> black men work less hard than white men. . . . This lesser effort,
> though, is a reflection not of indolence but of singleness. These men
> lack the motivation conferred by familial demands and the strength
> imparted by marital support. [p. 162]*

It has been generally accepted that most men in our society need to fulfill the provider role successfully to establish strong marital relationships and stable families. Yet Gilder suggests that men need to be married and have stable families to work hard and by inference, fulfill the provider role successfully. Thus, it is a case of the proverbial vicious circle. Which, then, is the more powerful point of intervention—employment or family—in the effort to break this cycle? The answer appears to be that employment provides the greater leverage. From a public policy standpoint, it is far more feasible and appropriate to provide opportunities for productive work than to promote family attachment. Moreover, a job is likely to promote the latter without any need for government intervention.

The need for public policy aimed at improving the status of young black males to emphasize jobs (i.e., deficiencies in the structure of employment) rather than family (i.e., deficiencies in the structure of black families) is not inconsistent with Wilson's premise in his book *The Declining Significance of Race* (1978). Although critics concluded (apparently primarily from the title) that Wilson rejected the idea that racism is an important factor in the income gap between black and white workers, he in fact made the case that, although important, racism is relatively less important than basic structural problems in the American economic system, including uneven economic growth, increasing technology and automation, industry relocation, and labor-market segmentation. He wrote:

> *In the final analysis . . . the challenge of economic dislocation in modern industrial society calls for public policy programs to attack inequality on a broad class front, policy programs . . . that go beyond the limits of ethnic and racial discrimination by directly confronting the pervasive and destructive features of class subordination. [pp. 153–154]*

The status of black males as a consequence of widely varying strategies implemented since the advent of the Civil Rights movement must be viewed as a dynamic, evolving aspect of this country's social and economic life. In a Rand research study of economic progress of blacks between 1940 and 1980, it was stated that in 1940, three-quarters of all black families were poor, similar to the male poverty rate, and between 1940 and 1960, reductions in black family poverty moved at the same rate as declines in black male poverty. However, after 1960 the percentage reduction in the proportion of black men in poverty was 70 percent larger than the percentage reduction in poor black families (Smith and Welch, 1986, p. 104).

Unfortunately, this apparent progress of black males has not led to a similarly dramatic increase in the overall quality of life in black communities. According to Smith and Welch (1986), the rapid increase in female-headed households among blacks has led to an increasingly segmented black experience: "[intact] black families participating in an affluent America while distressing numbers are left behind in the worst ravages of poverty" (p. 106).

Perhaps even more important, however, is the finding that much of the long-term reduction in the percentage of black men in poverty was due to a combination of economic growth and improving black labor market skills, principally through education (enhanced by black migration patterns) and job training. Affirmative action significantly shifted black male employment toward EEOC-covered firms with federal contracts and increased the representation of black male workers in managerial and professional jobs in those firms. However, there is little evidence that affirmative action has raised the incomes of black males as a group—that is, closed the wage gap between black males and white males. Moreover, since 1970, part but not all of the economic progress of black males was offset by black employment problems.

Since the end of World War II, the overall civilian labor participation rate has declined; however, the black male participation rate has been dropping much faster than the white rate. Furthermore, the trends in work participation of young black males have been the most unfavorable. In 1954, the nonwhite teenage unemployment rate was about 1.4 times the white rate. By the 1970s, black teenagers were on the average 2.3 times as often unemployed as white teenagers. By 1979, the rate had risen to 2.6 times the rate for white teenagers. In the summer of 1981, for the first time over 50 percent of young blacks were unemployed (U.S. Department of Labor, 1978, Table A–4, pp. 187–188; Table A–18, p. 210). This period represented the depths of an economic recession that did not see a recovery until 1983. Although the unemployment ratio improved for all black groups between 1983 and 1986, young black males continued to be unemployed about twice as often as young white males (Swinton, 1986, pp. 14–16).

The conclusion that can be drawn from this review of racial public policy over the past 40 years is that difficulties for black males in social functioning have been generated by circular and dysfunctional transactions among the three major ingredients of competent social functioning: family, school, and work. Thus, satisfactory performance in a work role is a necessary requisite for effective functioning in most other social systems, including the family. Adequate schooling is necessary to function effectively at jobs that pay a "living wage." At the same time, a stable family is the crucible in which skills needed to function effectively in school and later on the job are developed.

The Rational Policy Imperatives

In a militantly egalitarian society—at least in its political ideology—there is resistance to any public policy that openly and specifically seeks to provide benefits and privileges to one group that are denied others. Even in instances in which blacks have been clearly disadvantaged by public policies, their disadvantage was more than likely interpreted as a function of some nonracial attribute such as inadequate or inferior education or training or apathy. Therefore, any public policy that seeks to redress inequities currently experienced by young black males must be directed toward resolution of particular problems for which young black males are more vulnerable. For example, the foregoing review of racial public policy suggests that most problems disproportionately experienced by young black males generate and are generated by family instability, school failure, and unemployment. Thus, the outcomes for black males can be improved indirectly by improving the performance of public schools with respect to their nonwhite, poor student population; by providing adequate family income through improved employment and public assistance programs; and by indirectly supporting efforts to promote family cohesion and stability (Hefner, 1976, p. 71).

Education

The statistics reflecting the failure of the schools to educate low-income black students, especially young black males, are distressing. At the same time, however, some schools have achieved results, even when located in low-income, black communities. Efforts have been made to categorize and label the factors associated with schools considered to be effective. They include leadership (particularly increased autonomy for school-based leadership), teaching skill, clarity of expectations, pupil monitoring, and overall climate (Moody, 1986, p. 33).

Perhaps the most troublesome dilemma in regard to education in black communities arises as a consequence of society's inherent classism, which places less value on blue-collar employment than on management or the professions. The effect has been twofold: a tendency of public schools to place blacks into vocational education "tracks," regardless of their interest or potential for college and the professions; and, at the same time, a recognition by black families and children that these occupations are devalued and, therefore, a rejection of vocational education, even in cases of student interest and/or special aptitude. The question becomes, How do we create public schools where "tracks" are completely value-free and based solely on interest and special aptitude?

Melman (1983, p. 267) has identified the basic social attitudes in the workplace that sharply differentiate the functions of managers from workers. Decision making is not shared; therefore, occupations take on a primarily decision-making or a primarily production content. The attitude reflected in this structuring of work roles is that managers always have higher status and greater significance than the worker. The success of the Japanese management style has hinged on the renunciation of this strictly hierarchical arrangement and on providing for greater democracy in the workplace.

Yet, in many of the nonmanagerial occupations in the United States, workers have created alternative sources of status. For example, a child whose father is a machinist or a truckdriver or a construction worker is often socialized to a subculture that is defined by the fellow workers. Frequently, a folklore has been developed complete with heroes—for example, men in their occupation who had accomplished remarkable feats "on the job." Many of these children will grow up with a great respect for the father's occupation and others similar to it.

The labor union is often an important aspect of the blue-collar subculture. Blacks have had great difficulty in the past and to some extent in the present becoming a part of this subculture. Furthermore, low-income black children have less opportunity to be exposed to a male role model who has had steady blue-collar employment. Thus, their attitudes toward occupational roles are almost all derived from the schools and the literature, which do not hold blue-collar employment in high esteem.

If public-school education is to become more effective in educating young black males, it is essential that the importance of basic educational skills for *all* occupational roles be emphasized—not merely those needed for college or the professions. The importance of *all* occupational roles to the society should also be emphasized, along with the rewards—personal and economic—that accompany these roles. Representative Augustus Hawkins of California has introduced legislation that would create nationwide school programs modeled after those programs that have already demonstrated that urban, poor, and predominantly black schools can effectively educate students (Moody, 1986, p. 33). Policies that would encourage the development of programs aimed at changing the perceptions of the importance of occupations throughout the society could similarly be proposed.

Employment

The National Urban League recently addressed the problem of employment barriers during the development and writing of the Opportunities for Employment Preparation Act of 1986 (S. 2578) and the Aid to Families and Employment Transition Act of 1986 (S. 2579) (Glasgow, 1986). The first bill amends the Job Training Partnership Act (JTPA), and the latter amends the AFDC and Medicaid legislation (Titles IV and XIX of the Social Security Act). The intent of these two bills is to strengthen single and two-parent families who are long-term AFDC recipients or long-term unemployed.

If passed, provisions in these bills will:

1. Include vocational, adult, and postsecondary education programs as part of the employment training.
2. Create an outreach, preemployment, and vocational education component (a feeder system) within JTPA, which will target education and employment benefits to those most in need.
3. Target preemployment services to families who have participated in AFDC for two years or more and to individuals who have been unemployed for two or more years. These services will include a structured search for an eight-week internship with a private or public agency, educational preparation and basic skills development, career counseling, family counseling, and parenting skills targeted to teenage parents.
4. Authorize community-based organizations, such as the Urban League, to conduct and provide preemployment services.
5. Provide for unlimited support services, including child care and transportation.
6. Prevent participants in the proposed feeder system from losing other program benefits such as AFDC and food stamps as a result of employment and training benefits (e.g., scholarships and educational assistance).

Several assumptions inherent in this proposed legislation must hold if a significant positive effect on the employment rate of young black males will follow—namely, that more jobs are available than are workers to fill them, that the jobs available provide enough income to support a standard of living above the poverty level, and that the jobs will be available on a nondiscriminatory basis.

The economic difficulties of black males have been clearly related to aspects of the performance of the economy over the last 15 years (Swinton, 1986). Job growth has not been high enough to lower the unemployment rate significantly. Furthermore, job growth has occurred primarily in the lower-paying service, finance, and trade sectors rather than in the higher-paying goods production sector. This growth has also occurred to a larger extent in sectors that have traditionally employed more women than men.

Melman (1983) has pointed to the decline in productivity and the deterioration of the American industrial economy over a period of at least two decades, including "technical/economic incompetence of a quality and scope unprecedented in American history" (p. 263). The reasons, he suggests, include the orientation of managers toward short-term profit making, the lack of respect and consequent low status of blue-collar workers, and a military budget that is a major drain on the production capabilities of the society. Perhaps most importantly, Melman contends that the American economy is characterized by profits and power goals rather than production goals. Thus, what is important is that a profit is made, while the nature of the work that yielded the profit is only of secondary importance. This is illustrated most dramatically by the pervasive practice of giving huge bonuses to chief executives who earn a profit for the company rather than to workers based on their productivity. Yet, in order that all Americans will be able to find and hold useful jobs in the years ahead, a national economic policy for productivity growth will be required.

According to Melman, "the underlying requirements include initiatives by all the production occupations for progressively enlarged workplace democracy, moves toward production-oriented management, more decentralized decision-making and a substantially smaller military economy" (p. 291).

To the extent that the employment outcomes for young black males are dependent on the state of the American economy in general, Melman's analysis could be used to measure the potential of economic policy proposals for affecting the availability of jobs for young black males. Black leaders have seldom, with the exception of support for the Humphrey-Hawkins bill, devoted sustained political attention to such macroeconomic issues. Yet, if blacks and other allies of the poor were to exert political pressures in this area, the role of macroeconomic policies (such as a full employment policy) in shaping the employment outcomes for young black males may in time be altered.

Improved Public Assistance Programs

Recently, strong voices have been putting forth the premise that current social welfare programs act as a disincentive to work (Cogan, 1978; Gilder, 1980; Murray, 1984). However, there is considerable evidence that the rise in poverty in recent years is more likely due to multiple factors, such as increased automation that has eliminated unskilled and low-skilled jobs, an economy that has staggered between repetitive cycles of prosperity and recession, and the tidal wave of women and new immigrants who have moved into the job market, frequently displacing younger black workers. Yet, public assistance programs are based primarily on an assumption that work is generally available to all who need to work, and therefore, public assistance to anyone of working age should be available only on a temporary basis to those who are ill, unemployed, or caring for small children. Young black males in need of public assistance are most likely to be in the unemployed category. The unemployed in most instances are eligible only for general assistance, administered at the local community level and frequently in the form of vouchers for room and board in substandard living arrangements.

Almost everyone involved in the welfare reform debate agrees with the premise that welfare programs should help those who can work to work. Work is perceived as a primary source of status and positive self-concept, so that any provision of assistance that is not attached to a job is perceived as stigmatizing. However, the goal of productive employment could be more effectively achieved through a more radical social insurance program than incremental expansion of public assistance programs.

Social insurance programs, unlike welfare programs, do not depend on income or assets for eligibility. They work more like insurance programs, since they pay money at the time of a particular event such as retirement, loss of a job, or death of the wage earner. Yet, it is possible to conceptualize an entry age into the job market (e.g., age 18) in the same way that we define an exit age (e.g., age 65 or 70). Subsequent to entry, in any instance that a year elapses without employment, the person would become eligible for unemployment compensation. In addition, however, the participation in vocational education and utilization of preemployment services as indicated above would not only be provided but would be made a condition of eligibility for unemployment compensation. These and other support services would therefore be targeted to recipients of unemployment compensation rather than to recipients of the AFDC program. This would have the net effect of expanding unemployment insurance to include those persons who have never worked or who are looking for a job after a long period of unemployment.

Although our focus is on young black males, generally social insurance programs are designed to provide income maintenance for persons of either gender at all stages of the life cycle. Therefore, complementary modifications to other programs would need to be consistent with any new directions to be taken in efforts to bring about welfare reform. For example, three former public assistance programs were collapsed into the SSI program (Aid to the Blind, Aid to the Disabled, and Old Age Assistance) and are now administered by the Social Security Administration as the Supplemental Security Income program. Supplemental Security Income (SSI) and Social Security (OASDI) could be merged, dropping the SSI means test and reducing the grants only for earnings from work or income from investments or a pension fund. The disability provisions under Social Security would be extended to cover temporary disability. Most importantly, those persons who are blind, disabled, and therefore unlikely to be employed would be assisted by this program rather than an unemployment insurance program.

Still another example is a program of children's allowances, which are fixed monthly sums paid to parents to be used for the benefit of children. Kamerman and Kahn (1978) studied family policy in 14 countries—12 in Europe, the United States, and Canada—and only the United States lacked family allowances (p. 483). Jansson (1984) suggests that "serious consideration should be given to a family allowance . . . in which income is given to all families, either as a flat per-child grant or as graduated grants that vary with family income" (p. 342). The simultaneous establishment of these social insurance approaches to social welfare reform at a high enough benefit level could conceivably eliminate almost all official poverty in this country.

Ozawa (1986, p. 444) has referred to the development of such a network of social insurancelike programs as a public investment approach. She contends that if policymakers decided to adopt these new programs, current welfare and related programs, including AFDC, could either be eliminated or scaled down drastically. The portion of SSI that deals with disabled children could also be eliminated. The government might altogether revamp the Food Stamp program and public housing assistance. Dependent benefits for children under Social Security could be eliminated. Personal exemptions for children could be curtailed. The net cost of this investment approach would depend on the scope of the new programs and the extent to which the old were curtailed. However, there would be an increased opportunity for young black males to become eligible for jobs at a living wage or, if unemployed, to engage in alternative work-related activities (e.g., vocational training) without incurring the stigmatization associated with welfare dependency.

A comprehensive family policy would eliminate the stigmatizing situations in which some families—predominantly black and other racial/ethnic minorities—are identified as deficient, dysfunctional, or even pathological and for whom services are justified on these bases. Probably a variety of feasible and effective administrative models differentiated by varying relationships between public and private service delivery systems could be developed to implement such policy. However, there is some evidence to suggest that an appropriate organizational unit for implementing family policy should have power to coordinate a wide range of relevant programs as well as power enough to balance significant family interests and competing interests such as military defense or the environment (Kamerman and Kahn, 1978, pp. 489–490).

Family Stability

The problems of black families have been described primarily as a function of the inability of young black males to become effectively integrated into the economic life of American communities. This has been attributed to a range of factors, including a legacy of disrupted family life from the slavery period, employment discrimination, and more recently, weak economic conditions. However, there is general agreement that whatever the reasons the consequences of high unemployment or disproportionately low-income employment have been devastating to the establishment and maintenance of stable families in black communities.

There is not much agreement, however, on whether policy at national, state, or local levels should address the problem of family stability *directly* in specific legislation and/or programs or only *indirectly* through increased employment opportunities. Nevertheless, the interrelatedness of work, school, and family in the development of young black males who are able to function effectively in their social environment demands a multifaceted policy agenda. Neglect of any of the elements could weaken the efforts directed toward other elements—for example, a lack of attention to provision of resources needed to stabilize family life will lessen the probability that children will be socialized effectively enough to take advantage of educational and employment opportunities provided later.

The need to create the conditions in which the socialization of black male children for effective social functioning can take place is compelling. The need for quality education and adequate income has already been documented. In addition, families need to be able to provide adequate health care for their children before and after their birth. For example, county, state, or federal governmental agencies or some combination thereof could hire physicians or contract with private physicians to provide all expectant mothers with free prenatal and postnatal care. Free health clinics could be established as an integral part of the public school system, or a subsidized health insurance program for children might be developed similar to Part B of Medicare.

Current social welfare policy is inadequate and even counterproductive in insuring the optimal development of our country's low-income children, among whom black children are overrepresented. For the first time, in 1986 more than half (52 percent) of black children were in households below the poverty level. Their predicament is serious because the public appears less and less supportive of governmental expenditures for social welfare purposes. However, this trend of nonsupport could reverse itself. Currently, there are 19 elderly persons per 100 working-age individuals, but by the time the baby-boom generation of the 1950s and 1960s retires in the early years of the next century, there will be 38 elderly persons per 100 working-age individuals (Ozawa, p. 441). More significantly, the data imply that the degree to which the baby-boom generation will be economically secure in old age will depend largely on how productive current nonwhite children are when they reach adulthood. The development of the earning capability of nonwhites is now crucial in determining whether this nation can ensure a satisfying quality of life for the elderly of the 21st century.

The message is clear: The first line of defense in preparing young black males to take advantage of employment opportunities or to fight effectively against systemic employment discrimination is a nurturing family. Initially, at least, costs for a coherent, comprehensive network of services to children and their families may exceed current levels of support for social programs. However, spending on such programs would be justified because taxpayers consider it wise to invest in the nation's children—not only for the sake of the children but for the sake of their own individual interests as well. Furthermore, spending targeted to children insures provision regardless of the parents' employment status or earnings. Consequently, governmental resources would be used more effectively to promote the physical, mental, and intellectual development of children rather than to monitor, regulate, and control the behavior of the children's parents. Thus, the provision of a wide range of social welfare services would be normalized.

Conclusions

The need for radical reform in this nation's economic, educational, and social welfare systems is profound. Young black males are virtually being held hostage so that the current inequitable distribution of power and resources in our society can remain intact. The resulting fallout contributes to the wide range of social problems chronicled in earlier chapters of this book. Young black males who are unemployed and with little prospects of achieving economic stability all too frequently resort to exploitive relationships with women and detached relationships with their children. The children—males to a greater extent than females—all too often drop out of school. Without adequate education, young black males are vulnerable to recruitment by adults into criminal lifestyles.

There is enough dissatisfaction with the status quo that change—even somewhat radical change—may be possible. For example, there is both conservative and liberal support for what may be termed the most radical of the proposals—the need to provide a subsistence level below which no child should have to fall and the need for full employment at a living wage for all who want to work. With so much agreement, one should wonder why our current fragmented, inadequate, and even destructive "nonsystem" persists. At least two major obstacles to the approach to policy development were discussed in this chapter. The first is the ethic that has obscured an incredible control of wealth in this country by a few—wealth that could be shared by the public to insure the basic necessities of life for everyone. There is considerable apathy about the plight of the poor black male because of a belief system that justifies this striking inequality. It purports that individuals who achieve great wealth do so because they possess intrinsic qualities such as motivation, dedication to the work ethic, and intelligence to a greater extent than do other individuals, including most black males. Thus, black males do not deserve larger shares of the available resources.

Ryan (1981) has gathered evidence to support his contention that the relative economic position of the family one is born into is a far better predictor of one's own economic status than is the most complex array of internal traits and abilities (p. 64). From this latter perspective, the current range in annual incomes from one based on minimum wage to hundreds of millions is excessive, intolerable, and impossible to justify. The alternative is not a kind of socialism in which wealth is divided up among all of us but rather above a maximum level wealth is placed in the public sector and used to provide access to amenities that are shared by all— from libraries to day care to parks to homemaker chore services for the elderly.

A second obstacle to the kind of real reforms in the economic, educational, and social welfare systems that are needed if young black males are to improve their current socioeconomic status is the problem of the tremendous dislocation in the labor force which would be necessary in order to dismantle existing social welfare programs to implement a social investment approach. Large numbers of persons employed in public social service jobs are dependent on the current social welfare system. The threat of the possible elimination of a massive number of positions as suggested by the social investment approach will be sure to create active, even vehement, opposition. The reasons given for the opposition will not likely include fear of job loss but rather such perceived problems as excessive cost, potential abuses, or lack of administrative feasibility.

In the short run, the incremental approach to reforming those economic, educational and social welfare systems that negatively impact young black males may be the most feasible way to reduce that impact. However, the short-term changes should be consistent with the long-range vision of more radical reform involving guaranteed employment, including vocational training and other support services for those without marketable vocational skills and family allowances. In order to achieve these goals, it will be necessary to change public attitudes regarding the distribution of economic resources and to provide viable alternative employment for dislocated public employees.

References

Barker, L. J., and McCorry, J. J. Jr. (1976). *Black Americans and the political system*. Cambridge, Mass.: Winthrop Publishers.

Barnett, M. R. (1976). A theoretical perspective on American racial public policy. In *Public policy for the black community: Strategies and perspectives*, edited by M. R. Barnett and J. Hefner. New York: Alfred Publishing Co., pp 3–53.

Burkey, R. (1971). *Racial discrimination and public policy in the United States*. Lexington, Mass.: D. C. Heath.

Cogan, J. F. (1978). *Negative income taxation and labor supply: New evidence from New Jersey-Pennsylvania experiment*. Santa Monica, Calif.: RAND Corporation.

Duncan, G. J. (1984). *Years of poverty, years of plenty: The changing economic fortunes of American workers and families*. Ann Arbor, Mich.: University of Michigan, Institute for Social Research.

Frazier, E. F. (1950). Problems and needs of Negro children and youth resulting from family disorganization. *Journal of Negro Education* (Summer).

Gary, L. (1981). *Black Men*. Beverly Hills, Calif.: Sage Publications.

Gibbs, J. T. (1984). Black adolescents and youth: An endangered species. *American Journal of Orthopsychiatry* 54: 6–21.

Gilder, G. (1981). *Wealth and poverty*. New York: Basic Books.

Glasgow, D. (1986). Statement for the record (Before the Subcommittee on Domestic Marketing, Consumer Relations, and Nutrition Committee on Agriculture, U.S. House of Representatives, Hearings on Employment and Training/ Welfare Reform), September 26.

Guion, R. M. (1969). Employment tests and discriminatory hiring. In *Negroes and jobs*, edited by L. A. Ferman, J. L. Kornbluh, and J. A. Miller. Ann Arbor, Mich.: University of Michigan Press, pp. 323–338.

Hefner, J. A. (1976). The ghetto. In *Public policy for the black community: Strategies and perspectives*, edited by M. R. Barnett and J. Hefner. New York: Alfred Publishing Co., pp. 55–75.

Hill, R. B. (1986). The black middle class: Past, present and future. In *The state of black America, 1986*, edited by J. D. Williams. New York: National Urban League, pp. 43–64.

Jansson, B. S. (1984). *Theory and practice of social welfare policy*. Belmont, Calif.: Wadsworth.

Jordan, V. (1984). Exploding some myths about social programs. (Guest Editorial). In B. S. Jansson, *Theory and Practice of Social Welfare Policy*. Belmont, Calif.: Wadsworth, pp. 244–245.

Kamerman, S. B., and Kahn, A. J. (eds.). (1978). *Family policy: Government and families in fourteen countries*. New York: Columbia University Press.

Melman, S. (1983). *Profits without production*. New York: Alfred Knopf.

Moody, C. D. (1986). Equity and excellence: An educational imperative. In *The state of black America, 1986*, edited by J. D. Williams. New York: National Urban League, pp. 23–42.

Moynihan, D. P. (1965). *The Negro family: The case for national action*. Washington, D.C.: Office of Policy Planning and Research, United States Department of Labor.

Murray, C. (1984). *Losing Ground*. New York: Basic Books.

Ozawa, M. N. (1986). Nonwhites and the demographic imperative in social welfare spending. *Social Work* 31 (6): 440–447.

Ryan, W. (1981). *Equality*. New York: Pantheon Books.

Smith, J. P., and Welch, F. R. (1984). Affirmative action and labor markets. *Journal of Labor Economics* 2 (2): 269–302.

———. (1986). *Closing the gap: Forty years of economic progress for blacks*. Santa Monica, Calif: Rand Publication Series (February).

Sowell, T. (1984). *Civil rights: Rhetoric or reality*. New York: William Morrow.

Staples, R. (1975). To be young, black and oppressed. *Black Scholar* 7: 2–9.

Swinton, D. (1986). Economic status of blacks, 1985. In *The State of Black America, 1986*, edited by J. D. Williams. New York: National Urban League, pp. 1–21.

Turner, J. H., Singleton, R., Jr., and Musick, D. (1984). *Oppression: A sociohistory of black-white relations in America*. Chicago: Nelson-Hall.

U.S. Department of Labor. (1978). *Employment and training report of the president, 1978*. Washington, D.C.: U.S. Government Printing Office.

Wilson, W. J. (1978). *The declining significance of race: Blacks and changing American institutions*. Chicago: University of Chicago Press.

Chapter 10

CONCLUSIONS AND RECOMMENDATIONS

Jewelle Taylor Gibbs

> *This nation cannot continue to compete and pros-*
> *per in the global arena when more than one-fifth of*
> *our children live in poverty and a third grow up in*
> *ignorance . . . If we continue to squander the talents*
> *of millions of our children, America will become a*
> *nation of limited human potential. It would be tragic*
> *if we allow this to happen. America must become a*
> *land of opportunity—for every child.*
>
> Committee for Economic Development,
> *Children in Need: Investment Strategies for the*
> *Educationally Disadvantaged (New York: CED,*
> 1987).

Introduction

The portrait painted in the preceding chapters of young black males in contemporary American society is grim. Schools have failed them, so they have dropped out or been pushed out. Without education or skills, employers have rejected them or consigned them to menial dead-end jobs. Without jobs and legitimate income, they have gravitated to the illegitimate world of drugs and delinquency. Without security and stability, they have been unwilling or unable to assume family responsibilities for the children they father. Without hope or commitment, without benefit of power and privilege, these young men have succumbed to alienation, anger, and despair. They are destroying themselves and endangering their families and communities through drug addiction, homicide, and suicide. Like other species that have become extinct through manmade exploitation or neglect, young black males are truly an endangered group.

Three facts should be strikingly obvious from the multidisciplinary analysis of the social and economic status of young black males provided in the preceding chapters. First, the problems of this group have worsened in the past 25 years, in spite of a number of government-initiated efforts to alleviate them. Second, the problems are all interrelated, highly complex, and not amenable to short-term, piecemeal solutions. Third, a comprehensive set of policies and programs must be developed in order to address the causes of the problems rather than the symptoms. These policies and programs must focus on underlying social, economic, technological, cultural, and political factors that impact the lives of black families and influence the environmental context in which these young black males develop.

As Solomon noted in Chapter 9, the solutions to the problems of young black males are inextricably linked to the stability and effective functioning of the black family, improvements in their educational outcomes, and opportunities for regular employment and income. Solomon provides convincing historical, sociological, and political data to support proposals for a cohesive, coherent, and comprehensive family policy and network of services which, while targeted to all low-income American families, would particularly benefit black youth and their families, who are disproportionately represented among the poor in America.

In this concluding chapter, we briefly examine several current proposals for such a comprehensive family policy, which should minimally include provisions for a guaranteed annual family income, adequate health care, adequate housing, and equal access to education, employment, and training for youth and adult family members. Specific policies addressed to the needs and problems of low-income youth are also discussed, along with model programs that are targeted to serve inner-city disadvantaged youth, a high proportion of whom are black. Strategies of implementation are proposed for achieving these policies, translating them into effective programs, and disseminating these programs throughout the nation's urban areas. Finally, the concluding section of the chapter addresses the implications of these proposed policies and programs for other disadvantaged minority youth, for the revitalization of American cities, and for the prosperity and stability of the entire society.

Family Assistance Policies

In his excellent book *Common Decency*, noted public policy expert Alvin Schorr (1986) proposes the following five principles that should guide domestic social policies to achieve a truly democratic and just society:

1. Fair shares, or a more equitable distribution of income.
2. Mainstreamed social insurance and social services, or the elimination of means testing for basic income maintenance and adequate social services.
3. A full employment policy to produce sufficient jobs and income for those who are in the labor force.
4. Decentralization of federal government power to increase the flexibility and autonomy of state and local governments.
5. Racial integration to achieve equality of opportunity.

Schorr's proposals for a comprehensive set of policies to improve family functioning and to promote a sense of community in American society involve radical changes in current government social policies and programs which are beyond the scope of this book. However, his proposals reflect the goals outlined by Dr. Solomon in his advocacy for a refundable tax credit to improve the economic status of the working poor and for changes in the AFDC program to peg benefits to increases in the cost of living, to provide work incentives, and to extend coverage to unemployed two-parent families. In addition, Dr. Schorr proposes specific policies that would increase the supply of low-rent housing, improve access and delivery of health care to low-income families, improve educational opportunities for minority youth, and create full employment in the nation's economy. As he points out, all of these policies and programs will reduce poverty and thereby improve the status and stability of minority families who are overrepresented among the nation's poor families. Since nearly half of all black youth begin their lives in poor families, any policies and programs that address their multiple problems will have a direct impact on the health and welfare of these youth.

In 1986 the American Public Welfare Association (APWA) published a significant report, *One Child in Four*, which documented the plight of America's poor families and children. The APWA policy statement, jointly developed with the National Council of State Human Service Administrators, calls for the establishment of a family living standard (FLS), which would include basic family maintenance costs (housing, food, clothing, transportation, etc.)

and would be determined by state-specific standards. Low-income families would receive supplemental cash assistance to make up the difference between their income and the FLS, which would replace the current programs of AFDC, food stamps, and the low-income home energy assistance program (LIHEAP). In addition, this report proposes a range of programs to improve the self-sufficiency of low-income families, including comprehensive, mandatory welfare-to-work programs, child support enforcement, improved education for low-income children, and programs of adolescent pregnancy prevention and support services.

The Children's Defense Fund (CDF) has been a tireless advocate for a comprehensive family policy and has for many years effectively lobbied to improve benefits and services for poor families and children. In her book *Families in Peril: An Agenda for Social Change*, Marian Wright Edelman (1987) outlines a set of far-reaching proposals to improve the economic status of low-income families and to strengthen their capacity to rear their children in healthy environments. These proposals, many of which have been introduced into the legislative agenda of the 100th Congress, include increased family income supports for AFDC recipients and the working poor; extension of Medicaid benefits to all persons below the federal poverty level; extension of health services to low-income families through community health centers; increased funding of maternal and child health block grants; expansion of comprehensive education, training, and employment programs for AFDC recipients; and extension of food stamps to all eligible nonenrolled families as well as to non-AFDC low-income families who need supplemental food benefits (Edelman, 1987; CDF, 1987b).

Senator Daniel P. Moynihan (D-New York), the author of the controversial *Moynihan Report* (1965), has been one of the most vocal proponents of a rational family policy that would replace the current AFDC program. Since the publication of his book *Family and Nation* (1986), he has translated his ideas into legislation called The Family Security Act of 1987, introduced into the Senate as Bill S. #1511 in July 1987. The bill has been proposed as an amendment to Title IV of the Social Security Act, and its major provisions call for a comprehensive program of mandatory employment training for AFDC recipients (except for mothers of children under 3 years old), establishment of paternity and mandatory child support from absent fathers of dependent children, transitional Medicaid and child care benefits for up to 9 months for families who lose their welfare benefits due to an increase in earned income, benefits for all eligible children in one- or two-parent families, reevaluation of benefit needs and payment standards by states once every five years, and authorization of funds for demonstration projects for rehabilitation of housing for homeless welfare families.

In a critical analysis of the Family Security Act, McFate (1987) points out the following major flaws in its provisions:

1. The emphasis on establishing legal paternity in order to collect child support from fathers of out-of-wedlock children is "largely irrelevant to the current population of long-term welfare recipients" (p. 3) because they are often unmarried women who had children as teenagers. Since these women and their partners are likely to have limited education and work experience, mandatory withholding would yield very little income, even in cases where paternity could be established.
2. States should be required to offer educational services to long-term welfare recipients as well as to young mothers under age 22, in order to enhance basic skills in both groups.
3. States should be required to couple education and training programs with mandatory workfare, since studies show that compulsory work programs without these features are not effective in decreasing welfare dependency.
4. This bill does not address the current inequities in the levels of public assistance grants. These disparities would probably increase if up to 10 states are allowed to ask for a waiver in order to receive block grants which would be exempted from federal guidelines and eligibility requirements for up to five years.

Although these proposals range from the more radical and comprehensive reforms of Schorr (1986) and the Children's Defense Fund (1987b), to the more moderate remedies of the American Public Welfare Association (1986), to the more conservative proposals of Moynihan's 1987 legislation, they all share three significant social goals: to improve income supports for poor families and children, to increase the self-sufficiency of welfare recipients through education and employment training programs, and to provide adequate social services, health care, and housing to strengthen family functioning. While these proposals are not based on "racial public policy" as defined by Dr. Solomon, they reflect a public policy approach that is consonant with the goals of a heterogeneous democratic society and politically more feasible to achieve than policies specifically directed to minority groups (see Hamilton and Hamilton, 1986). Quite obviously, the cumulative effect of such policies would significantly improve the status of low-income black families, thereby creating much more stable and nurturant environments for the socialization of black youth.

Policies and Programs Targeted for Disadvantaged Youth

Since the "War on Poverty" initiative of the Johnson administration (1964–1968), a number of federal policy initiatives and programs have targeted disadvantaged youth, with a particular emphasis on urban minority youth. In more recent years, these policies and programs have been supplemented by efforts of state and local governments, foundations, businesses, higher education, nonprofit community organizations, churches, and professional/business/fraternal organizations to address the multiple problems of young black inner-city males in the areas of education, employment, delinquency and drug abuse, teenage parenthood, health and mental health, and high-risk behaviors. We will highlight several of these major policies and programs, evaluate their effectiveness, and suggest recommendations as to their future directions.

Educational Policies and Programs

It became quite fashionable in the 1970s to advocate "excellence" in education and to promote programs to enrich high school curricula, to strengthen college preparatory courses, and to enhance the skills of competent students. By the 1980s it was clear that this focus on educational "excellence" posed a threat to the drive for educational equality in the nation's urban school districts (see College Entrance Examination Board, 1985; NBCDI, 1985). It was also clear that the entire American educational system had a number of severe deficiencies which could not be corrected simply by pouring more money into existing programs. The series of reports on the nation's schools which have been widely publicized in the last five years have all emphasized the particularly critical problems of inner-city schools that serve minority students. While school reform is needed throughout all levels of the public school system, it is important for policymakers to remember that middle-class and well-to-do communities have larger tax bases and a range of resources not available to inner-city school districts. Middle-class families also have the alternative of sending their children to private or parochial schools, while low-income families have no choice but the public schools. There is already a growing "computer gap" between suburban and inner-city schools, which may further the disparity between achievement scores and work-related skills among white and black high school students. Thus, the educational issue needs to be redefined and reframed from simply keeping black youth in school to improving the kinds of schools they are kept in, as well as increasing their educational options while they are there.

If we begin with the assumption that every normal child can learn to read and write, then we can state categorically that our educational system has badly failed black youth, especially young black males. As was pointed out in Chapter 2, performance of black elementary and high school students on several educational measures has remained lower than that of any other ethnic group in the United States. In spite of fairly recent improvements on standardized achievement tests and college entrance examination scores, black male students generally obtain lower grades and achievement scores, have higher suspension and expulsion rates, higher school drop-out rates, and lower rates of college enrollment than black females.

Major Priority Areas. While there are numerous policies and programs that could improve educational achievement and enhance educational opportunities for black youth, several recent national reports on education have identified four major priority areas to be addressed in order to improve education for inner-city urban youth: (1) financing of education; (2) curriculum equality; (3) teacher recruitment, training, and placement; and (4) drop-out prevention programs (see Committee for Economic Development, 1987).

FINANCING OF EDUCATION. Early childhood education programs should be extended and adequately financed to cover all eligible preschool children. A Cornell University study of the long-term effects of 14 different preschool programs made two major conclusions: (1) ". . .most high quality programs were effective in raising achievement and IQ scores and improved self-esteem for the children who participated," and (2) ". . .any well-designed, professionally supervised program to stimulate and socialize infants and young children from poor minority families is effective" (Committee for Economic Development, 1987, p. 33). A major longitudinal evaluation of the Head Start Program in Ypsilanti, Michigan, showed that its participants, as young adults, had better educational, occupational, and social outcomes than nonparticipants (Berrueta-Clement et al., 1984), yet the national program currently reaches fewer than half of the eligible children.

The reductions in federal aid for compensatory education programs should be restored and these programs should be extended to embrace the majority of black youth who are eligible in elementary and high school. Disadvantaged elementary and secondary school student participants in Chapter I Compensatory Education

Programs have significantly improved their test scores, yet only half of the eligible children receive these services (CDF, 1986a). Vocational education programs must be improved to provide students with relevant skills and must be funded at levels to provide equipment, resources, and well-trained teachers who can prepare students for the contemporary labor market. Finally, school desegregation efforts should continue to be enforced and financed in view of the long-term positive educational and economic gains which are achieved by black students who attend integrated schools.

CURRICULUM EQUALITY.   Disproportionate placement of black students in nonacademic and vocational programs results in lower educational achievement and attainment. These practices must be monitored and greater options must be developed for increased access to academically challenging programs.

Blacks are also overrepresented in special education programs where they are often misdiagnosed and incorrectly placed. Since they frequently receive minimal academic instruction and inadequate remedial services, their potential for educational development is vastly diminished and their opportunity for economic mobility is severely impaired.

Students in predominantly black and low-income schools have limited access to microcomputers and to teachers who are trained in their use. If these resources are not equalized across school districts, black and other low-income students will fall further behind educationally and will be further disadvantaged in the labor market.

TEACHER   RECRUITMENT,   TRAINING,   AND   PLACEMENT. Teacher shortages indicate that there will be a 20 percent shortfall in the number of new teachers needed by 1988. This shortage will be partially due to the loss of the most academically able women and minorities to other professions. In order to reverse this trend, efforts must be made to increase teachers' salaries, to create more professional incentives, and to make the schools safe and more hospitable environments, particularly in inner-city neighborhoods.

Teacher training must also be drastically altered to increase teachers' substantive knowledge, their knowledge of normal and abnormal child development, their knowledge of cultural and cognitive differences in attitudes toward education and learning styles, and their abilities to interact with children and parents from culturally different backgrounds in order to teach these young people more effectively.

Placement of teachers should involve sensitivity to the need for positive role models for students in predominantly black schools as well as the need for the more experienced teachers to be assigned to the most difficult school settings, which might entail special incentives such as merit pay or additional teaching aids. Since it is projected that blacks will constitute only 5 percent of all public school teachers by the year 2000, it is crucial that efforts be increased to recruit and train able black college students as teachers so that some will be available for assignment to inner-city schools.

DROP-OUT PREVENTION PROGRAMS.   The Children's Defense Fund (1986a) has proposed a Dropout Prevention and Recovery Act, which would establish a uniform national reporting system for keeping accurate records of dropouts and truants. It would also support projects for identifying potential dropouts to keep them in school and projects for reenrolling students who have already dropped out of school. Comprehensive services are needed for emotionally troubled and academically deficient youth who are particularly at risk for dropping out, including tutoring, psychological services, family counseling, and income-support programs.

Work-study programs have been found especially effective in reducing drop-out rates among low-income minority youth, who often leave school prematurely in order to supplement family income or support a pregnant girlfriend. Cooperation with local businesses to provide part-time job opportunities targeted to this group would also result in lower drop-out rates.

Parental participation in all aspects of the educational system has been shown to be an effective tool in decreasing drop-out rates and increasing satisfaction with the schools, especially among minority parents. Parents should be involved with teachers and administrators in devising a flexible but challenging curriculum, increasing incentives for academic achievement, obtaining improved funding and resources, and increasing accountability for standards of excellence for both teachers and students.

Federal and State Efforts to Improve Inner-City Schools.   In addition to these major priority areas just listed, funds should be increased for the federal Chapter I Program, which provides remedial instruction in reading, mathematics, and other basic subjects for disadvantaged students in elementary and secondary schools. This program, which reaches only about 50 percent of those youth who are eligible, has improved test scores of participating students and has proven to be both successful and cost-effective (CDF, 1987b).

Increased funds are also needed to support effective schools in urban areas (Edmonds, 1979). The conditions of inner-city schools are deplorable, no matter what criterion is used. Yet a few examplary schools manage to educate children and inspire them to go to college or trade school in spite of depressed community conditions. As Drs. Reed and Solomon have noted, these schools are characterized by strong administrators, dedicated teachers, effective discipline, high expectations for student performance, and significant parent involvement. Effective inner-city schools also offer a range of innovative programs to expose students to role models, career options, and alternative value systems (see Comer, 1980). Funding of such model schools should be coupled with continued support of desegregation efforts in inner-city schools, since a large body of research has demonstrated that black students perform better in integrated school settings where there are ethnically and socioeconomically diverse student bodies. Magnet schools, which draw students from many areas of the city, as well as city-suburb transfer plans, have shown promise in increasing academic achievement of minority youth. School districts are more likely to develop such plans if they can obtain federal funds for transportation and other increased costs.

Several drop-out prevention bills have been introduced into the 100th Congress, including the School Dropout Demonstration Act of 1987, the School Dropout Retention and Recovery Act of 1987, and the School Dropout Demonstration Assistance Act of 1987. A significant feature of all of these bills is the provision of a variety of educational, psychological, and social support services for youth who are at high risk for failing or dropping out of school.

Many national and local foundations have financed programs in early education, compensatory education, and enrichment programs for inner-city youth, including the Carnegie Foundation, the Ford Foundation, the Rockefeller Foundation, the Robert Wood Johnson Foundation, and others.

Corporations and small businesses have developed national initiatives to improve inner-city schools through such groups as the National Alliance for Business, the Private Industry Council, and the Committee for Economic Development, which in 1985 published the report "Investing in Our Children: Business and the Public Schools."

In order to reinforce these widespread efforts to improve urban schools, parents, civic organizations, and churches in the black community should collaborate on recruiting volunteer aides to assist in classrooms, recruiting college students and retired persons to serve as tutors in after-school programs, and providing safe and supervised facilities for after-school enrichment programs. Black churches are excellent resources for recruiting volunteers, for providing facilities for after-school, weekend, and summer educational programs, and for raising funds for college scholarships and special enrichment classes for low-income black youth.

Such community efforts could be directed toward creating community learning centers, which would not only provide tutoring and enrichment activities for students but would also recruit school dropouts for alternative educational programs. Local banks might provide low-interest loans to underwrite the initial costs of such centers, which could be financed on an ongoing basis through business contributions, local government subsidies, and foundation grants.

A more radical proposal has been advanced by Dr. Samuel Proctor, a prominent black clergyman and educator, who has advocated the establishment of a national system of youth academies for disadvantaged inner-city youth who are failing in school and have no work skills. These academies would be located on unused military bases and would offer a combination of academic, vocational, and cultural subjects. By removing students from their ghetto environments, these academies would provide a more benign setting, emphasizing self-discipline, useful skills, and self-development. As Proctor (1987) notes about the multiple problems of these unsocialized youth, "We need an intervention—a practical, unambiguous, morally sound, educational functional approach that will break this lock-step that will vault one generation out of the morass of failure and futility, and give us a chance to engender a new strain" (p. 10).

Finally, federal loan and grant-in-aid programs for low-income youth to attend college should be increased rather than decreased. The recent drop in college enrollment of black students has been partially attributed to a reduction in financial aid as well as to a perception that colleges and universities are not as committed to affirmative action programs (Chronicle of Higher Education, 1987). Education has been the traditional route out of poverty for all minority groups, yet this route is being systematically closed off for today's black youth, even if they are sufficiently motivated to qualify for college admission. Without federal government assistance in the form of Pell grants and subsidized student loans, many black youth (and particularly black males) will be denied the opportunity for a college education and the potential resulting benefits of increased career options, higher income, and social mobility.

In summary, the policies which are required to provide educational opportunities for black youth can be viewed as investment strategies in human capital development and should be planned and implemented in three broad areas, as recently recommended by the Committee on Economic Development (1987): "(1) prevention through early intervention—programs that focus on children from birth to age five and on teenagers who are most at risk of premature parenthood; (2) restructuring the foundations of education—changes that are needed in the structure, staffing, management and financing of schools; and (3) retention and reentry—targeted programs that combine comprehensive educational, employment, health and social services for students still in school and for dropouts" (p. x). As the report graphically points out, each dollar spent now to prevent educational failure will actually save $4.75 in the cost of remedial education, welfare, and crime in the future (Committee on Economic Development, 1987).

Model Educational Programs. In addition to current federal and state efforts to fund programs of remedial education, improve and modernize programs of vocational education, develop innovative drop-out prevention programs, and promote school-to-work transition programs, there are a number of local programs sponsored by businesses, foundations, and nonprofit community organizations that are designed to motivate inner-city youth to complete high school and to obtain employable skills. One such program is the Cities in Schools Program, sponsored by a national nonprofit organization that brings together local schools, businesses, and government agencies in cities like Atlanta, Georgia, to provide a range of services, including an alternative school site, tutoring, counseling, health, and social services in order to prevent high-risk youth from dropping out. The National Urban League also has developed an Education Initiative Program in cities like Seattle, Washington, where the local Urban League Chapter signed a 1986 "Memorandum of Cooperation" with the Seattle public schools to mobilize the entire community in increasing the academic achievement of black and other minority students in the system.

The National Alliance for Business and the Private Industry Council have both encouraged local businesses to form partnerships with schools in order to provide them with resources (books, computers, language labs), technical assistance (computer instruction, field trips, science fairs), and volunteer personnel (tutors, mentors, etc.). Corporations such as the American Can Company and Xerox have given their employees release time to provide expertise to inner-city schools. In Fairfax, Virginia, a local business group has set up a foundation to provide tutoring, summer jobs, and counseling to a group of black seventh graders, who are guaranteed admission and complete financial aid to Virginia Polytechnic Institute and State Univeristy if they stay in the program for five years and can meet the college admissions requirements.

A number of national foundations have funded innovative demonstration projects in inner-city schools, with several goals, including drop-out prevention, higher achievement levels, and increasing the number of graduates entering college. The ABC Program (A Better Chance), originally funded by the Charles Merrill Foundation, identifies gifted minority youth in junior high school, recruits them for private high schools (primarily on the East Coast), and provides them with some supportive services until they graduate.

The New York City Board of Education contracts with community-based organizations to assist with drop-out prevention programs. An excellent example of a multiservice, community-based project is the DOME Project, which operates alternative classrooms for severely disruptive students in one district, provides truancy prevention services for the district's middle schools, and offers a variety of social, psychological, and health services to students and their families.

Many universities and colleges located in urban areas now have volunteer service programs in which students can frequently obtain credit for serving as tutors and teachers' aides in inner-city schools. Participating black students at universities such as Harvard, Yale, Brown, University of Chicago, University of California at Berkeley, Southern University, and Stanford also serve as role models and mentors to black males in fatherless families, providing them with cultural, recreational, and social experiences that offer them an alternative view of the world and a vision of hitherto unknown career options.

Finally, many black churches are reclaiming their traditional role in educating black youth for responsible roles in the community. Urban churches of all denominations are recruiting members and professionals in the community for a number of youth programs, ranging from tutoring to courses in black history and culture. They are donating their facilities for after-school enrichment courses and remedial instruction, art and music lessons, summer school, and weekend study centers. Such programs can be found in large churches like the Abyssinnia Baptist Church in New York, the Shiloh Baptist Church in Washington, D.C., and the Allen Temple Church in Oakland, California, and in smaller churches like the Dixwell Avenue Congregational Church in New Haven, Connecticut, and the Radcliffe Presbyterian Church in Atlanta, Georgia.

Employment Policies and Programs

As was pointed out in Chapter 3, three of the major factors in the high unemployment rate of black youth are lack of education and training, structural changes in the urban labor market, and lack of access to transportation to the new job markets. In addition to black youths' limited exposure to the world of work, they frequently are not exposed to adult male role models who are gainfully employed. Thus, they are doubly handicapped in developing appropriate attitudes toward work, good work habits, and specific skills that would make them attractive to employers. To remedy this situation and to facilitate the transition of black youth from school to work, the federal government should adopt monetary and fiscal policies to promote a *full employment policy*, which would create a range of new jobs and ultimately increase youth employment rates for minorities as well as all other groups. However, such an overall policy will be more effective for youth who already possess minimum skills and are able to find transportation to these jobs. "Hardcore" unemployed youth will also need special programs of job training and transportation subsidies in order to enter the job market. Thus, funds must be made available for job training programs and job relocation funds for those young adults willing to move to areas of high employment, and transportation subsidies to provide mass transit for inner-city residents to reach jobs outside of central cities.

Existing Employment Programs. Some federally funded programs which have attempted—some with more success than others—to increase the rates of employment of young black males and improve their attachment to the labor force are briefly described below.

SCHOOL-TO-WORK TRANSITION PROGRAMS. These include a variety of programs involving a collaboration between schools and businesses to facilitate the progression from the classroom to the work setting. Two federally funded projects that have achieved favorable results with minority youth are the School-to-Work Transition Project, which provided five to ten hours of job-related instruction weekly during the school year in 11th and 12th grades, and the Job Track Project, which consisted of two days of instruction and three days of support services, including clerical skills and counseling, to promote students' entry-level skills, attitudes, and information (Congressional Budget Office, 1982).

THE JOB TRAINING PARTNERSHIP ACT (JTPA). The Job Training Partnership Act, which shifts job placement for disadvantaged youth from the public to the private sector, has provided training for only 4 percent of those eligible. Critics have noted that this act was funded at a lower level than CETA, and that employers were training those workers who were most likely to be quickly employed rather than those who were "most in need." Funds for supportive services must be restored, and the selection of trainees must be more closely monitored in order to increase this program's usefulness to black youth. The budget for the Summer Youth Employment Program included in this act should also be substantially increased to provide more summer jobs for inner-city youth who have few options for summer employment.

THE JOB CORPS.   The Job Corps should not be eliminated, since it provides education and training for a group of black youth who are severely educationally and economically disadvantaged. A combination of remedial education and skills training has resulted in substantial gains in earnings and employment for this group.

Since it is cheaper to rehabilitate black youth in the Job Corps than to send them to prison or to subsidize the hidden costs of their unemployment, this program should be strengthened rather than reduced. States should sponsor youth employment services to provide job counseling and job referral for all youth, with specialized services for low-income minority youth. States should also sponsor Youth Conservation Corps, which would supplement Job Corps Programs and would provide remedial education and basic job skills, and involve black youth in meaningful community service.

In addition, an Urban Service Corps, modeled on the Peace Corps and Vista, would be a constructive alternative to military service for many black youth and would have the additional benefit of improving the city neighborhoods, parks, and facilities where these youth live.

THE TARGETED JOBS TAX CREDIT PROGRAM.   The Targeted Jobs Tax Credit Program has not been very successful in increasing the employment of black youth. Although employers can write off 85 percent of the wages for a disadvantaged youth, employers actually claimed credits for fewer than 3 percent of newly hired teens who were eligible, and one study found that 82 percent of the youths enrolled would have been hired without the subsidy, suggesting an employer preference for middle-class youth (Congressional Budget Office, 1982).

Proposed Employment Programs.   To supplement these federal programs, the Children's Defense Fund (1987b) has proposed the establishment of "youth opportunity accounts," which would provide high-risk teenagers with credits toward some type of education, training, or work in exchange for their achievement of an educational goal or involvement in community service.

Business and industry are also developing urban programs to provide part-time and summer employment to disadvantaged youth to teach them marketable skills and assist them in making the transition from school to work. The Private Industry Council has been in the forefront of developing such programs, providing thousands of jobs for minority youth in cities such as Boston, New York, and San Francisco. Many corporate leaders now recognize the serious problems of preparing skilled workers for the labor force of the 21st century, so they are cooperating with the schools and civic groups to develop innovative solutions to prevent drop-outs and to engage young black males in the labor force.

In addition, business executives can cooperate with inner-city schools to sponsor job fairs, career exploration courses, job search workshops, and work study programs. Most urban black teens are unfamiliar with the nuts and bolts of successful job hunting— information which middle-class youth learn from their parents and older siblings—for example, how to prepare a resume, how to dress appropriately for an interview, how to negotiate terms of employment, how to project a positive attitude, and how to match interests and talents to available jobs. Since black teens also usually lack the informal network of contacts and knowledge about the world of work, these in-school job-related activities will provide them with this essential information.

At the local community level, corporations, small businesses, professional associations, and labor unions should develop mentor programs in partnership with local schools, as has been successfully initiated in cities like Chicago, Boston, and Washington, D.C. While these mentor programs vary in structure, their goals and activities are remarkably similar in that they either provide re-sources for schools (e.g., computers, audiovisual equipment, ma-chine shop equipment, language lab facilities, etc.) and/or mentors who are paired with promising students in need of additional tutoring or social support. For many of these students, these mentors serve as excellent role models, big sisters or brothers, tutors, and confidantes. It is particularly important to recruit more adult black males as mentors, since so many young inner-city black men do not have fathers to provide them with career advice, support, and constructive work habits and attitudes. Black profes-sional organizations, fraternities, small business proprietors, and union members might concentrate more efforts in this direction in conjunction with their expressed concerns about the problems of black youth and the stresses of the black family. Annual scholarship awards are commendable but they actually reach a very small segment of disadvantaged youth. If more time and money were directly invested in providing for these black youth, these efforts would have a much more significant and long-range benefit to the black community and to the wider society than the time and money currently invested in elaborate conventions and expensive social activities regularly sponsored by these organizations.

Finally, there have been strong pressures for the federal government to institute a subminimum wage for teenage workers. Proponents of this proposal argue that it would provide an incentive for employers to hire unskilled youth and at the same time reduce competition for adult jobs, but opponents argue that a lower wage would not substantially increase youth employment, would reduce earnings of disadvantaged youth, and perhaps reduce their incentive to work. As Larson has noted, a subminimum wage would have a particularly negative impact on minority youth, who already earn less income when they are employable and who would have even less incentive to work for lower wages. Additionally, such a wage structure would further increase the earnings gap between low-income black youth and middle-income white youth, who are more likely to obtain jobs in industries willing to pay them higher wages—for example, clerical and technical jobs versus unskilled and service jobs.

It is really ironic that this proposal for a subminimum wage for teenage workers who are increasingly represented by nonwhites has been so passionately advocated at the same time that premium salaries of $50,000 to $65,000 are offered by the nation's top corporations and law firms to recent graduates of law and business schools, who are predominantly white. Of course, these exorbitant recruiting costs and salaries are passed on in higher costs to clients or in higher prices to consumers for the products. Thus, middle-class taxpayers are really subsidizing these excessive salaries, as well as paying proportionately more of the federal tax bill because they have fewer legitimate deductions (*San Francisco Chronicle*, 1987). If a similar analysis is applied to the subminimum wage, it is clear that such a policy would ultimately benefit middle-class employers who would receive higher profits at the expense of low-income youth, who would not only have lower earnings but would also have less bargaining power for higher earnings in subsequent jobs. In fact, the minimum wage should be *increased* in order to reflect chronic inflation which has reduced the real value of the dollar in recent years. Inflation has resulted in a significant decline in real earnings for all youth, but has been particularly severe for black youth who have such limited employment options.

From 1973 to 1985, the number of black male high school dropouts in their early 20s who did not earn any (legitimate) income increased from 12 percent to 43 percent (*Time*, 1987). This nation simply cannot afford to tolerate this unconscionable situation in which an ever-expanding pool of young black males will be both uneducated and unemployed, without any skills to become economically self-sufficient.

Model Employment Programs.   There are some promising programs aimed at rectifying the employment problem, but they have only begun to scratch the surface. Since the Job Training Partnership Act has not proven to be an effective vehicle for recruiting and training the most disadvantaged youth into the job market, the federal government initiated a special demonstration project called JOBSTART in 1985 to target low-income high school dropouts (Auspos and Price, 1987). As of January 1987, the program was operating in 15 sites, sponsored by community-based organizations, community colleges, and adult vocational schools, or nonresidential components of Job Corps Centers. JOBSTART provides instruction in basic skills and occupational skills, a range of support services, and job development and placement assistance. While this program faces some special challenges in recruitment, retention, and successful job placement of disadvantaged dropouts, it offers one of the most comprehensive and well-designed plans to increase the employability of young black males who have failed in all the traditional systems.

The Summer Training and Education Program (STEP) is a demonstration project designed by Public/Private Ventures, a national nonprofit organization, and funded by public funds from the federal Summer Youth Employment Program (SYEP) and local governments. Located in five cities (Boston, Seattle, Portland, San Diego, and Fresno, California), this project recruits low-income youth with significant educational deficiencies for an intensive summer program of remedial education in reading and math, work experience, life planning, and social support. Evaluation of this program has not only shown increased academic gains but also more knowledge about contraception, sexually responsible behavior, and the consequences of early parenthood among the participants (CDF, 1986c).

Conservation Corps and Urban Service Corps have also been effective in preparing inner-city youth for the world of work. Since 1983, the East Bay Conservation Corps in Oakland, California, has provided a year-round program for out-of-school disadvantaged inner-city youth ages 18–24, and a summer program for in-school youth ages 15–21. The predominantly black male corps members participate in remedial education, a structured work experience, and peer support groups, as well as workshops designed to enhance their self-esteem, social skills, and career options. This program is supported by federal summer youth employment funds, foundation grants, and corporate donations. Other conservation and urban service corps, which may be supported by a combination of federal, state, and local funds, afford an excellent opportunity to prepare these youth for the labor market, while simultaneously involving them in useful conservation and community development projects.

The Private Industry Council was the guiding force behind the "Boston Compact," an innovative partnership of public schools and private businesses which offers graduates of local high schools priority consideration for jobs. Intended to motivate potential dropouts to remain in school and to obtain minimum job skills, this compact has inspired similar models in cities like Minneapolis, San Antonio, and Hartford, Connecticut. While the drop-out rate in Boston schools has not been substantially reduced since the program was initiated in 1982, the superintendent of schools is currently collaborating with business and community leaders to reorganize the schools, create more alternative educational programs, increase the involvement of teachers, students, and parents in innovative efforts, and broaden the scope of the program to include middle schools and community organizations (Committee for Economic Development, 1987).

In New York City, a consortium of business and industrial leaders founded the New York City Partnership, Inc., which has sponsored a very successful summer jobs program since 1981, generating nearly 140,000 jobs for the city's 16–21-year-old disadvantaged youth (*Report to the New York City Partnership*, 1987).

Another effective partnership between the public schools and local business leaders is the Jobs for America's Graduates Program, in which approximately 10,000 low-income youth in 10 states have participated. This program facilitates the transition of high school graduates from school to work with such features as preemployment counseling, modeling of work-related skills, and job placement services.

Finally, it has been proposed that industries which employ skilled labor should establish apprenticeship programs for low-income youth, as have been developed in some European countries (CDF, 1987a). Such apprenticeships, which would have to be negotiated with the labor unions, would provide skilled training and occupational opportunities to noncollege-bound youth, and at the same time would increase the supply of skilled manpower and the earnings capacity of these young men, both of which would benefit the national economy.

Delinquency Prevention and Substance Abuse Prevention

The links between dropping out of school, unemployment, delinquency, and drug abuse have been documented repeatedly throughout this book. Results of studies by Dembo and Brunswick described in Chapters 4 and 5 suggest that strategies of primary prevention of delinquency and substance abuse among black youth should be directed toward maintaining teens in school and securing regular employment for those who are not in school. Other approaches that might prove to be effective if they are aimed at the appropriate target groups, adequately financed, and supported by a broad coalition of community groups should all reinforce these dual goals.

On the federal level, increased funding is needed for the prevention and rehabilitation projects authorized by the Juvenile Justice and Delinquency Prevention Act. As the recent *Children's Defense Fund Budget* (CDF, 1986a) noted, while there are a number of programs designed for delinquency-prone youth, all of these programs are threatened with severe funding cutbacks. In addition to the Child and Adolescent Service System Program (CASSP), which is aimed at improving the coordination among the child welfare, juvenile justice, mental health, and special education systems, other significant delinquency-prevention features are included in the Runaway and Homeless Youth Act, the Adoption Assistance and Child Welfare Act, and the Child Abuse Prevention and Treatment Act. These programs should be strengthened and expanded rather than reduced or eliminated in the current administration's efforts to cut social programs.

Federal funds for the Runaway and Homeless Youth Program, which provides emergency services and temporary housing to youth who run away or are pushed out of their families for a variety of reasons, should also be increased, particularly since homeless black youth are especially vulnerable to sexual exploitation, delinquency, and substance abuse.

States such as Florida, Kentucky, and Maryland have recently revamped their juvenile justice systems, increased funds for innovative programs of prevention and early intervention, and provided comprehensive services to high-risk, predelinquent teens (CDF, 1986a).

Delinquency Prevention. Approaches to black delinquents through the cooperative efforts of local agencies, businesses, and community groups must also be conceptualized in terms of primary and secondary prevention. Evaluation studies of preventive approaches to delinquency have generally indicated that most programs are ineffective for a variety of reasons, including a failure to specify the target population, failure to match treatment to type of delinquent, and failure to control for variables such as type of offense, age, SES and community support system (Thornton, James, and Doerner, 1982). Since black delinquents tend to be overrepresented among the category of socialized or subcultural delinquents (Gibbs, 1982), primary prevention efforts should be aimed at modifying their immediate environments to provide more recreational and cultural after-school and weekend activities and to coordinate efforts to reduce the school drop-out rate and the youth unemployment rate (Lewis, 1978). Black churches should be encouraged to donate their facilities and enlist their retired members as volunteer tutors, child-care workers, youth camp leaders, and counselors. It seems quite ironic that publicly funded recreational and cultural programs are usually available for youth in suburban middle-class communities, while few such programs or even adequate facilities are available for inner-city youth, who are forced to play in trash-littered lots, dangerous city streets, and abandoned buildings.

Secondary prevention or early intervention efforts should focus on the establishment of more diversion programs operated by youth service organizations within the community that could prevent the premature labeling and stigmatization as "delinquent" of those with first-time minor offenses. In addition, a range of comprehensive services, such as those offered by public and private agencies in Kentucky, must be available to the heterogeneous population of black delinquents—for example, prevention of truancy; home-based social and rehabilitative services for the delinquents and their families; day treatment programs which involve remedial education, counseling, and recreation; foster care for abused or neglected children; and residential treatment facilities for more seriously delinquent and disturbed youth (Lewis, 1978). If these approaches are going to be effective with black delinquents, they must be planned in conjunction with black mental health and social welfare professionals and community leaders, they must take into account the sociocultural values and indigenous institutions of the black community, and they must be staffed by people who are sensitive to those values and realities.

Substance Abuse Prevention. Substance abuse education programs should be introduced in inner-city elementary schools in recognition of children's early exposure to drugs in these communities. Effective drug prevention approaches for adolescents have included peer counseling, parent involvement, and cooperation among schools, social agencies, and the juvenile justice system. In order to stem the tide of substance abuse among black youth, such programs must take into account the social context, the subcultural values, and the realities of the inner city, where access to alcohol and drugs and patterns of drug use differ from those of middle-class communities.

Community groups can establish neighborhood "watch groups" to promote greater concern for the safety and welfare of children and adolescents and anonymous "hot lines" for reporting drug dealers and other illegal activities. Such groups can also involve black youth in community clean-up campaigns, escort services for the elderly, and constructive alternatives to lounging on street corners. Volunteer neighborhood associations could also set up community crime watch patrols, as have been initiated in several eastern and southern cities. While these crime watch patrols should avoid assuming the role of the police, they can make residents more aware of security precautions, report suspicious persons and activities to the police, and create an environment where criminal activity is neither rationalized nor reinforced.

Finally, as Brunswick has noted, drug abuse is not just a deviant activity, it is also a life-style and an industry. Any efforts to reduce the incidence of drug abuse in urban ghettos must be accompanied by a concerted community attack against the "hustling" life-style, with its rejection of the middle-class work ethic and its glorification of the ethos of hedonism, as well as a massive legal offensive against drugs as an underground industry. Unless the black community is willing to recognize the terrible toll of drugs and crime-related activities on all of its citizens and institutions and can confront the drug dealers, petty thieves, pimps, and prostitutes who openly ply their trade on street corners, in project hallways, and in alley "shooting galleries," legal efforts imposed externally and carried out sporadically will be inadequate and ineffective.

Programs to prevent delinquency and substance abuse must be closely tied to efforts to prevent school dropouts and to increase employment rates among young black males. Most experts would agree that these efforts, combined with a comprehensive set of policies to strengthen the functioning of low-income black families, form the basic blocks of primary prevention of delinquency and antisocial behaviors.

Model Delinquency Prevention Programs.   Programs that emphasize the development of self-sufficiency and enhance self-esteem contribute to lower rates of delinquency and substance abuse among black youth. Such model programs are supported by the Eisenhower Foundation, which funds community crime prevention programs in cities like Baltimore, Cleveland, Miami, Newark, and

Philadelphia (Polsky, 1986). Most of these demonstration projects target high-risk disadvantaged high school dropouts, predominantly minority males. One example is the Juvenile Awareness Education Program, which operates the House of Umoja in New Castle, Delaware, modeled after a successful program in Philadelphia. This program provides remedial education, life-skills training, employment skills, and counseling, as well as outreach efforts to reduce gang violence and improve conflict resolution techniques.

Some programs target the hard-core dropouts with a previous history of delinquency or drug abuse—those who have essentially been labeled as hopeless by the schools and other agencies. Several comprehensive programs in Washington, D.C., have been particularly effective in addressing this difficult group of black youth. "City Lights," for example, is a program that offers a range of innovative day treatment programs to disturbed and disadvantaged teens who participate in educational and therapeutic activities structured to help them continue to live in the community (Tolmach, 1985). The Junior Citizens Corps is a youth agency that serves delinquent and emotionally troubled black youth ages 10–19 through a variety of community-based programs, including job counseling and referral, social rehabilitation, remedial education, social services, and youth leadership training. These programs could be replicated in other inner-city communities where traditional programs have failed.

Finally, any programs of secondary or tertiary prevention (rehabilitation) for black delinquents should be linked to the improvement of educational skills and vocational training, since these types of programs have generally had the most positive outcomes and, particularly for this group, are more likely to attack the underlying socioeconomic causes of their antisocial behavior.

Model Drug Prevention Programs.   In terms of primary prevention, a recent review of evaluations of 127 drug abuse prevention programs concluded that these programs "produced only minor effects on drug use behavior and attitudes," with the 8 most effective programs designed with peer or process orientations rather than an information-only approach. Moreover, current programs of drug education, like sex education, rarely take into account ethnic differences in attitudes, usage patterns, and response to treatment (Beschner and Friedman, 1986; Nelson et al., 1974; Paton and Kandel, 1978). Such programs must also take into account the social context, values, and realities of the inner-city teenager's life-style, which are very different than those of suburban white middle-class youth. Urban black youth are exposed earlier to a variety of drugs, may be involved at an early age as "runners" or "spotters" or even drug dealers, and tend to accept the pervasive presence of drugs as a fact of community life. Most current high school drug education programs fail to recognize that inner-city youth usually have an earlier exposure and greater level of sophistication about drugs than middle-class suburban youth. To be effective, drug education and prevention programs must involve the cooperation of parents and community leaders, as well as peer counselors, all of whom must not only be willing to inform these teens about the dangers of drug abuse but also to set up supportive peer groups who will make mutual contracts to avoid drugs and will also develop alternative forms of socializing. Parents must be willing to monitor the behavior and moods of their children, to confront them about suspicious friends and activities, and to give them positive reinforcement for staying "clean." Moreover, parents themselves must be supported and reinforced by community leaders who are willing to take a public stance against drug dealing and drug use in the black community and by improved police surveillance and enforcement.

Community health centers and school-based clinics that offer comprehensive health care to black adolescents are important in that they provide education, counseling, and treatment for substance abuse. In communities like Kansas City, where comprehensive health clinics are located in the public high schools, use of alcohol and marijuana decreased in the first two years of clinic operation (CDF, 1986b).

Multiservice programs which combine drug and alcohol abuse education and treatment programs with health, mental health, education, employment, vocational counseling, and referral services are excellent approaches to prevention and early intervention. Programs such as "The Door" in New York City offer a range of services to low-income and minority youth ages 12–20; these programs, which are available after school and in the evenings and are free or at low cost (CDF, 1986c), offer a holistic approach toward the physical, emotional, social, and intellectual needs of youth—a perspective that is often lacking in substance abuse programs, but one that is particularly appropriate for black youth.

With regard to secondary and tertiary prevention, most federally funded drug counseling and rehabilitation programs are aimed at older youth and at the harder drugs such as cocaine and heroin. However, black children in the inner city are exposed to drugs at increasingly younger ages, so more locally sponsored community programs need to be developed with a focus on early intervention and prevention of long-term drug abuse. Since the preadolescent group is a somewhat more captive audience in elementary and junior high schools, these programs could effectively utilize parents and volunteers as well as people from youth organizations such as Boy Scouts and Girl Scouts, Little League and other team sports, and other recreational and cultural groups. Supervised youth activities could also serve as a vehicle for informal drug education and prevention programs involving parents and youth leaders in approaches specifically tailored to the attitudes and behaviors of this target group of teenagers. Such ongoing programs would be particularly effective in communities where schedules of intermittent reinforcement are necessary for many adolescents to maintain drug-free behavior.

Providing decent recreational facilities and sports equipment to black youth community organizations is a way of offering black adolescents an alternative to street life. Many of these youth live in neighborhoods without parks and pools, and their families cannot afford equipment for sports like tennis and hockey. More organized sports and recreational activities, particularly on weekends and in summer months, would probably contribute to a reduction in street crime. Churches could also donate facilities to be used for some of these youth activities. Churches are also a source from which older youth could be recruited for volunteer activities with younger children and elderly church members who are in need of services. Thus, volunteer service could be a component of youth development and delinquency prevention.

Finally, blacks as individual citizens must be willing to use anonymous hotlines and other measures to report known drug dealers and criminal activity in their neighborhoods. The only way that inner-city areas will ever be restored to any semblance of order and decency is for blacks to act aggressively to rid their communities of the criminals and drug dealers who are parasites, insidiously destroying the bodies, minds, and souls of black youth.

Teenage Parenthood

In Chapter 6, Connors reviews findings that teenage fathers are more likely to drop out of school or attain fewer years of education and a lower occupational status, to earn lower wages, and to have more spells of unemployment. Moreover, when compared with their peers who have not fathered children, they are also more likely to have larger families and to experience unstable marriages. Although most teenage pregnancy prevention efforts have been aimed at adolescent females, as noted in Chapter 6, it is imperative to focus attention on black males in order to reduce the rates of out-of-wedlock pregnancy and paternity in this population.

Several recent analyses have suggested that there is a strong correlation between unwed fatherhood and unemployment for young black men—that is, as unemployment rates increase, marriage rates decrease without a concomitant decrease in rates of childbearing among young black couples (Wilson and Neckerman, 1984; CDF, 1987a). The economic and social consequences of teenage parenthood for black youth have been clearly delineated in numerous studies, but the indirect costs to the black community are less obvious. It has been predicted that 94 percent of black children born in 1980 will spend the majority of their childhood until age 18 in a single-parent, female-headed household (Hofferth, 1985). If this prediction is accurate, it will ensure a generation of black youth who will grow up in fatherless families, many on welfare, deprived of constructive male role models, and further isolated from the norms of mainstream middle-class society.

Senator Moynihan's proposed Family Security Act requires unwed mothers on AFDC to identify the fathers of their children so the government can collect child-support payments and thus reduce the overall costs of the welfare program. Although this idea has merit in terms of reinforcing the notion of paternal responsibility, it is doubtful that it will generate any appreciable funds from young black fathers, many of whom are unemployed. Another feature of this same bill which holds more promise of success is the proposal to extend education and training benefits to unemployed young men who are living with their families.

Since declining rates of employment and income among young black males are related to declining rates of marriage among young black females, it seems reasonable to assume that increased training of these men would improve their employment prospects and, correspondingly, provide incentives for them to marry and form families.

Alternatively, improved educational and employment opportunities would presumably motivate young black males to postpone paternity or at least to marry in the event their partners become pregnant. However, this is only one part of the problem of out-of-wedlock births to black youth. Research also indicates that low-income black youth have negative attitudes toward contraception, and males, particularly, tend to equate paternity with masculinity. Fathering children may very well be one of the few sources of self-esteem and status available to young black males who, unemployed and uncommitted, do not derive their major source of satisfaction and status from the world of work, the preserve of the white male. Unfortunately, young black males fail to understand that paternity without responsibility deprives them of any significant role in society.

Model Teenage Pregnancy, Prevention, and Parenting Programs. Efforts to postpone paternity among black males must be tied to efforts to provide them not only with knowledge of contraception but also with tangible sources of self-esteem and status in the wider society. Sex education programs in grades K-12 must be designed to provide accurate and developmentally appropriate information to males as well as females. The Family Life Education Program (FLEP), recently approved by the New York State Department of Education, provides a flexible curriculum that can be adapted to local community needs, values, and interests. Early indications are that teenage pregnancy rates have dropped in districts which implemented this program.

Family planning and contraceptive services should be easily accessible, available, and free or very inexpensive in inner-city areas. Communities like St. Paul, Minnesota, which have set up comprehensive teen health clinics in the junior and senior high schools, have found them effective in reducing pregnancy rates. Peer counseling about sexual attitudes and behaviors can also be included in schools as well as in youth groups, athletic teams, camps, and boys clubs.

Successful programs have recognized this connection and have linked information on sexuality and family planning with self-esteem building, job counseling, health, and recreational activities. Examples of such programs are the Young Men's Clinic Center at Presbyterian Hospital in New York City, the Multi-Service Family Life and Sex Education Program of the Children's Aid Society in New York City, Family Focus Community Family Center in Evanston, Illinois, and the Teen Services Program of Grady Memorial Hospital in Atlanta, Georgia (CDF, 1986b).

The National Urban League has initiated an "Adolescent Male Sexual Responsibility Project" through its local affiliates. This program will involve young black males in projects to increase their knowledge of family planning as well as to promote more responsible attitudes in their sexual relationships.

Black churches must begin to tackle the teenage pregnancy problem directly through pastoral sermons and youth programs on responsible sexual attitudes, values, and behaviors and, indirectly, through support of sex education and teen health clinics in the schools, family planning clinics in the community, and constructive and well-designed programs on related topics sponsored by local community organizations. One demonstration project in a Washington, D.C., black church involves pairing adult males to serve as counselors and role models to young males in the neighborhood with the goal of delaying sexual activity and promoting sexual responsibility.

The National Council of Negro Women and the major black fraternities and sororities have also made sexual responsibility a high priority on their national agendas. These groups have been cooperating with the Children's Defense Fund in its efforts to alert the black community to the damaging consequences of teenage parenthood and to develop programs of primary prevention of out-of-wedlock pregnancy as well as early intervention to strengthen parenting skills and economic self-sufficiency of young parents (CDF, 1986b, 1986c, 1986d, 1987a).

Finally, teen parenting programs should encourage the participation of young fathers as well as mothers in order to increase their involvement with their children and to develop a sense of shared responsibility for their children's welfare. The Teenage Pregnancy and Parenting Program sponsored by the San Francisco General Hospital offers comprehensive services to teen fathers, including counseling, job referral, and follow-up support services.

Health and Mental Health

In addition to short-range changes in Medicaid and long-range changes in a comprehensive national health system, Medicaid health services should be extended to all children ages 5–18 in low-income families, and to all youth ages 18–21 who are in school, in job training programs, or working. This extended coverage will assure minimum levels of health care for nearly all black children and youth up to age 21.

Minnesota was the first state to provide comprehensive outpatient health care insurance coverage for children from birth to age 6 whose families had incomes up to 185 percent of the federal poverty level. Through passage of the "Right Start" health insurance program for the working poor, the state of Minnesota offers coverage to families whose income makes them ineligible for Medicaid benefits or who cannot afford private coverage. For those low-income youth 21–24 in the labor force, a proposal for all employers to provide health insurance for their employees, as has been proposed in the state of Massachusetts, provides another model of insuring the working poor (*New York Times*, 1987).

Health clinics and special teen clinics located at school sites are particularly important in reaching inner-city black youth with preventive care, early detection of health problems, and low-cost treatment of health problems. These programs should receive additional funding through the Maternal and Child Health block grants to the states. Local school districts should set up teen clinics in inner-city junior and senior high schools to provide these youth with comprehensive health services, family planning services, and counseling for emotional problems. Such clinics, in addition to addressing the health needs of black males, could also help to reduce teen pregnancy rates by educating males and females about birth control measures. Moreover, on-site school clinics could develop ongoing health education programs aimed at improving dietary practices, reducing smoking, preventing drug and alcohol abuse, and generally reinforcing health-promoting behaviors among black youth.

The mental health needs of black youth have been sorely neglected. As noted in Chapter 7, a dual system of care has developed in which minority youth (and black males, in particular) have been processed through the juvenile and adult criminal justice systems for behavioral and psychological problems, while white youth have been referred to the mental health system for similar problems (Lewis and Balla, 1976). In order to reverse this insidious trend, mental health professionals must develop better techniques for early identification of troubled black youth, for improved assessment measures that take into account cultural differences in presenting symptoms, and for expedited referrals for appropriate services of early intervention and treatment.

While school-based clinics and community health centers are two important links in a comprehensive system of adolescent mental health, several other programs offer preventive services and counseling for disadvantaged high-risk youth, and special funds are often available. For example, there are Title XX Social Services Block Grants to the states, and mental health funds are available in the Alcohol, Drug Abuse and Mental Health Block Grants and the Juvenile Justice and Delinquency Prevention Programs. The Child and Adolescent Service System Program (CASSP) focuses on coordinating the multiple youth-serving systems and agencies in order to improve the delivery of essential mental health services for severely emotionally disturbed youth. This excellent program deserves additional funding so that it can be strengthened and expanded to all 50 states. Legislators must be convinced that increased allocations for these mental health programs of prevention and early intervention will result in long-range savings from reductions in the costs of institutionalization, rehabilitation services, chronic antisocial behavior, community violence, and police and criminal justice services.

A major way to improve the delivery of health and mental health services to blacks is to recruit and train more black physicians, dentists, and mental health professionals (DHHS, 1985). This recruitment process is obviously dependent on more effective educational policies and programs from the elementary school through college levels, as well as financial aid policies that will offer equal opportunity to low-income black students. As noted in Chapter 7, economic incentives must also be offered to young black health professionals to locate in inner-city areas where the need may be greatest but the rewards poorest.

Model Health Care Programs. Teenagers and young adults have special health and mental health needs that cannot always be met in traditional medical settings, particularly when those settings frequently do not have any specialists in adolescent medicine or mental health. This is especially true for low-income black youth, who feel doubly alienated from the predominantly white and middle-class health care system. If this group is going to obtain adequate medical and mental health services, then the current health care system will require some modifications in facilities, staffing, and delivery of services.

Programs that have effectively addressed the health needs of black youth have been "accessible, affordable, and appropriate" (CDF, 1986b). The pioneer adolescent health services program of the St. Paul, Minnesota Maternal and Infant Care Project, with clinics located at high schools and junior high schools, has been replicated in several cities around the country. In addition to school-based clinics which provide comprehensive services, there are also many hospital-based youth clinics such as the Community Adolescent Health Center at Johns Hopkins University Medical Center in Baltimore and the Young Adult Clinic at Presbyterian Hospital in New York City. A third model is the community-based youth clinic such as "The Door—A Center for Alternatives" in New York City, which provides comprehensive health and mental health services as well as educational and prevocational services, social services, and legal services to a heterogeneous and multi-ethnic group of youth (Committee for Economic Development, 1987). Although most of these programs serve more females than males, they attract more black males as they build a record of trust and reliability in their communities.

The ability to reach out to black males will be a significant asset for these clinics as the number of AIDS cases increases among black youth (Morgan and Curran, 1986). It will be crucial for health workers to develop innovative ways to educate the black community about ways to prevent the spread of AIDS. As of December 1987 only 17 states and the District of Columbia mandated education about AIDS in the public schools, yet this is the primary avenue for reaching black youth who are more likely than whites to engage in unprotected sexual intercourse in early adolescence (*New York Times*, 1987b). Since blacks are more likely than whites to contract AIDS through the use of infected intravenous needles, the campaign to prevent AIDS must also be linked to drug prevention as well as to safe sex practices. Comprehensive services must be accessible for black youth who are truants, runaways, emotionally disturbed, or from "multiproblem families" to reduce their risk of becoming delinquents or drug abusers.

Violence and Life-Threatening Behaviors

The alarming rates of homicide, accidents, and self-destructive behaviors among young black men have serious implications for the health and welfare of the entire black community, not only in terms of direct costs of interpersonal violence and criminal activity, but also in indirect costs of delayed family formation, potential years of life lost, and a general level of fear and paranoia.

This problem is so pervasive in urban ghettos that it is accepted as a way of life in the inner cities of Chicago, Detroit, New York, and Los Angeles. To modify this phenomenon will be a difficult challenge, but to ignore it will be an invitation to anarchy. While these high-risk behaviors are seemingly intractable and impervious to change, there are a number of approaches which, in combination, may reduce the incidence of violence and life-threatening behaviors in this group.

The increase in suicide rates and violent self-destructive accidents among black youth can probably best be addressed indirectly through policies and programs of primary prevention that will reduce their feelings of helplessness, hopelessness, depression, and alienation—all of which have been related to suicidal behavior in adolescence (Grueling and DeBlassie, 1980; Gibbs, 1987). As noted earlier, such programs should be aimed at alleviating the social and economic conditions that have made young black men more vulnerable to school withdrawal or failure, unemployment, unwed fatherhood, drug abuse, and delinquency.

First and foremost, policies and programs that specifically address reduction of violence in young black males include the need for a strong gun control policy on the federal, state, and local levels. Thus far, efforts to achieve such a policy on the federal level have failed because of the effective lobbying of the National Rifle Association and other opponents of gun control. Advocates of gun control must form more effective coalitions and use more forceful strategies to achieve their goals, particularly in view of escalating random acts of gun violence on freeways, in hostage situations, and in urban drug wars. As these violent episodes increase in our society and spread beyond the ghettos, it may become clearer to the general public that a civilized society cannot afford to permit the unrestricted sale of handguns and the easy availability of even more dangerous weapons.

Gun control, however, is essentially a third-order level of violence prevention, since those people who are most likely to use guns are probably more prone to violent behavior and have chronic difficulties with impulse control. Two other preventive approaches should be used to promote nonviolent behaviors. A primary prevention approach has been instituted in the public schools through programs which teach all children conflict-reduction skills. These programs have been targeted to schools in low-income, inner-city areas with high rates of criminal victimization and violence. The goal of such programs is to teach black youngsters how to resolve their differences without resorting to physical violence and to develop more constructive ways of relating to each other.

A secondary prevention approach would target those children and youth who are at high risk for violent behavior because of a history of child abuse and family violence. These children should receive counseling and other needed services, including foster care, through the Child Abuse Prevention and Treatment Act, child welfare services, and Title XX services. Without treatment, these youth are likely to grow up aggressive and hostile, using violence to abuse others as they were once abused.

Another area of intervention is the mass media, which features an inordinate amount of violence, even in the Saturday morning TV cartoons. Since black youth are known to look at more television than white youth, they are subjected to a steady diet of images of sexual aggression, drug abuse, criminal activities, and police violence. For many of these youth who are culturally isolated and psychologically immature, these repetitive images shape their vision of the world outside their ghetto walls and reinforce their feelings that violence is a justifiable means to any number of desirable goals—sex, money, cars, clothes—whatever the screen makes glamorous.

Model Violence Prevention Programs.   A very effective program of primary prevention of interpersonal violence has been instituted in four Boston public high schools. Developed by Dr. Deborah Prothrow-Stith, a black psychiatrist, the curriculum focuses on conflict-resolution techniques and "is specifically aimed at raising the individual's threshold for violence, by creating a nonviolent ethos within the classroom and by extending his repertoire of responses to anger" (Prothrow-Stith, 1986, p. 235). Over 500 minority students have participated in this well-designed program, which offers students alternatives to aggressive responses when they feel angry or frustrated.

The Breakthrough Foundation sponsors a Youth at Risk Program for violent juvenile offenders in Boston, New York, and San Francisco. This program, which involves a ten-day intensive residential component and a 6- to 12-month follow-up evaluation, offers instruction in communication, impulse management, life-skills development, remedial education, and counseling. A 1984 evaluation of the program concluded that recidivism rates among these delinquents were significantly reduced after they participated in the program (Prothrow-Stith, 1986).

Two other programs could be models for reducing interpersonal violence in minority youth. The Nebraska Commission on Drugs developed a program that emphasizes improvement of self-esteem and communication skills in peer group dynamics sessions. Strike II, a joint project of the Baltimore County Juvenile Justice System and the Adolescent Health Program of Johns Hopkins University Hospital, is a program that mandates participation of first-time violent offenders on probation and offers comprehensive health, education, recreation, job readiness, and psychological counseling to these delinquent inner-city youth. Evaluations of both of these programs indicate that they have been successful in changing attitudes and/or behaviors for these aggressive youth (Prothrow-Stith, 1986).

Strategies of Implementation

Achieving radical change in a democracy characterized by competing interests is not an easy task, but dismantling the current welfare bureaucracy with its entrenched hierarchy may be an even more formidable challenge. However, the welfare system in this country has become so unwieldy, so inflexible, and so unresponsive to those most in need that it has finally drawn the wrath of both liberals and conservatives, who now find themselves in an uneasy alliance as advocates of welfare reform. Moreover, a national consensus is emerging over the need to improve the public educational system, the need to provide affordable health care to all families, and the need to provide a minimum standard of living for the nation's poor children. Both business leaders and labor unions are increasingly becoming concerned about America's ability to maintain its economic growth and the quality of the future labor force in order to ensure the country's competitive position in international trade. Civil rights organizations are reevaluating their traditional agendas and formulating new strategies to address the problems of education, employment, and family stability.

With the recognition that black youth and black families are in many ways worse off in the 1980s than they were in the 1960s, in spite of over 20 years of special programs designed to improve their status, these organizations have been joined by black political leaders, black professional and fraternal groups, black educators, and black religious leaders in calling for strong measures to combat these problems (Joint Center for Political Studies, 1987). Now that the leaders of black organizations have admitted the gravity of the situation, labeled the problem as a "crisis" for the black family, and mounted a national campaign to dramatize the issues, the time seems especially propitious to orchestrate a massive, well-planned, and well-coordinated attack on the problems of black youth, capitalizing on the widespread concern and confusion about how to develop effective solutions to their plight. In the 1980s, we have seen broad-based coalitions to promote "Live-Aid" for starving Ethiopians, "Farm-Aid" for bankrupt farmers, and "Friends-Aid" for victims of AIDS. The time has now come to organize "Ghetto-Aid" to save endangered black youth.

The following 12 strategies of implementation are proposed to achieve significant change in federal, state, and local social policies and to foster innovative and effective programs that are appropriately targeted to meet the needs of inner-city black youth and their families.

1. *Coalition-building.* Advocacy groups with overlapping interests in the welfare of children and families should form coalitions at the national, state, and local levels to maximize their political, educational, economic, and social programs. These organizations include civil rights, social welfare, education, health, labor unions, women's rights, family, and child advocacy groups. Their strategy should emphasize the importance of a comprehensive family policy which will benefit *all* vulnerable American families, the majority of whom will be white.

2. *Lobbying.* Advocacy groups must develop effective lobbying techniques, public education campaigns, and direct action strate-

gies to convince federal, state, and local legislators and government officials to adopt their social agenda. In order to build bipartisan support and to avoid the "special interest group" label, lobbying efforts should constantly focus on the benefits to all families, benefits to the economy, and long-term cost savings in the social welfare, health care, and criminal justice systems, through the provision of adequate income and social services to low-income families.

3. *Political participation*. Black organizations and individuals should actively participate in both political parties in order to have an impact on the choice of candidates for all levels of government and in order to avoid being ignored by one political party (Republicans) or being held hostage by another (Democrats). Total allegiance of a minority group to either political party limits the ability of that group to have a continuous influence on successive administrations when there is a transfer of political power. Clearly, blacks should diversify politically for greater leverage in both parties, particularly since the black vote is now a crucial swing vote in the major industrial states and in many southern states. In October 1987, the significance of black voting majorities was dramatically demonstrated when many conservative southern senators voted against the confirmation of Judge Robert Bork, whose nomination to the Supreme Court had been strongly opposed by civil rights groups.

4. *Economic development*. Business leaders need to make a greater commitment to promoting job opportunities, job training, and job advancement for young black males. The National Alliance for Business and the Private Industry Council should continue to recruit corporations and small businesses for their social programs and to promote these programs on the basis of economic self-interest. In addition to creating more job opportunities for low-income minority youth, large corporations and financial institutions should develop "social capital" investment accounts. These funds could be used in a number of ways—for example, to "adopt" schools in inner-city areas, to finance the development of small black-owned businesses, to provide money for community improvement projects, to give loans to black professionals to set up offices in the inner city, and to provide funds for the rehabilitation of low- and middle-income housing in order to encourage more upwardly mobile blacks to return to inner-city neighborhoods.

5. *Affirmative action*. The federal government should continue to monitor employers very closely to assure their compliance with nondiscriminatory policies in hiring and promotion practices, in lending, in real estate sales, in consumer interest rates, and so

forth. While it has often been claimed that affirmative action policy primarily benefits middle-class blacks, there is some recent evidence that many of the blacks who were hired for entry-level positions in businesses in the 1960s and 1970s have not progressed very far and have often left large corporations for jobs in smaller, less pressured firms (Monroe, 1986). This phenomenon has occurred in all segments of the economy, including higher education, the military, the entertainment industry, and the government itself. Higher education may have helped many young black men learn how to join the team, but it has not generally taught them the informal rules and bureaucratic skills really required to play the game successfully. Thus, employers who are truly committed to an integrated work force must design in-house programs of mentorship and career development, particularly for black males, who appear to be at a greater disadvantage than any other group in the executive suite.

6. *Community development*. Federal and state government programs are not the panacea to cure all the ills of the inner cities. These inner-city areas could be revitalized by a combination of business investment, foundation grants, community organization projects, and local government initiatives. Nonprofit community organizations such as the Urban League and the Urban Coalition have teamed up with local businesses and professional and civic groups to sponsor education, employment training, health, delinquency prevention, teenage parenting, and a wide range of other projects aimed at providing employable skills and life options for black youth. Many of these programs require a minimal investment of funds, use volunteer staff, and involve members of the community in their planning and implementation; thus, there is a leveraging effect for every dollar spent, creating an excellent return on the original investment.

7. *Church involvement*. The black church has traditionally been the central axis around which the rest of the community revolved. For over a century, it has served as a refuge for blacks from racial discrimination, social oppression, and economic exploitation. Black clergymen have functioned as spiritual leaders, teachers, politicians, legal advisers, social workers, and counselors. Since the height of the civil rights movement in the 1960s, when black clergymen were organizing the protests and black churches were centers of the movement, the role and functions of the church have shifted from a focus on civil rights back to a focus on social services. Many urban churches are now in the forefront of social activism, with programs of Head Start, child care, youth groups, educational programs, leadership workshops, credit unions, and so

on. Governing bodies of the major black denominations should support the development of youth-oriented programs in all churches; local churches should collaborate with community organizations to sponsor communitywide youth projects, develop outreach efforts to assist homeless families, provide mentors for troubled youth, and "adopt" poorly functioning families by pairing them with stable families who will share their resources with them and expose them to constructive life-styles. For urban black churches, the time has come to focus on saving the minds and bodies of black youth in this life rather than saving their souls for the life hereafter.

8. *Foundation involvement.* Foundations can continue to play a very important role in providing grants for local demonstration projects in education, employment, adolescent pregnancy prevention, health care, delinquency and substance abuse prevention, and reduction of high-risk behaviors. While several foundations have made long-term commitments to urban problems and to minority issues, they generally use their funds to initiate programs rather than to support them indefinitely. There are obvious advantages as well as disadvantages to this philosophy, since some innovative programs have been terminated for lack of funds after very promising beginnings. Optimal results are obtained when these demonstration projects are part of an ongoing organizational structure that can absorb them when the foundation support runs out.

9. *Higher education involvement.* Colleges and universities, many of which launched ambitious minority recruitment drives in the 1960s and 1970s, have appeared to lessen their commitment to an integrated student body. Just as black college enrollment in predominantly white colleges has declined since its peak in 1976, the retention of black students has also become more problematic on many campuses. Because of future demographic changes in the youth population, it will be essential for institutions of higher education to recruit more black students and to provide them with financial aid and adequate support services so that they will perform well academically and graduate. A major barrier to black student retention is the perception by black students that they are outsiders in the academic world, aliens in a hostile environment (Fleming, 1984; Gibbs, 1983). To counter this self-defeating perception, university faculty and administrators must make greater efforts to hire black faculty and professional staff members, to enrich the curriculum with courses on minority group history and culture, and to foster a campus environment where racial and cultural diversity is not simply tolerated but actively celebrated.

10. *Black professional, business, fraternal, and civic organizational involvement*. These groups are an excellent resource for direct "hands on" involvement with black youth to provide part-time or full-time jobs, sponsor recreational and sports programs, fund summer camperships, provide facilities for youth programs, serve as volunteer or resource specialists in the schools, and underwrite college scholarships. Since many of these black leaders no longer live in the inner cities, it is important for them to maintain their ties and to provide visible models of achievement to all black youth. Just as churches can reach out to unstable black families, organizations and individuals could "adopt" a needy black family or a black youth to lend them financial, social, and emotional support. The traditional baskets at Thanksgiving and Christmas need to be replaced by long-term contributions of time, money, and social support for black youth and black families who are less fortunate and less successful than their middle-class counterparts. The motto of the late Mary McLeod Bethune, founder of Bethune-Cookman College in Florida and a selfless public servant, should be adopted by all successful blacks: "Each one, teach one."

11. *Mass media involvement*. The mass media has played positive and negative roles in influencing the lives of black youth. Television coverage of the graphic brutality against blacks in the civil rights protests of the 1960s can be largely credited with awakening the conscience of white America to the widespread racial discrimination in this society, ultimately generating public support for the two landmark federal civil rights bills in 1964 and 1965. On the other hand, television has also fostered negative stereotypes of black men as criminals, drug addicts, buffoons, and hustlers, and black women are portrayed as meddling matriarchs, sexy "Sapphires," dumb domestics, and welfare widows. These images of blacks (with the notable exception of "The Cosby Show," in which everyone is almost too good to be true) offer very few positive role models for black children. With the exception of black athletes and celebrity entertainers, most of the smart, successful, and self-confident males who appear on TV are white. Moreover, black males who do appear in regular television series are often cast in police roles where they reinforce the legitimacy of violence and aggression. Thus, black youth, who watch television regularly, are bombarded with negative images of adult blacks, as well as a steady diet of aggression and violence, frequently performed by or directed against nonwhite males. If the television industry is unwilling or unable to clean its own house by rejecting scripts and advertisements with demeaning and deviant images of blacks and by minimizing violence and pornography in its prime time programming, then civil rights and child advocacy groups should exert

economic pressures on sponsors of these programs to cancel their support, as well as continued efforts to change industry hiring practices to employ more black writers, directors, technicians, and actors.

The print media should also be held accountable for its portrayal of blacks, its inadequate and biased coverage of the black community, and its poor record in hiring and promoting minority journalists. The mass media can and should be a powerful voice for equality and justice in a democratic society, yet it has sometimes abdicated this responsibility in order to pander to popular tastes and to increase profit margins. The major challenge of the next decade for the mass media will be the role it chooses to play in preparing America to live harmoniously in a multiracial society, where adapting to ethnic reality may be a great deal more difficult for many people than absorbing exotic images on the television screen.

12. *Black family involvement*. There is an old southern saying, "The good Lord helps those who first help themselves." Many low-income black families function very successfully, rear law-abiding children, and are economically self-sufficient (see Frazier, 1967). These families are stable forces in inner-city neighborhoods, leaders in their churches and civic organizations, political organizers, and community activists. If these families could be mobilized to form support networks for single-parent families, to set up child care and food cooperatives, to establish crime watch committees, to form car pools, to organize youth recreation and sports activities, and to volunteer as aides in the schools, the community would gradually be transformed from a disorganized ghetto to a liveable urban neighborhood. Many inner-city families have passively accepted the deterioration of their neighborhoods, but others are beginning to organize to save their communities from the equally undesirable alternatives of abandonment to the squatters or gentrification by the yuppies, and to reestablish a sense of shared community. An example of this commitment is currently occurring in Harlem, where many younger professional blacks have been involved in "urban homesteading"—that is, moving back "uptown" to stake their claims on their traditional neighborhood, to renovate and rehabilitate once elegant townhouses, and to recreate a sense of racial identity and cultural pride.

Concluding Comments

The United States is rapidly moving toward a true multiracial society, not simply a society with a number of minority groups. If this society is going to prosper in the 21st century, if the economy is going to maintain its competitive edge over the other industrialized nations, and if the nation is going to maintain its political leadership of the free world, it is imperative for the leaders of government, industry, higher education, and foundations to cooperate in formulating solutions to the problems of black youth. Policies and programs that address the multiple problems of young black males and their families will also improve the social and economic status of other low-income minorities such as Hispanics, Asians, and American Indians. This nation cannot maintain its economic growth without preparing minority youth for productive work roles. It cannot maintain its political leadership without solving its internal racial and social conflicts. And, most obviously, this nation cannot portray itself as a model of democratic freedom and justice as long as one-fifth of its young people are denied equal access to education, employment, health care, housing, and fair treatment in the criminal justice system. America must move from a society based on white privilege, power, and prejudice to a society based on multiracial community, cooperation, and compassion.

It is important not to minimize the effects of racial discrimination, which is still a pervasive factor in the employment opportunities for black males. While structural unemployment and changing labor markets have undoubtedly been major causes of black male unemployment in urban areas, Kasarda (1985) points out that educational levels alone do not account for significant racial differences in central-city unemployment rates. He notes that

> *black male central city residents in the northeast and southern regions who attended college had higher rates of unemployment in 1982 than did white central-city residents in these same regions who did not complete high school. Putting aside possible racial differences in the quality of schooling, such discrepancies do suggest that problems of racial discrimination may be compounding the structural disadvantage central-city blacks face given their overall educational distributions.* [pp. 57–58]

As a sociologist, Kasarda clearly sees the connection between discrimination and unemployment for black males. It is curious that so many economists have difficulty in interpreting their regression equations to explain this same phenomenon. The "unexplained variance" of black male unemployment, when all other factors have been accounted for, is most likely employer discrimination—a variable that is admittedly difficult for economists to measure, but apparently even more difficult for them to conceptualize and to articulate.

The future status of black youth in this country is inextricably tied to the fortunes of all Americans, white and nonwhite, young and old, rich and poor, urban and rural, liberal and conservative. If the schools continue to fail them, the nation will not have a sufficient pool of educated manpower for a highly skilled labor force. If employers continue to reject them, the economy will not be able to maintain a competitive edge in the world, and the social security system will not be able to support the growing number of elderly citizens (who are predominantly white). If these young adult males cannot get jobs, they will be less likely to marry and more likely to father children out of wedlock, thus expanding the welfare rolls and inflating the costs of the welfare bureaucracy. If the criminal justice system fails to divert minor offenders or to rehabilitate chronic offenders, communities will pay the price in increased levels of fear, increased costs for police and security measures, and increased taxes for more jails and prisons. If low-income black families are not provided with adequate food, health care, and housing for their children, these youth will grow up with chronic health problems due to poor nutrition and housing, resulting in greater burdens on the health care system and greater total costs for tertiary and long-term medical care.

Finally, if these young men see no hope for their future and no meaningful roles for themselves in legitimate society, they will inevitably turn to drugs and criminal activities in order to support themselves and to provide an alternative role structure and status system. Clearly, the cost to society of these activities is extremely high in terms of victimization rates, drug-related prevention, treatment and enforcement programs, police services, and all of the physical and psychological costs to victims and their families. Ultimately, the primary victims are these young men, whose despair, frustration, and anger enmesh them in a life-style of self-destructive and life-threatening behaviors which make them likely candidates for death at an early age—from homicide, drug overdoses, accidents, or suicide.

Any society that persistently exploits, oppresses, and discriminates against certain classes of its citizens ultimately bears the seeds of its own deterioration and destruction—whether it be Nazi Germany, the Union of South Africa, or the United States. The social, economic, and moral fabric of this nation is slowly being eroded by the high costs of discrimination, the waste of human resources, and the escalation of violence and fear in urban areas. Some states are spending millions of dollars to build new prisons rather than allocating sufficient funds to prevent school dropouts, delinquency, and drug abuse among the very young men who will occupy those prisons. One major study by health economists has estimated that direct and indirect costs for AIDS victims will exceed $66.4 billion by 1995 (Scitovsky and Rice, 1987), yet there are almost no effective education and prevention programs in black communities, which are producing one-fourth of the new adult cases and nearly 60 percent of the pediatric cases (Centers for Disease Control, 1986). Japan and other industrial nations are aggressively challenging America's economic supremacy with highly skilled labor forces and advanced technological developments, yet this country still will not commit itself to the necessary educational reforms to assure that minority children will be educated and that minority youth will learn employable skills. Our housing market is one of the most luxurious and expensive in the world, with the average single-family home selling for over $100,000 in major urban areas (*San Francisco Examiner*, 1987), yet we cannot provide housing for the homeless and sufficient low-rent housing for low-income families, forcing them to live and rear their children in unsanitary and unsafe conditions. Corporate law firms and Wall Street brokerages offer exorbitant beginning salaries to young professionals, yet many of these same corporate leaders support efforts to reduce the minimum wage for teenagers, which would reinforce the growing gap between the "haves" and the "have-nots" in the United States.

The United States has allocated billions of dollars for national defense to build weapons that do not work, millions for foreign aid to support countries that are not stable, and millions for farm subsidies to grow crops that are destroyed. Yet this government cannot find the funds to raise 2 million black families above the poverty line, to feed 4 million poor black children, and to provide jobs for one million young black men.

The mayors of America's large cities have appealed to the current administration for more money to revitalize their central cities, but their pleas fall on deaf ears. Urbanologists have clearly recognized that the fate of American cities is closely linked to the fate of poor minority groups who live in their central core (Peterson, 1985). If these cities are ever going to regain their economic and cultural vitality, federal, state, and local governments must collaborate on attracting new jobs, increasing the supply of low- and middle-income housing, improving transportation and other urban services, reducing crime rates, improving the schools, and expanding park and recreational facilities. These improvements must be accompanied by significant efforts to rehabilitate inner-city neighborhoods, provide job training programs for minority youth, and strengthen the functioning of low-income families through comprehensive social services. The ghettos cannot be permanently sealed off from the rest of the central city and, without their economic and social rehabilitation, the future of America's cities will also be endangered, with tragic consequences for the nation and the world.

Just as the fate of the cities is tied to the fate of poor blacks, so too are the fortunes of middle-class whites and blacks linked to the fortunes of the black "underclass." In 1968, the Kerner Commission predicted that America was drifting toward a divided society of blacks and whites, yet 20 years after the urban riots it is clear that the black "underclass" is alienated from middle-class blacks as well as whites (Report of the National Advisory Commission on Civil Disorders, 1968). In those 20 years, their condition has actually deteriorated—there are more black families below the poverty line, more black families on welfare, more black children born out of wedlock, more black youth in prison, and more blacks involved in the self-destructive world of drugs and violence. As this "underclass" grows and becomes more socially isolated, more frustrated, and more alienated, no ghetto walls will be strong enough to contain their hostility and rage. When this rage erupts, blacks will not only turn it on themselves as they did in Watts and Liberty City; it is quite likely that they will also invade the peaceful suburban enclaves of power and privilege. If and when that day comes, no gates, no steel bars, and no alarm systems will protect the "haves" from the "have-nots." The only real protection is prevention, and that message has not yet fully penetrated the protected domains of the wealthy and powerful groups in our society.

In 1968, Martin Luther King, Jr., the prominent civil rights leader, was assassinated as he marched for economic and social justice in Memphis, Tennessee. Five years earlier, at the 1963 March on Washington, this Nobel Laureate had inspired thousands of civil rights marchers with his passionate "I have a dream" speech, yet in 1988 his dream of racial equality is still far from reality and today's black youth are worse off in many ways than those who marched with him in the nation's capital 25 years ago.

A few individuals with foresight and genuine compassion are trying to make a difference in the lives of disadvantaged black youth. One such person is retired New York executive Eugene Lang, who gave a graduation speech in 1981 at his former New York elementary school and promised to provide scholarships to college for all of the graduates who completed high school successfully. Looking at these bright-faced, ebullient black and Hispanic students, Mr. Lang spontaneously made his offer to be their benefactor and friend through their high school years. He related to each youth as an individual (not three-fifths of a person) and recognized each person's potential (not one was "invisible"). He treated these youth with respect and dignity, and communicated his high expectations for their success. They responded by fulfilling his faith in their ability to perform and to achieve at significantly higher levels than their peers. After four years of investing his time and interest in these "disadvantaged" teenagers, Mr. Lang recently reported that 50 of the original class of 61 students had finished high school, and half of them were happily accepting his offer of tuition scholarships to finance their college education. From this initial vision, Mr. Lang established the "I Have A Dream" Foundation in order to help other concerned philanthropists establish similar programs for disadvantaged minority youth. By 1987 the program was sponsored by over 100 businesses or individual donors and involved over 4,000 students in 15 cities, including Boston, Chicago, Dallas and Washington, D.C. (Committee for Economic Development, 1987).

Mr. Lang and his co-benefactors did not waste their time analyzing the deficiencies of these students or criticizing the lifestyles of their families. Rather than blaming the victims for the consequences of their victimization, he offered them hope, tangible assistance, and a chance for a better life. The positive outcome of this quasi-experiment in motivation challenges the assumptions of the conservatives who insist that "those people" cannot respond to positive incentives but will only alter their behavior if they are threatened with punitive measures and termination of benefits.

Our legislators and policymakers might learn some lessons from Mr. Lang's experiment. Labeling poor blacks with terms such as "underclass," "disadvantaged," and "dysfunctional" may serve a descriptive purpose, but these terms simply obscure the underlying causes of their behavioral problems; nor does labeling per se inform or advance public policy. If black youth are given real opportunities for education, if they are provided with meaningful jobs, if they have adequate income to care for their families, if they have hope for future mobility, then they will act responsibly and will contribute their fair share to the larger community. Then, and only then, will the promise of American democracy be fulfilled for all of its citizens.

References

American Public Welfare Association. (1986). *One child in four*. New York: APWA.

Auspos, P., and Price, M. (1987). *Launching jobstart: A demonstration for dropouts in the JTPA system*. New York: Manpower Demonstration Research Corporation.

Berrueta-Clement, J., Schweinhart, L., Barnett, W., Epstein, A., and Weikart, D. (1984). *Changed lives: The effects of the Perry preschool program on youths through age 19*. Monograph No. 8. High Scope Educational Research Foundation. Ypsilanti, Michigan: The High/Scope Press.

Beschner, G., and Freidman, A., eds. (1986). *Teen drug use*. Lexington, Mass.: Lexington Books.

CDF. See Children's Defense Fund.

Centers for Disease Control (1986). Update—Acquired immunodeficiency syndrome—United States. *Morbidity and Mortality Weekly Report* 35 (Dec. 12): 757–766.

Children's Defense Fund. (1986a). *A children's defense budget*. Washington, D.C.: CDF.

———. (1986b). *Building health programs for teenagers*. Washington, D.C.: CDF.

———. (1986c). *Model programs: Preventing adolescent pregnancy and building youth self-sufficiency*. Washington, D.C.: CDF.

———. (1986d). *Welfare and teen pregnancy: What do we know? What do we do?* Washington, D.C.: CDF.

———. (1987a). *Declining earnings of young men: Their relation to poverty, teen pregnancy and family formation*. Washington, D.C.: CDF.

———. (1987b). The new congress and children, *CDF Reports* 8: 1–20.

Chronicle of Higher Education. (1987). More young black men choosing not to go to college. December 9, p. 1.

College Entrance Examination Board. (1985). *Equality and excellence: The educational status of Black Americans*. New York: The College Board.

Comer, J. P. (1980). *School power*. New York: The Free Press.

Committee for Economic Development. (1985). *Investing in our children: Business and the public schools*. New York: CED.

———. (1987). *Children in need: Investment strategies for the educationally disadvantaged*. New York: CED.

Congressional Budget Office. (1982). *Improving youth employment prospects: Issues and options*. Washington, D.C.: Congress of the United States.

Department of Health and Human Services. (1985). *Report of the secretary's task force on black and minority health*, vol. I. Washington, D.C.: DHHS.

Edelman, M. W. (1987). *Families in peril: An agenda for social change*. Cambridge, Mass.: Harvard University Press.

Edmonds, R. (1979). Effective schools for the urban poor. *Educational leadership* 37: 15–24.

Fleming, J. (1984). *Blacks in college: A comparative study of students' success in black and white institutions*. San Francisco: Jossey-Bass.

Frazier, E. F. (1967). *The Negro family in the United States*, rev. ed. Chicago: University of Chicago Press.

Gibbs, J. T. (1982). Personality patterns of delinquent females: Ethnic and sociocultural variations. *Journal of Clinical Psychology* 38: 198–206.

———. (1983). Counseling black college students: Problems, needs, and strategies. In *College admissions counseling*, edited by W. R. Lowery. San Francisco: Jossey-Bass.

———. (1987). Conceptual, methodological, and sociocultural issues in black youth suicide: Implications for assessment and early intervention. McCormick

Award paper presented at the Annual Meeting of the American Association of Suicidology, San Francisco, May.

Grueling, J., and DeBlassie, R. (1980). Adolescent suicide. *Adolescence* 15: 589–601.

Hamilton, C., and Hamilton, D. (1986). Social policies, civil rights, and poverty. In *Fighting poverty: What works and what doesn't,* edited by S. Danziger and D. Weinberg. Cambridge, Mass.: Harvard University Press.

Hofferth, S. L. (1985). Updating children's life course. *Journal of Marriage and the Family* 47: 93–116.

Joint Center for Political Studies. (1987). A policy framework for racial justice: Black initiative and governmental responsibility. Washington, D.C.: JCPS.

Kasarda, J. (1985). Urban change and minority opportunities. In *The new urban reality,* edited by R. E. Peterson. Washington, D.C.: The Brookings Institution.

Lewis, J. (1978). A comprehensive approach to delinquency prevention and treatment. *Child Welfare* 57: 675–84.

Lewis, D., and Balla, D. (1976). *Delinquency and psychopathology.* New York: Grune & Stratton.

McFate, K. (1987). Welfare reform bill calls for new direction. *Focus* 15: 3–7.

Monroe, R. (1986). A perennial favorite. *The Crisis* 93: 38–64.

Morgan, M., and Curran, J. (1986). Acquired immunodeficiency syndrome: Current and future trends. *Public Health Reports* 101: 459–65.

Moynihan, D. P. (1965). *The Negro family: The case for national action.* Cambridge, Mass.: MIT Press.

———. (1986). *Family and nation.* New York: Harcourt, Brace, Jovanovich.

National Black Child Development Institute. (1985). *Excellence and equity, quality and inequality.* Washington, D.C.: NBCDI.

Nelson, S. et al. (1974). A national study of the knowledge, attitudes and patterns of use of drugs by disadvantaged adolescents. *American Journal of Orthopsychiatry* 44: 532–37.

New York Times. (1987a). Massachusetts considers proposals to assure health insurance for all, August 21, p. 7 (national edition).

———. (1987b). States mandating class on AIDS triple in year, December 4, p. 17 (national edition).

Paton, S., and Kandel, D. (1978). Psychological factors and adolescent illicit drug use: Ethnicity and sex differences. *Adolescence* 13: 187–200.

Peterson, R. E., ed. (1985). *The new urban reality.* Washington, D.C.: The Brookings Institution.

Polsky, D. (1986). The Eisenhower grants: Redirecting juvenile delinquents. *Youth Policy* 10: 3–4.

Proctor, S. (1987). A national youth academy. *Youth Policy* 9: 10–12.

Prothrow-Stith, D. B. (1986). Interdisciplinary interventions applicable to prevention of interpersonal violence and homicide in black youth. In *Report of the secretary's task force on black and minority health,* vol. V. Washington, D.C.: U.S. Department of Health and Human Services.

Report of the National Advisory Commission on Civil Disorders. (1968). Washington, D.C.: U.S. Government Printing Office.

Report to the New York City Partnership: Summer Jobs '86. (1987). New York: The New York City Partnership.

San Francisco Chronicle. Poor are paying more taxes, Congressional study says. November 11, p. A-21.

San Francisco Examiner. Housing prices up 10% a year. September 6, p. F-1.

Scitovsky, A. and Rice, D. (1987). Estimates of the direct and indirect costs of acquired immunodeficiency syndrome in the United States, 1985, 1986, and 1991. *Public Health Reports* 102: 5–17.

Shorr, A. (1986). *Common decency: Domestic policies after Reagan.* New Haven: Yale University Press.

Thornton, W., James, J., and Doerner, W. (1982). *Delinquency and justice.* Glenview, Ill.: Scott, Foresman.

Time. (1987). The ghetto: From bad to worse. August 24.

Tolmach, J. (1985). There ain't nobody on my side: A new day treatment program for black urban youth. *Journal of Child Clinical Psychology* 14: 214–19.

Wilson, W. J., and Neckerman, K. M. (1984). Poverty and family structure: The widening gap between evidence and public policy issues. Paper prepared for Conference on Poverty and Policy: Retrospect and Prospects. December 6–8, Williamsburg, Virginia.

INDEX